God's Good Covenant

God's Good Covenant

Poetic Beauty in Hosea Enhanced by Counting

Loren F. Bliese

RESOURCE *Publications* • Eugene, Oregon

GOD'S GOOD COVENANT
Poetic Beauty in Hosea Enhanced by Counting

Resource Publications
An Imprint of Wipf and Stock Publishers
199 W. 8th Ave., Suite 3
Eugene, OR 97401

www.wipfandstock.com

PAPERBACK ISBN: 978-1-7252-9623-7
HARDCOVER ISBN: 978-1-7252-9624-4
EBOOK ISBN: 978-1-7252-9625-1

(I wrote the UBS copyrighted article "Symmetry and Prominence in Hebrew Poetry with Examples from Hosea" using excerpts from a discourse-analysis study of the complete text of Hosea that I developed while teaching at Mekane Yesus Seminary in Addis Ababa. I was also serving as a United Bible Societies Translation Consultant along with Dr. Ernst R. Wendland the editor, and many colleagues studying discourse analysis. The full manuscript, including the excerpts in that article, has been revised and expanded in the present book. —Loren Bliese)

06/25/21

I dedicate this book to the many students who participated in my exegesis courses during my twenty years with Mekane Yesus Seminary, Addis Ababa, Ethiopia. The structural analysis presented in this study of Hosea was done over many years together with my students. I thank them for their feedback and participation, and wish them God's blessing in their ongoing service.

Contents

Preface | ix

Abbreviations | xi

Hebrew Alphabet with Numerical Values | xii

Chapter 1: Method of Numerological Analysis | 1
- Introduction: Numerical Patterns in Hosea | 1
- Literary Features in the Poetry of Hosea | 3
- Symbolic Numbers Used in Hosea | 7
  - Symbolic Numbers Highlight a Possible Thematic Goal in Hosea | 10
- Word and Lemma Counts in Structural Units of Hosea | 12
  - Table 1: MT Word and Lemma Counts in 9 Blocks and 5 Parts | 13
  - Table 2: Cumulative MT Word and Lemma Sums by Blocks and Parts | 15
  - Comparing Symbolic Lemma Values | 17
  - Table 3: Total Counts of Lemmas Having the Same Value | 18
- Chronology for the Introduction of Literary Counts | 23

Chapter 2: Structural Display and Analysis of Hosea 1–3 | 25
- Key to Formatting of the Following Poetry: | 25
- Part One 1:1—3:5 | 25
  - First Block 1:1—2:8[10], Key Words "Children" and "That Day" | 25
  - Second Block 2:9[11]—3:5, Key word "Return" | 51

Chapter 3: Method of Discourse Analysis of Hebrew Poetry | 71
- Theoretical Comments on Poetic Structure | 71
- A. Structurally Defined Peak | 71
  - Identification of Secondary Peaks | 72
  - Types of Poetic Features Prominent in Peak Lines | 79
  - Chart of Distribution of Features of Prominence | 99

B. Overall Structure of Hosea | 100
Structural Chart of Poetic Lines in Parts and Blocks in Hosea | 102
A Part 1, 88 poetic lines of Judgment and Salvation | 102
B Part 2, 88 poetic lines of Judgment | 102
C Central Part 3, 50 lines of Judgment | 102
B' Part 4, 88 lines of Judgment | 102
A' Part 5, 88 lines of Judgment and Salvation | 102
Words that Occur Chiastically Balanced Between Parts in Hosea | 105
Words that Occur Chiastically Balanced Between Blocks in Hosea | 106
C. Chiastic Symmetry Helps to Interpret Problematic Texts | 110
D. Line Divisions that Show Sentence Boundaries | 111

Chapter 4: Structural Display and Analysis of Hosea 4–14 | 113
Part Two 4:1—7:2 | 113
Third Block 4:1—5:4, Key words: "Know the LORD" or "Spirit of Harlotry" | 113
Fourth Block 5:5—7:2, "Israel, Ephraim and Judah" | 129
Central Part Three 7:3—8:13, Fifth Block, "Kings and Princes" | 144
Part Four 8:14—10:1 | 161
Sixth Block 8:14—10:1, Key word "Multiply" for evil | 161
Seventh Block 10:2—11:7, 254 words, "Be destroyed or Lifted up" | 173
Part Five 11:8—14:9[10] | 185
Eighth Block 11:8—13:3, "I am the LORD your God" | 185
Ninth Block 13:4—14:9[10], "The LORD and Fruit" | 197

Chapter 5: Translating Peak and Chiasmus | 213

Appendix: A Test of Textual Variants to See if they Produce More Symbolic Numbers | 217
Table 4: Revised Word and Lemma Counts in Blocks and Parts | 217
Table 5: Cumulative Revised Word and Lemma Sums by Blocks and Parts | 221
Table 6: Summary of *Word* Counts in MT & Revised, Plus Cumulative | 222
Table 7: Summary of *Lemma* Counts in MT & Revised Plus Cumulative | 223

References | 225

Author Index | 231

Subject Index | 233

Scripture Index | 237

Preface

MY RESEARCH ON HOSEA began in 1981 when my family and I were waiting out a violent demonstration in Nairobi, Kenya. We could not leave the Mennonite Guest House, giving me an opportunity of several days to count Hebrew words in the poems of Hosea. I did this to test a theory that biblical poetry includes metrically chiastic line-length. I found sufficient examples, and pursued the study after returning to Addis Ababa, Ethiopia, where I served as a United Bible Societies Translation Consultant. In November, 1982 I presented a paper to translation colleagues in Nairobi on the first three chapters of Hosea. In it I developed the dichotomy I found in biblical Hebrew poetry of homogeneous metrical lines with end emphasis versus metrically chiastic lines with central emphasis. The counts are based on words or hyphenated word units. I later taught Hosea at Mekane Yesus Seminary in Addis Ababa, and analyzed the rest of the book with input from my students over many years. Copies of the study were updated each year for new students. In 1994 excerpts from the teaching manuscript were published by the United Bible Societies as a chapter "Symmetry and Prominence in Hebrew Poetry: With Examples from Hosea" in *Discourse Perspectives on Hebrew Poetry in the Scriptures* edited by Ernst R. Wendland.

After retirement in 2004 I did research on symbolic numbers in scripture, and in 2018 published *Count God In: Theological Numbers in the Song of* Songs. Since then I have added numerical research to the teaching notes on Hosea, which had focused on the discourse study of poetic structures. I found that besides the *alphabetical number 22* and its related products of 11, which I originally described as essential to the overall structure, the *theological number 26* and related products of 13, 17, 23, and 32 are used in similar ways in Hosea as they were in Song of Songs. The numerical use of both the alphabetical and theological sets is realized in many ways. I found that it comes in lemma (lexical root) alphanumeric values giving prominence to high points, and counts in the whole book, counts in structural units, and counts in individual poems.

Chapter 1 below is a study of these numerical patterns in Hosea. In Chapter 2 the first three chapters of Hosea are discussed in terms of structure, word-stresses in poetic lines, and symbolic numbers, all relating to prominence. This is intended to serve as an introductory application of the hypotheses proposed in the book. A theoretical discussion of the relationship between structure and peak on the basis of the whole book is found in Chapter 3. Chapter 4 is an application of these principles of analysis to Hosea 4–14, which is displayed symmetrically and commented on in terms of structure, symbolic numbers, and prominence. Chapter 5 points out applications of this study to translation. An appendix shows the possibility of adding more symbolic numbers by using variants suggested in textual studies.

I thank my grandson Joel Meyers for adapting the Excel program he worked out for Song of Songs so that it would count the value of lemmas (lexical roots) which I extracted from the Hosea data in Westminster Hebrew Morphology (1991). Joel's program adds the value of each letter according to its numerical sequence in the Hebrew alphabet and gives the total "value" for each lemma. I also thank my son Paul Bliese for his continuing help with a new computer and advice in calculations for statistical probability. I have used Kristopher J. Preacher's www.quantpsy.org on-line calculator for the many chi-square results below. The large number of calculations with probability give credence to details in the analysis that may otherwise look like chance.

Abbreviations

ASV	American Standard Version
BCE	Before the Christian Era
BDB	Brown, Driver, Briggs. *A Hebrew and English Lexicon of the Old Testament*
BHK	*Biblia Hebraica.* Edited by Rudolph Kittel
BHS	*Biblia Hebraica Stuttgartensia.* Edited by K. Elliger and W. Rudolph
BHQ	*Biblia Hebraica Quinta. The Twelve Minor Prophets.* Prepared by Anthony Gelston
CEV	Contemporary English Version
GNT	Good News Translation
LXX	Septuagint
MT	Masoretic Text
NEB	New English Bible
NIV	New International Version
NJPS	New Jewish Publication Society Translation
NRSV	New Revised Standard Version
REB	Revised English Bible
RSV	Revised Standard Version
SIL	Summer Institute of Linguistics
UBS	United Bible Societies
WHM	Westminster Hebrew Morphology (1991)

Hebrew Alphabet with Numerical Values

Hebrew	Transliteration	Alphabetical Value	Mathematical Value
א	ʾ	1	1
ב	b	2	2
ג	g	3	3
ד	d	4	4
ה	h	5	5
ו	w	6	6
ז	z	7	7
ח	ḥ	8	8
ט	ṭ	9	9
י	y	10	10
ך/כ	k	11	20
ל	l	12	30
ם/מ	m	13	40
ן/נ	n	14	50
ס	s	15	60
ע	ʿ	16	70
ף/פ	p	17	80
ץ/צ	ṣ	18	90
ק	q	19	100
ר	r	20	200
ש/שׂ/שׁ	ś/š	21	300
ת	t	22	400

The total alphanumeric value of the sum of the letters in words or lemmas (lexical roots) in the text below are given with an equal sign followed by the value, such as *YHWH*=26 for the value of *Y*=10, *H*=5, *W*=6, and *H*=5.

Chapter 1

Method of Numerological Analysis

Introduction: Numerical Patterns in Hosea

THIS STUDY OF HOSEA shows interesting numerical patterns for both words and lemmas (lexical roots) in the literary sections of the book. The significance of these counts is related to the symbolic numbers in (1) the *twenty-two* letters of the Hebrew alphabet, and (2) the alphanumeric value of YHWH or *twenty-six* along with some extensions that will be explained below.

Number symbolism comes already in the first two words after the title, *dbr YHWH* 'word-of the-LORD.' The alphanumeric value of both lemmas is 26 (*d*=4, *b*=2, *r*=20 totaling **26**, and *Y*=10, *H*=5, *W*=6, *H*=5 totaling **26**). These two words come together again in 1:2a making an inclusio for the introduction with double 26s, and introducing the first episode of God's call to Hosea to marry a "wife of harlotry." "Word of the LORD" comes a third time in 4:1 making another double set of 26s at the beginning of the second major part of the book.

Another important example is the total of words in the first literary block, which begins with the title "HOSEA" through 2:8 [Hebrew 2:10].[1] Block 1 has 286 Masoretic Text (MT) words. Factors of 286 are **26x11** and **22x13**, representing both the theological set with 26 and the alphabetical

1. Note the paragraph divisions at the end of 2:8 in NIV and CEV. Block 1 ending at 2:8[10] is the half-way point with the first 44 poetic lines of the 88 poetic lines of part 1, which ends at 3:5 at a clearly obvious major juncture. Details are given in section B "Overall Structure of Hosea" in chapter 3. The structural boundaries for five parts and nine blocks were done prior to my 1994 article on Hosea (Bliese, "Symmetry and Prominence," 67–68), and without reference to numerical counts of words and lemmas.

set of 22 used in Hosea. Note that each of the main symbolic numbers 26 and 22 are matched with the *basic* prime number factor of the other, 11 and 13. This is important since in the observed patterns of symbolic numbers any multiples of these *basic* numbers are used, such as **11**, 22, 33, 44, etc., and **13**, 26, 39, 52, 65, 78, etc., up to the total counts in the book of 2382 for words and 3093 for lemmas. I propose that 286 was purposely chosen for the number of words in block 1 because 286 so beautifully combines these two symbolic sets by being the convergence of these two correlates of 286. The fact that the book opens with the above noted doublet of words with the value of 26, and that the intertwined factors of 286 involving both symbolic sets are in the *first* block, suggests that they are *clues at the beginning of the book* for a general plan to use these symbolic numbers.

As will be detailed below, after the introduction, the first poem in 1:2c-d, which is the first message, is unique in having *the highest percentage of multiples of lemmas with divine-name numbers, and the last poem 14:9[10] has the second highest.* Included in these divine-name lemmas, each poem has one *YHWH*=**26**, and doublets of contrasting key words, *znh* 'harlotry'=**26** in 1:2c-d, and *byn* 'understanding'=**26** in 14:9[10]. This makes an inclusio for the book of poems based on divine-name numbers as well as key words. The second poem of the messages, 1:4b-c, also has a pattern of numbers with the *third highest percentage (15.15%) of lemmas with the alphabetic set.* It has one 22, three 66s, and one 77. These are made up of two singletons (hapax)—*yhw'* 'Jehu'=22 and *mmlkwt* 'kingdom'=77—enclosed by the second and third *yzr''l* 'Jezreel'=66. These three peripheral poems form a beautiful inclusio with the highest use of *divine-name* numbers on the outside, augmented by the second poem with the strong *alphabetical* inclusio of 66, 22, 77, 66.

A related special symbolic number comes in block six, which has 242 or **22x11** words. The use of 242 reinforces the importance of the alphabetical set by being the product of both 22 and its basic factor 11.

A very interesting example of a numerical pattern with *lemma values* comes with the largest value of all lemmas in Hosea. It is 104 with *tmrwrym* 'bitterness(es)' in 12:14[15] in the last part 5, with factors of **26**x4 (and **13**x8). The next highest lemma value with symbolic factors is 78 with *n'pwpym* 'adultery' in 2:2[4] in part 1, with factors of **26**x3 (and **13**x6). This pattern of the two lemmas with the highest alphanumeric values in consecutive multiples of 26 (3x26 in part 1 of Hosea, and 4x26 in the last part 5) is striking. It also adds to the significance of the three "word-of the-LORD" double 26s in the beginning of the book, and the inclusio of highest percentage of symbolic numbers including YHWH and double key words with values of 26 in the first and last poems of the messages.

These are examples that will be discussed along with many more below of how symbolic numbers are used in Hosea. This study will show that the text of Hosea shows a variety of ways used to beautify the message by symbolic numbers. The patterns include (1) the strategic use of individual lemmas with symbolic values such as 26s for *dbr YHWH*, (2) word and lemma counts that are symbolic within structural units such as 286 words in Block 1, and (3) total counts of words and lemmas such as for the two key characters 26 Elohim (God) and 44 Israel in the book. The discussion of symbolic numbers will continue after the next section describing special literary features promoted by the author and used in this book.

Literary Features in the Poetry of Hosea

In this study the poetry of Hosea is analyzed into symmetrical structures. The effort was begun after a word-stress count of the lines in *Biblia Hebraica Stuttgartensia* (BHS) showed some perfect and near perfect metrical chiasms. The traditional system of counting stress units by means of *words or hyphenated units* has been the basis of the counts.[2] In going through the 402 lines of poetry in Hosea, fifteen sections fit most naturally into a series of homogeneous lines with nearly identical rhythm, with either four, five or six word-stress units per line. A *line* normally forms both a semantic and metrical unit in a poem. Alter identifies it as the essential unit of Hebrew poetry.[3] This *homogeneous* type of structure has been generally recognized in Hebrew poetry. However, thirty sections are most naturally defined as metrically *chiastic* poems with from two to seven word-stress units per line. These chiasms are built on the structure of metrical inversion, where the first and last lines have basically the same number of word-stress units, and the second lines from each end also agree in number of rhythmical units, with the pattern continuing to the center, as in the Greek letter Chi or X. This chiastic type of metrical structure is proposed by the author as part of

2. See Zevit ("Poetic," 351); Freedman ("Poetry," 18–27 on "quantity"); and van Grol ("Zephaniah," 191–92).

3. Alter, *Biblical Poetry*, 9. Also see Alter ("Ancient," 611–24), and Freedman ("Acrostic," 408–31). Kugel (*Idea*, 2–3) uses both "line" and "verse." O'Connor (*Verse*), Margalit ("Ugaritic," 298) and traditional studies call this "line" a "verse" made up of "lines," "versets" or "cola." Watson (*Poetry*, 13) uses the term "strophe," and notes that it is made up of from one colon to several cola, bicola being the norm. Kugel (*Idea*, 297) dismisses meter in Hebrew poetry, but does rightly point out that the problem has been trying to force everything into lines which "are roughly equal in length in a given passage of poetry." In noting the close relation between music and prophecy Kugel (*Poetry*, 24) quotes from Robert Lowth's "Lectures on the Sacred Poetry of the Hebrews" that "the predictions of the prophets are metrical." Also see Andersen ("Analyzing," 68–87).

the essence of Hebrew poetry. In the past such variations in line length have been described as irregular, but in this study they are considered to be more highly structured.

A description of the metrical structure of the Hebrew *poetic line* is important. Except for short lines with only two or three units, all other lines divide semantically with a caesura, thus forming two cola per line, or in some cases three cola. As is generally the case in Hebrew and Ugaritic poetry, tetrameter lines (with four word-stresses) and hexameter lines (with six stresses) normally divide in the middle, although sometimes hexameter lines are tricola with two feet in each colon. Pentameters and heptameters normally have the larger colon first, 3+2 and 4+3. A few examples of tricola heptameters were also found, and some hexameters and heptameters divide 4+2 and 5+2.

Boundaries of poems and their stanzas are sometimes marked by extra feet in lines at the break (anacrusis), or by changes from normal meter, such as 3+2 cola meter to 2+3 in pentameters. Boundaries are also sometimes marked by short bimeter or trimeter monocola lines either at the beginning or end of the unit.

The lines of Hosea normally group into *strophes* made up of couplets with two lines with closely connected ideas.[4] The repetition and parallelism in these *couplets* are just as exemplary of Hosea's style as is internal colon to colon parallelism within a single line.[5] Sometimes triplet strophes and single-line strophes are also found. Short monocolon lines are usually counted the same as full lines in strophic analysis. The analysis of the text below marks strophic boundaries with *, while structurally marked stanzas are marked with #.[6]

The symmetrical patterns which were observed, usually fit into the traditional divisions in the text as indicated in BHS or versions. In some places different junctures are proposed below. Many metrical chiasms are also supported by *semantic chiasmus*. (Good examples are 7:3–7 and 10:9–15. See the displays of individual poems in chapter 4 below for Hosea 4–14, and in chapter 2 for Hosea 1–3.) On the other hand, homogeneous metrical poems are more likely to have a "*terrace*" pattern of words repeated in

4. Couplets are called "verses" by some, but this is not to be understood as the numbered verses, which are made up of various combinations of lines in the MT. See Dearman (*Hosea*, 15) who notes, "Verses may comprise two bicola or more." He also gives examples of verses with "two bicola + one" and "two tricola."

5. For example, Willis ("Parallelism," 62–63) has noted that Hos 4:6b-c and 10:1c-f exemplify "alternating parallelism" in that the two lines of each couplet have the same semantic structure.

6. Korpel and de Moor ("Fundamentals," 38–60) describe stanzas as "canticles."

pairs (either contiguous or interlocking) building up to a final climax.[7] (See 2:14–17[16–19], 22[24]; 13:4–6.) A final climax in a homogeneous type may also be emphasized by a semantic chiasm that has the second half of the inversion on the last line. (See 7:14.)

The efforts to find structural features which mark the boundaries and peaks of poems were limited in early studies of Hebrew poetry.[8] However, in recent decades good progress is being made in text and discourse analysis. Several studies have noted patterns similar to what is called metrical chiasmus here.[9] The description of *inclusio* or inclusion as outlined by Freedman and developed by Alter, and others, is especially relevant to this study.[10] They point out the metrical as well as the semantic identity or similarity of the first and last lines of some poems in Hosea. See especially the discussion of Hosea 4:1–10, 11–14 and 8:9–13 in Lundbom ("Rhetoric" 301–8, and "Contentious" 52–70). Andersen and Freedman in their commentary (*Hosea*, 140–41) also point out lexical and semantic inclusion as important in defining units in Hosea. My analysis goes beyond inclusio and describes the *rhythmical symmetry of the whole poem*, using traditional *word-stress units* rather than syllable counts.

7. Boadt ("Reflections," 161) summarizes my 1994 article on Hosea "Symmetry and Prominence in Hebrew Poetry" writing, "Loren Bliese argues that when the climax is in the middle (chiastic) then the middles will be less parallel than the ends; if the climax comes at the end, however, then 'terrace patterns' will appear in the parallelism as it approaches the end. Such final climactic prominence is often achieved by doubling line ideas or lengthening significantly the number of syllables in a line." On page 159 Boadt also notes that Bliese highlights "the essential role of 'symmetry and prominence' to detect poetic divisions." This present study is an expansion of that 1994 article.

8. O'Connor (*Verse*, 141–42) in commenting in 1980 on "features that set off whole poems or major classes of them," states, "This group of features is not widely believed to exist." On 460 he notes as one of "three useable items" for defining "gross poetic structure," "a general notion of symmetry." in 1982 Sawyer ("Prophets," 240) noted that past studies emphasized smaller units, but that structuralists remind us that "there are still questions to be asked about literary units, whole chapters, even whole books, which have been neglected in much modern scholarship." A major contribution is van der Meer and de Moor's *The Structural Analysis of Biblical and Canaanite Poetry* giving studies representing the research in Kampen.

9. De Moor ("Rhythmical," 13–17) describes metrical symmetry in terms of "embracing patterns," which are based on feet per lines in Ugaritic poetry. Shea ("Chiasmus," 13–25) describes a crescendo:decrescendo structure based on number of cola per couplet. Halle and McCarthy ("Psalm 137," 161–67) describe a similar chiastic structure based on syllable counts. Christensen ("Jonah," 29–48) analyzes the book of Jonah as a five-part poetic structure on the basis of syntactic-accentual units. His analysis is very similar to what I have found in poetic books, with each part "arranged concentrically from a metrical point of view" and key verbs appearing "at the structural center of metrical configurations" (41).

10. See Freedman ("Prolegomenon," xxxvi–viii), and Alter ("Psalms," 255–58).

The recognition of the *center of chiastic poems* as special in Biblical poetry is also developed here (also see Kosmala, "Form," 442–45; and Breck, "Chiasmus," 70–74). Especially note Lundbom ("Rhetoric" 306), "There would seem to be at least some indication then, that Hosea uses the centers of his poems for embellishment. I offer this as a provisional conclusion which further research can perhaps corroborate." This study of Hosea proposes that the *center line of poems with chiastic rhythm* is usually the peak of the poem. In contrast, the *final line* of poems with homogeneous lines is usually the peak. The stronger claim is that these are the thematic peaks of the poems. A weaker, but nevertheless empirically demonstrable claim (see probability calculations in chapter 3), is that they are the structural peak. I propose that the structural peaks help to identify the thematic peaks. For chiastic poems "crux" or "pivot" might be a useful designation, and for homogeneous poems "climax" would indicate the function of emphatic structural closure. The Hebrew audience would presumably distinguish if the poem had a homogeneous rhythm and expect a final peak. If line lengths varied, they would expect a chiastic structure with a central peak.

Another observation detailed in chapter 3 regarding structurally related emphasis is that in *chiastic poems with a couplet (two lines) in the center, secondary peaks* are often found at the *beginning and end of the poem.* A third place of predictable prominence is at the *quarter lines of long chiastic poems.* These have also been designated here as secondary peaks.

Various literary devices are used to give prominence to these primary and secondary peaks. The high percentage of peaks which have references to the "LORD" and "God" is especially significant. Chiastic inversions, unique line length, and dropping or interrupting previous parallelism are examples of changes of style at peak. (Various literary features for primary and secondary peaks are tabulated, calculated for relevance, and discussed below in "Structurally Defined Peak" in chapter 3 A.)

In many cases metrical patterns are discernable using the Masoretic Text (MT) with the lineation as in BHS. This is especially true where long or short line-length gives prominence to a chiastic peak. Where MT is not found to be symmetrical, hyphenation options other than those with MT maqqēp are presented as examples of how the poet might have fit the words into a regular pattern. Shoshany ("Prosodic," 175) gives the following guideline: "The assignment of hyphens by the Masoretes seems to reflect their own performance of the text, rather than a transmitted tradition. Hence, the reader of a given poetical text may assign stress to the 'small words'—whether connected with a hyphen or bearing an accent mark—according to prosodic considerations." My departures from the MT hyphenation of word-stress units in determining lineation is acknowledged as being largely subjective and conjectural. However, the changes from MT in this study are not presented as normal speech patterns, but are only suggestions of how the basically homogeneous or chiastic structures could have been actualized in a metrical performance of song or oral poetry.

Besides the whole of Hosea which has been analyzed below, the author has made a tentative perusal of much of Biblical poetry, and has found similar metrical chiasms as well as the previously known homogeneous units. See the references "Psalms 1–24," "Psalm 23," "Count" (for Song of Songs), "Joel," "Amos," "Obadiah," "Micah," "Nahum," "Habakkuk," and "Zephaniah" under Bliese in References. Also see Bliese's Society of Biblical Literature review of David E. Orton's *Poetry*. Undoubtedly the following reconstructions of word-stress units, lines, and poem and block boundaries can be disputed. However, the following study, particularly with its presentation of metrical chiasmus and symbolic number patterns, hopefully will show that meaningful boundaries and peaks can be found by adding *metrical* considerations to discourse analysis and thematic studies. On the basis of the symbolic *numerical patterns* found in both poem and book levels, I propose that the formation of the text of Hosea and other books should be seen as having included a plan to achieve literary beauty by counting a variety of literary units. I see this type of analysis as a powerful exegetical tool.

We will turn now to a description of the *basic symbolic numbers* in Hosea and biblical Hebrew literature.

Symbolic Numbers Used in Hosea

(1) The most important theological number is **26**, which is the alphanumeric value of *YHWH* calculated by adding the value of each of the four letters, *Y*=10, *H*=5, *W*=6, and *H*=5. The *theological number set* includes multiples of the prime number base of 13, plus multiples of each of the three individual letters *Y*=10, *H*=5, and *W*=6. The set includes a short count of 17 related to *YHWH*. It probably represents a hypothetical archaic *ʾHWH*=17 where *alep* has the value of one, related to the *alep*-initial root *ʾHYH* 'I AM' in Exod 3:14 for the name YHWH.[11]

11. See Labuschagne, "Numbers" (89) with diagrams of the counts for 26 and 17, and *Numerical* (90) where he notes that 26 and 17 "have been explained as referring to the divine name in the Jewish tradition and their status of divine name numbers has been firmly established and accepted." In *Numerical* (103) Labuschagne gives an example from the non-poetic introduction and epilogue of Job where the name *YHWH* and the name *Job* both occur exactly 26 times. The theologically symbolic numbers 26, 17, 23, and 32, along with 10, 6, and 5 are also noted as significant in my *Count God In: Theological Numbers in the Song of Songs* (63–65). However, Song of Songs does not use the alphabetical

(2) The alphabetical set is based on the **22** letters in the Hebrew alphabet. The prime number base of the set is **11**. Acrostic psalms with lines beginning with the consecutive letters of the alphabet are a well-known example of the use of 22 in Hebrew literary structures (see Ps 119 and Lamentations).

(3) An extension of the theological set comes with **23**. Twenty-three is based on *kbwd* 'glory' with *k*=11, *b*=2, *w*=6, and *d*=4, totaling **23** for the full *kbwd.* A short form *kbd* without *w* is used in construct or genitive forms in the Pentateuch including references to God's glory (Exod 29:43; 33:18, 22; Num 14:22; and Deut 5:24, the only "glory" in Deuteronomy). It has the value of **17**, supplementing the reason for 17 as a divine name number, which can also be based on *YHWH* with *Y*=1 as well as on *'hwh* as noted above.

(4) There is evidence in Hosea that **32** was also used along with 26, 17, and 23 as divine name numbers. Counting with the *mathematical* set of alphanumeric values rather than the alphabetically sequential values gives *k* the value of 20 rather than 11. The value of *kbd* is then **26**, the same as *YHWH*, and *kbwd* with mathematical values is **32**. (See Labuschagne, *Numerical*, 90–91, 122).[12] The data in Hosea indicates that these numbers were considered symbolic at the time the text of Hosea was finalized. Since this is important in Hebrew number history, I have collected the following examples of 32 and 64 (or 32x2) in Hosea that add prominence to the poetic structure.

{1} The word *kbwd* 'glory' comes three times. The first two have the suffix "their," referring to the "priests" in 4:7, and to "Ephraim" in 9:11. The third in 10:5 has the suffix "it" referring to the calf of Beth-aven. The "glory" of the priests and of Ephraim in the first two is understood by many to refer to God.[13] 9:11 is the one most clearly referring to God. *Numerical*

11, 22 set, except in special cases like the combination of 7 and 11 in 77. (Seven comes from another well-known set of symbolic numbers symbolizing fullness.)

12. Claus Schedl (*Baupläne*, 51) proposed that the 23–32 significance is based on a Babylonian geometrical pattern of a triangle of numbers 1–10, where the sum of the corners and center are 23, and the sum of numbers between them is 32. This has been used in Jewish mysticism where the letters of the divine name are expanded by lines in a triangle from Y to YH to YHW to YHWH. Although Labuschagne based the significance of 23 and 32 on the values of *kbd* and *kbwd* rather than Babylonian geometry, both Schedl and Labuschagne saw the total of 23+32=55 to be significant in Biblical texts with 55 words that divide into 23 and 32 words. (See Labuschagne, *Numerical*, 121–27.)

13. See for example Ps 3:3[4] "But you, O Lord, are a shield around me, my glory, and the one who lifts up my head." Also see Exod 33:22 "while my glory passes by I will put you in a cleft of the rock, and I will cover you with my hand until I have passed by;" and Zech 2:5[9] "I will be the glory within it" (Jerusalem).

enhancement is found with a plethora of ten lemmas with the value of 23, 32, or 64 in the poem 9:10–10:1. There are four 23s, and three 32s (*ʿnb* 'grapes'=32, *mṣ ʾ* 'found'=32, and *śwh* 'yield'=32, which is a singleton), and three 64s with a play on words with the same value—Israel=64 x2, and the singleton *šqwṣ* 'disgusting'=64. MT has 98 word-stress units in the poem, which was found to be significant in my study of Song of Songs, and 98 is the sum of the four divine-name numbers 17, 26, and both counts 23 and 32 of *kbwd*. Furthermore, the word "God" comes in the fifth line from the end, chiastically matching "glory" in the fifth line from the beginning. I see this plethora of *kbwd* numbers as being intentionally added to mark *kbwd* here as a divine reference. The presence of three 32s and three 64s, with each having a singleton, gives good support to seeing the use of 32 as being included in the inventory of divine-name numbers, in this case based on *mathematical* values as well as alphabetical-sequence values.

{2} The last two words in the list of five characteristics of God's good covenant in 2:19–20[21–22] are *rḥmym* 'mercy,' which has the value of 64 or 32x2, and *ʾmunh* 'faithfulness' with the value of 39 or 26+13. Both of these are singletons (hapax) in Hosea, which can be evidence of a choice to end the list with two words pointing numerically to YHWH.

{3} The first word of the poem 3:1b-d *ʿwd* 'again' has the value of **26**, and the contextually strange last lemma *ʿnb* 'raisins' has **32**, making an inclusio of divine numbers that add focus on the reference to *YHWH*=**26** in the central peak of 3:1c.

{4} The inclusio with *ryb* 'accusation, accuse'=**32** in 4:1b–4a, is supplemented by the repetition of *ʾyš* 'man'=**32** in each colon of the final line 4a.

{5} As noted above, in 9:10 there is a play on numbers with *yśr ʾl* 'Israel'=64 (**32**x2) in "As grapes in the desert I found *Israel*," and the singleton *šqwṣ* 'disgusting'=64 (**32**x2) in "they became as *disgusting* as the thing they loved." This may relate to the prominence of *znwnym* 'harlotry'=64 twice in the first prophecy in 1:2, "Take for yourself a wife of *harlotry* and offspring of *harlotry*."

{6} Especially note the numerical chiasm around kbwd 'glory=32 mathematically in v. 11 with two **32**-value lemmas before "Israel"=64 (**32**x2) in 9:10— *ʿnb* 'grapes,' and *mṣ ʾ* 'found'—and the singleton *śwh* 'yield'=**32** that comes after the second "Israel" in 10:1 of the same poem. Note that the three 64's are also only in 9:10 and 10:1 chiastically enclosing *kbwd* .

{7} The last line before the final Wisdom closure is 14:8[9] "I am like a *r ʿnn* 'green' (=64 or **32**x2) cypress, it is from me that your fruit is found" (*mṣ ʾ*=**32**). (Cypress *brwš*=49 with 7x7 possibly relates to final fullness in this final poem of the main message.) YHWH's identification as a "green"=64 cypress with the theological symbolism of 32 as a divine-name number looks to me like a number play, especially with the last word of the book before the Wisdom closure "found" having the value of 32.

{8} The final Wisdom poem is connected to the previous poem with *ḥkm* 'wise'=32 in 13:13 and 14:9[10], near the beginning of each poem forming anaphora. Note 13:13 "he is an un*wise* son;" and 14:9[10] "Who is *wise*?" These are the only two occurrences of *ḥkm* in Hosea. The use of *ḥkm*=32 here may reflect a later Wisdom redactor's interest in the 32 divine number count.

{9} Enhancement using structural counts may be evident with the 32 words in 6:4–6, and the 256=32x8 words in block 8 (11:8–13:3).

Symbolic Numbers Highlight a Possible Thematic Goal in Hosea

Seven lemmas whose *total occurrences* each have strong symbolic numbers stand out in Hosea. These *seven* lemmas have the following symbolic counts found only on these lemmas, which is the reason they stand out. In the theological set *YHWH*=26 comes 46 or 23x2 times, and "Elohim" 26 times as the only words with 46 and 26 occurrences. The key verb *šwb* 'return' comes 23 times as the only word with 23 occurrences. The verb *ʾhb* 'love' and noun *ʿam* 'people' both come 17 times as the only lemmas with 17 occurrences. In the set based on 22 of the alphabet, "Israel"=64 or 32x2 comes 44 times as the only 44. The MT *ʾl* 'to' preposition comes 30 or 10x3 and 5x6 times as the only lemma with 30 occurrences. These words can be put together in what I propose as a thematic goal in Hosea, "YHWH loves his-people; return, Israel, to your-God" (*ʾhb yhwh ʿm, šwb ysr ʾl ʾl ʾlhym*). The surface words beginning with the participle *ʾōhēb* would be *ʾhb yhwh ʿmw, šwbh ysr ʾl ʾl ʾlhyk*. This adds the suffixes *w* 'his,' *h* for the plural imperative, and *k* 'your,' which are not included in lemma counts. *This makes 26 letters* in Hebrew. I propose that these key words with symbolic numbers fit so nicely into an overall goal for the book that an intentional plan like this can be suggested, especially because these are the only lemmas that have these total counts. Besides the total counts of 26 for *ʾlhym* 'God' and of 44 or 22x2 for Israel, the *kbwd* divine-name values with the YHWH count of 46 or 23x2, and of Israel with 64 or 32x2 make these two main characters of the book especially prominent.

I'll add some references where this theme occurs with *sequential* numbers for word and lemma counts in the book. I see the symbolic products of these numbers as potential markers of prominence to their contexts. The frequently repeated theme of YHWH loving Israel is stated well in 3:1 in the poem where Hosea is commanded to love the wife who went astray, as an action prophecy to show that "YHWH loves Israel." YHWH comes beautifully in 3:1 its 11th time as the 676th or **26x26** lemma, and the 490th or 70x7 word. This looks like an intentional placement of YHWH on these numbers, not only the theological 26x26, but also the 70x7 of the fullness set. "Loves" (*ʾhb*) in 3:1 stands before YHWH as the 675th or **5**x135 or **5**x**5**x27 lemma, which may also be significant with the 5s as in the two *H*s of *YHWH*. "Israel" in 3:1 is the 679th lemma with factors of 7x97, and the 483rd word with factors of 7x69, and **23**x21 or 23x3x7. Besides the theological factors of 26 and 23, the fullness factor 7 is thereby tied to both YHWH and Israel. The lemma *hlk* 'go' also comes in this command in 3:1 as the 667th or **23**x29 lemma, with "*Go*, love a woman." It also comes its final 22nd time in the last verse of the book 14:9[10] "the righteous *go*" in the ways of YHWH. Among the 17 "loves" also note 11:1 "When Israel was a child, I loved him," with "loved" the 1824th word or **32**x57. Also note 14:4[5] "I will love them freely," with "love" as the very strong symbolic 3010th lemma or **10**x301, or **5**x602, or 7x430.[14] These symbolic factors on the sequential counts of these key words enhance the thematic messages.

The even more frequent second theme "Return to your God" is stated clearly at the end of part 1 in 3:5, "Afterward the Israelites shall *return* and seek the Lord their God." It also comes twice in the final chapter as a *command*, as proposed above for a theme. In 14:1[2] Hosea pleads, "*Return*, O Israel, to the Lord your God," where *šwb* 'return' is the 2278th or **17**x134 word. And in 14:2[3], "*return* to the Lord; say to him, "Take away all guilt" "return" is the 2289th or 7x327 word. The final **23**rd "return" (as translated in RSV) in 14:7[8] is the 3042nd or **26**x117 lemma, giving a strong closing theological number. It can also be translated "again" modifying "dwell" as in NRSV and NIV. The key word *šwb* has many meanings in Hosea including "turn away from God," "return," and "repent" as in 3:5 (see BDB, 997, "turn back to God {=seek penitently}"). Also note that in 14:1[2], which is very similar to the above command, the preposition "to" is *ʿd*=20, which comes 5 times, while that in 14:2[3] is *ʾl*=13, which comes 30 times.[15] Since both have theological counts, either would fit in

14. Dearman (*Hosea*, 2010:36) writes concerning 14:4[5], "Hosea shares with Deuteronomy the vocabulary of "love" (*ʾāhab*) as a motivation for YHWH's choice of Israel. Surprisingly, that vocabulary does not occur in Amos, Isaiah of Jerusalem, or Micah, Hosea's prophetic contemporaries, though each of them presupposes that God had graciously drawn Israel and Judah to himself." Dearman (p. 58–59) also points out the role of "love" in covenantal treaties, "International treaties employ the terminology of "love" to describe the relationship established between suzerain and vassal. Such a cultural context may have influenced the Deuteronomic language of YHWH loving his people or the people being commanded to love him."

15. Dearman (*Hosea*, 190) notes that *ʾel* is the typical preposition for returning "to"

the above theme as a symbolic lemma with two letters to fit in the 26-letter line. However, the unique count of 30 occurrences for *ʾl* gives it preference over the count of 5 for *ʿd* since there are 23 lemmas with 5 occurrences.[16] (The 22-count lemmas *ʾmr* 'say,' and *kl* 'all' also come in 14:2[3] making a symbolic connection to the alphabetic set.) These references show how the theme of *šwb* 'return' is emphasized as an inclusio both at the end of part 1 in 3:5 and at the end of the book. I propose that the author tailored the *totals* of these seven key thematic words to fit these key symbolic numbers, and also arranged several of these words strategically so they would have symbolic *sequential* counts.

Word and Lemma Counts in Structural Units of Hosea

The tables below use the junctures from my 1994 structural analysis, and therefore come before I began analyzing the use of numbers in Hosea.[17] The junctures are therefore not influenced by lemma and word counts. As previously noted, the number of *poetic lines* per structural unit in Hosea is analyzed as being based on a 44, 88 series related to the 22 letters of the alphabet. The analysis has four *parts* with 88 lines of poetry and a central 50-line part. The four 88-line parts are also divided into *blocks* with 44 poetic lines each, which when added to the central part/block make nine blocks. The following table 1 diagrams the total counts that these literary divisions produce for MT words and lemmas and indicates those that are symbolic numbers. "Prime numbers" means they have no factors, and those listed as "not symbolic" have none of the factors in the theological set (13, 17, 23, 32, and 6 and 5) or the alphabetical set based on multiples of 11.

YHWH in Hosea, except in 14:1[2] where *ʿad* comes, and that Deut 30:2 and 10 also illustrate both prepositions for this phrase.

16. Along with the symbolic 23-count for 5, it is also interesting that other total counts of lemmas with values related to the divine-name letters *YHW* also have symbolic counts—there are *five* lemmas with the value of both 10 and 12, and *twenty* (10x2 and 5x4) with the value of 6.

17. See Loren Bliese, "Symmetry and Prominence in Hebrew Poetry: With Examples from Hosea," (In *Discourse Perspectives on Hebrew Poetry in the Scriptures*, edited by Ernst R. Wendland. United Bible Societies, 67–94).

Table 1: MT Word and Lemma Counts in 9 Blocks and 5 Parts

Blocks	MT Words	MT Lemmas
1st, Title–2:8[10]	**286=22x13, 11x26**	376 not symbolic
2nd, 2:9[11]–3:5	271 prime number	**390=13x30, 26x15, 10x39, 6x65, 5x78**
Part 1 totals	557 not symbolic	767=13x59
3rd, 4:1–5:4	**276=23x12, 6x46**	361 not symbolic
4th, 5:5–7:2	257 prime number	336=6x56
Part 2 totals	533=13x41	697=17x41
5th, 7:3–8:13	301 not symbolic	357=17x21 (Block 5 the same as Central Part 3)
6th, 8:14–10:1	**242=22x11**	307 prime number
7th, 10:2–11:7	254 not symbolic	**319=11x29**
Part 4 totals	496 not symbolic	626 not symbolic
8th, 11:8–13:3	**256 32x8**	347 prime number
9th, 13:4–14:9[10]	239 prime number	**299=13x23**
Part 5 totals	**495=11x45, 5x99**	646=17x38

As noted above there are 286 (**=22x13** and **=26x11**) MT *words* in block 1 combining the most important symbolic numbers for Hosea—the alphabetic 22, and theological 26, together with the basic factors 13 and 11 of the other set. The MT *lemma* count 390 in block two is also highly symbolic. Besides **13**, it has factors of **26**, **10**, **6** and **5**.[18] The presence of such strong symbolic numbers in *both* blocks of part 1 strengthens the case that they

18. Amazingly, all of these five symbolic factors for 390 are combined with factors with further symbolic numbers. Note for 13x30 the factor 30=5x6, for 26x15 the 15=5x3, for 10x39 the 39=13x3, for 6x65 the 65=13x5, and for 5x78 the 78=26x3 as well as the sum of 13+26+39. The number 78 with all of these symbolic factors is used strategically to show theological emphasis in Song of Songs (see Bliese, *Count*, 50, 63) where it is the total count of the preposition *l* 'to.' In table 4 in the Appendix a suggested revision from 390 to 391 has an alternative option with two divine name symbolic factors 17 and 23 for block 2.

are not mere chance. Support for the importance of symbolic numbers in Hosea comes from the use of the number 143, which has factors of **13x11,** combining the base numbers of the theological set with 13 for 26 and with 11 for 22. The total occurrences of the preposition *l* 'to' is 143. The total of MT word-stress units in the longest poem 13:12—14:8[9], which comes just before the final Wisdom closure is 143. Also, the block 1 word total of 286 is double 143 where 286 adds the factors of 26x11 and 22x13. The location of 286 and 143 with their convergences of symbolic factors in the beginning and end of the book gives them likelihood of being intentional. I propose that these highly significant numbers are further evidence of an intentional *plan to use symbolic numbers in the structure of Hosea.*

Of the twenty-six structural numbers in Table 1, thirteen are symbolic, five of thirteen for words, and eight of thirteen for lemmas). This is not statistically probable. However, the presence of five numbers with *corollaries* (more than one symbolic factor, including those with both factors symbolic such as the above 242=**22x11**) supports a proposal that these numbers are not just chance but were likely targeted. This becomes most powerful for multiples formed by a *convergence* or *corollary* of more than one set of factors such as the above 286 with **22x13** and **26x11**. When these corollaries are included in the counts by counting all the symbolic numbers, the two symbolic factors with the highest number of occurrences are 13 with five occurrences, and 11 with four (13 and 11 are significantly the base numbers of the theological and alphabetical symbolic sets). Next come 17 and 6 which each have three occurrences, then 22, 23, 26, and 5 where each have two, and 32 and 10 where each have one occurrence. A statistical comparison can be made of the 13 and 11 base numbers of the two main symbolic sets over against the base numbers 5, 6, and 10 from the YHWH-letter set. The two occurrences noted above for 26 are added to balance the three YHWH-letter numbers. This gives a matrix of categories of **1028** possible hits for 11, 13 and 26, and **2329** possible hits for 5, 6, and 10, compared to groups with **11** actual hits for 11, 13, and 26, and **6** actual hits for 5, 6, and 10.[19] Yates' chi-square on Kristopher J. Preacher's www.quantpsy.org calculator is 7.69 with p= 0.0056 or 99% positive probability. This indicates that a targeting of the main symbolic numbers with factors of 11, 13, and 26 more than of 5, 6, and 10 is probable.

In order to compare the symbolic numbers with random numbers, I tested the twenty structural numbers in table 1 with the large factors 12, 14, and 27, compared to small 7, 8, and 9. These numbers were chosen to be near the above six symbolic numbers. The results are three 7s, three 8s, no 9, one

19. The calculation was done by dividing each symbolic number into the MT word total of 2,382 less 213 unused numbers or 2169, and the lemma total of 3,093 less 273 unused numbers or 2820.

12, one 14, and no 27. The counts include corollaries (more than one symbolic factor), although the only number with corollaries is 336, of which the small factors 7 and 8, and the large factors 12 and 14 are counted. (It also has 2, 3, 4, 6, 16, 21, 24, 28, etc., as a very potent number used in ancient geometry because of all the factors that converge on 336.) The low result of eight total in this test group compared to nineteen for symbolic numbers gives further support to the proposal that theological and alphabetical symbolic numbers have been intentionally targeted in forming the numbers in the parts and blocks of Hosea. The predominance of the six lower random numbers with 7, 8, and 9 as over against only two hits with 12, 14, and 27 is mathematically expected, and shows how the MT predominance of the symbolic numbers 11, 13, 22, and 26 over lower numbers is exceptional. Although the actual hits are too few in the test group for reliable calculation, chi-square for a matrix of potential small of 1994 compared to actual small of 6, and potential large of 1010 and actual large of 2 comes to .02 with p= .88, indicating no probability for these random numbers compared to the above good probability of 7.69 with p= 0.0056 or 99% positive probability for the symbolic numbers.

Calculations were also done to determine if the use of symbolic numbers extends to *cumulative* totals. Table 2 lists the cumulative totals from the beginning of the book to the end of each block and part. Block 1 is the same as in table 1, so parentheses are added to it.

Table 2: Cumulative MT Word and Lemma Sums by Blocks and Parts

Blocks/Parts	Cumulative Words	Cumulative Lemmas
(Block 1, Title–2:8[10]	**286=22x13, 11x26**	376 not symbolic)
Block 2 & Part I, Title–3:5	557 prime number	766 not symbolic
Block 3, 4:1–5:4	833=17x49	1127=23x49
Block 4 & Part II, 4:1–7:2	1090=10x109, 5x218	1463=11x133
Block 5 & Part III, 7:3–8:13	1391=13x107	1820 26x70, 13x140, 10x182, 5x364
Block 6, 8:14–10:1	1633=23x71	2127 not symbolic
Block 7 & Part IV, 8:14–11:7	1887=17x111	2444 not symbolic
Block 8, 11:8–13:3	2143 not symbolic	2793 not symbolic
Block 9 & Part V, 11:8–14:9[10]	2382=6x397	3092 not symbolic

Table 2 shows a contrast between the number of symbolic numbers in MT words compared to lemmas. Cumulative words have seven of nine blocks symbolic or 77.78%, while lemmas have only three of nine or 33.33%. Words have eight factors with *large* numbers, while lemmas have only four. (Both words and lemmas have two small symbolic numbers each.) The overall picture suggests that a plan to include cumulative counts may have been used for words, but not as likely for lemmas. This will be discussed further and confirmed by a test in the Appendix.

The high proportion of *large* symbolic factors is noteworthy as in Table 1. Including the corollaries or multiple symbolic factors on the same number, there are twenty-six large number factors (with 11, 13, 17, 23, and 32), and ten small (with 6 or 5). For statistical probability 11, 13, and 26, can be compared to 5, 6 and 10 as was done with Table 1. The matrix has the categories of **1028** for total possible hits for 11, 13 and 26, and **2329** total possible hits for 5, 6 and 10, compared to groups with 7 hits for 11, 13 and 26, and 4 hits for 5, 6 and 10. Yate's chi-square is 4.17 and p is 0.04 or 96% positive probability, although there is a status warning for the low group numbers.

The text of Hosea is considered one of the most difficult because of many unknown words and seemingly ungrammatical forms.[20] Generations of scholars have proposed many changes to make sense of what they see as a corrupted text. The above study and tables 1 and 2 are based on the MT, and show it to be sufficiently reliable to find numerological patterns with near statistical probability. These counts of MT words and lemmas recommend an investigation of the possibility that the nine blocks and five parts originally had even more symbolic numbers, and that *textual variations* might give possibilities for changes that could make other counts symbolic.

A test was set up to make comparisons to MT. The many textual variations suggested in BHK, BHS, or BHQ were checked for possibly improving the counts. The choices to use any of them are not based on current scholarly acceptance of the proposed revisions, nor on my own evaluation of whether they are likely or not. Twelve of the fifteen suggested revisions are based on the LXX and one on a Dead Sea text, so they are not purely conjectural. Although some are widely accepted, others are not. The changes were chosen only to increase the number of symbolic factors. The proposed changes are noted in tables 4, and summarized in tables 5, 6, and 7 in the Appendix "A

20. Garrett (*Hosea*,26) notes that "Hosea contains possibly the most difficult Hebrew in the Bible . . . but few scholars today feel free to rearrange, delete, and modify Hosea at will. For the most part, our confusion with the text of Hosea is a matter both of our ignorance of his dialect and of the intentionally elliptical and obscure nature of the book. It is not in most cases a matter of the text having been badly transmitted."

Test of Textual Variants to See if they Produce More Symbolic Numbers." The success of the test is shown in that *the revisions made all parts and blocks have totals of words and lemmas that contain symbolic number factors*. The test also confirms the preference for the large (11, 13, 17, 23, 32) symbolic numbers and their multiples as observed in MT. Calculations were also done for *cumulative totals* at the end of each part to see if they were significant. The cumulative totals for lemmas stayed low, similar to MT totals. However, the *revised cumulative word totals have increased symbolic factors confirming what was observed in table 2 with MT*. This is significant since the revision focused only on structural part and block totals, so the cumulative totals resulting from them became mathematically random. The presumed reason for the increase with *words* is that the original had controlled word totals cumulatively at structural junctures of parts and blocks, as well as focusing on the totals of each unit. Therefore, improving counts in the units also would get closer to original cumulative counts. However, the counts for *lemmas* was only on the unit totals so cumulative totals did not improve when unit totals improved. The tables and discussion in the Appendix give the details and statistics for these assertions.

Comparing Symbolic Lemma Values

As noted above, lemma *values* are a common form of numerical symbolism in Hebrew. I have proposed in my study of Song of Songs that Classical Hebrew scribes developed competence in automatically recognizing common symbolic lemmas, and in adding up the alphanumeric values of those they didn't know. Evidence shows that they also categorized lemmas according to their values as in the groups in table 3 below.[21] So that those reading this paper can have access to the results of such competence I have added an equal sign (=) followed by the alphanumeric lemma value after the symbolic lemmas in this study. Any lemma can also be calculated using the "Chart of Hebrew Alphabet with Numerical Values" before chapter 1.

I want to emphasize Labuschagne's proposal that Hebrew authors and editors used lemma values for aesthetic decoration and to mark prominence in their work.[22] This resembles authors of many languages adding rhyme and rhythm to beautify their work and emphasize high points. If this is so, lemma values that are symbolic should be more frequent than the rest. The

21. See Bliese, *Count*, 34–35 for "competence," and 63–65 for grouping by values.

22. Labuschagne ("Compositional," 587) proposes that those who did these patterns did not do them for "the reader or the listener, but for their own satisfaction to show their craftsmanship and, more importantly, to the glory of God."

numbers in table 3 below give evidence to support that this process was going on in Hosea, although not as strong as the evidence in Song of Songs.[23] The use of symbolic *lemma values* goes along with structural patterns with symbolic *counts of words and lemmas* as part of the multifaceted inventory of tools used to enhance and beautify scripture.[24]

The following table lists groups marked by # of lemmas having the same alphanumeric value. Column one lists the symbolic numbers based on 11, 13, 17, 23 and 32. This lemma value number is followed by x (times) and the total number of lemmas with that value. Columns two and three have other nearby numbers aligned to **compare** with the symbolic first column. The large counts of prepositions obviously skew the totals, so the lemmas with highest occurrences have been listed in parentheses to help with evaluating them. In order to save space, when the listed lemmas do not equal the total for that number, the totals of "other" small-count lemmas are often noted to fill the picture of the total for each number. The numbers for lemmas with values from 7–104 are all listed if there are any.

Table 3: Total Counts of Lemmas Having the Same Value

Symbolic # Values with their Total Counts	Adjacent #s to Compare	Other Numbers Nearby
#11x82 (80 *k* and 2 *ḥg*)	#12x167 (143 *l*, 20 *hw* ʾ, 3 ʾ*k*, 1 ʾ*wh*) (24 besides *l*)	#7x1 (*dg*); #8x18 (16 ʾ*hb*); #9x16 (11 *bw* ʾ)
#13x110 (=22x5, 11*x*10) (65 or 13x5 *l* ʾ, 30 ʾ*el*, 7 ʿ*al*, 3 ʾ*ēl*, 1 ʾ*ḥd*, 1 ʾ*yb*, 1 ʾ*hbh*, *1 ghh*, *1 zw*)	#14x26 (9 *lb*, 6 *yd*, 4 ʾ*ēm* 4 others)	#10x1 (*bdd* 'alone')

23. In Song of Songs the frequencies of the values of the twenty-four groups of lemma frequencies, except one group with a factor of 7 and another with 11, are combined in groups of totals related to the theological YHWH-numbers 5, 6, 13, 17, 23 and 32. Seven and eleven represent the fullness and alphabetical symbolic sets also used to a lesser extent in Songs (see Bliese, *Count*, 62–68).

24. I personally also see the role of divine inspiration in the amazing variety and complicated interchange of the ways symbolic numbers are used. I believe God gave guidance to discover what possibilities there are to enhance the beauty of scripture, and inspired his servants to put in the hard work to count elements and adjust the text. I interpret their dedication to glorify God by embroidering symbolic numbers into the tapestry of biblical texts, to be a response to God's inspiration.

#17x**28** (=7x4) (6 *zabāḥ*, 5 *dm*, 5 *zebaḥ*, 5 *ṭwb* adjective, 2 *ṭwb* noun, 2 *gdwd*, 2 *ʾwy*, 1 *yhb*)	#15x4 (2 *ʾbl*, 1 *gm*, 1 *hwd*)	#16x45 (25 *bn*, 12 *gm*, 5 others)
#22x**28** (=7x4) (6 *dmh*, 5 *rb*, 3 *ph*, 2 *ndd*, 2 *ʾš*, 2 *ḥbl*, 2 *yḥd*, 2 *ʾyk*, 1 *ʾzn*, 1 *ḥwḥ*, 1 *yhwʾ*, 1 *ʿbd*)	#18x43 (13 *hm*, 6 *mh*, 12 others)	
#23x**96** (=32x3) (47 *ʾt*, 22 *kl*, 8 *ḥyh*, 3 *ṭmʾ* {vb}, 3 *kbwd*, 3 *yām*, 2 *ʾdmh*, 2 *ʾph*, 1 each *kḥd*, *yʾl*, *gbwl*, *ṭmʾ* {adj}, *my*, *ʾrb*)	#24x35 (14 *ʾkl*, 4 *bt*, 4 *bly*, 9 others)	
#26x**110** (=**22**x5, **11**x10) (46 *yhwh*, 13 *znh*, 10 *ʿwd*, 7 *yld*, 7 *dbr*, 5 *dābār*, 4 *gbʿh* {& 2 hills}, 4 *rʾh*, 3 *byn*, 2 *pdh*, 7 singletons: *bayin*, *bll*, *ḥmh*, *ḥwl*, *yeled*, *ʾml*, *zōnâ(h)*)	#27x88 (58 *mn*, 8 *nby*, 7 *rb*, 5 others)	#28x97 (48 *ʿl*{prep}, 22 *hlk*, 16 others)
#32x**42** (6x7)(10 *ʾyš*, 8 *mṣʾ*, 6 *ryb*, 5 *nʾp*, 2 *ʿnb*, 2 *ḥrd*, 2 *ḥkm*, 2 *yrb*, 5 singletons: *ṣmʾ*, *šbṭ*, *ḥwṣ*, *ḥll*, *šwh*)	#31x17 (3 *ʿgl*, 2 *ḥšb*, 12 singletons)	
Symbolic Multiples:		
#20(=10x2, 5x4)x**38** (27 *hyh*, 4 other lemmas totaling 11)	#19x12 (3 *gwy*, and 9 singeltons)	
#25(=5x5)x**65** (=13x5) (*ʾyn* x15, *ʾny* x12, *kn* x10, 16 others)	#21x90 (69 *ky*, 6 *dgn*, 8 others)	
#30(=10x3, 5x6)x**87** (16 *ydʿ*, 15 Judah, 7 *śdh*, 24 others)	#29x103 (28 *ywm*, 23 *šwb*, 16 *ʿam*, 14 *ʿim*, 14 others)	
#33(=11x3)x**45** (7 *ʿlh*, 7 *yšb*, 18 others)		
#34(=17x2)x75 (22 *ʾmr*, 15 *byt*, 8 *šām*, 7 *rwḥ*, 1 *ʿṣ*, 14 others)	#35x35 (9 *ʿnh*, 8 *drk*, 5 *ʾšm*, 10 others)	#36x77

#39(=**13**x3)x**76** (20 *ʾrṣ*, 9 *lqḥ*, 6 *ʾḥry*, 5 *mdbr*, 22 others)	#38x44 (5 *rpʾ*, 4 *zkr*, 24 others)	#37x15
#40(=10x4, 5x8)x**46** (**23**x2) (10 *qrʾ*, 7 *pqd*, 5 *škḥ*, 5 *ḥṭʾt*, 13 others)	#41x87 (26 Elohim, 8 *śr*, 7 *rḥm*, 23 others)	#42x60 (12 *ʾšr* 'that')
#44(=**11**x4)x**30** (6 *kšl*, 4 *śym*, 3 *nṣl*, 14 others)	#45x**26** (3 *šbt*, 3 *ysr*, 16 others)	#43(26+17)x41 (5 *ksp*, 4 *npl*, 3 *zrʿ*)
#46(=**23**x2)x**23** (5 *ʿyr*, 13 others)	$47x36 (5 *yšʿ*, 5 *pry*, 19 others)	
#50(=10x5)x**25** (12 *ntn*, 3 *šmʿ*, 8 others)	#49 (7x7) x**17** (3 *znwt*, *šaḥar*, *zrwʿ*, *ḥrš*, *ḥārāš*, 7 singletons)	#48x29
#51(=**17**x3)x**24** (3 *mlḥmh*, 3 *šḥt*, 13 others)	#53x24 (4 *krt*, 3 *bʿlym*, 3 *twrh*, 11 others)	#57x12
#52(=**13**x4, **26**x2)x**10** (2 *npš*, 2 *tḥt*, 2 *lʾ-ʿmy*, 4 others)	#54x**23** (5 *bryt*, 4 *pnym*, 3 *šmr*, 10 others)	#58x10
#55(=**11**x5 and **23**+**32**) x**17** (3 *srr*, 3 *byt-ʾwn*, 2 mʿśh, 2 *prṣ*, 7 single)	#56x7 (8x7) (2 *ʿšq*, 5 singletons)	#59x4 (2 Lo-ru*ḥ*amah, 2 singletons)
#60(=10x6, 5x12)x**8** (6 *mšpṭ*, 2 others)	#61x44 (37 Ephraim)	#62x**13**
#65(=**13**x5)x4 (2 *pšth*, 1 *mspr*, 1 Hezekiah)	#64 (**32**x2) x58 (44 Israel)	#63 (7x9) x3
#66(=**11**x6, 22x3)x**6** (5 Jezreel, 1 *štym)*	#67x1	#68 (**17**x4) x0 (none)
#69(=**23**x3)x1 (*ḥṣṣrh)*	#70(10x7, 5x14)x1 (Beth-arbel)	#71x3 (3 singletons)
#77(=**11**x7)x1 (*mmlkwt*) (last lemma with factor of **11** or 7)	#76x3 (3 *mʿllym)*	#74x21
78(13x6, **26x3**)x1 (*nʾpwpym*, 2nd highest with a theological number)	#79x7 (13+17+23+26) (6 *tyrwš*), *#80 (10x8)x0*	*#92 (23x4)x0, #96 (32x3) x0* (none)
104(13x8, **26x4**)x1 (*tmrwrym*, the highest lemma value with a strong 26 and tied to the above 78=26x3)	#81x1, #82x1, #89x1, #88 *(11x8)x0, #90 (10x9)x0*	#93x1 (*šʿrwry* 2nd highest #) (missing #s have no lemma with their values)

Lemmas with values of the theological numbers 13, 26, and 39 stand out as having higher counts than their adjacent non-symbolic numbers. Amazingly, both 13 and 26 have **110** occurrences (**5x22** and **10x11** with both the theological numbers 10 and 5, and the alphabetical **22** and **11**). The 110 occurrences of **26** include 46 YHWH, which looks like an intentional double of the related divine-name number **23**. The adjacent numbers for 26 have significantly less occurrences with 25x65 and 27x88 (including 58 *mn* 'from,' a word-lemma which is reduced to a clitic *-m* 56 of the 58 times). The 110 **13**s include 65 (13x5) *lʾ* 'not,' which is always a word.[25] The adjacent 14 has only 26 occurrences. The other adjacent number 12 has 167 occurrences, but this would be only 24 without its 143 *l* prepositions that never stand alone as words. Except for 12 with 167, *twenty-six and thirteen with their 110 count stand out as the highest lemma counts with values of seven or more.* The next theological number in the 13, 26 set is **39**, which also stands out with 76 occurrences versus the adjacent 38, which has 44 occurrences, and 40, which has 46. Labuschagne (*Numerical*, 128–30) credits Schedl with the recognition of 39 as the sum of YHWH=26 and *ʾḥd* 'one'=13 referring to Deut 6:4, *YHWH ʾḥd* 'YHWH is one.' Labuschagne ("Numbers," 97–98) also gives a strong example in Deut 3:1–10 showing that its structure can be analyzed with three sections with 39 words each, and each is divided into 17 and 22 word units.

The two highest lemma *values* with symbolic factors are *tmrwrym* 'bitterness(es)' in 12:14[15]a with the value of 104 or **26**x4 and **13**x8, and *nʾpwpym* 'adultery' in 2:2[4] with the value of 78 or **26**x3, **13x6**, and 39x2, as well as the addition of **13+26+**39. These two lemmas amazingly have consecutive factors with 26x3 in part 1, and 26x4 in the final part 5. 104 is especially remarkable since the next largest number for any lemma value is *šʿrwry*=93 (which is not symbolic), leaving a gap of eleven numbers between 93 and 104. This looks like an intentional effort to incorporate the 26x4 highest number with its factors of 26 and 13. It also relates to the first two lemmas of the book after the title, *dbr YHWH* 'word-of YHWH,' which both have the value of 26, and the first poem naming Hosea's children which has **104** letters besides 26 words and two 26-letter lines.

The numbers 10 and 11 also end with a likely intentional cutoff. Both end on a multiple of seven, ending a full series of factors from one to seven. Ten ends on 70, with factors of **10**x7, with no 80, 90, or 100. Eleven ends on 77 or **11**x7, with no 88 or 99. (Note there are 79, 81, and 89 adjacent numbers.) (Also note that 77 also plays an important role in Song of Songs,

25. The importance of 65 as a symbolic number is noted by Labuschagne ("Numbers," 89–96), who analyses Ps 79 with two balanced parts of 65 words, which along with their total of 130 are based on the divisor or factor of 13.

especially as the value of a near inclusio with a thematic reversal of *šḥrḥr* 'darkened' and *šlhbtyh* 'flame of YH,' Bliese, *Count*, 44, 99.)

The number 55 or **11x5** has the divine-name number **17** for its total occurrences, which marks 55 with three symbolic numbers 5, 11, and 17. Fifty-five is also the sum of the two divine name numbers based on *kbwd*, which has the value of **23** alphabetically and **32** mathematically. A play on numbers occurs with lemmas with the value of 23 significantly including *kbwd*=**23**, and 23's having 96 or **32**x3 occurrences. 32 is based on the mathematical value of *kbwd* where *k* =20 instead of the alphabetical 11. 32 has 42 occurrences or **6**x7, which has both theological and fullness symbolism. These symbolic numbers give support for placing *mathematical* counts along with alphabetical counts within the inventory of those who created the number patterns in Hosea.

Multiples of 7 also seem to be treated as symbolic as with the value-numbers 17 and 22, which both have 28 or 7x4 counts. Another fullness number 40 has 46 or **23**x2 occurrences, which combines theological factors of both the divine name number 23, and of 40 with its own factors of **10** and **5**.

Note that there is only *one* lemma with the value of **10**. It is in 8:9 *bdd* 'alone.' This makes a nice play on the word "alone" by having only this one lemma with the value of 10. Theologically the 10 may have been seen to relate to the first letter Y=10 of YHWH, who is referred to often in the Hebrew Bible as the "only one" using the related noun *bd* (see 2 Kgs 19:15; Isa 37:20).

A chi-square test was done comparing the *four divine-name numbers 17, 23, 26, and* 32, to non-symbolic numbers close to them, 16, 24, 27, and 31. The matrix of 859 potential symbolic hits and 865 potential non-symbolic hits was compared to 231 actual symbolic hits and 127 actual non-symbolic hits. Chi-square is 26.95 and p is 2.1e-7 or positively nearly 100% probable. This gives strong support to positing an intentional utilization of these four divine-name numbers.

Note that although the *multiples* related to 26 continue with the high count of 76 occurrences for 39 (13x3), high counts do not continue beyond 39 since the value 52 (13x4 or 26x2) has only ten occurrences, 65 (13x5) only four, and 78 (26x3) only one. Multiples with **17** continue with 34 with 75 occurrences, and 51 with 24. Multiples with **23** have an intriguing **23** occurrences for 46, but then 69 has only one occurrence. A probability test on the sum of the *doubles* (17x2=34, 23x2=46, 26x2=52, 32x2=64) of the four divine-name numbers compared to the sum of the nearby numbers 32, 48, 54 and 62 with the matrix of 429 symbolic possible hits, and 433 non-symbolic possible hits gives chi-square of 10.13 with p of 0.00146 or 98% positively probable. This supports positing an intentional use of *divine-name x2 multiples in Hosea as symbolic.*

Although not in the table, note that single-letter particles (clitics) greatly increase low numbers. The lemma value of 5 includes 117 *h* articles, and of 6 includes 352 *w* conjunctions, and the number 2 has only one lemma, 129 *b* prepositions. This increases the totals of these basic theological numbers in comparison to their adjacent counts. There is only one singleton lemma (*dg* 'fish') with the value of 7, one singleton (*'b* 'father') with the value of 3, and none for 4.

In summary, lemmas that had the sum of their letters match the divine-name values of 17, 23, 26 and 32 have higher frequencies than nearby non-symbolic numbers, indicating that these four divine name values were selected for use. The sum of frequencies for the doubles for 17 (34), 23 (46), 26 (52), and 32 (64) also have a significantly higher count than their nearby non-symbolic numbers. (46 is smaller than its adjacent numbers, but this may be because its 23 lemmas were purposely limited in order to match its base number 23.) The symbolic counts of *lemma groups* in the above Table 3 use the same symbolic base numbers (5, 6, 11, 13, 17, 23, 32) as in the earlier tables with symbolic counts for *words and lemmas in structural units*. The basic unity of these numbers within a variety of applications makes a strong case for seeing these symbolic numbers as tools used to add beauty and emphasis to the final form of biblical Hebrew texts. They also were likely done out of spiritual devotion to honor God. Labuschagne (*Numerical*, 95) proposes that biblical number patterns "were constructed essentially to the glory of God."

Chronology for the Introduction of Literary Counts

When were these numerical patterns incorporated into the Hebrew text? Forbes ("Method," 34) gives information about the pre-exilic time before the widespread inclusion of vowel letters (which are called "Bible spelling" and are included in the above MT value counts for lemmas), "For the early period, up to the destruction of Jerusalem by the Babylonians in the sixth century, there is enough evidence from these documents to show that Bible spelling is later; it has been adjusted fairly uniformly to the standards of post-exilic times." On p. 35 Forbes points to the other end of the period of changes referring to the "stable" spelling of Hebrew and Aramaic, "This suggests that the corpus of the Hebrew Bible was finally closed, and its text—including its spelling—was fixed sometime in the fourth century BCE." Andersen ("Qumran," 72) and Andersen and Freedman ("4QTestimonia," 250) generally support the fourth century, but add that the time line could have continued to "the third century." As I see it, the observed symbolic numbers based on lines, words, and lemmas could possibly have predated the Babylonian exile, but the number of MT *letters*, and patterns with *values* of lemmas could not be worked out until the spelling was standardized for individual books after the fifth century return from exile. A likely situation would be that the lemma counts were adjusted at the same time that the spelling of earlier books was standardized since revision was being done anyway. The change from Hebrew to Aramaic script may also have facilitated other innovations such as number patterns. Freedman ("Evolution," 10) states that this standardization was realized progressively from the Torah, which has "fewer vowel letters." He goes on to note that in the rest of the Hebrew Bible "the spelling of the Former Prophets is less full than that of the Latter Prophets," while in the Writings generally "the poetic books are somewhat more conservative than the prose works (e.g., Ezra-Nehemiah), which reflect the latest and fullest spelling in the Hebrew Bible."[26] Hosea coming in the Latter Prophets would be after the Torah and Former Prophets in this development of "Bible spelling." The fourth century seems likely to me for Hosea. Song of Songs uses the same theological numbers including the mathematical count with *kbwd*=**32**, and its MT form is dated as late as the third or second century. Therefore the numerical tradition apparently has a history of use through several centuries including both new writings such as Song of Songs and redactions of previous books such as eighth century Hosea.

26. Andersen and Freedman ("4QTestimonia," 251) list "the career of Ezra" as one of the factors in their dating of when the spelling system was put in place to "as early as the first Return or as late as the fourth century." Andersen and Freedman ("4QSamb," 206) in discussing the "double switch of -h to -w and of -w to -yw" note, "This is only one of many indicators of major overhaul of biblical texts during that period, and tradition associates this with the career of Ezra, and with the adoption of the square (Aramaic) character."

Chapter 2

Structural Display and Analysis of Hosea 1–3

Key to Formatting of the Following Poetry:

Peak lines are in **bold** font, secondary peaks and structurally significant key words are in *italics*, and words repeated in relation to the peak and secondary peak lines are underlined in the text below. The Hebrew hyphen (maqqēp) is indicated by =, and normal hyphens—show the set of English words used to translate any one Hebrew word. Places where another option instead of the MT hyphenation is proposed to fit a poetic structure are indicated by parentheses around deleted hyphens (=), and a plus sign in parentheses (+) between words that are joined.

Part One 1:1—3:5

(13 Poems; 88 Poetic Lines; Words: MT 556, Possible revision 558=6x93; Lemmas: MT 767=13x59, Possible revision 768=6x128)

First Block 1:1—2:8[10] Key Words "Children" and "That Day"

(7 Poems; 44 Poetic Lines; Words 286, the confluence of the primary theological and alphabetical factors **26x11=286** and **22x13=286**; Lemmas MT 376, Possible revision 377=13x29 by adding *mn* in 2:1[3] for conjectural improvement of lemma counts in structure, see table 4)

Title: **הוֹשֵׁעַ HOSEA** (one word, which is included in word and lemma counts)
Introduction 1:1–2a
(Chiastic Metrical Poem 5 7 5, with a final 3-foot closure; 4 lines; 25=5x5 words; 7 theological lemmas with divine-name factors of 13, 17, 23, or 32 equal 24.14% of 19 lemmas)

A 1 The-word-of=the-LORD which was
to=Hosea *son-of*=Beeri, (5)
B **in-the-days-of Uzziah, Jotham, Ahaz, Hezekiah**
kings-of Judah, [5+2](7)
A' and-in-the-days-of Jeroboam *son-of*=Joash
king-of Israel. (5)
*

2 *The-beginning-of the-word-of=the-LORD by-Hosea.* (3)

The first two words after the title, *dbr YHWH* 'word of-the-LORD,' both have the value of 26 by adding the value of their letters (*d*=4, *b*=2, *r*=20 totaling 26, and Y=10, H=5, W=6, H=5 totaling 26). They are followed three words later by the name "Hosea." The same sequence "word, LORD, Hosea" in 1:2a ends these introductory lines. This repetition gives strong emphasis by forming an inclusio of the theologically strongest 26-value doublet *dbr YHWH*. The same doublet of "word of-the-LORD" comes in God's covenant with Abram in Gen 15:1 and 4. The lines here show a possible rhythmical structure in that the first sentence has five words, the second seven, the third five, and the last three, as displayed above. This can make a metrical chiasm of 5 7 5 with a final three-foot closure. The structure gives prominence to the Judean kings in the center of the chiasm. This fits with the view that the center line may be a later Judean addition after Israelite priests brought the book to Judea from northern Israel.[1] This central peak is set off structurally by being the longest line, and also has prominence with the words "in-the-days-of" and "king" repeated in the next line where "king" also begins the second colon. The word "son-of" comes in the cola on each side of the central list of kings, giving balance. Without the central line there would be only the two pentameter lines and a final emphatic closure. The structural

1. Mays (*Hosea*, 21) writes, "The Judean kings are given the preferred place by being listed first, a clue to the Judean provenance of the editor." Dearman (*Hosea*, 79) gives as an explanation of the "emphasis on the Judean kings rather than on those in Israel" that "the origins of the book we now have likely comes from Yahwists who moved southward in the aftermath of Israel's demise." He also notes on p. 20 that "their updating for presentation in Judah may have continued into the exilic period."

emphasis would then be on the final "the-word-of-the-LORD by-Hosea," which has prominence from the inclusio with the first line. In the above structure this final monocolon is counted as a secondary peak because of its shortness. (See the discussion on structural identification of secondary peaks in chapter 3 A below.) With the list of Judean kings, the lines before the final closure form a triplet rather than a normal couplet typical of Hosea. Including the final colon with the previous introductory paragraph is supported by MT with a paragraph marker after it.[2]

All symbolic lemma values with factors of 5, 6, 11, 13, 17, 23, and 32 will be listed in each episode in the book to provide data, and those that suggest to me a possible choice by the author/redactor will be pointed out in the discussion as above with the inclusio of 26s. Obviously many of the symbolic numbers occur by pure chance. In contrast to the *structural* study where the alphabetical series beginning with 11 and 22 were found to be stronger, in the following *analysis of each poem* the numbers relating to the theological set for 26 and multiples of its base of 13 are the strongest. Multiples of the other divine numbers 17, 23 and 32 are also important, and to a lesser extent the multiples of 5 and 6. Other lemmas in 1:1–2a with symbolic values are הוֹשֵׁעַ *hwšʿ* (*h*=5, *w*=6, *š*=21, ʿ=16) 'Hosea'=48 or **6**x8 x3, *ʾšr* 'which'=42 or **6**x7, *hyh* 'be'=20 or **5**x4 or **10**x2, *ʾl* 'to'=**13**, *bʾry* 'Beeri'=33 or **11**x3 , *ywtm* 'Jotham'=51 (**17**x3), *yḥzqyhw* 'Hezekiah'=65 (**13**x**5**), *mlk* 'king'=36 or **6**x**6** x2. *yhwdh* 'Judah'=30 or **10**x3 and **5**x**6**, and *w* 'and'=**6**. Having "king" and three names with theological values "Jotham," Hezekiah," and "Judah" in the central peak adds prominence. The total of symbolic numbers in 1:1–2b is 16 of the 29 lemmas or 55.17%. There are 7 large divine-name numbers or 24.14%, 8 small theological numbers or 27.59%, and one 33 of the 22 set or 3.45%.

Episode One: The Marriage of Hosea 1:2b–3

1:2b And-said YHWH to=Hosea: (4 words)

The *waw* 'and' together with the imperfect aspect verb, marks the narrative line—even at the beginning of the story. The three words are best taken as a prose introduction to the following poem. All five lemmas have theological values, *w* 'and' equals **6**, *ʾmr* 'said' equals 34 or **17**x2, YHWH=**26**, *ʾl* 'to' equals **13**, and Hosea equals 48 or **6**x**8**.

2. NRSV "When the Lord first spoke through Hosea," connects the final line to the next paragraph, as do NIV and GNT. Garrett (*Hosea*, 50) recognizes this option, but also points out that "the phrase reads almost like a title and could be translated as "The Beginning of the Lord's speaking to Hosea."

1:2c-d Pentameter Couplet: God Commands Hosea to Marry

(2 lines; 13 words; 48 letters; 11 word-stresses; 16 lemmas of which 9 are large theological lemmas with values of 26, 39, or 64 equaling 56.25% of the 16, *the highest percentage of divine-name lemmas of all 45 poems*)

"Go, (anacrusis) (1)

Take=for-yourself a-wife-of harlotry

and-offspring-of harlotry, (26 letters with "Go") (5)

Because=by-harlotry the-land has-committed-harlotry

from-after the-LORD." (22 letters) (5)

The total of letters in the first line including "Go" is **26**, the main theological number equivalent to the value of YHWH. The second line has **22** letters, the same number as the Hebrew alphabet. This ties it numerically to the central line of the book in 8:2 with its 22 letters. The poem has **13** words, the base of the 26 theological set, and **11** word-stress units, the base of the alphabetical set. These counts related to 26 and 22 in this first poem after the introduction serve as an introduction to the importance of these symbolic numbers in the book. They serve the same purpose as the symbolic factors of the total words in block 1 with the confluence of theological and alphabetical factors **26x11**=286 and **22x13**=286 where the main symbolic number of one set is multiplied by the mathematical base of the other set. There are 16 lemmas, and 9 of these are divine-number multiples. This gives a percentage of 56.25%, *the highest of all 45 poems* for this first poem of Hosea's message. The last poem of the book 14:9[10] is the second highest with 35%. I see this numerical inclusio of the highest divine-number percentages as further evidence of a plan that counted and controlled theological numbers in the book. The nine lemmas here are also unique in that they are all large theological numbers 26, 39 or 64. There are also one each of small theological 5, 6, and 12, but no multiples of the alphabetical 11.

The first word of YHWH to Hosea after the introduction is "Go." The lemma *hlk* for "go" comes **22** times in Hosea. This is significant in the beginning because it also relates to the overall structure of the book, which is based on multiples of the alphabetic number 22. The second word *lqḥ* 'take' has the value of 39 (the sum of 12+19+8), which equals the main theological number 26 plus its base 13 and the Hebrew for "God (is) one."

As in the final MT line 1:2d, the basic pattern of this poem is pentameter—a five-foot rhythm that is also used in dirges. The first line in MT has six words, but "Go" is analyzed here with anacrusis—an additional word introducing the first line. It can be shown to not be a 3+3 rhythm because the six-foot MT line does not divide syntactically into two cola since they would separate the genitive "wife-of" and "harlotry." The syntactic division is after the first "harlotry," the expected place when "Go" is not counted. So the poem is analyzed as having an introductory "Go" plus two five-foot lines each divided syntactically after the third word-stress unit giving regular 3+2 cola.

As in other poems with a homogeneous metrical line sequence, the final line is the climax or peak. The occurrence of the divine name YHWH with its value of **26** as the final word is significant in the peak line here as well as in many other poems. It is also significant as the 52nd lemma in the book or 26x2. The *repetition* in the infinitive absolute translated "by *harlotry*" plus the verb "has committed *harlotry*" is another feature of emphasis in the final peak. Their lemma *znh* 'commit harlotry, prostitution' has the value of **26** (*z*=7, *n*=14, *h*=5) and comes **13** times in Hosea, which enhances its status as a key word, especially when seen with its prominence in this first message with other symbolic numbers. The two *znh* 'commit harlotry' lemmas with the value of 26 form a contrasting inclusio with two *byn* 'understanding'=26 in the last poem 14:9[10], and each poem has one YHWH=26. As noted above, this poem has the highest percentage of divine-number lemmas for the 45 poems, and the final poem has the second highest. I propose that the semantic contrast between "harlotry"=26 and "understanding"=26 in relation to YHWH=26 is an intentional component of the inclusio of highest divine-name percentages.

The metaphor of harlotry for idolatry is used by Hosea and other prophets to emphasize the seriousness of failing to be faithful to YHWH. The related thematic noun *znwnym* 'harlotry'=64 or **32**x2 is prominent with the factor 32, which is one of the four divine-name numbers. It is significantly repeated at the end of each colon in the first line. The double occurrence of these two words suggests a "terrace pattern" (Watson, *Poetry*, 208–12), which repeats words in pairs, leading to a final peak. The final peak line also has two lemmas with the value of **39** (or 26+13), *ʾrṣ* 'land" and *ʾḥry* 'after,' and the article *h* 'the'=**5** on "land." The conjunction "because" can also be noted as an example of more difficult syntax in the peak line—a recognized feature of prominence. The peak also has prominence by departing from normal expectations in not having the parallelism of the other line. (See chapter 3 A, "Structurally Defined Peak" below for a discussion of features which add prominence.)

For God to command a prophet to marry a harlot seems inappropriate. However, Isaiah, Jeremiah, and Ezekiel were also told to do shocking things in order to illustrate their message. Dearman (*Hosea*, 2010:82) writes, "Bizarre behavior is thus not out of the question for prophetic signs!" The "harlotry" of Gomer is not defined by any details, so there are various interpretations including prostitution, or participation in a Baal sex rite.[3] Garrett (*Hosea*, 51) recommends "promiscuous woman" as the meaning, and on p. 52 notes that Hosea implies that she was "habitually licentious."

The description of the children as "children of harlotry" using the same word *znwnym* is especially problematic. Again, there are several proposals of what this says about them. Garrett (54) evaluates the various possibilities and concludes that the term is used since the three children represent the individual Israelites who were unfaithful to God, and "we should not use this language to try to flush out more details about his family life or Gomer's background." On p. 55 Garrett adds, "The children are themselves oracles, and they are the theological framework of Hosea's message." As I see it the change to positive names for the children supports this analysis of "children of harlotry" as a literary representation of Israelites in general here and in 2:4 rather than a description of specific immorality of the three children.

Other lemmas with symbolic values in 1:2c-d are *lqḥ* 'take'=39 or **13x3** or **26+13**, *l* 'for'=12 or **6x2**, *w* 'and'=**6**, and *yld* 'child'=**26**. This totals 12 for the poem, making 75% of the 16 lemmas with theological symbolism. There are nine large number factors (without the small YHW 10, 5, and 6)—four 26s, three 39s with factors of 13, and two 64 with the factor of 32. The three small theological numbers are one each of *w* 'and'=6, *l* 'for/to'=12 or 6x2, and *h* 'the'=5. There are none with the factor of 10 or with the alphabetical 11, 22 factors.

1:3 Narrative of Marriage and Birth

(10 words, and together with the next speech introduction 13 words)

And-he-went, and-he-took Gomer the-daughter-of=Diblaim, (4)

and-she-conceived, and-she-bore=to-him a-son. (3)

All three narratives (1:3, 6, 8) where God commands Hosea to name Gomer's children have the lemmas *hrh* 'conceive' and *yld* 'bore' with numerical allusions to symbolic numbers (*hrh*: *h*=5, *r*=20, h=5 for 30 or **10x3** and **5x6**; and *yld*: *y*=10, *l*=12, *d*=4 for **26**). The consistent use of these words with values that refer to YHWH in the three narratives of conception and birth anticipates Hosea's teaching of YHWH as the source of conception and birth. The lemma *lqḥ* 'take'=39 (for a wife), and "Gomer" (*g*=3, *m*=13, *r*=20) with the value of 36 or **6x6**, add to this symbolism. Other symbolic

3. Dearman (*Hosea*, 367) writes, "Gomer's form(s) of sexual infidelity could include one or more acts of commercial prostitution, adultery, ritual copulation to enhance fertility, and possibly sex to pay a sacred vow."

lemmas are four *w* 'and'=**6**, the *'t* object=**23**, *bt* 'daughter'=24 or **6**x4, and *l* 'to'=12 or **6**x2. This narrative has seven words and is divided syntactically after the first four as in poetic seven-foot lines. However, since the following narrative line has only three words, there is no adjacent heptameter line to fill a typical couplet. The verse is prose.

Episode Two: The Naming of Jezreel 1:4–5

1:4a Narrative Introducing the Divine Command

And-YHWH said to-him: (3)

The pattern is parallel to episode one in that the command is introduced in a minimal three-word narrative formula. The only difference is "him" instead of "Hosea." All four lemmas have theologically symbolic values, *w* 'and'=**6**, YHWH=**26**, *'mr* 'said'=34 or **17**x2, and *'l* 'to'=**13**.

1:4b-5 Chiastic Poem 5 66 5 God Commands Hosea to Name his Son Jezreel

(4 lines; **26** words; 104 or **26**x4 letters; **22** word-stresses for both MT and the chiastic rearrangement below; **33** lemmas of which 9 or 27.27% are multiples of the large theological divine-name lemmas, 13, 17, 23, or 32, as the 14th highest poem; and 5 lemmas with multiples of the alphabetic set 11 making 15.15%, the third highest of the 45 poems, 3 of these are 66, which also is a multiple of 6, representing *W* of *YHWH*)

A *"Call his-name <u>Jezreel</u>,*
for=in-just a-little-while (20 letters) (5)
B **I-will-punish the=blood-of <u>Jezreel</u>**
on(=)the-<u>house</u>-of Jehu, (26 letters) (5/6)
B' **And-I-will-end the-kingdom-of the-<u>house</u>-of(+)<u>Israel</u>.**
* (enjambment)
5 **And-it-will-be in-that day,** (32 letters) (7/6)
A' *That-I-will-break the=bow-of <u>Israel</u>*
in-the-valley-of <u>Jezreel</u>." (26 letters) (5)

This poem of four lines has **26** words, the full value of the lemma *YHWH*, as compared to half that or 13 in the previous poem. It also has **22** word-stress units, the full number of letters in the alphabet, as compared to 11 in the previous poem. The total number of letters is 104 or **26**x4. The first line of the central peak and the last line, which is a secondary peak, both have 26 letters giving numeric prominence to these lines. The line between them has 32 letters, with the divine-name number of *kbwd* by mathematical counts. Note that the previous poem 1:2c-d had only two lines, with 26 letters in the first line, and 22 in the second, giving a total of 48, which is 6x8, with the 6 equal to the W of YHWH. The arrangement of numbers in these two first poems of the message is evidence of a special effort to enhance the beauty of the book by symbolic numbers.

The above proposed 5665 metrical chiasm emphasizes the thematic lines of "punishment of Jehu in Jezreel" and "ending the kingdom of Israel" in the center lines where chiastic emphasis normally occurs.[4] The key word of this poem is 'Jezreel.' It comes chiastically in the central peak and as an inclusio in the first colon and last word. The value of Jezreel (*y*=10, *z*=7, *r*=20, ʿ=16, ʾ=1, *l*=12) is 66, which is 11x6, combining the base of the alphabetical set with 6, which represents the *W* of YHWH. Sixty-six is also the sum of 17+23+26, the three numbers that symbolically represent YHWH that are based on the sequence of the alphabet.[5] The meaning of "Jezreel" is "God sows," which is thematically important in Hosea's proclamation to the agrarian Israelites that YHWH, not Baal, is the true God who controls the crops. The peak line "I will punish the blood of Jezreel on the house of Jehu" has been interpreted as the result of Jehu going too far in his carrying out God's command to exterminate Ahab's line to avenge the blood of the prophets and servants of YHWH in 2Ki 9:7–8. Sherwood (*Literary*, 123), however, notes that the destruction of Ahab's line by Jehu in Jezreel is presented in Hosea not "as a positive act of vengeance" but "as a moral outrage to be avenged." She adds that in this way "Hosea's sign 'Jezreel' does not mimic history but recreates history by radical reinterpretation." Garrett (*Hosea*, 57) proposes that pāqad 'visit, punish' followed by "blood" in 1:4 should not be "punish," but "seems to mean 'visit upon' in the sense that God would bring upon Jehu's dynasty the same violent destruction that befell Omri's dynasty." Dearman (*Hosea*, 2010:92–93) notes both of these possibilities

4. The 22 word-stress units of MT can be made into a metrical chiasm by moving a hyphen in the third line to the second. This may be done as illustrated above by separating *ʿl* 'on' from "the-house" in B, and joining "house-of(+)Israel" in B'. This makes both lines regular 3+3 hexameters. Such metrically motivated changes are obviously subjective, but I propose that they are within possible adjustments performers could make to fit a poetic rhythm.

5. Sixty-six is also used in Song of Songs as a theologically important symbolic number because of the addition of 17+23+26. Songs also has three other symbolic numbers 98, 79, and 78, based on addition of combinations of the four numbers representing YHWH including 32 which is calculated by the mathematical system (Bliese, *Count*, 63).

that "the blood of Jezreel" indicates either "judgment" or "a matter of joining a well-known place of fighting (cf. 1Kgs. 21) with the coming fall of the ruling dynasty."

"Israel" also comes chiastically connecting the central peak and last line. It comes 44 times in Hosea or double the alphabetical **22**. It's lemma *yśr ʾl* has the value of 64 or **32**x2. The repetition of *byt* 'house' with the value of 34 or **17**x2 coming in each line of the peak adds prominence to the center of the chiastic inversion along with "Jezreel" and "Israel." The chiasmus is filled in with "Jezreel" on the ends, and time phrases "in just a little while" and "it will be in that day" between them.[6] Except for *ʿl* 'on'=28, all lemmas in the central peak have symbolic values as multiples of the full set including 5, 6, 11, 13, 17, 23, and 32. The symbolic lemmas in the peak are *w* 'and'=**6** x2, *pqd* 'punish'=40 or **10**x4 or **5**x8, *ʾt* object=**23**, *dm* 'blood'=**17**, *yzrʿʾl* 'Jezreel'=**66**, *yhwʾ* 'Jehu'=**22**, *šbt* 'end'=45 or **5**x9, and *mmlkwt* 'kingdom'=**77**. The value of *mmlkwt* is prominent as 77 or **11**x7, combining the base of the alphabetical set with the 7 fulness set. Note that "Jehu" and "kingdom" are singletons suggesting they are chosen especially to fill the 22 and 77 slots in this poem.[7]

A *double* rather than single peak line in the center regularly indicates further prominence in the peripheral lines of Hebrew poems. Such initial and final lines are therefore called secondary peaks in this study. In the first line *ʿwd* 'again, still, just' has the value of **26** (ʿ=16, *w*=6, *d*=4), *qrʾ* 'call'=40, and *šm* 'name'=34. The object marker *ʾt*=**23** (ʾ=1, t=22), is repeated chiastically in the peak and last line along with "Jezreel" and "Israel." Other lemmas with symbolic values in the last line are *hyh* 'be'=20, *h* 'the'=**5**, and *hwʾ* 'that'=12. There are 25 symbolic lemmas in the poem or 75.75% of the 33 lemmas. Of these 9 or 27.27% are with multiples of the large theological divine-name numbers 13, 17, 23, and 32, tying with 7:3–7 for 12th highest. There are 11 or 33.33% with small theological numbers 5, 6, and 10. The remaining five are multiples of 11, the base of the alphabetic set, making 15.15%, *the third highest of the 45 poems*. They are Jezreel=66 x3, kingdom=77, and Jehu=22, of which one of each comes in the central peak. This is significant since the first poem of the 44 messages, 1:2c-d, is the highest

6. Garrett, (*Hosea*, 57–58) presents a diagram and gives reasons for "incomplete" elements in a chiastic structure incorporating all of 1:4b–5 "Call his name Jezreel (A) For it is just a little while (B) And I will bring the bloodshed of Jezreel (C) upon the house of Jehu (D) And I will put an end (C) to the kingdom of the house of Israel (D) 5 And it will be in that day (B) And I shall break (C) the bow of Israel (D) In the valley of Jezreel. (A)."

7. Garrett, (*Hosea*, 56–57) discusses the inconsistency of condemning Jehu here when he is commended elsewhere. It may be that the attraction of the 22-value of Jehu's name influenced this choice of ruler.

of the divine-name numbers and has *no lemmas with values as multiples of 11*. The high number of alphabetical values in this 1:4b–5 is enhanced by the totals of 22 word-stress units and 33 lemmas in the poem.

Another interesting structural feature is that the first two and last two lines both have structures breaking from normal semantic connections in their bicola by having the second colon of the first lines connect to the following lines instead of to the first cola. Both of the second cola, "for in just a little while" and "and it will be in that day," are semantically parallel as time clauses, which further emphasizes the similarity. The stronger semantic break between 4b and 5 is marked with a * stanza juncture to show the enjambment in this line. The colon "And it will be in that day" aligns metrically with the last colon of verse 4, but aligns semantically with verse 5. Such enjambment is very common in the following poems. This structural pattern and the analysis as a metrical chiasm are both repeated in the next poem in 1:6b–7.

Episode Three: The Naming of "Not Pitied" 1:6–7

1:6a Narrative Report of Birth of Daughter, and the Divine Speech

And-she-conceived again, and-bore a-daughter;
and-He-said to-him; [2+2+2](6)

There is no "to him" after "bore" as in 1:3, either here or in the next birth account in 1:8 "And she conceived and bore a son." This has prompted speculation that these two are not Hosea's.[8] However, these are best taken as abbreviations since it is not clearly stated they were not his. The three narrative tenses with initial *w* identify the line as a prose introduction to the following poem. After the initial *hrh* 'conceive' with the value of 30, the contiguous lemmas *ʿwd* 'again" and *yld* 'bore' both have the value of **26**, which give numerical prominence. As in the narrative in 1:2b, all lemmas have theological values, here including *bt* 'daughter,' which has the value of 24 or 6x4 (with *b*=2 and *t*=22), *ʾmr* 'say'=34, *l* 'to'=12, and *w*=6 x3.

1:6b–7 Chiastic Poem 7 66 7 God Commands Hosea to Name the Daughter "No Mercy"

(4 lines; 30=10x3 or 5x6 words; 27 MT word-stresses or **26** revised; 41 lemmas of which 11 or 26.82% have values that are multiples of large divine-name theological lemmas, the 17th highest)

8. Kidner (*Hosea*, 23) sees the omission of "to him" as a denial of "paternity," which is reinforced by the name "Not My People" for the third child.

A *"Call her-name "No mercy,"*
For I-will-not(+)add again (8/7)
B **To-have-mercy on-the=house-of Israel** AB
that=I-forgiving forgive for-them; CC' (6)
B' 7 **But-on-the=house-of Judah I-will-have-mercy.** B'A'
* (enjambment)
And-I-will-save-them by-YHWH, their-God; (6)
A' *And-I-will-not save-them by-bow and-by-sword,*
nor-by-battle by-horses and-riders." (7)

1:6b–7 has 30 words, which has factors of all three letters of YHWH, with Y=10, W=6, and H=5. MT has 27 word-stress units. However, to show a metrical chiasm, the above display adds a hyphen between the negative "not" and "add," as is more normal for negatives. This makes **26** word-stress units, the value of YHWH, which is the basis of the theological set used in Hosea. This compares to the previous poem with 22 word-stress units, the basis of the alphabetical set. The name YHWH with the value of **26** comes in the peak the sixth of the 46 or **23**x2 times in the book. It is expanded with "Elohim" in "YHWH their-God." This is significantly the *first* of the **26** Elohim in Hosea. These divine names together with their symbolic total counts add prominence to the theme of YHWH's salvation coming here for the first time in the book in the same peak colon, "I will save them by YHWH, their God." The key word of the first stanza is "mercy" emphasized by the shocking name *l ʾ rḥmh* 'No Mercy' for the girl.[9] The key word of the second stanza is *yšʿ* 'save.' They are both repeated, coming once in the central peak, and respectively in the secondary peaks at each end. "Save" is also repeated twice in part 5 at 13:10 and 14:3[4], forming a double inclusio for the book. The lemma *sws* 'horse' is also part of the book inclusio coming only here and in 14:3[4]. After the name Lo-Ruhamah 'No Mercy' in the first line, the lemma *rḥm* 'have mercy' comes in each line of the peak and six times in part 1, but then does not occur until its seventh final time in 14:3[4]. The lemma *nśʾ* 'forgive,' which has prominence with its infinitive absolute "forgiving forgive," also comes in 14:2[3] adding to the salvation inclusio for the book. It has the value of 36 or **6**x**6**. The two peak lines give thematic emphasis to

9. Sherwood (*Literary*, 118) notes, "The coupling of children and non-love is striking and perverse, and it is reasonable to suggest that it would have appeared so in any society and any historical context." On pp 123–24 she points out how this also "subverts the equation between God and love and mercy that occurs frequently in the Hebrew Bible."

"mercy" by an inverted parallelism: (a) mercy (b) on the house of Israel; (b) on the house of Judah (a) mercy (see Andersen and Freedman, *Hosea*, 241). The repetition of both "mercy" and "house" in the peak lines is enhanced by *byt* 'house' having the value of 34 or 17x2, and being repeated in each line of the previous peak at 1:4. Except for the initial "surely the land has committed harlotry from after the LORD" in 1:2, neither this nor the following poem on "Not-My-People" add information concerning the offense that will not be forgiven. The metaphor of "harlotry" will be developed as idolatry in Hos 2.[10]

Other lemmas with symbolic values in the peak are *yśr ʾl* 'Israel'=64, *yhwdh* 'Judah'=30, *ʾt* (object)=23, *l* 'for'=12, and *w* 'and'=6 x2 in peak and x4 in the last secondary peak line. The focus on the center with "mercy" in the first line and central peak, and "save" in the central peak and last line, supports the proposed chiastic metrical structure. The two central peak lines both end with the suffix *-hem* "them/their" giving further balance by rhyme. The Hebrew word *ʾrḥm* 'I-will-have-mercy' with the suffix *-ēm* 'them' also comes in the first cola of both peak lines. The thematic change from "mercy" to "save" in the second colon of B' resembles the break in the last lines of the previous poem, and can be identified as enjambment at the strophe break. "And I will save them by YHWH their God" aligns metrically as the last peak colon, but semantically as the first colon of the final strophe. The *waw* conjunctions in both poems at the point of enjambment and again beginning the clause following the enjambment also show the similar pattern in each poem. The semantic alignment of the second colon of the first line with the second line, is also the same as in the previous poem with *ki* 'for.' *Ki* also comes in the peak at 6c as "that."

The double line in the center theoretically suggests prominence in the ends. The naming of "No Mercy," and the value of 26 for *ʿwd* 'again' give the first line prominence. "Again" also comes in the prose introduction "conceived again," and in the first line of the previous poem forming anaphora. Lemmas with symbolic values in the secondary peak of the first line are *qr ʾ* 'call'=30, *šm* 'name'=34, and *l ʾ* 'no/not'=13, which comes twice in the first line including with "No mercy" and in the last line with "not save." In the last line the key word *yš ʿ* 'save' and the *list* of military terms add prominence. The preposition *b* 'by' comes five times in the last line besides once in the peak with "by the LORD." Stuart (*Hosea*, 32) notes the chiasm in the last line of "bow-sword," "battle" and "horses-horsemen," arranged so that the

10. Sherwood (*Literary*, 127) writes, "The linchpin of the signifying chain in Hosea 1 is sexual intercourse. Intercourse is an icon of idolatry but on a literal level leads to children: the implication is that as surely as sex leads to conception and birth, so idolatry leads to the wrath of Yhwh."

"foot-soldiers" with bows and swords and "mounted combatants" enclose the central "warfare/battle." The value of *ḥrb* 'sword' is 30 (10x3, 5x6), *sws* is 36 (6x6), and *mlḥmh* 'warfare' is 51 or 17x3, giving numerical prominence to the last line. Eleven of the 41 lemmas of the poem or 26.82% are with multiples of the large symbolic divine-name numbers—two 13s, two 23s, two 26s, four multiples of 17, and one multiple of 32. Fourteen are with YHW small numbers—six *w*=6, three multiples of 10, and five multiples of 6. There are none with multiples of 11.

The reference to "Judah," in 7a is taken by many commentators to be a positive interpolation after Assyria conquered Israel.[11] If there was an early text without the third line, the poem would still recommend a chiastic structure of 7 6 7, with the peak in the center and with the last line a condemnation, consistent with the central peak's emphasis on "no mercy."

Episode Four: The Naming of "Not My People" 1:8–9

1:8–9a Narrative Report of the Birth of the Next Son
(8 words, 11 lemmas)

8 And-she-weaned No-Mercy,
    and-she-conceived and-bore a-son. (6)
9a And-He-said: (1)

This narrative section carries forward the time line, and introduces God's next speech. Garrett (*Hosea*, 169) notes that weaning at that time was normally "some three years" after a birth. Again, the narrative tenses with *w* show that it is prose, distinguishing it from the following poem. "And-he-said" is an even more abbreviated prose introduction than earlier forms. Of the ten lemmas, "wean," "No-Mercy," and "son" do not have symbolic values, but the three *w* 'and' conjunctions have 6s, and the four lemmas repeated from previous speech introductions have the following theological values: "conceive"=30 or 10x3 and 5x6, "bore"=26, "said"=34 or 17x2, and *ʾt* object=23.

11. See Wolff (*Hosea*, 20–21); Mays, (*Hosea*, 29); and Dearman, (*Hosea*, 99) who does not exclude Hosea as a possible redactor. Instead of this positive interpretation concerning Judah, Andersen and Freedman (*Hosea*, 188–194) propose continuing the negative of 6 through 7a. For reactions see Emmerson (*Hosea*, vii–viii, 88–95); Garrett (*Hosea*, 60); and Dearman (*Hosea*, 97).

1:9b–d Three Line Tetrameter Poem, Command to Name "Not My People" (3 lines; 12=6x2 words; 11 word-stresses; 12 lemmas, 4 of which or 33.33% have large divine-name values with three multiples of 13 and one of 17, the 4th highest of the 45 poems.)

"Call his-name
    "*Not~my-people*," (4)
For you-are
    not my-people; (4)
And-I AM=not for-you." (3)

1:9b-d has 11 word-stress units, matching the first poem in this series on Hosea's family in 1:2c-d. The first poem between them has 22, and the second has a proposed word-stress adjustment from 27 to 26, which will make word-stress units in all four poems numerically symbolic. This poem is only a line and a half in the BHS display of MT. One way to describe this structure is to say that the third clause is "balancing the others" (Buss, *Prophetic*, 41). The effect is a dramatic cut-off ending this historical section of the children's names. Another way to analyze the structure fits the homogeneous line option of many other poems in Hosea—such as the first couplet in 1:2 commanding Hosea's marriage. This homogeneous analysis is portrayed above. The first two lines are tetrameter. The last is trimeter as in the MT, which gives added emphasis by the change at the end. The peak line in such a homogeneous sequence (as distinguished from chiasmus) is predictably the final one. It is very emphatic with the hinted reference to the divine name, *ʾhyh* 'I AM' of Exod 3:14. The "not" before it after the two previous names beginning with "not" gives the clue that this is intended to refer to YHWH as "I AM." "For you" is a clear reference to the covenant form "I will be God for you, and you will be people for me" (see Exod 6:4–7; Deut 29:12–13; and Jer 11:2–4). "I am not for you" is therefore a pronouncement ending the covenant (see Garrett, *Hosea*, 70, and Dearman, *Hosea*, 99). This negation of *ʾhyh* 'I am/will be' for you is reversed in an inclusio for the book with a positive "*I will be* as dew to Israel" in 14:5[6]. These are the only two "I am/will be" forms of *ʾhyh* in Hosea, although one narrative tense in 11:4 has the same form after its initial *waw*, "*And I was* to them as those who lift the yoke on their jaws, and bent to him feeding." The lemma *hyh* 'be' has the value of 20 or 10x2 and 5x4.

The repetition of *lōʾ ʿammî* 'not my people' in the second cola of each of the first two lines builds up to the last line which also has the same *lōʾ* in "I am not." Such buildups by repetition are common in homogeneous poems, and help to emphasize the end. The first *ʿammî* comes in the name *lō ʾ ʿammî*, but it is not hyphenated, so the two lemmas are counted separately. The count for *ʿammî* in Hosea is therefore 17, giving the lemma prominence from its association to one of the four numbers representing YHWH. The name comes once more in 2:23[25] where it is written with a *maqqēp* or hyphen indicating that it is a name.[12] The combined value of the name *lō ʾ= ʿammî* is 52 or **26**x2, adding strong theological symbolism to the name. "Not," which comes three times in this poem, has the value of **13**. *Qr ʾ* 'call' has the value of 40 or **10**x4 and **5**x8, and *šm* 'name' has the value of 34 or **17**x2. The full emphatic pronouns *ʾtm* 'you' plural and *ʾnky* 'I' are interesting since both have the value of 36 or **6**x**6** adding a numerical play on words building up to "I" in the final peak. There is also a *w* conjunction=**6**, and the pronoun *l* 'for'=12 or **6**x2 in the final peak. Of the twelve lemmas, six are with YW small factors 10 and 6 giving 50% of the twelve, and the four others are two 13s, one 34 based on 17, and one 52 based on 26, making 33.33% or the 4th highest poem in the book. This is significant since the poem has the divine "I AM" reference. There are no lemmas with multiples of 11.

This analysis also gives an interesting structural pattern to all of the four poems about Hosea's family, with homogeneous sequence lines at the beginning and the end, each with 11 word-stresses, and two structurally similar chiastic poems in the middle with 22 and 26 word-stresses. The only occurrences of "The LORD" or "God" are significantly in the *peak* last lines of the homogeneous first (1:2d) and last poem with its "I AM," and in the *peak* central section of the chiastic third poem (1:7a). The third person *lāhem* 'for them' reference at the end of the first line of the peak of the "No-mercy" poem in 1:6 is changed to the more personal and thus more emphatic *lākem* 'for you' in the last word of the "Not-my-people" poem in 1:9. The total for the preposition *l* in Hosea for both the MT and for the suggested revised total count is 143 or **13**x**11**.[13] This is a powerful symbolic number since the factors 13 and 11 are the two basic numbers for the theological set of 26 and the alphabetical set of 22. The **26**th *l* comes with God

12. Andersen and Forbes, ("Count," 302) in discussing what the MT scribes counted note, "was *mappeq* considered a spacer? That items ligatured by *maqqep* might have been counted as single words at some places and times seems to us (and to Weil) likely." My own counts here and in Song of Songs have counted only *names* with maqqēp as single words. I have added ~ in the above display to show that *lō ʾ~ ʿammî* is also a name.

13. Bliese, (*Count*, 43) notes that Song of Songs has seventy-eight *l* 'to/for' prepositions, and that 78 is a very potent symbolic number with factors of 13x6, 26x3, and 39x2, as well as the sum of 13+26+39=78. Also see page 200 where *ʿammî* 'my-people' in Song 6:12 is noted to be the 936th word with factors of 13x72, 26x36, 39x24, and 78x12.

making a "covenant" in 2:18[20]. These numbers add evidence to support intentional counting and adjusting of lemmas in Hosea in order to beautify "the word of YHWH."

1:10—2:1 [Hebrew 2:1–3] Chiastic Poem 546 44 645 Israel's Restoration (8 lines; 46=23x2 words; 60 lemmas 10x6, 5x12, of which 17 or 28.33% have divine-name multiples, the 11th highest poem, a possible revision adds a lemma making 61)

A 10 *But-the-number-of the-children-of=Israel will-be*
as-the-sand-of the-sea, (5)
B Which-is not=measured
And-not counted. (4)
*
C And-it-will-be-that in-the-place
where=it-was-said to-them,
"You-are not=my-people," [2+2+2](6)
D **It-will-be-said to-them,**
"Children-of the-living=God." (4)
*
D' 11 **And-they-will-be-gathered, the-children-of=Judah**
and-the-children-of=Israel together, (4)
C' And-they-will-appoint for-themselves
one leader;
and-they-will-go-up from=the earth; [2+2+2](6)
* {enjambment since 11c also connects to 11d}
B' Because great
is-the-day-of Jezreel, (4)
A' 1 *Say to-your-brothers, "My-People,"*
and-to-your-sisters, "Mercy." (26 letters) (5)

Some commentators consider this poem to be "loosely connected" sayings of Hosea put together by an editor in a "diffuse style" (Wolff, *Hosea*, 1965:26). However, BHS displays MT as a chiastic poem with perfectly metered lines of 546 44 645. The couplets all show semantic parallelism regardless of the different metrical length of each of the lines. Internal parallelism can be noted in cola relating to each other in lines B (not measure//not counted), D' (children of Judah//children of Israel) A' (to your brothers//to your sisters). The second line of the peak, D', also has inverted semantic parallelism, which is a common feature of emphasis in peak lines: (a) "gather" (b) "children" (b) "children" (a) "together." The value of *qbṣ* 'gather' has the value of 39 or 26+13 giving it theological prominence. The repetition of "children of" in the first line and three times in the central peak points to it as a key word. Such repetition between the first line and the central peak is a feature often found in chiastic poems. "Children of Israel" comes six times in Hosea, while "children of Judah" comes only here. "Children of the living God" also comes once in the central peak. If "children of Judah" is a later addition, the pre-Judean total for "children of" would have been seven. *Yśr ʾl* 'Israel' has the value of 64 or **32x2**, and is repeated chiastically in the first line and central peak. Also in the peak *yhwdh* 'Judah' has the value of 30 with factors of **10**, **6**, and **5**. The central peak of the chiasm is thematic, especially the emphatic colon "say to them, 'children of the living God.'" *Lāhem* 'to them' is the same word in the denial of forgiveness in 1:6, and the same preposition *l* as at the end of 1:9 "I am not for you." Now the reversal comes with the seventh *l* preposition. The previous order when the names were given has been changed in 1:10[2:1]d with the originally *final* "not my people" reversed to "children of the living God" coming *first* before the other names.[14] *ʾēl* 'God' has the value of **13**, the base of the 26 set. In the last strophe "My-people" comes in the final secondary peak line between the names "Jezreel" and "Mercy." The word *ʿmy* (16+13+10) 'My-people,' including the *y* 'my' suffix, is analyzed as a name as in NRSV, NJPS, Garrett, and WHM. It has the value of 39 or **13x3** or **26+13**. The divine numbers relate numerically to *yzrʿʾl* 'Jezreel' (God sows) with the value of 66 or **6x11** or **26+17+23** in the final secondary peak.[15] The first lemma of the peak and of the last secondary peak line is *ʾmr* 'say'=34 or **17x2**, chiastically tying the center to the end. "Say" also comes in the line before the peak giving balance with that in the other half. The conjunction *w* 'and'=**6** comes twice in the central peak, twice in the first secondary peak, once in the last secondary

14. Dearman (*Hosea*, 104) writes concerning "children of the living God," "This affirmation is at the same time part of the reversal of the declaration that Israelites were "children of harlotry" (1:2) and "not God's people" (1:9). One might say that the phrase *children of the living God*, which occurs only in Hosea, is a corporate reversal of the name Not My People."

15. The literary importance of the three children is obvious in chapters 1–3. Garrett (*Hosea*, 36–37) also sees the symbolism of "the three children" shaping "the text" of the following chapters 4–7, and notes structural triads reflecting the number of Hosea's children continuing through the book.

peak, and three times in other lines. On each side of the center the hexameters are exceptional tricola of two feet per cola [2+2+2] adding to the symmetrical balance. The tricola analysis is followed here from BHS.

The double lines DD' in the central peak structurally point to secondary peak emphasis at the ends in this final reversal from the negative names. The final line has special numerical status with **26** letters. The repetition of "say to . . . and to" in the last line, repeating "say to" in the peak and in 10c adds prominence, making a total in the poem of four *l* 'to'=12 or **6x2** along with three *ʾmr* 'say'=34 or **17x2**. The repetition of the root *ʾḥ* 'brothers' and *ʾḥwt* 'sisters' along with the preposition *l* 'to' also adds prominence to the last line. *Gdwl* 'great' has the value of 25 or **5x5** adding to the numerical symbolism with reference to the *H*=5 x2 of YHWH. The LXX has "brothers" and "sisters" *singular* and is followed by most versions to fit with the singular brother and sister of chapter 1. This change is also suggested in the Appendix as a possible revision in 2:1[3] adding a lemma *mn* 'from' when the plural -*m* suffixes become prefixes on the following words. The last couplet is also distinguished by having no hyphens (unlike the other lines). Each beat has only one word, slowing down the cadence for emphasis. It also changes from third to second person *ʾtm* 'you' =36 or **6x6**, giving a more personal emphasis, which is a common feature of prominence in peak lines. This recalls the same third person to second person change between 1:6 and 1:9 above in the poem where God announces that the covenant with "my-people" has ended.

The double lines in the center also suggest looking for emphasis in the first line of the poem. This is realized in the key phrase noted above, "children of Israel," and the reference to the patriarchal blessing "as sand of the sea" (Gen 22:17; 32:12). Numerically *ym* 'sea' has the value of **23**, and *ḥwl* 'sand' of **26**. "Sand" is also the 143rd word in Hosea with factors of **13x11**, the two base numbers of the two major symbolic sets. Since "sand" occurs only here in Hosea, its placement together with the main symbolic number 26 has a good likelihood of being intentional. Other lemmas with symbolic values in the first line are *w* 'and'=**6**, *hyh* 'be'=20, *yśr ʾl* 'Israel'=64 or **32x2**, *k* 'as'=**11**, and *h* 'the'=**5**. Also in the first line *mspr* 'number'=65 or **13x5** has prominence from both the numerical factors and from repetition of the same root with *spr* 'count' in the second line. "Not measured and not counted" in the second line also has theological values—*lʾ* not'=**13** twice, and *spr* 'counted' (*s*=15+*p*=17+*r*=20)=52 or **26x2**.

In the line before the central peak, besides "say"=34 or **17x2**, there is also *mqwm* 'place'= 51 or **17x3**. In the line after the central peak there are four lemmas with symbolic multiples, two from the alphabetical 11 set, and two from the theological 13 set, as follows: *śym* 'appoint'=44, *ʿlh* 'go up'=33, *ʾḥd* 'one'=13, and *ʾrṣ* 'earth'=39 or 13x3.

Many translations ignore the MT clause break and connect "and they will go up from the earth" in 1:11[2:2]b with the following "because great is the day of Jezreel" instead of the former clause as above. If this poem were dealt with in isolation, making this change could be considered, although it would undo the parallel structure of tricola [2+2+2] on both sides of the peak. As displayed above without enjambment, MT clauses can be arranged in a beautifully chiastic metrical structure with couplet strophes throughout the poem with no changes in MT hyphenation. On the other hand, a comparison with the three major poems at the end of chapters 2 and 3, shows the same trademark of a semantic break or enjambment between the two cola at the beginning of the last strophe. Enjambment was also noted above in the previous two chiastic poems. In 2:23[25] we find the same ambiguous situation of a colon meeting both the semantic parallelism of the preceding line, and/or opening a new line. The variously interpreted, "go up from the earth," is therefore ambiguous. It may either be interpreted in relation to Jezreel, "God sows," as GNT does with, "grow and prosper in their land" (see Dearman *Hosea*, 2010:106, and see 10:8 for this use of the verb *ʿlh* 'go up'), or the structure of the tricolon may relate the phrase semantically to the preceding 'be gathered' (*qbṣ*), which supports the New American Bible, "come up from other lands," as is found in 2:15[17] " I brought her up from the land of Egypt." (For *qbṣ* in a similar context, see Isa 11:12 "*gather* the dispersed of Judah from the four corners of the earth," and Isa 43:5 "I will bring your offspring from the east, and from the west I will *gather* you.") Also note Wolff (*Hosea*, 24) who applies it to Israel's land: "take possession of the land." The ambiguity is described by Wolff (*Hosea*, 28) as "various allusions," by Mays (*Hosea*, 33) as a "riddle," and by Yee (*Hosea*, 74) as "multifaceted." Besides the play on *ʿlh* 'come up/grow up' further prominence comes in that three of the four lemmas have symbolic values: *ʿlh*=33 or 11x3, *h* 'the'=5, and *ʾrṣ* 'earth'=39 or 13x3. In the preceding phrase of this line "they will appoint for themselves one leader" every lemma is symbolic: *śm* 'appoint'=44 or 11x4, *l* 'for'=12 or 6x2 (also twice earlier), *rš* 'head, leader'=42 or 6x7, and *ʾḥd* 'one'=13.

Other symbolic lemmas in the poem are: *ʾšr* 'which'=42 or 6x7 x2, *lʾ* 'not'=13 x3, *hyh* 'be'=20 or 10x2 or 5x4, *mqwm* 'place'=51 or 17x3, and *ʾtm* 'you' plural=36 or 6x6. Of the 60 lemmas 17 or 28.33% have divine-name factors, four have multiples of 11, and 25 have multiples of 5 or 6.

2:2–8[4–10] Chiastic Poem 366552555 7 555255663 The Adulterous Wife Deceived by Her Lovers

(19 lines; 102 words; 141 lemmas, 34 or 24.41% that are divine-name multiples)

2:2–3[Hebrew 4–5] Stanza I, Plead with Your Mother Lest I Destroy Her

A 2 *Plead with-your-mother, plead,* (3)
B For=*she* is-not my-wife,
and-*I* am-not her-husband; (6)
*
C And-let-her-remove her-harlotry from-her-face,
and-her-adultery from-between her-breasts, (6)
D 3 Lest=I-strip-her naked,
and-make-her-bare as-the-day of-her-birth; [2+3](5)
*
E *And-make-her as-a-desert,*
and-set-her as-a-dry land, [2+3](5)
F *And-kill-her with-thirst.* (2)

All of 2:2–8[4–10] is one metrical unit indicated by the above A, B, C, D, E, F letters, which will continue in following stanzas to J and back to A' representing the metrical inversion 366552555 7 555255663. However, it will be discussed separately for each stanza. First I'll note an *inclusio for the whole poem* with the series *hy'* 'she,' *l'* 'not'=13, and *'nky* 'I'=36 or **6x6.** These three words come in the first verse 2:2[4] "For *she* is *not* my wife, and *I* am not her husband" and last verse 2:8[10] "*She* did *not* know that *I* gave her." "She" comes only in these two places in Hosea making the inclusio especially powerful. "I" *'nky* comes **11** times in the book, but these are the only two in this poem. "Not" *l'* comes 65 or **13x5** times in the book and seven times in this poem of which the first and last are those in the inclusio. "Husband" *'yš*=**32** is matched chiastically inside the three words of the inclusio coming in this poem only in 2:2[4] and in 2:7[9] "I will return to my first *husband.* "Husband" is important in the thematic metaphor where the husband represents God, so its value of 32 as one of the four numbers used to represent God is especially significant.

There is also a pattern in the first half of the full poem 2:2–8[4–10] with *znwnym* 'harlotry'=64 or **32x2** here in 2:2[4] and in 2:4[6] with "children of harlotry," the only occurrences in this poem, but twice in the first command to Hosea to marry of wife of *znwnym* and have children of *znwnym*. The lemma *n'pwpym* 'adultery' comes between them in the last colon of 2:2[4] of the first stanza here with the value of 78 or **26x3**, **13x6**, and 39x2 by multiples, as well as **13+26**+39 by addition. This is the only place in the Hebrew Bible where *n ʾpwpym* comes. I propose the high numerical symbolism of 78 influenced its inclusion here.

The first half 2:2[4] of Stanza I is a plea for the wayward wife to change, with emphasis in the repetition of *ryb* 'plead'=**32** twice in the short first line. The repeated *ryb* numerically builds up to *ʾyš* 'husband'=**32** in the second line of the poem and ties to the repetition of *ʾyš*=**32** near the end of the poem as a numerical inclusio. The second half 2:3[5] of the first stanza is a threat, most emphatic on the final colon, "And kill her with thirst." There is a buildup of three threats with *k* 'as'=**11** before it with "make her bare *as* the day of her birth," "make her *as* a desert," and "set her *as* a dry land." The progression from "make her as a desert" to "kill her with thirst" illustrates the more specific seconding in the second half of the parallelism. Other symbolic lemmas in this stanza are interesting. There are two 26s: *byn* 'between'=**26**, and *yld* 'birth'=**26**; two 32s: *ṣmʾ* 'thirst'=**32**, and the above *ʾyš* 'husband'=**32**; and two 39s: *mdbr* 'desert'=39, and *ʾrṣ* 'land'=39. There is also a series of 11s with *ṣyh* 'dry'=33 or **11**x3, *śym* 'make'=44 or **11**x4, and the singleton *ʿrwm* 'naked'=55 or **11x5** or the sum of 23 and 32. Three of the last four lemmas make another buildup to "kill with thirst" with alliteration of *ṣ* in *ʾrṣ*, *ṣyh*, and *ṣmʾ* 'thirst.'

The first and last lines of this stanza illustrate the principle of identifying monocola lines as secondary peaks because of their short emphatic nature. "*Plead with-your-mother, plead*" has only three words; "*and-I-will-kill-her with-thirst*" has only two. This final bimeter line along with the pentameter line before it "*And make her as a desert, // and set her as a dry land*" are the center of the first half of the full poem 2:2–8[4–10]. Such lines at the quarters of long chiastic poems have been identified as places with a structurally marked high point, as observed in all the long chiastic poems in Hosea as well as other books. They are printed in italics to point them out as secondary peaks.

Besides parallelism at the couplet level as in the previous poems, this poem has clear internal semantic parallelism relating the cola in each line: (B) not wife//not husband, (C) harlotry//adultery, face//breasts (D) naked// bare, (E) desert//dry land. The heightened emphasis of the second part of the parallelism comes by comparing the two lines of each *couplet*, rather than in line-internal parallelism. Note "mother" becomes "not my wife" in the first strophe, the warning against "adultery" becomes the punishment of stripping in the second, and making her as a "desert" becomes "killing her with thirst" in the third strophe. The very strong imagery of God's punishment in Hosea while elsewhere describing God's love and mercy illustrates what Sherwood (*Literary*, 252) describes for Hosea, that it "simultaneously pursues one kind of action (blessing, reconciliation) and its opposite (denunciation, violence, imprisonment and curse)." Such "contradictions" (p. 243) seem inappropriate to Western expectations for scripture, leading to interpretations that obscure Hosea's full message by focusing only on the final good outcome. This picture of God is even more violent in 13:7–8 where God is like beasts—a lion, leopard, and bear—that tear open and devour Israel.

"Her" is emphasized by eleven repetitions of its final *-ah*/*-â* giving the stanza rhyme and a build-up to the end. The lemma *ʾyš* 'husband, man' comes ten times in Hosea, of which the occurrence here in the first strophe is the first time. Also *ʾšh* 'wife, woman' comes five times. The statement ending the marriage in 2:2[4] is symbolic of the ending of the covenant between God and Israel.[16]

2:4–5[6–7] Stanza II, There will be No Mercy for Chasing after False Providers

G 4 And-on=her-children I-will-not(+)have-mercy,
  for=children-of harlotry are-they; [2+3](6/5)
H 5 For their-mother played-the-harlot,
  she-who-conceived-them acted-shamefully; (5)

*

I For she-said, "I'll-go
  after my-lovers, (5)
J The-givers-of my-bread and-my-water,
  my-wool and-my-linen,
    my-oil and-my-drink." [3+2+2](7)

"Children of harlotry" is best understood as recommended for "offspring of harlotry" in 1:2 referring to Israelites in general, and not focused on Hosea's three children. The last line J is the center crux of the overall chiasm of 2:2–8[Hebrew 2:4–10], and is therefore in an emphatic position structurally. The agricultural list has a "key function"[17] pointing out the

16. Other lemmas in 2:2[4]–5[7] with symbolic values are *lʾ* 'not'=13 twice here and seven times in the whole poem, and *w* 'and'=6 six times here and 24 times in the poem.

17. Andersen and Freedman (*Hosea*, 227) note, "this half-verse has a key function because of its thematic connections with other parts of the discourse." Also see Mays

delusion of Israel in expecting Baal to provide food, clothing and pleasure when the only true "giver" is the LORD God. The first lemma in the peak, *ntn* 'give,' has the symbolic value of 50, the product of Y=10 and H=5, which represent the short name YH. The theme and numerical significance are repeated in the last verse of the poem 2:8[10] with God identifying himself as the one who *ntn* "gave her the grain, wine and oil." This ties the central peak to the end in a typical chiastic pattern. Other lemmas in the peak that have numerical significance are *lḥm* 'bread'=33 or 11x3, *mym* 'water'=36 or 6x6, *ṣmr* 'wool'=51 or 17x3, and *pšth* 'linen'=65 or 13x5.[18] This peak line is given further prominence by its metrical length, being the only heptameter line in the long poem. The 3+2+2 tricola structure is exceptional for heptameters, where 4+3 is normal. The peak line is also marked with alliteration since every word ends in *-y*. The ends of its first and last cola have rhyme with *-ay*, which gives further balance to the peak line. Garrett (*Hosea*, 80) refers to a suggestion by Tängberg ("*pištî*," 1977:222–24) that the line with the list may be "a fragment of a fertility cult hymn that Hosea's contemporaries sang." This would give strong prominence to this peak line. Both couplet parallelism and internal cola parallelism noted in the first stanza continue in the first two lines of this stanza. However, the last two lines have parallelism only at the couplet level—"lovers" // "givers." This dropping of internal parallelism in the central couplet serves to mark the central peak of the chiasm. Dropping of parallelism is discussed in chapter 3 as a feature of peak lines.

2:6–7[8–9] Stanza III, The Hedged-In Disillusioned Adulterous Wife

I' 6 Therefore, behold(=)I-will-hedge
your=way with-thorns, (4/5)
H' And-build a=wall-against-her,
so-her-paths she'll-<u>not</u> find; [2+3](5)

*

G' 7 And-she'll-pursue her=lovers,
but-<u>not</u>(=)overtake them; [2+3](4/5)
F' *And-she'll-seek-them, but-<u>not</u>(+)find.* (3/2)

*

E' *And-<u>she'll-say</u>, "<u>I'll-go</u>,*

(*Hosea*, 39).

18. Besides these six in the peak line, other lemmas with symbolic number values in 2:4[6]–5[7] are *ʾt* object marker=23 x5, *hm* 'they'=18 or 6x3, *znh* 'adultery'=26, *hrh* 'conceive'=30 or 10x3 and 5x6, *ʾmr* 'said'=34 or 17x2 twice, and *ʾḥry* 'after'=39 or 13x3.

and-return to=my-first <u>husband</u>, [2+3](5)

D' For-it-was better(GOOD) for-me

then than-now." (5)

The structure of this stanza has been called "irregular" (Harper, *Hosea*, 236; Collins, "*Line-forms*," 265; Andersen & Freedman, *Hosea*, 234). The reason proposed in this paper for the so-called irregularity is that the rhythm is conforming to the overall chiasm of 2:2–8[4–10] and is not integral to this stanza alone. The 555255 proposed here balances I through D above. The last line is a regular pentameter (although BHS has a different arrangement of lines).[19]

The line "And she'll seek them, but not find" (7b) should be taken as an intentional dramatically shortened line, signaling her ultimate despair and readiness to turn back, which is developed in the last line. This short line is next to the center of this half of the poem (7c), bringing two secondary peaks together. In the overall metrical chiasm 7c is parallel to the two-foot climatic line ending 2:3[5] "And kill her with thirst." Adding a hyphen to "but-not(+)find" makes both lines parallel as bimeters. *Bqš* 'seek' has the value of 42 or **6**x7, and *mṣ'* 'find' has the value of **32** and comes earlier in this stanza also along with "not." The repetition of *l'* 'not'=13 here and in the two preceding lines makes a buildup to "not find." This is the sixth of seven "not" in this poem. The last is in the final verse 2:8[10] "But she did *not* know." The direct object marker *'t*=**23** comes three times before the short climax, also adding to the buildup. These are the last of its five occurrences in this poem. In the quarter secondary peak 2:7[9]c, "go," which comes **22** times, and "return," which comes **23** times, are key words in the book of Hosea and are notable coming in the center of this half. This is the first occurrence of the 23 *šwb* 'return' in the book. As pointed out earlier, such lines at the quarter points regularly have prominence in Hosea's long poems and are counted as secondary peaks and printed in italics. "I'll go and return to my first husband" with *'yš* 'husband'=**32** in this secondary peak makes a reversal to its occurrence in the first strophe of this poem "I am not her husband." Other lemmas in the secondary peak 2:7[9]c with symbolic values are *'mr* 'said'=34, and *'l* 'to'=**13**. "Better" in the last line 2:7[9]d is the first of

19. The first line is improved by reading "behold" and "hedge" separately to make a regular pentameter. The third line also could have a hyphen removed from the negative to make a pentameter. Another possible solution is to keep the MT here and read 2:4[6] above as a tetrameter by combining the four words in the second colon into two units. This would also remove the anomaly of the 2+3 pentameters in G and G'. However, the combined forms in 2:4[6] seem more awkward than keeping the 2+3 pentameters.

five occurrences of the key word, the adjective *ṭôwb*. It also comes in 4:13, the central poem at 8:3, 10:1, and last major poem at 14:2[3]. The five are structurally significant by coming once in each of the five parts of the book, as does "COVENANT" forming the theme "God's Good Covenant." The lemma *ṭwb* also has the theologically symbolic value of 9+6+2=**17**. These first occurrences point to the thematic importance of this strophe with "I'll return to my first husband, for it was better for me then than now."[20]

2:8[10] Stanza IV: She Mistook Her Provider

C' But-*she* did-<u>not</u> know

that(+)*I* <u>gave</u> her (7/6)

B' The-grain and-the-wine and-the-oil;

* (enjambment)

and-silver I-increased for-her; (6)

A' *But-gold they-used for-Baal.* (3)

The final stanza 2:8[10] ends the poem with a hexameter couplet and a final trimeter colon. The second colon can be read naturally with a hyphen after *ky* 'that' to make a hexameter line. The reference to "knowing" God is the first in the book introducing the emphasis of the whole book as found in the central line 8:2 with Israel crying to God "we know you," and in various boundaries and peaks. Numerically *yd*ʿ 'know' has the value of 30=**10x3** or **6x5** with factors equivalent to Y, W, and H of YHWH. Its significance is further enhanced in that "know" comes fifteen times, which is 3x5 or the sum of Y=10 and H=5 for the short divine name YH. The final lemma in the poem is *bʿl* 'Baal,' which also has the value of 30 as 2+16+12, making a near inclusio for the stanza of lemmas with the value of 30. The final verb *ʿśh* 'make/use' has the value of 42 or **6x7**.[21] "Silver" and "gold" are both object-fronted for emphasis. They often occur together in Hebrew and Ugaritic poetry, and are considered a fixed word pair. The final short line is also marked by the change from the wife metaphor "she," to "they" representing Israel.

The chiastic structure of the whole poem 2:2[4]–8[10] recommends putting the final trimeter line separately. This results in another case of enjambment where the first colon of B' connects backwards, while the second

20. Other lemmas in this stanza with symbolic values are *l* 'for'=12 (x5 in the poem), *kn* 'so'=25 or 5x5 (together with *l* as "therefore"), *hnh* 'behold'=24 or 6x4, *drk* 'way'=35 or 5x7, *syr* 'thorns'=45 or 5x9, and *h* 'the'=5 x4.

21. Another lemma *tyrwš* 'new wine' has the value of 79, which is used symbolically in Song of Songs as the sum of 13+17+23+26 (Bliese, *Count*, 63.)

colon about "silver" connects forwards. This is a device noted above near the end of several of Hosea's poems. The strophic pairing of *couplets* is maintained by means of this enjambment since the half lines are counted as one of the lines in each couplet.

In summary, the poem 2:2–8[4–10] is structurally a large metrical inversion, a chiasm 366552555 7 555255663. The poem can be divided into two sections with the first half ending after the thematic central seven-foot line. This line is paralleled in the list of crops at the end along with the lemma "give" with its value of 50 or **10x5**, tying to the value of YH. The two dramatically shortened lines inside each half as well as the initial and final short lines all give climactic emphasis: "Plead with your mother, plead," "Kill her with thirst," "Seek them but not find," and "But gold they used for Baal." These are all counted as secondary peaks. Symmetry is also evident in cola structure. E and E', and G and G' (if taken as pentameters) all have the irregular pattern of the two-foot colon before the three-foot. As noted in the introduction to this poem, three key words "she," "not" with its value of **13**, and "I" with its value of 36 or **6x6** in the second line of the poem are repeated in the third line from the end, forming an inclusio. The wife's "I'll go" in 5B and 7C also add to the chiastic balance by coming in each half of the poem in stanzas two and four, first in sin and then in repentance. As noted above, "go" is one of the three lemmas with 22 occurrences in the book. These are the third and fourth. "Go" is also the first word YHWH speaks to Hosea in 1:2, and Hosea's response is the second in 1:3.

There are 141 lemmas in 2:2–8[4–10] of which 34 or 24.41% are divine-name multiples. These include three 26s, seven 13s and five other multiples of 13, one 17, four multiples of 17, five 23s, seven 32s, and two 64s. The small theological numbers 5 and 6 have 51 multiples. In the alphabetic set there are three 11s, and four with multiples of 11, giving 4.96%. Obviously, most of these are pure chance. However, there are places noted above that support the possibility of intentional choice such as the seven 32s and two 64s here; or where symbolic values cluster or have patterns such as the inclusio here of *'yš* 'husband'=**32**, *l'* 'not'=**13** (which also comes 65 times or **13x5** in the book), and *'nky* 'I'=36 or **6x6**; or where singletons occur such as *n'pwpym* 'adultery' in 2:2[4] with its high value of 78 or **26x3**, **13x6**, and 39x2 by multiples, as well as **13+26+39** by addition.

The number of poetic lines (not counting narrative introductions) to this point is 44—double the Hebrew alphabet of 22. The number 22 and its multiples (especially 44 and 88) are significantly used throughout the book of Hosea as the basis of organization (see the section on overall structure in chapter 3 B below). The dominant key word in this first block is "children"—both of Hosea, and of God. The word *ben* 'child' or plural 'children' occurs ten (=Y) of its twenty-five (**5x5** or HxH) times here, and is thematic, especially in the introductory section on Hosea's children and the following 1:10–2:1[2:1–3]. The central peak in 1:10[2:1] presents the goal of the children of harlotry becoming "children of the living God." The only two places in Hosea where "children of harlotry" occur are in this block at 1:2 with the only synonym *yld* 'children'=**26,** and at 2:4[6] with one of the twenty-five *ben* 'children.' The poem 1:10–2:1[2:1–3] is in the center of the block with a middle 22nd poetic block line coming on the second line of its peak with "children of Judah" and "children of Israel." The fact that a positive poem is the center of the block with condemnatory poems on both sides helps to see the 44 poetic lines of block 1 as intentional structuring. As noted above, the importance of symbolic numbers is especially evident in the word count of 286 with its four important symbolic factors **26x11** and **22x13** for block one 1:1—2:8[10].

Second Block 2:9[11]—3:5, Key word "Return"

(6 Poems; 44 Lines; Words: MT 271, Possible revision: 272=**17x16** by adding *lî* in 2:16[18]; Lemmas: MT 390=**26x15**, **13x30**, **10x39**, **6x65**, **5x78**, Possible revision 391=**17x23** with *lî* at 2:16[18])

2:9–13[11–15] Punishment and Destruction, Ten Pentameters plus introduction and conclusion

(12 or **6x2** lines; 66 or **6x11** words; 92 lemmas with 19 divine-name multiples or 20.65%)

9 *Therefore I-will-reverse (return),* (2)

And-I-will-take my-grain in-its-time,

and-my-wine in-its-season; (5)

And-I-will-*recover* my-wool and-my-linen,

which-was-to-cover (ʾt)her=nakedness. (5)

*

10 And-now I-will-uncover (ʾt)her=lewdness

in-the-eyes-of her-*lovers*, (26 letters) (5)

And-no=one will-*recover*-her from-my-hand.

* (enjambment)

11 And-I-will-stop all-her=celebrations, (5)

Her-feasts, her-new-moons, and-her-Sabbaths,

and-all her-festivals. (5)

*

12 And-I-will-destroy her-vineyards and-her-fig-trees,
of-which she-said, (5)
"Gifts are-these to-me
which(+)my-*lovers* gave=to-me." (6/5)
But-I-will-make-them into-a-thicket,
and-the-beasts-of the-field will-eat-them. [2+3] (5)

*

13 And-I-will-punish(+)on-her (ʾt)the=days-of the-Baals
when she-offered-incense(+)to-them; (7/5)
And-decked-herself with-her-rings and-her-jewelry,
and-went after(+)her-*lovers*. (6/5)
But-(ʾt)me she-forgot, says=the-LORD. (3)

2:9–13[11–15] is a judgment poem made up of Qinah lament pentameter lines plus an introductory monocolon line of two feet and a final monocolon peak line of three feet with the emphatic two-foot "But me she forgot" and the closure "says the LORD." The final line has been identified by Wolff as the "climax" (*Hosea*, 1965:40). Ending the poem with YHWH=**26**, the basis of symbolic theological numbers, gives strong final emphasis. "Me" in the final peak is a suffix on the direct object marker *ʾt* with the value of **23**. The direct object marker *ʾt* comes four times in the poem in pairs typical of buildups to final peaks. The first pair is at 2:9–10[11–12] on "nakedness" and "lewdness," and the second pair is in 2:13[15] on "days of Baals" and "me" referring to YHWH in the final peak. The value of *škḥ* 'forgot' is 40, with factors of *Y*=**10** and *H*=**5**. "Forget" recalls its synonymous "not know" near the end of the previous poem. It also forms a near inclusio with the final climax of the first poem in the final block nine with "Therefore they forgot me" in 13:9. Again, the peak line is the only line with the divine name as in most of the previous poems. "Says the LORD" also occurs in 11:11 in the next to the last block, giving symmetry to the book by balancing the same words which come only there, and here in the second block in three poems at 2:13[15], 16[18] and 21[23]. After this condemnation the other three occurrences are in positive promises.

Metrically the initial two-foot line and final three-foot line together make up the equivalent of a pentameter as found in all other lines. This makes the total of word-stress units 55 or **11x5** with the above adjustments to the MT 56 units. The two peripheral lines also fit together semantically with the accusation in the final trimeter line, and the judgment in the initial bimeter. This suggests the possibility of an intentional relationship like the "discontinuous bicola" Lundbom ("Rhetoric," and "Contentious,") describes in 4:4b–9a, 4:11b–14, and 8:9–13.

Besides the two pairs of *ʾt* direct objects noted above, groups of repeated suffixes and words give a kind of terrace build-up to the final peak. The 'I-my' suffixes with final *-î* on verbs and nouns dominate in 9[11] with six occurrences, and continue on the initial words in 11[13], 12[14]a, 12[14]c, and 13[15]a, the two occurrences of "to me" in 12[14], and the final emphatic initial "me" in 13[15]c. The 'she-her' *-â*/*-ah* suffix begins at the end of 9 and ends with the seventeenth occurrence on the "she forgot" at the end (Buss, *Prophetic*, 39). The word *nṣl* 'recover' in 9[11] and 10[12] with the first occurrence of "lovers" between them also suggests a terrace pattern. This is enhanced by a play on *nṣl* with two contexts of "take away" (cloth) and "rescue" (the woman). Numerically *nṣl* has the value of 44 as another multiple of 11. The word "lovers" (lemma *ʾhb*) occurs three times, in 10[12], 12[14]b, 13[15]b. The "my" suffix is on the central 12[14]b and the "her" suffix on the other two, making a chiastic pattern. The first part of 2:10[12] ending with "lovers" is a **26**-letter line giving it prominence. "Gave to me" in this central 12[14]b ties it into the key word "givers" in the peak 2:5[7]c of the previous poem. The value of *ntn* 'gave' is 50 with factors relating to *Y*=**10** and *H*=**5**. The use of a *quotation* in "Gifts are these to me, which my lovers gave to me" also adds prominence to 12[14]b. Repetitions make a terrace build-up to the end with "her lovers" being the last word before the short climax.

I will recover 9[11]
  <u>her</u> lovers 10[12]b
    recover 10[12]c
      <u>my</u> lovers 12[14]d
        <u>her</u> lovers 13[15]d
          LORD ME . . . SHE (The two suffixes "me" and "she" are repeated throughout 9–13[11–15] besides on the above words.)

The poem divides into four strophes with three lines in each strophe if the enjambment after 2:10[12] is ignored. Otherwise the enjambment in the middle of the second triplet makes 10[12] and 11[13] each a separate strophe of one and a half lines or a total of five strophes.[22]

This poem resembles the previous one in that most lines have internal colon to colon parallelism. The exceptions are the quote couplet in 2:12[14]b, and the line with enjambment noted above. This poem and the preceding one are also related in many thematic ways. One structural relationship is that the agricultural items from the *central peak line* of the preceding chiasm are repeated in the *first couplet* of this poem (a feature noted in other Biblical poetry, for example five times in Neh 9, see Bliese, "Nehemiah," 214). Here in 2:9[11] the "clothing" doublet of "wool and linen" is moved to the end of the list, which anticipates the following words on stripping. As noted earlier, the value of *ṣmr* 'wool' is 51 or 17x3, and of *pšth* 'linen' is 65 or 13x5, giving further prominence to the word pair.[23] The move of wool and linen to the end also makes a chiastic arrangement of the pairs tying this poem to the previous one: wool and linen 5[7], grain and wine 8[10]//grain and wine 9[11]a, wool and linen 9[11]b.[24] This repetition comes across the juncture of blocks one and two (anadiplosis), and ties these two blocks together as part 1 in the structure of the book. Such links between blocks of text are common in Hosea.

Three Poems of God's Covenant of Love 2:14–23[16–25]

(22 lines)

2:14–17[16–19] Love Poem 1: Renewed Courting and Vows

22. Metrically, although some of the combinations are long, and reach the maximum of six syllables noted by van Grol ("Zephaniah," 191), hyphens can be added to combine "which-gave-to-me" in 2:12[14]a, "and-I-will-visit(+)upon-her" and "which-she-offered" in 13[15]a and "after-her-lovers" in 13[15]b. 10–11[12–13] have been divided into three bicola lines, instead of two tricola as in BHS. This causes enjambment in the middle line, but allows for regular 3+2 pentameter lines.

23. Other lemmas with symbolic values in 2:9–13[11–15] not already noted are *l* 'for'=12 (x5 in the poem), *kn* 'so'=25 or 5x5 (together with *l* as "therefore"), *w* 'and'=6 x18, *lqḥ* 'take'=39, *mwʿd* 'season'=39 x2, *l* 'to'=12 x2, *ʾt* object=23 x4, *glh* 'uncover'=20, *ʿyn* 'eye'=40, *ʾyš* 'man'=32, *lʾ* 'not'=13, *šbt* 'stop'=45, *kl* 'all'=23 x2, *ḥg* 'feast'=11, *ḥdš* 'new moon'=33, *šbt* 'Sabbath'=45, *gpn* 'vineyard'=34, *tʾnh* 'fig'=42, *ʾšr* 'which'=42 x3, *ʾmr* 'said'=34, *ʾtnh* 'gift'=42, *hm* 'them'=18, *śym* 'set/make'=44, *yʿr* 'thicket'=46, *ʾkl* 'eat'=24, *ḥyh* 'living thing, beast'=23, *h* 'the'=5, *śdh* 'field'=30, *pqd* 'punish'=40, *qṭr* 'burn incense'=48, *ʿdh* 'decked'=25, *nzm* 'ring'=34, and *ʾḥry* 'after'=39.

24. See Andersen & Freedman (*Hosea*, 241). They also note the chiastic ending with "went after-her lovers; but me-she forgot" because of the "deliberate" fronting of the object "me," deferring the effect of the verb "forgot" until last (262). Note the same verb in the peak at 13:6.

(10 Tetrameters; 48 or 6x8 words, or 49 by adding *lî* 'to/for me' in 16[18]Ba as in the following clause in 16[18]Bb filling 273 words in block two; 39 or 26+13 MT word-stresses, or adjusted as below to 40 or 10x4 or 5x8 word-stresses; 69 or 23x3 lemmas, of which 17 or 24.64% have values as multiples of divine-name numbers)

14 Therefore behold,
  I will-allure-*her*, (4)
And-I-will-lead-*her* to-the-desert,
  and-I-will speak to=*her*-heart; (4)
*
15 And-I-will-give to-*her*
  her=vineyards from-*there*, (4)
And-the=Valley of-Achor
  for-a-door of-hope. (4)
*
And-she-will-answer *there*
  as-in-the-*days*-of *her*-youth, (4)
And-as-the-*day* I-brought-*her*-up
  from-the-land-of(=)Egypt; (3/4)
*
16 And-it-will-be in-that=*day*
  says(=)the-LORD, (3/4)
"You-will-*call*[add -*lî*= 'to/for'-me], 'My-Husband,'
  and-you-will-<u>not</u>=*call*=me <u>again</u>(+)'My-*Baal*.'" (5/4)
* (26 letters without *ly*)
17 And-I-will-remove the=<u>names</u>-of
  the-*Baals* from-*her*-mouth; (4)
And-they-will-<u>not</u>(=)be-brought-to-remembrance
  <u>again</u> by-their-<u>name</u>. (3/4)

2:14–17[16–19] and the following two poems are positive in contrast to most of the preceding poems. All three have the phrase "in that day" where God promises a future time of renewed fellowship with God. The switch from the previous lament style of Qinah pentameters to these tetrameter lines marks the change from judgment to salvation.[25] The use of "desert" (*mdbr*=39) also shows this reversal. In 2:3[5] God threatens "I will make her a desert, and set her like a dry land, and kill her with thirst." Now in 2:14[16] the desert is the place to which God will "lead her," "speak to her heart," and "from there" "give her vineyards to her." The initial positive relationship in the desert referred to in 2:15[17]with "in the days of her youth" when God "brought her up from the land of Egypt" is referred to again in 9:10 with "as grapes in the desert I found Israel, as first-fruit on a fig tree" and in 13:5 "I knew you in the desert in the land of drought."[26]

Only the second line of 16 has internal cola parallelism in this poem, "You will call me My Husband//but you will not call [me] my Baal." However, the rest of the poem has parallelism in the couplet strophes. The first strophe has "I will allure her" // "I will speak to her heart," The second and third strophes illustrate the feature of parallelism with the *more specific* information in the second part with "vineyards" // "valley of Achor for a door of hope," and "days of her youth" // " days I brought her up from the land of Egypt." The last strophe has "remove the names" // "not brought to remembrance by name."

Dearman (*Hosea*, 351) defends the interpretation of "Baal" in Hosea as a reference to syncretism with "Canaanite deities" rather than a metaphor for "human political figures" as proposed by some scholars. He points to 2:16[18] "you will not call me again 'My Baal" as especially important evidence that YHWH was venerated as another Baal. Although the veneration of deities was included in political treaties, Dearman identifies the polemic using the name "Baal" in Hosea and Jeremiah as basically against "religious" syncretism.

The last line with "not be brought to remembrance" referring to Baal, can be taken as a climactic reversal of the over-all theme of the previous two poems referring to YHWH with "not know me" and "forget me" at the ends (semantic epiphora by synonyms). The last word *šm* 'name' is climactic, having the value of 34 or 17x2, and being repeated from the previous lines' play on the "names" "My Husband" and "My Baal." The lemma *ʿwd* 'again' in the final peak has the value of **26**, and is repeated from the third line from

25. Four hyphens may be adjusted from the MT to make homogeneous tetrameter lines; i.e., to separate "land-of Egypt," "says the-LORD," and "not-remember," and to combine "again(+)My-Baal."

26. Dearman (*Hosea*, 35) contrasts the two uses of *mdbr* as the "arid, foreboding" desert of 2:3[5] which comes from the "perspective of existence in the land of promise," in contrast to the "positive setting" in 2:14[16] serving as "part of the typology of marriage for covenant, with the 'wilderness,' the former place of covenant making, serving as the future place of marriage renewal."

the end. The final climax is emphasized by the following terrace pattern building up to the end noted above by the underlined and italicized words, and by the repetition of the suffix "her" as in the previous poem:

> 15[17] there there (*šām* 'there' has the same value of 34 as *šēm* 'name' at the end)
>
> 15–16[17–18] days day day
>
> 16[18] *qr* ʾ 'call'=40 to me . . . not call me to me again ʿ*wd*=26
>
> 16–17[18–19] Baal (*b* ʿ*l*=30) names (*šm*=34)
>
> 17[19] Baals not again name. (*l* ʾ 'not' has the value of 13, and is repeated from 16[18])[27]

The final *double number switch* with "Baal(s)" and "name(s)," together with an interlocking terrace repetition, also gives emphasis to the final climax with "again," "Baal," "names," "Baals," "again," "name." The line 2:19[21] with the play on "husband" and "Baal" has **26** letters if the suggested *ly* is not added.

Although a major break is often placed after 15[17] (Wolff *Hosea*, Mays *Hosea*, and Stuart *Hosea*), the repetition of "day" twice before, and once after the break, gives support for considering 2:14–17[16–19] as a unit. Furthermore, both this and the preceding poem have anaphora beginning with "Therefore," and both have ten homogeneous major lines and five strophes each. Sherwood (*Literary*, 205) points out that the third "therefore" in 2:14[16] is not the usual use of therefore in "advancing an argument and building upon it . . . 'Therefore' . . . becomes in this poem a pivot between antitheses and a sign of discontinuity." I see this as a buildup with two negative "therefore" in 2:6[8] and 2:9[11] resulting in punishment, changing in the final third "therefore" to a positive word of hope.

Word-stress units qualify for numerical symbolism either with MT of 39 as 26+13, or as the proposed revision to 40 with factors of 10 and 5 as in YH. The 48 MT words have a factor of 6 equal to *W* in the theological set, or the suggested addition of *lî* makes 49 or 7x7 in the fullness set. This poem together with the previous poem has the significant total of 22 lines, and this

27. Other lemmas with symbolic values in 2:14–17[16–19] besides those noted are *l* 'for'=12 (x4 in the poem), *kn* 'so'=25 or 5x5 (together with *l* as "therefore"), *hnh* 'behold'=24, ʾ*nky* 'I'=36, *pth* 'allure'=44, *w* 'and'=6 x10, *h* 'the'=5 x3, *mdbr* 'desert'=39, *dbr* 'speak'=26, *ntn* 'give'=50, ʾ*t* direct object=23 x3, *krm* 'vineyard'=44, ʿ*mq* 'valley'=48, *tqwh* 'hope'=52, ʿ*nh* 'answer'=35, *k* 'as'=11 x2, ʿ*lh* 'go up'=33, ʾ*rṣ* 'land'=39, *hyh* 'be'=20, *hw* ʾ 'that'=12, *YHWH*=26, *qr* ʾ 'call'=40, ʾ*yš* 'man'=32, and *ph* 'mouth'=22.

poem together with the following two poems of the covenant of love also has a total of 22 lines.

2:18–20[20–22] Love Poem 2: Covenants of Peace and Marriage
(Chiasm 56 55 65; 36 words **6x6**; **32** word-stresses; 63 lemmas of which 9 or 14.29% have values with multiples of divine-name numbers, one of three poems tying for 8th highest at 14.29%)

A 18 *And-I-will-establish for[l]-them a-COVENANT*
in-that day (26th *l*) (5)
B With=the-beasts-of the-field
and-with=the-birds-of the-sky
and-the-creeping-things-of the-ground. [2+2+2](6)
*
C **And-bow and-sword and-war**
I-will-destroy from=the-land. (5)
C' **And-I-will-make-them-lie-down in-safety.**
|# (enjambment, C' has 26 letters)
19 **And-I-will-betroth-you to-me forever;** [2+3](5)
B' And-I-will-betroth-you to-me
in-righteousness and-in-justice
and-in-loyalty and-in-mercy; [2+2+2](6)
A' 20 *And-I-will-betroth-you to-me in-faithfulness;*
and-you-will-know the=LORD. (26 letters) (5)

2:18–20[20–22] is a beautiful chiastic poem on God's good covenant. MT has a perfect inverted rhythm of 56 55 65. Word-stress units have the divine name number of **32**. This poem also has enjambment as several previous poems. The semantic break in the two stanzas is unique in that the two cola of the second peak line are used to summarize each of their adjacent stanzas: "lie-down in-safety" for the first stanza, and "betroth-you to-me forever" for the second, making this the thematic line in the peak of the chiasm. Both of these cola end with lemmas that are singletons in Hosea, *škb* 'lie down' together with *bṭḥ* 'safety' in first cola, and *ʿlm* 'forever' in the second. The peak line C' with enjambment also has **26** letters, giving it prominence. There are other singletons: *rmś* 'creep' and *ʾdmh* 'ground' in "creeping things of the ground" at the end of the line before the peak, *rḥmym* 'mercy' at the end of the line after the peak, and *ʾmwnh* 'faithfulness' at the end of the first colon of the last line, totaling seven singletons in the poem. The line with the enjambment has a reversal of the expected feet in its two cola by having 2+3 first rather than the regular 3+2. This gives symmetrical balance to the peak with 3+2, 2+3. The change of pronouns from "them" to "you" also marks the stanza juncture in this line. Prominence also comes with the anthropomorphic *ʾrś* 'betroth" (=42 or **6**x7) for God in the peak, and then repeated in each of the following lines. The central peak has the important word pair "bow and sword" also found in 1:7. The lemma *ḥrb* 'sword' has the value of 30 or **10**x3 and **5**x**6**. Also in the peak at 2:18[20] *mlḥmh* 'war' has the value of 51 or **17**x3. Two other symbolic lemmas come in the central peak, *ʾrṣ* 'land'=39 or **13**x3, and the singleton *škb* 'lie down'=34 or **17**x2. The two tricola 2+2+2 lines B and B' come at corresponding places in the inversion giving further balance to the chiastic structure.

Since the structure is split with two lines C and C' in the center, emphasis is expected at the two ends. The *final line*, which is structurally marked as a secondary peak, has the last word of the poem YHWH=**26**, the only divine name. The line also has **26** letters giving it theological prominence. The repetition of "betroth" in the center and following two lines (19[21] a and b), also gives prominence as a buildup to its occurrence in the final line. The four lemmas in the last colon, *w ydʿ ʾt YHWH* 'and know direct-object LORD,' all have theological values—6, 30, 23, and 26—adding to the climax. These are the only occurrences of these lemmas in the poem. This is important to note in regard to the overall theme of "know the LORD" found at significant places in the book, and along with its antithesis "forget" as semantic epiphora with the previous three poems. Note how "know" encloses "forget" and "not brought to remembrance" in the series with two condemnations followed by two positive references: 2:8[10] "didn't *know* (that I gave)," 2:13[15] "forgot" (me), 2:17[19] (Baals) "not brought to remembrance," 2:20[22] "you will *know* the Lord." "Know" also comes in the central peak line of the book at 8:2 "My God, we know you."

The *first line* is also structurally identified as a secondary peak because of the double line in the central peak. The first line is thematically important with the key word *bryt* 'covenant'=54 or **6**x9 and the eschatological "in that day" with the article *h* 'the'=**5** (followed by four more in the poem) plus *hwʾ* 'that'=12 or **6**x2. The poem-initial *w* 'and'=**6** (followed by 13 more), and the preposition *l* 'for'=12 or **6**x2 in "for them" (followed by five more *l* in the poem) also add symbolic number prominence to the first line.[28] This is the first occurrence of the five *bryt* 'COVENANT,' which is structurally marked by coming once in each of the five parts of the book. The preposition *l*, which is especially linked to covenant language, comes its **26**th of 143 times here in "establish for [*l*] them a COVENANT" (143 is significant as **13x11**). The *l* in covenant language comes with "I will be a God to [*l*] you, and you will be a people to [*l*] me" in Exod 6:7, etc. It also comes in the covenant after the flood in Gen 9:10 where the *final summary phrase* has an *l* 'with' *lcl ḥyt h ʾrṣ* "every living creature on earth" (NIV) as here, while the preceding prepositions are all *ʿm* 'with' for people, birds, and various animals in 9:9–10 as here in 2:18[20]. The peaceful coexistence with animals recalls the garden of Eden of the original creation, and connects to "lie down in safety" in the central peak. Dearman (*Hosea*, 126) notes that the Gen 9:10 "covenant" is an "everlasting" (*ʿōlām*) covenant with "all living creatures" having "overtones" with 2:19[21] "betroth you to me forever" (*ʿōlām*). These intertextual overtones give further prominence to the peak here. The first line is also one of the central eleventh lines of the 22 in this group of three salvation poems. Since the last line and the second line of the central peak each have **26** letters, the whole poem 2:18–20[20–22] is especially marked for its theological message. It is one of only three poems in the book with more than one 26-letter line (see also 4:4b–9a, and 13:7–11). The thematic emphasis is on God's *good "covenant"* symbolized by a betrothal of God to Israel. The allusions to Gen 1 with similar animal groups and its seven-fold repetition of "good" add to the idea of the goodness of the covenant here. The central poem of the book, 8:1–4, brings the two key words "good" and "covenant" together in an accusation that Israel "broke my covenant" and "spurned the good," negatively recalling the goodness of this first statement of the covenant. Here the goodness of the covenant is emphasized by the list of five words in 19–20[21–22] all with the preposition *b* 'in': *ṣdq* 'righteousness,' *mšpṭ* 'justice'=60, *ḥsd* 'loyalty,' *rḥmym* 'mercy'=64, and *ʾmwnh* 'faithfulness'=39. This is the *first time in the book* that any of these basic good words occur, tying to the first occurrence of "covenant" here. Three of them have theologically prominent numbers; 60 is equal to **10x6** and **5x12**, 64 is equal to **32x2**, and 39 is equal to **26+13**. The last two are *singletons* in Hosea adding to their likelihood of being chosen to end the list because of relating to the divine-name numbers 32 and 26. The total of five in the list is also numerically significant. The location of *ḥsd* 'loyalty' in the *center* of the five, points to its importance in relation to "covenant," as does "faithfulness" at the end.

28. Other lemmas with symbolic values are *ḥyh* 'beasts'=23, *śdh* 'field', *ʿwp* 'bird'=39, *rmś* 'creeping thing'=54, *ʾdmh* 'ground'=23.

2:21–23[23–25] Love Poem 3: The Answer of Restoration

(Six Pentameters; 40 words; 30 or 10x3 or 5x6 word-stresses; 59 lemmas with 14 or 23.73% having divine-name multiples)

21 And-it-will-be in-<u>that</u> day
    I-will-*answer*, says=the-LORD: (5)
I-will-*answer* the=heavens,
    and-they will-answer the=*land.* [2+3](5)
*

22 And-the-*land* will-*answer* the=grain
    and-the=wine and-the=oil; (5)
And-they will-answer Jezreel (or <u>ʾet=God</u>-<u>*sows*</u>);
    23 and-I-will-*sow*-her(+)for-myself in-the-*land.*
* (6/5)
And-I-will-have-*mercy*-on *No Mercy*;
    and-I-will-<u>say</u> to-*Not*=<u>My-People</u>, (26 letters) (5)
"You-are(=)<u>my-people</u>;"
    and-<u>he</u> will-<u>say</u>, "My-<u>God</u>." [2+3](4/5)

2:21–23[23–25] is a beautiful poem with a homogeneous structure pointing to a final climax. The final line is God's reversal of their negative name to "my people," and ends with the people's response "My-God." The buildup of a terrace pattern begins with God speaking the key word *ʿnh* 'answer'=35 or 5x7, which resounds four more times involving the heavens, earth, and Jezreel meaning "God sows." There is a near inclusio of divine names with YHWH coming as the last word in the first line and "my-God" the final word of the poem. *YHWH* has the value of **26**, and *ʾlhym* 'God' comes **26** times in the book. The surface form *ʾĕlōhāy* 'my-God' is a key word repeated in several places including the MT reading of 8:2, which is central to the whole book. The lemma *w* 'and'=**6** is in a buildup, coming on the first word of the poem *hyh* 'be'=20, and then the tenth time on the first word of the final colon *hwʾ* 'he'=12 or **6**x2. The pronoun "he" forms an inclusio with the identical *hwʾ* 'that'=12 in the first colon of the poem. The lemma *ʾmr* 'say' in the middle of the final peak colon has the value of 34 or 17x2. "Say" also comes in the colon before the final line adding prominence by balancing God's "I will say" with the response of the people "he will say." Seven repetitions of *ʾet*=**23** also add to the buildup to the end, in spite of the object marker normally being minimized in poetry. See the figures in Andersen and Forbes (*Vocabulary*, 271) where Hosea has 44 occurrences making a frequency of 85 per 10,000 words similar to Psalms with 78 with per 10,000, and Proverbs with 40. This contrasts with Joshua with 567 per 10,000, Genesis with 493 per 10,000, and Leviticus with 646 per 10,000. Note ʾ*et* in the following buildup to the final peak.

21[23] answer answer ʾ*et* they answer ʾ*et*

21–22[23–24] land land (ʾ*rṣ*=39)

22[24] answer ʾ*et* ʾ*et* ʾ*et* they answer ʾ*et*

22–23[24–25] Jezreel sow 23 land (*yzrʿʾl* 'Jezreel'=66, means 'God sows')

23[25] mercy ʾ*et* No Mercy (*l*ʾ no=13)

23[25] say Not~My-People (*l*ʾ~ ʿ*my*=52)[29]

23[25] my-people, say My-God

There are 40 words with the factors of 10 and 5, and 30 word-stress units with the factors of 10, 6 and 5 relating to YHWH. Hyphenation changes are suggested in two lines. In 23[25]a the normal option of connecting the preposition *l* 'for' to its preceding verb by a hyphen is proposed rather than the MT without a hyphen. In the last line ʿ*my*= ʾ*th* 'my-people(=)you-are' can be read as two words by deleting the hyphen. This will fit the pattern in Hosea of final emphatic lines normally being slowed down. All lines will then have pentameter rhythm, and the MT 30 count for word-stresses will be maintained.

Harper (*Hosea*, 244) makes a division of this section into three stanzas of trimeter movement. The first stanza is the first couplet whose boundary is also structurally marked by its exceptional final line with 2+3 instead of 3+2 feet. The second stanza ends with "Jezreel," following the full stops in the BHS (and most translations except RSV). This division has much to say for it, since both stanzas then end with the parallel, "And they answered . . ." The divisions can then be compared to the previous poem, 2:18–20[20–22] and the poems in 3:3–5, and 1:10—2:1 [2:1–3]. The analysis would place a break in the last colon of the middle couplet at the same point in all four poems. In this poem, "And I will sow her for myself in

29. Other lemmas with symbolic values in this poem are *h* 'the'=5 x7, *hm* 'them'=18 x2, *l* 'for, to'=12 x2, and possibly *tyrwš* 'wine'=79 or 13+17+23+26 by addition rather than factors.

the earth," verse 23[25], would then begin the last stanza. It is important to point out these similarities to the former poem to show their close relationship. However, the above display has departed from the BHS lineation in order to show a possible rhythmical structure as a homogeneous poem. The three couplets are all semantically well-formed with parallelism between lines. The beginning "LORD," middle "God sows," and final "God" also give cohesion with divine names in the three strophes. The conclusion is that this poem has both its own normal couplet structure, as well as an obvious similarity to the exceptional structure of the preceding poem, 2:3–5[5–7], and especially to 1:10—2:1 [2:1–3] which is also ambiguous. Similarities can also be seen in the anaphora of "that day" in the first line of this and the previous poem, as well as both having six lines, and the scarcity of clear internal colon to colon parallelism in both poems.

The penultimate line has special prominence in having **26** letters, and having the names that God gave the children in the first chapter, "No Mercy" and "Not My People." "No Mercy" is changed to "Mercy" also in this line. The line balances with the final line metrically with a regular 3+2 cola matching the 2+3 of the last line. This suggests the possibility of counting the whole strophe of two lines as the final peak, as is done in some other poems. The return to the topic of the three children's names gives unity to the content of the first two chapters. This final poem in chapter two emphasizes the graciousness of God symbolized by the changes in the condemnatory names. The thematic unity of God's good covenant of love in the three last poems is reinforced by the cohesion suggested by their total line count of 22 lines, an alphabetical number important in the overall structure of the book. The progression in the three poems from "allure" to "betroth" to "answer/respond" is also significant. The eschatological phrase "in that day" significantly unites these three poems. It comes in the middle of the first poem and in the first lines of the other two, as previously noted. (This is similar to "therefore" which begins the first of these three poems in 2:14[16] and its predecessor in 2:9[11], and begins a stanza in the preceding poem at 2:6[8].) "That day" is unique to part 1 coming only in block 1 at 1:5 and in block two in these three poems (Mays, *Hosea*, 47). It is also noteworthy that "last days" in 3:5 are the last words of part 1 forming an inclusio with "that day" in 1:5.

3:1–5 Hosea Renews his Marriage

3:1a Narrative Introducing the Divine Command to Hosea

And-the-LORD said to-me, (3)

The main stylistic feature is the first person "me" autobiographical account. The first chapter was all biographical, with "him" in reference to Hosea. All four lemmas have symbolic values, *w* 'and'=6, *YHWH*=26, *'mr* 'said'=34, and *'l* 'to'=13.

3:1b–d The Divine Command to Hosea to Love an Adulteress

(Chiastic Poem 7 4 7; 20 words; MT 17 word-stresses, or 18 if adjusted for chiasmus; 24 lemmas of which 7 or 29.17% have divine-name values, one of three poems tied for the 8th highest values)

Again go, love(=)a-woman
loved-of a-friend, and-an-adulteress; (6/7)
As-the-LORD loves
the=children-of Israel. (4)
But-they turn to=other gods,
and-love cakes-of raisins. (7)

NRSV, CEV, NJPS, Jerusalem Bible, and New American Bible place "again/further" in the previous narrative. However, including it in this poem makes the 26-value *'wd* 'again' a theologically symbolic first word recalling the first two words of the book *dbr YHWH* 'the word of YHWH' each with 26 letters in 1:1. Placing "again" here also adds to the poetic line length making it possible to balance it with the final heptameter. I have followed translations that connect "again" to the following command (RSV, GNT, and American Standard Version have "Go again"; and see NIV which connects "again" with "love.")

The identity of the woman in chapter 3 is left ambiguous. However, most studies see her as Gomer, the wife of Hosea in chapters 1–2 (See Mays, *Hosea*, 55–56, Garrett, *Hosea*, 48–49, 97–99, and Dearman, *Hosea*, 132). The point is not the historical details, but that the woman's adultery (*n'p* the first time here of five in chapters 3–7) is symbolic for Israel's unfaithfulness to God. She is described as *znh*=**26** 'playing the harlot' thirteen times in chapters 1–9 also as a symbol of unfaithfulness to God in a term that in chapters 1–2 describes her adultery. I propose that the numerical symbolism of the strongest number 26 for *znh* may be behind having it come in the first message of 1:2, and thirteen times in the book since 13 is the base of the 26 set. "Commit adultery" (*n'p*) is also symbolic with its value of **32** used for a numerical representation of God in the mathematical rather than sequential alphabetical value for *kbwd* of 23. The 5 occurrences of *n'p* is also symbolic since the value the *H*'s in YHWH is 5.

The structure of this pronouncement in 3:1b–d is chiastic. The middle tetrameter "as the LORD loves the children of Israel" is the thematic peak. The divine name comes significantly in the center. Four lemmas in the peak have symbolic values, *k* 'as'=11, *YHWH*=26, *ʾt* object =23, and "Israel"=64 or 32x2. Wolff (*Hosea*, 60) emphasizes the climactic nature of this line by noting, "With the use of the third person ("Yahweh"), the intention to proclaim suddenly interrupts what is stylistically a report." The center also has prominence with syntactic complexity since the whole line is a comparative *k* 'as' clause. "The children of Israel" is also in the next peak in 3:5 and was also in the peak of 1:11 and the initial secondary peak of 1:10, prompting my choice of "children" for the theme of part 1. The key word *ʾhb* 'love' comes chiastically in the center and in an inclusio, occurring in the first and last cola. It is further emphasized by its repetition in four of the six cola. The repetition emphasizes that the renewed marriage is to be based on love in spite of Gomer's adultery, and that this is symbolic of God's love for Israel in spite of their apostasy. "Love" also has numerical symbolism since it occurs 17 times, which is one of the divine name numbers.[30] The first word of the poem *ʿwd* 'again' has the value of 26, and the last lemma *ʿnb* 'raisins' has 32, making an inclusio of divine numbers with YHWH=26 in the center. The unusual climax of "love raisin cakes" may reflect a choice to balance the 32 of *n ʾp* 'commit adultery' in the first line. More specific seconding in line parallelism comes in the first line where "woman" is defined in the second colon as "loved of a friend, an adulteress." Three of these consecutive lemmas have number symbolism in the first line: *r ʿ* 'friend'=36 or 6x6, *w* 'and'=6 (which also comes twice on the other side of the peak), and *n ʾp* 'commit adultery'=32. Four consecutive lemmas follow the peak: *w* 'and'=6, *hm* 'they'=18 or 6x3, *pnh* 'turn'=36 or 6x6, and *ʾl* 'to'=13. The cola on each side of the center have negative references, to adultery and idolatry. The three-line metrical chiasm follows MT with the two long lines balancing each other, so it is not necessary to say that the final line is extra (Buss, *Prophetic*, 42).

The number 20 for total words has theological factors of 10 and 5 recalling YH. MT has the divine-name number 17 for the word-stress count, although the above suggested chiastic adjustment to 7 4 7 makes 18 or 6x3. Metrically the object "woman" can be given full stress making seven feet in the first line to match the final line.

3:2 Narrative of Hosea Buying His Wife

30. Seventeen is the count for Westminster Hebrew Morphology (1991). The Paratext count of UBS and SIL is 18 by also counting *hēbû* in 4:18. WHM analyzes *hēbû* with the lemma *yhb*. BHK and BHS propose deleting it as a dittograph of the previous *ʾāhăbû* since it is not translated in the LXX.

And-I-bought-her for-myself
    with fifteen silvers, (5)
And-a-homer-of barley
    and-a-lethek-of barley. (4)

"And-I-bought" is narrative tense (*waw* plus imperfect). The verse is prose although the nine words may also have a rhythmic structure, with the awkward repetition of "barley" filling the final phrase. The reason for the repetition is more likely to point to detailed bargaining in the negotiations than to fill a poetic line. A *ltk* 'lethek' is 110 liters or 50 homers, so the homer looks like the final bit that settled the deal. It seems Hosea did not want to pay more than he had to for her. Lemmas with symbolic values in 3:2 are *w* 'and'=6 four times, *krh* 'bought'=36 or 6x6, *l* 'for'=12 or 6x2, and *ltk* 'lethek'=45 or 5x9.

3:3a Narrative Introducing the Pronouncement of Hosea

"And-I-said to-her,"

These two words introduce the following poem, which has a full rhythmical sequence without them. The three lemmas have symbolic values, *w* 'and'=6, *ʾmr* 'said'=34, and *ʾl* 'to'=13.

3:3b–5 Seven Line Hexameter Poem, Hosea's Pronouncement to His Wife and to Israel

(47 words; 43 MT or 26+17 word-stresses, or revised to 42 or 6x7; 61 lemmas of which 15 or 24.59% have values that are multiples of divine-name numbers)

3b *Many* <u>days</u> you-will-dwell with(*l*)-me;
    you-will-not be-a-prostitute; [4+2](6)
And-you-will not-be for(*l*)-a-man;
    and-also(=)I <u>to(ʾl)</u>-you. (5/6)

*

4 Because *many* <u>days</u>
    <u>the-children-of</u> <u>Israel</u> will-dwell (6)
Without <u>king</u> and-*without*(+)prince,
    and-*without* sacrifice and-*without*(+)pillar, (8/6)
And-*without* ephod or-teraphim.

* (enjambment)

5 **<u>Afterwards</u> the-<u>children-of</u>(+)<u>Israel</u> will-return,** (7/6)

And-seek the(ʾt) =<u>LORD</u> their-God,

and (ʾt)David their-<u>king</u>; (6)

And-they-will-tremble <u>before(ʾl)</u>(=)the-<u>LORD</u>

and-<u>before(ʾl)</u>=his-goodness in-the-<u>last</u> <u>days</u>. (5/6)

In spite of the BHS prose display for 3:3b–5, these seven lines can just as well be considered a hexameter poem with a final peak.[31] "Afterwards," serves to emphasize this climax to part 1—a final prophetic announcement of blessing in the last days. It also sets off this section by a near inclusio, with *ʾḥr* 'afterwards' having the same root as *ʾḥryt* 'last.' The repetition of "before" using the unusual *ʾel*=13, which is normally "to," also gives prominence to the last line. The same preposition comes in 3c (translated "to"), giving lexical cohesion for the whole poem. The structure of the last two lines before the final "in the last days" is similar with a third person plural verb followed in the penultimate line by two direct objects both having the object marker *ʾt*=**23**, and in the final line by two prepositional phrases with identical prepositions, *ʾel* 'before.' This unity, plus the inclusio around it, recommend counting all of 5 as the peak. This is reasonable since it is also the conclusion of chapters 1–3, which is part 1 of the book. The only occurrences of divine names come in the final verse 5 with YHWH x2, and Elohim. The reference to "David their king" gives prominence by recalling Israel's messianic hope based on the first King David. The thematic "children of Israel" noted in previous peaks also comes in 5.

A terrace pattern builds up to the final peak with the majority of repeats typically in the climax at 5 (in caps) as follows:

many days (v. 3) (*rb* 'many'=22)
dwell (3) (*yšb*=**33**)
not-not to (3) (*lʾ* 'not'=**13**, *ʾl* 'to'=**13**)
many days (v. 4) (*rb* 'many'=**22**)
dwell (4) (*yšb*=**33**)
children of Israel (4) (*yśr ʾl*=64 or **32**x2)
king (4) (*mlk*=36 or **6**x**6**)

31. Hyphens can be added after the second "without" in each colon. MT hyphens can be deleted between "also" and "I" in 3 and between "before" and "LORD" in 5. This brings the 43 MT word-stresses down to 42 or 6x7.

without (4) (5 times) (*ʾyn*=25 or **5x5**)

AFTER (v. 5)

CHILDREN OF ISRAEL (5) (*yśr ʾl*=64 or **32x2**)

ʾet YHWH=**26** (their God) *ʾet* (5) (*ʾt* object marker=**23**)

KING (5) (*mlk*=36 or **6x6**)

TO (5) (*ʾl* 'to'=**13**)

YHWH=**26** (5)

TO (5) (*ʾl* 'to'=**13**)

AFTER ("LAST") (5)

DAYS (5)

The lemmas with symbolic values in the peak are: *bqš* 'seek'=42 or **6x7**, *ʾt* object=**23** x2, *YHWH*=**26** x2, *ṭwb* 'goodness'=17, and *h* 'the'=**5**.[32] The concentration in v. 5 of repeated key words including those from other lines of the poem, namely, "children of Israel," "king," "YHWH," and "days," also supports calling the whole final verse the peak. This compares with 6:3 which also has a final peak strophe beginning with anacrusis, instead of just one peak line. See similar climaxes in Ps 3:7–8 (Bliese, "Psalms 1–24," 272–3) and Joel 2:26c–27 (Bliese, "Joel," 66–67). The enjambment before 5 resembles those in the poems in 1:4b–5, 1:6–7b, and all of those in chapter two except the ten-line tetrameter. In all six poems there is enjambment in which a line is split, so that the final colon of the line aligns semantically with the next strophe, usually the last strophe or stanza. Here "Afterwards the children of Israel shall return" shares line metrics with verse 4, but semantically is part of the final strophe. The remarkable similarity looks almost like the signature of the poet in these poems.

There is limited internal line parallelism (see 4b with four "without" and the last two lines in v 5 with parallel direct object markers *ʾt* and prepositions *ʾl*). Couplet parallelism helps to identify three strophes in this poem: (1) (3b) "not be a prostitute" // (3c) "not be for a man," (2) (4b) "without" x4 // (4c) "without," and (3) (5b) "seek" plus two objects // (5c) "tremble" plus two prepositional phrases as noted above. The second colon in the enjambment in v. 5 joins its adjacent couplet as if they were tricola parallel to the last bicola line.

32. The lemma for the noun "goodness" is *ṭûb*, which also comes in 10:11 modifying a "heifer's neck," in contrast to the key word *ṭôb*, an adjective that comes five times, once in each part, as a key word of the book.

The progressive development and conclusion in the poem are noteworthy. The first strophe has the unusual restriction against not only immorality but even against marital intercourse if its last line is understood to apply to the two of them. The second strophe interprets this with a list describing political and religious dissolution, including both the good and bad as in the first strophe. The lemma *zbḥ* 'sacrifice' in the list has prominence with the value of 17. The last peak strophe is God's wondrous reinstatement of both correct government under David (see Emmerson *Hosea*, 95–113), and worship of the LORD, with all the ensuing blessings. The first two strophes begin with "many days" referring to a specific and limited time of restriction. The last strophe looks forward to the "last days" as an eschatology of God's "goodness." These anaphoric time references at the beginning of each strophe give cohesion to the poem.

The interpretation of "I also to You" in 3:3 is not clear since it can relate either to the previous colon as an extension of the negative restricting Hosea from relations with his wife (NRSV, Mays, and NIV 2011 "I will behave the same way toward you"), or to the first colon chiastically with a positive meaning of "I will also dwell with you" (NIV 1984, Andersen and Freedman. Garrett *Hosea*, 103 translates, "and then I shall be yours"). It may be purposely ambiguous. Since "many days" as a limited time comes in both of the two first strophes in contrast to "Afterwards . . . in the last days" (3:5) in the third strophe, the first two strophes could refer to a period after the exile when they are bought back by God and he is "with" them, but the former full political and religious structures are restricted. The list of being "without" both legitimate ("sacrifice" and "ephod") and condemned religious practices ("pillars" and "idols") in 3:4, looks like an application of the restrictions in 3:3 "you will not be to a man, nor I with you."[33]

There is an inclusio with the word "days" both first and last in the poem. "The children of Israel" comes in the lines both preceding and following the center of the poem. Metrically it is also possible to analyze the poem as a 556 44 655 chiasm, with the first four "without" in the peak. This would require only three changes in MT hyphens rather than the four above. However, the weight of the above terrace pattern leading to the final climactic couplet together with its initial anacrusis favors the homogeneous line analysis above.

Thematically this poem shows the denouement of the problem of the adulterous wife, just as the last poem in chapter 2 showed the denouement

33. See Dearman (*Hosea*, 136) "Hosea's abstinence is a continuation of the prophetic symbolic act initiated with his marriage. As the following verse indicates, Israel shall live for some time without the normal sociopolitical and religious institutions for a state. This is a period of its purification, a road to be taken along the way to restoration."

of the problem of the condemnatory names of the children. The lemmas *l' znh* 'not be-a-prostitute' add prominence in this denouement with their theological values of **13** and **26**. The two climactic poems thereby serve as powerful examples of God's ultimate faithfulness in bringing "goodness."

This second block of 44 lines in part 1 is bounded thematically by its only two occurrences of the word *šûb* 'return' in the first line 2:9[11], and next to last line in 3:5. The lemma *šûb* significantly comes **23** times in the whole book. The various meanings of *šûb* make it useful as a key word in the book, and as a theme for block 2. In the first line 2:9[11] God "reverses," and takes back his blessings as punishment, and at the end in 3:5 Israel "returns" to the LORD their God. The effect of God's reversal is repeated in the series of "without" in 3:4, and the effect of Israel's return is the "goodness" of God "in the last days" in the peak at 3:5.

The total of all the lines defined as poetry (excluding prose introductions) in chapter 1–3 is 88, the equivalent of four alphabets. The whole 88 poetic lines of this part 1 have significant reversals as inclusios: (1) the two marriage stories, with the four "harlot" occurrences in 1:2 matching the four "love" occurrences in 3:1 (Andersen & Freedman, *Hosea*, 395), (2) the key word "after" negatively in 1:2 and positively twice in 3:5, and (3) the judgment on "that day" in 1:5 corresponding to God's "goodness" in the "last days" in 3:5.

Chapter 3

Method of Discourse Analysis of Hebrew Poetry

Theoretical Comments on Poetic Structure

A. Structurally Defined Peak

A VALUABLE OUTCOME OF the metrical analysis described above in "Literary Features in the Poetry of Hosea" is that the peaks of poems can usually be structurally defined. *Chiasms* regularly have the primary peak in the *center*. For an example of the thirty metrically chiastic poems in Hosea I'll repeat my diagram for 3:1b-d with the key words "love" and "children of Israel," and the only divine name YHWH in the central peak.

Again go, love(=)a-woman
  loved-of a-friend, and-an-adulteress; (6/7)
As-the-LORD loves
  the=children-of Israel. (4)
But-they turn to=other gods,
  and-love cakes-of raisins. (7)

Homogeneous poems, which have basically the same number of word-stress units in every line, normally have the peak in the *last line*. For an example of the fifteen homogeneous poems in Hosea I'll repeat my diagram for 1:9b-d. It has typical serial repetition, with the key word "my-people" twice, and "not" building up to the final line where it comes with the divine name reference "I AM."

"Call his-name
"<u>Not</u>~my-people," (4)
For you-are
<u>not</u> my-people; (4)
And-I AM=<u>not</u> for-you." (3)

These metrically defined primary peaks consistently have more features of prominence than secondary peaks or non-peak lines. This is shown with probability calculations below in "Types of Poetic Features Prominent in Peak Lines."

On the basis of prominence and thematic emphasis, *secondary peaks* have also been noted to be related to structural parameters as noted in the following section.

Identification of Secondary Peaks

Secondary peaks in this study have been identified by four criteria. First, metrically *chiastic poems with a couplet* instead of a single line in the center have been observed to have their *peripheral* lines as secondary peaks. The final line seems to be more consistently climactic, but for purposes of structural consistency, both lines are counted in this analysis. In the displays, secondary peak lines are in italics, while full peak lines are in bold print. The four short four-line chiastic poems in Hosea are problematic since all lines become either peak or secondary peaks. However, sufficient other climactic features occur to recommend counting four-line poems in this way along with the longer chiastic poems.

Secondly, any short *bimeter or trimeter monocolon line* is marked in that it breaks the metrical pattern which is otherwise with bicola or to a lesser extent tricola lines. The terseness of most of these monocola lines supports counting them as secondary peaks if they are not in peak position. Note the trimeter peaks in 4:2b and 14:9[10], and the bimeter in 13:6b illustrating monocola lines as full peaks. However, note that many other features of prominence are minimal because the shortness of monocola lines limits opportunities for more features.

Thirdly, *long chiastic poems have secondary peaks in the middle of each half*, besides the primary peak in the center of the poem. Long poems are proposed to be 19 lines or more for Hosea. In 9:1–9 the mid-half lines are single tetrameter lines. In 7:8–16 the first half has a trimeter and a hexameter together as the mid-half strophe, while the second half has a trimeter followed by a bimeter. In the other four there are trimeter lines adjacent to the mid-half lines. Since these are also considered secondary peaks marked by their shortness, this results in series of three lines in 9:10—10:1, and in series of two lines in 2:2–8[4–10], 7:8–16, 12:2[3]—13:1, and 13:12—14:8[9]. The concentration of several lines together for secondary peaks seems to be justified by their climactic nature. 10:9–15 is a 17-line poem with trimeters in each half which might also have been included. However, the possible secondary peak lines which would be added at the mid-halves seemed less climactic, so the definition of long poems was placed at 19 lines. The structural similarity of all of these longest chiastic poems gives weight to this analysis.

Details are presented next for these three types of secondary peaks. The occurrences in each group of secondary peaks below are listed along with features of prominence supporting their peak status. Key words in the peaks that are repeated elsewhere in the poem are underlined, and other key words and features are noted as supporting evidence of prominence. I'll copy the structural display for the first four poems in the list. The examples in the list that do not have their structural displays repeated here can be understood better by referring to the poems in the structural displays in chapters 2 and 4.

1. Peripheral Secondary Peak Lines of Poems with a Couplet Chiastic Center

1:4b and **5**—Features of Prominence in the Secondary Peaks—The key word of the poem "Jezreel" comes in both peripheral lines as well as in the central peak, and "Israel" comes in the center and final line, which has **26** letters.

A 4b *"Call his-name Jezreel,*
for=in-just a-little-while (20 letters) (5)
B **I-will-punish the=blood-of Jezreel**
on(=)the-house-of Jehu, (26 letters) (5/6)
B' **And-I-will-end the-kingdom-of the-house-of(+)Israel.**
* (enjambment)
5 **And-it-will-be in-that day,** (32 letters) (7/6)
A' *That-I-will-break the=bow-of Israel*
in-the-valley-of Jezreel." (26 letters) (5)

1:6b and 7—Features—Repetition of God's "I will not" in both peripheral lines; the key words repeated in the central peak: 1st line "mercy," last line "save;" and the military list with four "by" prepositions.

A 6b *"Call her-name "No mercy,"*

for(+)I-will-not add again (8/7)

B **To-have-mercy on-the=house-of Israel** AB

that=I-forgiving forgive for-them; CC' (6)

B' 7 **But-on-the=house-of Judah I-will-have-mercy.** B'A'

* (enjambment)

And-I-will-save-them by-YHWH their-God; (6)

A' *And-I-will-not save-them by-bow and-by-sword,*

nor-by-battle by-horses and-riders." (7)

1:10 and **2:1** [**2:1** and **3**]—Key words, 1st line: "children of Israel" repeated in the central peak, "as the sand of the sea" referring to the patriarchal covenant; last line: "My-People," "Mercy" reversing the earlier condemnatory names, and repetition of the root of *'ḥ* 'brothers/sisters,' **26** letters.

A 10 *But-the-number-of the-children-of=Israel will-be*

as-the-sand-of the-sea, (5)

B Which-is not=measured

And-not counted. (4)

*

C And-it-will-be-that in-the-place

where=it-was-said to-them,

"You-are not=my-people," [2+2+2] (6)

D **It-will-be-said to-them,**

"Children-of the-living=God." (4)

*

D' 11 **And-they-will-be-gathered, the-children-of=Judah**

and-the-children-of=Israel together, (4)

C' And-they-will-appoint for-themselves

one leader;

and-they-will-go-up from=the earth; [2+2+2] (6)

* (possible enjambment)

B' Because great

is-the-day-of Jezreel, (4)

A' 1 *<u>Say to</u>-your-brothers, "<u>My-People</u>,"*

and-<u>to</u>-your-sisters, "Mercy." (26 letters) (5)

2:18[20]a and **20[22]**—The first line has the key word "covenant," which comes once in each of five parts, and the **26**th preposition *l* of 143 or 11x13 in Hosea. "To" [*l*] gets its significance from the patriarchal covenant formula "I will be God *to* you, and you will be a people *to* me." "To" [*l*] also comes three times in the central peak, and once in each of the last two lines with the key phrase "And I will betroth you *to* me," beginning in the central peak. The last line is also prominent with "you will know YHWH," a major theme in Hosea. The line has **26** letters, which is significant coming in the only line with YHWH.

A 18 *And-I-will-establish for<u>[l]</u>-them a-COVENANT*

in-that day (26th *l*) (5)

B With=the-beasts-of the-field

and-with=the-birds-of the-sky

and-the-creeping-things-of the-ground. [2+2+2] (6)

*

C **And-bow and-sword and-war**

I-will-destroy from=the-land. (5)

C' **And-I-will-make-them-lie-down in<u>[l]</u>-safety.**

|# (enjambment, C' has 26 letters)

19 **<u>And-I-will-betroth-you to[l]-me [l]</u>forever;** [2+3] (5)

B' <u>And-I-will-betroth-you to[l]-me</u>

in-righteousness and-in-justice

and-in-loyalty and-in-mercy; [2+2+2] (6)

A' 20 *<u>And-I-will-betroth-you to[l]-me</u> in-faithfulness;*

and-you-will-know the=LORD. (26 letters) (5)

More chiastic poems with double lines in the center and peripheral secondary peaks:

4:4b and **9a**—(peripheral both short trimeters) key words, "people" and *khn* 'priest'=30 in both, first line *ryb* 'contend'=32.

5:5a and **7b**—(peripheral both short trimeters),

1st line repeated in 7:10 "pride of Israel testifies . . .," first 4 words have symbolic values, *w* 'and'=6, *'nh* 'testify/answer'=35, *g'wn* 'pride'=24, and *yśr'l* 'Israel'=64,

last line "new moon devour them" figurative language; last 4 words have symbolic values *'kl* 'eat/devour'=24, *ḥdš* 'new moon'=33, *'t* 'with'=23, and *ḥlq* 'portion, field'=39 (a singleton).

5:8a and **9b**—1st line 22 letters, imperative "Blow the trumpet (*špr*=64)

last line key word "sure"; "Israel"=64.

5:10a and **11b**—1st line: key words "princes of Judah like removers of boundaries," singletons *swg* 'remove'=24, and *gbwl* 'boundary'=23,

last line singletons *ṣw* 'command'=24, and *y'l* 'determine'=23 (matching first line with its 24 and 23).

6:7 and **7:2b**—key words, 1st line "Adam," "covenant," "they," "betrayed-me," "there,"

last line "their-works surround-them," "my-face" (note "they/them" and "me/my" in both).

7:3 and **7b**—key words 1st line "king"=36, "princes,"

last line "kings," final lament of God "not one calls to me" the only "me" in poem.

13:12 and **14:8[9]b**—1st line the only single-line strophe, word pairs: "iniquity"-"sin" and "bound up"-"stored," key word "Ephraim" relating to "fruit" in the last line,

last line metaphor of God "I am as a green cypress" with final 78th or 26x3 *k* 'as,' *r'nn* 'green'=64, and *brwš* 'cypress'=49 or 7x7 numerical fullness, "from me," "fruit," "found."

2. *Short Bimeter and Trimeter Secondary Peaks*

1:2a—extra final line repeating the initial "The word of the LORD by Hosea," divine name *YHWH*=26, *dbr* 'word'=26.

2:2[4]a—opening line repetition of *ryb* 'plead'=32 x2 (divine name number).

2:3[5]c—mid line, strong language "kill" with *ṣm* ʾ 'thirst'=32; (2:3[5]c and 7[9]b are also quarter points of a long poem).

2:7[9]b—mid, positive-negative with *bqš* 'seek'=42 or 6x7, and *l* ʾ 'not'=13, *mṣ* ʾ 'find'=32.

2:8[10]c—end, "Baal" delayed identification of evil.

2:9[11]a—opens poem, key word *šwb* 'return' comes 23 times in Hosea.

4:11b, 14d—key word *ʿm* 'people' in both peripheral lines, enclosed by "heart" and "understanding"

1st line: "heart," *lqḥ* 'take'=39 or 13x3,

last line: *l* ʾ 'not'=13, *byn* 'understanding'=26, and *lbṭ* 'be ruined'=23.

6:5b—key words: ambiguous *mšpṭ* 'judgment/justice'=60, and metaphor "light."

7:1b—deictic *kî* 'Indeed,' key words "deal falsely" *šqr* 'false'=60 and *p ʿl* 'deal/do'=45.

8:9a, 13c—key word *hm* 'they'=18 in both lines,

1st line: deictic *kî* 'Indeed,' key words: *ʿlh* 'went up'=33, and *ʾšwr* 'Assyria'=48,

2nd line: key words: "Egypt return" (chiastic discontinuous bicolon "went up to Assyria // to Egypt return"), "Egypt" x13, *šwb* 'return' x23 in book.

9:10d, 17b—key words in a parallel frame: Verb, Predicate, Prepositional Phrase:

1st half: "and-became," *šqwṣ* 'disgusting'=64 (the same value as "Israel" in 9:10a), "as the thing they loved,"

2nd half: "and-they-will-be," *ndd* 'wanderers'=22, "among the nations."

9:16a—stanza introduction, two key words "Ephraim," "blighted."

10:10b, 14b—1st half: *štym* 'double/two'=66, a play on words with the surface *ʾsrm* 'tying them' of *ʾsr* 'bind'=36 having the same consonants as *ʾsrm* 'I will chastise them' of *ysr* 'chastise'=45 in the previous line 10a, and *ʿyn* 'eye'=40 although the qire reading is *ʿwn* 'iniquity'=36;

2nd half: All 4 lemmas have symbolic values: *k* 'as'=11, *šd* 'devastation'=25, *šlmn* 'Shalman'=60, and *byt- ʾrb ʾl* 'Beth-arbel'=70 and the last 2 are singletons.

12:1[2]b—keywords *rbh* 'increases,' *kzb* 'falsehood'=20, and *šd* 'violence'=25.

12:2[3]a—keywords *YHWH*=26, *ryb* 'indictment'=32, *yśr ʾl* 'Israel'=64 or 32x2.

12:6[7]a—keywords "God" x 26, "return" x23.

12:12[13]a—keywords "Jacob," *brḥ* 'flee'=30, *ʾrm* 'Aram'=34.

13:1b—keywords *ʾšm* 'guilty'=35, by *b ʿl* 'Baal'=30 and "died."

13:14c—key words *nḥm* 'compassion'=35, *ʿyn* 'eye'=40, "hidden."

13:16c [14:1c]—key words *hryh* 'pregnant'=40, "split open" (atrocity).

14:2[3]b—key words *kl* 'all'=23, *ʿwn* 'iniquity'=36, *nś ʾ* 'forgive'=36.

14:3[4]c—key words *ytwm* 'orphan'=51, *rḥm* 'mercy' (the name of Hosea's daughter); line quoted from Ps 10:14.

14:6[7]a—key words as *lbnwn* 'Lebanon'=48, "shoots," *nkh* 'strike/sprout'=30.

3. Secondary Peaks in the Middle of Each Half of Long Poems of 19 or More Lines

2:3[5]b—1st line: *śym* 'make'=44 (11x4), as a *mdbr* 'desert'=39, as *ṣyh* 'dry'=33 (11x3), *ʾrṣ* 'land'=39, with a buildup to "kill with thirst" in the next line with alliteration of *ṣ* in *ʾrṣ*, *ṣyh*, and *ṣm ʾ* 'thirst'; 2nd line emphatic bimeter monocolon, with more specific seconding: "kill her" with *ṣm ʾ* 'thirst'=32 (2:3 and the following 2:7 are in one poem.);

2:7[9]c—reversal for wife: *ʾmr* 'said'=34 "go" x22, *šwb* 'return' 1st of 23x, *ʾl* 'to'=13, *ʾyš* 'husband'=32.

7:10a—key words *ʿnh* 'answer'=35, *g ʾwn* 'pride'=24, *yśr ʾl* 'Israel'=64, and *pnh* 'face'=36;

(7:10b—added to the above quarter line because of its thematic message with divine names: "But they do not return to the LORD their God nor seek him in all of this") all lemmas except *b* 'in' have either a symbolic value or a symbolic count : *w* 'but/nor'=6 twice, *šwb* 'return' x23, *bqš* 'seek'=42 with rhyme both verbs ending in *û*, *l ʾ* 'not'=13 twice of 65 or

13x5 times in the book, *ʾl* 'to'=13, *YHWH*=26, "God" x26 in book, *kl* 'all'=23 and *zʾt* 'this"=30;

7:14b—ABBA chiastic with 14a, key words "grain and new wine," extreme worship "they gash themselves," rejection of God "they rebel against me."

9:3a—Every lemma has symbolic value, *lʾ* 'not'=13, *yšb* 'live'=33, *ʾrṣ* 'land'=39, *YHWH*=26;

9:7c—the key word of the block *rb* 'great/multitude'=22, key words *ʿwn* 'iniquity'=36, and "hostility." The whole line also has syntactic complexity by being a prepositional phrase *ʿl* 'because of.'

9:11–12a—anacrusis as an extra word *kî ʾm* 'even if,' syntactic complexity "<u>if</u>," key word *kbwd* 'glory' with both the theological value of 23 by the alphabetical sequence, and 32 by the mathematical count. It is also the 22nd word in the poem. Repeated root *ʿwp* 'bird/fly'=39, *škl* 'bereave'=44 also in central peak as 'miscarry,' *k* 'as'=11, list of 3 with alliteration of *m* 'without' on "birth," on *bṭn* 'womb/pregnancy'=25, and on the singleton *hrywn* 'conception'=55 (5x11 or 23+32);

9:16b—syntactic complexity *kî* 'if,' key words: "children," *yld* 'bear'=26, "kill," "precious offspring," 17a "<u>God</u>," "reject," and *šmʿ* 'hear/obey'=50.

12:5[6]—ABA' chiasm, repetition *YHWH*=26 twice here, x46 in book, plethora of divine names: "<u>LORD</u>," "<u>God</u> (x26 in book) of hosts (singleton)," "<u>LORD</u>," *zkr* 'name';

12:12[13]b—repetition "for a wife," key words: *brḥ* 'fled'=30, *śdh* 'field'=30, *ʾrm* 'Aram'=34, *ʿbd* 'serve'=22, *yśrʾl* 'Israel'=64, *šmr* 'guarded'=54, and "Jacob."

13:15a—key words "son," "brothers," *prh* 'bear fruit'=42, *qdym*=46 'east wind';

14:5[6]—simile (twice), key words "dew," "<u>Israel</u>," *prḥ* 'blossom'=45, "lily," n*kh* 'strike'=30, "roots."

Types of Poetic Features Prominent in Peak Lines

The following discussion of the distribution of various poetic features between peak, secondary peak and non-peak lines gives an overview of how peak is emphasized in Hosea. The intent is to show that peaks defined by reference to the metrical structures of a poem can be verified to be high points by testable data. These poetic features are not newly identified, but are those commonly discussed in the literature on Hebrew poetry and discourse analysis.[1] This study will especially focus on those features which can be statistically verified to be more frequent in peak lines of Hosea. In some cases, such as parallelism, this means peak lines show a decrease in a normal feature of Hebrew poetry in general.

Divine Names as a Feature in Peak

The frequency of references to "the LORD," and "God" are especially significant in the center of chiasms and at the end of homogeneous poems.[2] Twenty-one of the forty-five poems in Hosea have a divine name in the peak, and six more in a secondary peak. (Many others have divine words of advice or judgment, or the "I AM" reference, which have not been counted.) The table below gives the percentage for the number of occurrences of divine names divided by the number of lines in each category. Entering the "Line" numbers as conditions and the "Occurrences" as groups into a matrix 60,28, 64,11, 278,33 gives chi-square 23.97 meaning a 99.9% positive probability of being a significant variation from the expected average. (Even if the two references in 7:10b are moved to non-peak, chi-square is 23.4 also with 99.9%.)

	Occurrences	Lines	Percent
Peak	28	60	46.6
Secondary	11 (if 7:10b is not counted 11 is 9)	64	17.2
Non-peak	33	278	11.9

Divine names come in the following peaks and secondary peaks (the latter are enclosed in parentheses): 1:(2a), 2d, 7a, 7a, 10d; 2:13c, (20), 23c; 3:1c, 5, 5, 5; 4:6c, 10b, 16a; 5:4a, 4b, 6a; 6:3, 6; (7:10a, possibly also 10b); 8:2; ix (3a), 5, (17a); 10:12b; 11:9c; 12:(2a, 5, 5, 5, 6), 9, 9; 14:1[2], 1[2], 2[2], 9[10]b.

1. Watson (*Poetry*) gives a good description of these and other "poetic devices." See for example, "Gender matched parallelism" (123–27), "Number parallelism" (144–49), "Chiasmus and chiastic patterns" (201–7), and "Keywords" (287–94). Also see Schoekel (*Poetics*) for poetic features in Hebrew, and Longacre (*Discourse*, and "Text") for literary features giving prominence at peak.

2. Bliese ("Joel," 76–77) notes a 64% ratio in peak lines, 19% in secondary peaks, and 18% in non-peaks in Joel. Also in his discussion of "Psalms 1–24" see 1:6; 2:7; 3:8; 4:8; 5:8; 9:16; 11:4; 12:5; 13:3; 15:4; 16:7, etc. Shoshany ("Prosodic," 190–200) includes divine references as a feature of strong lines in quatrains of Jeremiah, for example, "The prosodic marker GOD reflects the strength of the first couplet" (190). Similarly, Stuart (*Meter*, 112) notes that LORD comes in the center 21b of Num 23:18–24. Youngblood ("Number," 174 ff.) notes the divine names in the center of Ps 85 and many others.

Repetition of Roots as a Feature in Peak

By comparing roots or lemmas (excluding affixes) within each line, the following list of repeated words in peak, secondary and non-peak lines was drawn up. Repetition *within* single cola was found to be more significant in relation to peak, so only that is tabulated in the diagram. The broader repetition within a whole line, although listed below in the references, is not statistically significant.[3] This is to be expected since parallelism is often represented by the same root in consecutive cola, and parallelism will be shown to be a general poetic feature often dropped in peak. In calculating chi-square from the table below, secondary peaks were not included since there is only one occurrence. Probability has therefore been calculated with only peak and non-peak. Yates' chi-square on these two is 24.78 or 99.7% positive probability, although there is a warning regarding the low number of occurrences. The low number means that chi-square probability is less accurate. However, comparing it with the peak percentage below gives assurance that repetition of roots is a feature of peaks.

	Occurrences	Lines	Percent
Peak	7	60	11.7
Secondary	1	64	1.6
Non-peak	14	278	5.0

Peak (Secondary peaks in Parentheses, those in the same colon underlined) 1:2d harlotry [infinitive absolute], 1:6 forgive [infinitive abs.], 1:11 children-of; (2:2[4]a plead); 3:5a object marker *ʾt*, 3:5b before; 4:2 bloodshed, 4:6a reject, 4:6b forget; 6:3 know [with anacrusis]; (7:10 and-not); 8:11 altars, 8:11 for-sinning; 9:5 for-the-day-of (9:7 great, 9:11 bird/fly); 10:5 over-it, 10:12 till/untilled; (12:5[6] LORD, 12 wife); 13:2 they; 14:2[3] to *ʾel*.

Non-peak 1:2c harlotry, 1:10 not; 2:2[4] not, 2:4[6] children, 2:6[8] wall, 2:11[13] stop/sabbath, 2:12[14] give, 2:12[14] to-me, 2:16[18] you-will-call, 2:18[20] with, 2:21[23] answer, 2:22[24] object *ʾt* [2+1=3 times], 2:22–23[24–25] sow; 2:23[25] mercy, 2:23[25] not; 3:1b love, 3:4 without [2+2=4 times]; 4:1 no [2+1=3 times], 4:4 man, 4:4 not, 4:5 stumble, 4:5–6 destroy, 4:10 and-not, 4:12 harlotry, 4:13 on, 4:14a on, 4:14a because, 4:14b with, 4:15 and-don't, 4:16 stubborn, 4:18 indulged-in-harlotry; 5:5 stumble, 5:13a *ʾt* object, 5:13c not, 5:14b I; 6:2 day, 6:4 What, 6:4 shall-I-do, 6:4 with-you, 6:11 restore-fortune; 8:4 and-not, 8:7–8 swallow, 8:13 sacrifice; 9:4 not, 9:7 days-of, 9:7 have-come, 9:12 them, 9:14 give; 10:1 multiplied,

3. The repeated lemmas within lines are 16 in peak or 26.6%, 6 in secondary or 9.2% and 65 in non-peak or 23.5%.

10:1 prospered/improved, 10:4 speak/word, 10:6 shame, 10:8 up/on, 10:15a wickedness/evil, 10:15b completely/destroy [infinitive abs.]; 11:4b yoke/on, 11:12[12:1] with; 12:3[4] object *ʾt*, 12:10[11] prophets; 13:6 became-full, 13:14 Where; 14:3[4] not.

Syntactic Chiasmus or Inverted Parallelism as a Feature in Peak

Syntactic chiasmus (or inverted parallelism) within lines has been tabulated. Chiastic structures extending beyond a single line are not tabulated, but are listed at the end of the section since they also give prominence to peaks. Besides the function of emphasis, grammatical chiasmus often occurs at boundaries, and ten such places are noted in the non-peak list by being enclosed in square brackets. These ten occurrences show another function of inverted parallelism, that of opening or closing units, so they have not been included in the counts. Including them gives 10.4% for non-peak which is not statistically significant in comparison to peak's 15%. Since short lines reduce the possibility of having many features, single colon lines are subtracted, leaving 33 full lines. Yate's chi-square for the three groups below is 28.84 or 99.7% positive probability. Since secondary 6.1% and non-peak 6.8% are close, the significance is the high percentage in peak lines as over against the others.

	Occurrences	Lines	Percent
Peak	9	60	15.0
Secondary	2	33 full	6.1
Non-peak	20–10=19	278	6.8

The occurrences found are listed below according to their type, with V for verb, P for prepositional phrase, S for subject, O for object, and 1 for root identity. The root is identified in quotation marks.

Peak Line Chiasmus

V S1S1 V—1:11 "children."

O V1V1 O—4:6 "reject."

OVVO—4:10–11; 5:6 (although both verbs in 1st colon).

V P1P1 V—6:3b "as."

P1 VV P1—7:12b "as."

PVVP—(7:14b secondary peak).

VOOV—13:2.

P1 SS P1—10:5 "on it."

VSPV (7:2).

V-Infinitive O; P Verbal-Participle—6:3a.

Note that the first nine examples (eight in peak and one secondary peak) have two pairs of the same categories arranged chiastically. This shows special care in the formation of chiasmus in peak lines as over against non-peak lines. Chiasmus in peaks which extends beyond one line was also noted in 1:6–7; 8:14; and (9:7b–8a).

Non-peak Line Chiasmus (Those at juncture are in square brackets)

[VOOV—2:6[8]b (opens stanza); 4:9b (begins poem).]

VSSV—4:13c; 10:14.

S V1V1 S—8:7c–8 "swallow."

[S1 VV S1—4:4a "man" (ends poem).]

[SVVS—6:1b (3rd line from final peak, all with chiasmus)]; 10:6b; 11:10b.

PVVP—10:10a.

V P1P1 V—12:2[3]b "as."

VPPV—9:3b; 12:12[13]b; 13:3.

PSSP—14:6[7]b.

[P P1P1 P—13:7 "as" (begins poem).]

VOSV—5:3; 10:3b.

[VPOV—7:2 (2nd line before peak ending 4th block).]

VOPV—8:1b (line before central peak of book); 8:12.

OVVP—12:6[7]b.

[P V1V1 O—13:6 "full" (last full line).]

P Adjective1 V1 S—4:16 "stubborn."

Pronoun1 S Complement Pronoun1—8:6a "he."

[Conjunction S Verbal Verbal S P—13:1 (last full line).]

Tricola Lines:

[VP, PV, VP 6:2 (line before final couplet peak).]

VO, OV, VO 10:13.

[VP, SOV, PV 12:10[11]a (begins stanza).]

Nineteen of the above three groups have at least two pairs of the same grammatical categories paired chiastically, such as VP, PV. These especially well-formed examples within the lines of each category are 8 or 13.3% in peak lines, 1 or 3% in secondary, and 10 or 7.2% in non-peak. Yate's chi-square for these three groups is 6.51 with p= 0.0385 or positively 96%, although there is a caution for the small numbers.

Irregular Bicola Structure Not a Peak Norm

Just as well-formed chiasmus is a feature in peak, regular patterns of bicola structure have been found to be more normal in peak than non-peak. Irregular cola structure has been counted whenever there is a deviation from the regular 3+2 to the irregular 2+3 in pentameters, a departure from 3+3 to 2+2+2 or 4+2 or 2+4 in hexameters, and a change from 4+3 to 3+4 or 3+2+2 or 2+2+3 or 2+3+2 in heptameters. Bimeter and trimeter lines do not divide, so without them the line total category numbers are peak 49, secondary 59, and non-peak 210. The counts show 10.5 or 21.43% irregular cola in peak, 5 or 8.47% in secondary peak, and 67.5 or 32.14% in non-peak lines. Yate's chi-square for the matrix of 11,49, 5,59, 68,210 is 7.895 and p-value is 0.0195 or positively 98%. This indicates that well-formedness rather than irregularity is the norm for cola structure in peaks and secondary peaks.

A closer look at other functions beyond prominence for irregular cola adds support to seeing regular cola as normal in peaks. One function is symmetrical balance for the whole poem. The heptameter in 14:1[2] in the way it is divided with the largest colon last, forms a chiastic structure with the second line of the couplet peak, 2+2+3; 3+2+2. This may also be the reason for the 2+3 irregular peak lines in 2:18[20]d–19[21]a and 6:11a which follow regular 3+2 lines also in central couplet peaks. Similarly, 7:5 has a balanced 2+2+2 irregular couplet in its peak. The secondary peak lines in 13:15a [5+2] and 14:5[6] [3+2+2] also show balance.

This kind of symmetrical arrangement of irregular lines is also noteworthy in non-peak lines. 2+3 pentameters come on both sides of a central peak in 7:12–13. Trimeter hexameter 2+2+2 lines in 1:10c and 11b and 2:18b and 19b are adjacent on both sides of peaks and thereby add to the chiastic structure marking the center. Similarly, a 2+4 line precedes, and a 2+2+2 line follows a central peak in 9:4c and 6a. Irregular hexameters also give balance at the borders of poems. In 4:15a and 19 the first and last lines both have 4+2 cola structure. Heptameter irregular non-peak lines have this same function of giving symmetry. 7:4b and 6b are 3+4 heptameters coming next to both lines of a central peak. The irregular heptameters in 8:4b and

8b are the first and last lines of a poem, and those in 12:8[9]a and 10[11] are the second lines on each side of a central peak.

Subtracting these lines that illustrate the function of symmetrical balance significantly lowers the peak percentage from 21.43% to 9.18% as in the ratios in the diagram below. Secondary peaks are the most regular, followed by peaks, leaving non-peak lines with 24% or over twice the percentage of peak lines. Yate's chi-square is 8.63 (df of 2 with p=0.013) or over 98% positive probability for a preference for regular colometry in peak and secondary peak lines.

	Irregular Cola	Lines	Percent
Peak	10.5 minus 6=4.5	49	9.18
Secondary	5 minus 2=3	59	5.08
Non-peak	67.5 minus 17=50.5	210	24.05

Another function of irregular cola structures is juncture. From peak lines the irregular 2:19[21] and 14:1[2] begin stanzas. The secondary peak 13:5a also begins a stanza. Non-peak lines with irregular cola are also common at juncture. The pentameters in 8:1a and 11:5a begin poems, and 2:4[6]a; 9:13, 12:4[5]b and 12:13[14]b–14[15]a begin stanzas. Irregular hexameter lines also begin a poem in 14:9[10]a and end one in 13:11, and the above-mentioned hexameters in 4:15a and 19 enclose a poem. Irregular hexameters also begin stanzas in 10:13a and 12:7[8] and 11[12], and the irregular heptameter in 12:10[11] ends a stanza. After subtracting these occurrences at juncture, Yate's chi-square is 8.93 (df of 2 with p=0.0115) or almost 99% probability.

	Irregular Cola	Lines	Percent
Peak	4.5 minus 3=1.5	49	3.06%
Secondary	3 minus 1=2.0	59	3.39%
Non-peak	50.5 minus 12=38.5	210	18.33%

In summary, both peak and secondary peak lines have lower percentages of irregular lines than non-peaks in all the above calculations. Irregular colometry also has the function of marking juncture and symmetry, and if lines with these functions are not counted, peak and secondary peak lines predominately conform to well-formedness, with non-peak lines six times more irregular.

A comparison of heptameters counted as irregular show further support for greater regularity in peak lines. Three heptameters (2:5c; 13:2c; 14:2[3]), have 3+2+2 structures with the expected largest colon first in tricola lines. The secondary peak in 14:5[6] has the same structure (the other secondary heptameter in 13:15a has 5+2). Only 14:1[2] has the longest colon other than first among peak heptameters, and this has already been shown to give balance to the central lines. None of the non-peak heptameter lines have the largest colon first, and are therefore more irregular (6:4b, 6b; 8:4b, 7c–8a; 12:8[9]a, 10[11]). As an indication that 4+3 is the norm for heptameters it should be noted that 16 regular forms were found as over against 12 irregular heptameters of all kinds.

References for irregular cola in peak and (secondary peak) are 1:1, 9; 2:(3a, 3b), 5c, (7c), 18d–19a, (23c); 6:11a; 7:5, 6; 11:7a (half line); 13:2c, (15a); 14:1[2], 2[3], (5[6]).

Unique Line Length as a Feature in Peak

Longacre (*Discourse*, 32) lists "change of pace" such as "length of units (clauses, sentences . . .)" as a feature of peak in literature. All the poems in Hosea were tabulated as to whether they have a uniquely long or short line, and whether it was peak, secondary peak, or non-peak. Five poems have a uniquely long line, and four are peak lines, giving strong probability to uniquely long line length as a marker for peak. Of the sixteen uniquely short lines eight were peaks, seven were monocola secondary peaks, and only one was non-peak. Calculating the probability of unique line length for the three categories, the following percentages resulted. Yate's chi-square is 30.8 (with a df of 2 and p=2e-7) or over 99% probability, although the low number 2 causes a warning. (The warning disappears if non-peak is experimentally raised to 12 instead of 2. This gives a p of 0.002 or almost 99%, which makes the actual 99% look reasonable.)

	Occurrences	Lines	Percent
Peak	12	60	20.0
Secondary	6	64	10.9
Non-peak	2	278	0.7

References in peaks, (secondary peaks), and Non-peak lines:

(a) Short: 1:(2a), 9; 2:(9a); 3:1b; 4:2b; 4:10b–11a; (6:5b; 7:1b); 8:6b; (9:16a; 12:1[2]b); 13:6b, 9; (14:6[7]). Non-peak 10:2a.

(b) Long: 1:1; 2:5[7]c; 12:7[8]b; 13:2; (note also 14:1–2[2–3] tricola heptameters with bimeters on each side). Non-peak 8:4b.

Single Line Strophes as a Feature of Peak

Most strophes in Hosea are couplets. There are also 89 triplets. Both couplets and triplets are normal patterns of Hebrew poetry. However, occasionally the semantic relationship between lines calls for identifying a single line as a strophe of its own. These have been counted in the three categories, showing that peak lines are much more likely to have single line strophes. Yate's chi-square for the three comes to 10.57 (with a df of 2) and p= 0.005 or a 99% probability (There is also a status warning for the low numbers).

	Occurrences	Lines	Percent
Peak	9	60	15.0
Secondary	6	64	9.4
Non-peak	8	278	2.9

References in peak and (secondary peak) are in 4:(4b, 9a, 11b,) 13b, (14c); 6:6, 11; (7:14b); 8:2, 6; 9:5, (11); 11:3; 12:1[2]c; 13:2c, and 9; and in non-peak are 5:12, 15a; 7:4b, 6b; 11:1, 4b; and 14:9[10]a.

Switches to Second Person as a Feature in Peak

Hosea is very free with grammatical changes, often for the same referent. Longacre (*Discourse*, 29) notes the role of a "shift to more specific person" such as "third person to second person" and "plural to singular" in literary peaks. Changes into second person have been tabulated below. The data below give a chi-square of 5.396 (with df of 2 and p=0.067) or a 93% probability (with a warning for the low number). (Yate's chi-square is 3.73 with p=0.15, or 89.5%, which just misses probability.) Individual examples obviously help to set off peaks such as in 9:5, the only second person plural line in its poem, and 13:9 and 14:1[2] which mark major transitions. The secondary peak example in 2:1[3] is a final line and the change in person obviously helps to give emphasis.

	Occurrences	Lines	Percent
Peak	6	60	10.0
Secondary	6	64	9.4
Non-peak	10	278	3.6

The references in peak and (secondary peak) are 2:(1[3]), 19[21]; 6:(5), 11; 8: 2; 9:5, (7); (12:6[7]); 13:9; 14:1[2], (3, 8); and in non-peak are 2:6[8], 16; 4:13; 5:3, 13; 8:5; 9:10, 14; 10:12; 13:14. Places where a second person peak switches to another person in the line after the peak also support this function. See (2:2[4]); 4:6–7; 6:11; 9:5–6, (7–8), 14b–15, and 12:9[10].

Many stanza breaks coincide with changes in person showing another function of this switch. See 2:6[8]; 3:4; 12:7[8], 10 and 14:4[5].

Plural to Singular Switch as a Feature in Peak

Following Longacre's observation (*Discourse*, 29) that grammatical switches from plural to singular characterize peak, they were calculated in Hosea yielding the following results. Yate's chi-square is 3.5 and p=0.07 or 93% probability.

	Occurrences	Lines	Percent
Peak	10	60	16.7
Secondary	3	64	4.7
Non-peak	23	278	8.3

The references for peak and (secondary peak) are 2:19[21] "them-you"; 4:6; v. 11; 6:(5), 10; 7:5; 8:11; (9:7); 10:5; 11:3, 7(also plural to singular showing turbulence); (12:12[13]); 13:9; and for non-peak are 4:8, 19; 5:3; 7:4, 6, 11; 8:3, 5, 6, 7, 9; 9:13; 10:1, 6, 11, 13, 15; 11:4, 6, 12; 13:14; 14:4[5], 7[8].

Switch of Number for the Same Referent, a Feature in Peak

A grammatical feature which is found in peak but rare elsewhere is for the number (singular or plural) of a referent to change (enallage). Calculations have been done here on changes within a line. Changes between Israel and its inhabitants are especially noteworthy. Note 11:3 and 7 where the changes occur in one colon, and 12:1[2]b-c where the change occurs between adjacent secondary and primary peaks. Such grammatical "shifts" add to the "turbulence" and "heightened vividness" characteristic of peak in literature as described by Longacre (*Discourse*, 28–29). No occurrences were found in secondary peaks. Yate's chi-square for the peak and non-peak ratios is 9.85 (df of 1) and p=0.001 or over 99% probability.

	Occurrences	Lines	Percent
Peak	7	60	11.7
Non-peak	5	278	1.8

References in peak are 1:6c, 7a; 2:16–17; 8:2, 6; 11:3, 7b; and in non-peak are 8:9b; 9:3b; 10:5a, 8, 9.

Imperatives as a Feature in Peak

Imperatives, including three jussives and a cohortative, total nine in peak or 16.7%, eight in secondary peak or 10.9%, and twenty-six in non-peak or 9.4%. Yates' chi-square of 0.916 does not meet statistical probability. References in peak are 5:8b; 6:3a, 3b; 9:14; 10:12; 9:1; 14:2[3]a, 2[3]a, 2[3]a.

Another factor is the frequency of imperatives used to begin poems, sometimes singly but often in a series. Fifteen of the twenty-six non-peak imperatives and five of the eight secondary peak imperatives open poems. The fifteen non-peak examples are 1:2c, 2c, 9b; 3:1b, 1b; 4:15a, 15b, 15b, 15c; 5:1a, 1a, 1b; 9:1a; 14:9[10]a, 9[10]a. Of the other non-peak imperatives two in 10:8 end a poem, two in 10:12a are in a series continuing into an imperative peak, two in 12:6[7]b follow in a series begun in a secondary peak, and 14:2[3]c follows in a series begun in a peak. The imperative in 6:1a is the first word of a quotation and is followed by the cohortative. This leaves only 8:5a and 9:7, or two out of the 26 non-peak imperatives, without a close relationship to juncture or peak. Of the secondary peak examples, the five in lines that open poems are 1:4b, 6b, 2:2[4]a, 2[4]a and 5:8a. One is in a closure line (2:1[3]), one is connected to a central peak (14:2[3]b), and one is in a mid-half line (12:6[7]a). Subtracting just these imperatives that begin poems as in the following table gives Yate's chi-square of 7.59 with p=0.022 on a df of 2 or over 97% probability (although there is a warning for the low numbers).

	Occurrences	Lines	Percent
Peak	9	60	15.0
Secondary	8–5=3	64	4.7
Non-peak	26–15=11	278	4.0

Lists of Three or More as a Feature in Peak

The data below show the same cline of highest in peak, followed by secondary peak, with non-peak the lowest. Yate's chi-square is 33.11 or 99.6% probable (although there is a warning with the low numbers).

	Occurrences	Lines	Percent
Peak	7	60	11.7
Secondary	3	33 full	9.1
Non-peak	15	278	5.4

Occurrences of lists in peak and (secondary peak) are 1:1b, (7b); 2:(3[5]b-c), 5[7], 18[20]c, 4:13b; 6:3c; (9:11). Also 4:2 and 8:14 are part of lists beginning with the previous line, and have been included. Non-peak lists noted are 1:7; 2:7[9], 11[13], 18[20], 19[21], 22[24]; 3:4; 4:1c, 2, 3; 5:1–2; 8:14; 13:3, 7–8; 14:9[10].

Enjambment as a Feature in Peak

Enjambment, a semantic break between cola so that the cola of a metrical line align with adjacent lines rather than with each other, was noted above as a common feature in Hosea. Four and a half lines have enjambment at peak in 1:4d, 6; 2:18d, 3:5a and the half line at 11:7a. There are no secondary peak occurrences. The six and a half non-peak occurrences are 1:11b; 2:8[10]b, 10[12]b; 7:6b; 8:9; 11:6b, 13b–14a. On the matrix 5,60, 7,278 Yate's chi-square is 2.94 (with a df of 1 and p=0.086) indicating 91% positive probability.

	Occurrences	Lines	Percent
Peak	4.5	60	7.5
Non-peak	6.5	278	2.3

Anacrusis as a Feature in Peak

The observed occurrences of anacrusis or introductory words not counted in the metrical line, are very few, with peak occurrences in 2:5[7] and 6:3, and secondary peak in 9:11. They do not have statistical probability when compared with the three occurrences in non-peak. However, as a means to bring turbulence at peak, anacrusis is important. It should be noted that non-peak examples all come at junctures—two begin poems (1:2c and 6:7) and one (9:6) begins a stanza. Peaks which have a previous short line may be considered to be set off with a function similar to anacrusis. See 6:6; 12:1[2] and 14:1–2[2–3].

	Occurrences	Lines	Percent
Peak	2	60	3.3
Secondary	1	33 full	3.0
Non-peak	3	278	1.1
(Non-peak not opening poems	1	278	0.4)

Syntactic Complexity as a Feature in Peak

A predictable feature for peak in literature is "syntactic complexity." Complicated grammar sets off peaks as illustrated by subordinate clauses, apposition, ellipsis, etc. A categorization of the conjunction *kî* 'because, while, that, indeed, truly' follows, showing a major difference between peak and non-peak.[4] The chi-square calculation with these two categories is 0.127 or 87.73% slightly missing the 90% statistical probability. (For all three categories chi-square is only 2.96 with p of 0.228.)

	Occurrences	Lines	Percent
Peak	15	60	25.0
Secondary	8	64	12.5
Non-peak	42	278	15.1

The peak and (secondary peak) *kî* occurrences are 1:2, (4, 6b) 6c; 4:6, 10, 13; 5:4, (11); 6:6; 7:6; 8:6, (9), 11; (9:12, 16, 17); 10:5; 11:9; 13:9, (15); 14:1[2], 9[10]; and the non-peak occurrences are 1:9, 11; 2:2[4], 4[6], 5[7], 5[7], 7[9], 8[10]; 3:4; 4:1, 12, 14, 14, 14, 16; 5:1, 1, 3, 7, 14; 6:1, 9; 7:1, 13, 13; 8:6, 7, 10; 9:1, 4, 6, 12, 15; 10:3, 13; 11:1, 3, 5, 10; 13:13, 16; 14:4[5].

Other examples of syntactic complexity noted in peaks are as follows: (apposition): 2:5[7]; (12:5[6]); (infinitives): 4:10; 5:4a; 6:3; 10:12; (ellipsis excluding gapping): possibly 1:6–7; 13:9; ("I–we" clash or discontinuous construct): 8:2.

Avoiding Parallelism of Syntax in Peak

One type of parallelism is repeating syntactic structures from one colon to the next. Such similarity within lines was calculated, namely, where a pattern of syntactic features in the same order in consecutive cola was observed. Since the verb is the essential unit, the cases of gapping where one verb served two cola, were not counted even if other elements were similar. Small variations in elements such as additional genitives, adjectives, pronouns, adverbs, prepositions and conjunctions were allowed. One tricolon had similarity in all three cola (10:11c), and four had similarity in two of three cola (2:18[20] b, 19[21]b; 9:6a, 7a). The ratio shows that syntactic similarity is not preferred for peaks in Hosea. (Also see Shoshany "Prosodic," 190–92 on "syntactic parallelism" as a characteristic of weak lines.) This follows the pattern observed

4. This comparison illustrates Longacre's observation (Discourse, 38) that the "incidence of particles" often changes either by addition or loss as a feature of peak.

with dropping parallelism in peak lines. In both cases a normal poetic feature is used less at peak. Although the percents mark the decrease of syntactic parallelism in peak lines, chi-square is below probability with only 88.7%.

	Occurrences	Lines	Percent
Peak	3	60	5.0
Secondary	2	33 full	6.1
Non-peak	40	278	14.4

References in peak and (secondary peak) are (2:3[5]b); 4:6c; 5:11a; 12:1[2]; (13:12); and in non-peak are 2:2[4]b, 5[7]a, 14[16]b, 18[20]b, 19[21]b; 3:4b; 4:10a, 13a 14b, 15b; 5:1b, 12, 13b, 14a; 6:1b, 4a, 5, 10b; 7:10b, 11b; 8:4, 7; 9:4a, 6a, 7a, 7b, 7c, 8b, 9b; 10:2b, 11c, 12a, 11:2b, 8a, 8b; 12:3[4]; 13:14a, 14b, 15c; 14:9[10]c.

Dropping Parallelism as a Feature in Peak

Parallelism has many forms in Hosea including both internal colon to colon parallelism and line to line or couplet parallelism. Many obvious occurrences have some form of the historic categories of repetition, contrast, or syntactic development, and often illustrate more specific "seconding" of an idea from a previous colon. Others have sound-repetition, or grammatical parallelism. Breaks where *semantic parallelism is dropped* have been calculated with significant results, showing a greater percentage of such breaks in peaks than non-peaks. Yate's chi-square of the data in the three categories is 11.65 (with df of 2 and p=0.003) giving over 99% probability of non-chance. This indicates that dropping parallelism rather than the presence of parallelism can be considered a feature of peak. A rough count of line-internal colon to colon parallelism also showed only 33% in peak as over against 44% in non-peak. Longacre (*Discourse*, 25) writes, "routine features . . . may be distorted or phased out at Peak."[5]

	Occurrences	Lines	Percent
Peak	12	60	20.0
Secondary	8	64	12.5
Non-peak	13	278	4.7

5. Shoshany "Prosodic," 201 states the difference clearly: "A structure containing repeated or parallel elements is generally of lesser syntactic complexity than a corresponding structure containing non-repeated or non-parallel elements; hence, syntactic complexity reflects strong constituents while repetition and syntactic parallelism reflect weak ones."

References in peak and (secondary peak) are 1:2d; 2:13[14]c; 4:2b, 13b; (5:7b, 11b); 6:(5b), 11a; 7:5, (10); 8:2, 6b; 9:(3a); 12:(1b); 13:2c, 6b, 9, (14c); 14:(3[4]c), 9[10]b; and in non-peak are 1:11b; 2:7[9]d, 10[12], 17[19]a; 4:17; 5:2; 6:10a, 16c; 8:12; 10:12c; 11:11b; 12:8[9]b, and 14:4[5]b.

This feature does not exclude parallelism from occurring in well-formed peaks. Examples of parallelism in peaks are 1:11a; 3:5b; 4:6b, 6c, 10b-11a; 5:4b, 8b, 11a; 6:3b, 6; 7:2b, 12b; 9:5, 14b; 10:5b; 11:3a, 9c; 12:1[2]; and in secondary peaks are 2:1[3], 3[5]a, 3[5]b, 7[9]b; 5:8a; 12:5[6]; 14:5[6]. At least two poems show parallelism throughout and end with a final line of close parallelism, namely 6:6 and 12:1[2]. Both of these poems are unique in having one short monocolon line which breaks the parallelism. In both cases this break comes in the line just before the final peak, thereby setting off the peak. Parallelism in these cases follows the same pattern of the rhythm, which is consistently hexameters except for the short trimeters before the hexameter peaks. Both rhythm and parallelism may be seen as a buildup, with the exceptional lines drawing attention to the final peak lines.

As was noted in the introduction, Hosea groups lines into couplets which also exhibit parallelism in many cases. Some examples are 1:10c-d; 2:15[17]c-d, 17[19]; 7:8, 9, 13a-b; 9:10a-b; 10:1b-c.

Avoiding Word-Pair Parallelism in Peak

A feature of Hebrew and Canaanite literature is the poetic use of pairs of words that commonly come together. They are counted as a word-pair if the pair is repeated in more than one place. In many cases these fit with parallelism. A tentative count of such semantically related pairs in Hosea's parallelism showed that peak and secondary peak lines are significantly less likely to have them. See the percentages below. Chi-square for the data is 5.44 with p-value of 0.0658, or 93.4% probable. The pairs below are listed with an H if repeated in Hosea, and a B if only once in Hosea but elsewhere in the Hebrew Bible.

	Occurrences	Lines	Percent
Peak	12	60	20%
Secondary	8	33 full	24%
Non-peak	111	278	40%

The references counted in peak and (secondary peak) are 1:11a Judah, Israel–H; 2:(1[3] brothers, sisters–B; 2:3[5]a return, seek–H; 2:3[5]b desert, dry land–B; 2:7[9] seek, find–H); 2:23[25]c my people, my God–B; 3:5b

God, king–B; 4:10b-11a forsook, keep–B; (5:8a trumpet, horn–B); 5:11 oppress, crush–B; 6:3 showers, spring rain–B; 6:6 sacrifice, burnt offering–B; 6:10b Ephraim, Israel–B; (7:3 king, princes–H; 7:10b return, seek–H); 8:14c cities, strongholds–B; 9:5 festival, feast–H; 9:14 womb, breasts–B; 12:1[2] Assyria, Egypt–H; (13:12 iniquity, sin–H; bound up, stored–Ugaritic).

As examples of some of the 111 in the above diagram that I counted in non-peak see 2:11 feast, festival–H; 3:4b, 8:10, 13:10b king, princes–H; 4:13a, 10:8c mountains, hills–H; 4:15a, 6:5b Judah, Israel–H; 5:3, 10:6b, 11:8a Ephraim, Israel–H; 5:3 harlotry, defiled–B; 5:15a return, seek–H; 7:11b, 11:2 call, go–H; 9:16 root, fruit–B; 14:9[10] wise, understand–B (Ps 107:43); and some noted by Dearman (*Hosea*): 4:8, 8:13, 9:9 iniquity, sin; 4:13a and 11:2b sacrifice, burn incense; 5:12 moth, rottenness; 6:2 live, rise; 7:15 chastise, strengthen; 9:6 nettles, thorns; 11:11a Assyria, Egypt; 13:14 ransom, redeem; 13:14 death, Sheol; and 13:14 plague, destruction.

Avoiding Number-Switch Parallelism in Peak

Cola which have an obvious contrast between singular and plural in the parallelism of the line have been counted. In some cases nominal forms, and in others verbal forms contrast. Although Yates' calculation is lower, chi-square is 3.37 or 90% probable, indicating that this type of parallelism is also avoided in peak and secondary peak lines, in contrast to non-peak lines.

	Occurrences	Lines	Percent
Peak	3	60	5.0
Secondary	1	33full	3.0
Non-peak	31	278	11.2

References in peak and (secondary peak) are (6:6); 9:14b; 12:1[2]c; 13:2c. Non-peak examples are 1:2c; 2:10[12], 15[17], 19[21]b, 21[23]b; 4:12b, 18b, 19; 5:1; 6:2; 7:1, 3, 4a; 8:13a; 9:1, 9b, 10a, 10b, 12a, 15b; 10:1b, 1c, 4a, 5a; 11:8b, 8c; 12 [12:lb]; 12:11[12]a.

Avoiding Parallelism of Rhyme in Peak

The number of lines which had the same final sound in both cola—a repeated vowel or consonant or combinations of both—were counted. The three groups calculated as below miss statistical probability. However, combining peak and secondary into one group with a matrix of 93,12, 278,60 gives chi-square of 2.35 or 93% probability. This indicates that rhyming is sometimes avoided in peaks as with parallelism in general. It gives balance rather than the irregularity preferred at peak and secondary peak.

	Occurrences	Lines	Percent
Peak	9	60	15.0
Secondary	3	33 full	9.1
Non-peak	60	278	21.6

References in peak and (secondary peak) are (1:5b), 7a; 2:5[7]c; 3:5b; 4:2b; 5:4a, (8a), 8b; 7:5b-6a, 12b; (9:12a); 14:1[2]; and in non-peak are 1:2c, 10c, 11c; 2:5[7]a, 9[11]b, 11[13]b, 12[14]b, 13[15]a, 16[17]b; 3:1c, 3a; 4:10a, 13a, 14a, 14b; 5:4, 5b, 7a, 13, 15a; 6:1b, 9; 7:8b, 11b, 13a, 13b, 14a, 16b, 16c; 8:4, 7a, 7b, 9b, 10a; 9:1c, 6a, 6b, 9b, 12b, 15b, 15c; 10:2b, 3a, 9b, 10a, 13c, 14c; 11:2, 6, 8c; 12:4[5]b, 8a, 11; 13:11, 14a, 15c, 16b; 14:3[4]b, 7[8]b, 9[10].

Alliteration was also noted in the following peak and (secondary peak) lines, with the letters in italics: (*b* in 1:7b); -*y* ending every word in 2:5[7]c; -*w/u* (dropped in peak after a previous colon and line) 4:11; -*l* in 4:13b; -*u*-(assonance) in 5:11; -*m* in 9:11–12; -*w* in 10:5; (-*u* assonance besides rhyme 10:8); -*m* in 13:2.

(Gender Switch as a General Poetic Feature)

A favorite form of parallelism is to contrast nouns in each cola by balancing feminine against masculine. The occurrences in the three categories are nearly identical indicating that this is a general feature of Hebrew poetry rather than a feature of peak. Although the differences are not statistically verifiable, the lower percentages in peaks and secondary suggest a tendency of avoidance in peak as in the previous features of parallelism.

	Occurrences	Lines	Percent
Peak	5	60	8.3
Secondary	2	33 full	6.1
Non-peak	25	278	9.0

References in peak and (secondary peak) are 2:22[24]a; 6:6, 6; (7:14a); 8:14; (9:7c); 12:1[2]c. Non-peak examples observed are 2:2[4]b, 21[3]b; 3:4b; 4:1c; 5:1, 8; 7:3, 4a; 9:9b; 10:12, 13a, 13b; 11:4, 4, 6, 6b-7, 12[12:1]; 12:1[2]a, 3[4], 14[15]b; 13:5, 12, 15c; 14:6[7]a, 8[9]b.

(Positive-Negative Contrast as a General Feature)

The lines where a positive-negative contrast or antithetical parallelism occurred were counted. The ratio with peaks is slightly lower than non-peak, but not enough to show statistical probability. This suggests that the feature is general for Hebrew poetry as a form of parallelism, with possibly some avoidance in peak as in the forms of parallelism noted previously.

	Occurrences	Lines	Percent
Peak	4	60	6.7
Secondary	2	33 full	6.1
Non-peak	21	278	7.6

References in peak and (secondary peak) are (2:7[9]b); 5:4b, 6b; (9:11b);11:7b, 9c; and in non-peak are 2:6b, 7a, 16b; 3:3b, 3c; 4:15a; 5:3a, 14b; 7:7b, 9a, 9b, 14a, 15; 8:6a, 13a; 9:4c, 16b; 10:3b; 11:9d; 13:11; 14:9[10]c.

(Metaphor Has Only a Slight Preference in Peaks)

Metaphor is a poetic feature that is expected to be more frequent in peak (note its use described in Bliese, "Joel," 80). Although peaks have higher frequencies in Hosea, the preference in peaks is not statistically verifiable. The cline in percentages reflects a positive use of metaphor for prominence in peaks.

	Occurrences	Lines	Percent
Peak	4	60	6.7
Secondary	3	64	4.7
Non-peak	11	278	4.0

References in peak and (secondary peak) are 1:2, 4c, (5); 2:18[20]; (5:7b; 6:11); 10:12; and in non-peak are 6:7; 7:8b; 8:1, 7, 7, 9; 9:13; 10:1, 11; 11:1; and 13:8b.

Simile has a small negative ratio in Hosea with peak at 16.7% (10 references), secondary at 17.6% (12 references), and non-peak at 18.4% (51 references).

(Rhetorical Questions a General Poetic Feature)

Rhetorical questions occur in peaks in 4:16 and 9:5. For Hosea this is not a frequent peak feature, although it still gives heightened effect when it occurs. Most rhetorical questions occur in non-peak lines, which is different from results in similar studies (Bliese, "Joel," 79–80), Nah 1:6 and 3:19 (Bliese, "Nahum," 55, 70–71, 77), and Isa 40:13, 18; 45:11; 50:8 (Bliese, "Second Isaiah"). Hosea 6:4a; 11:5; 13:10, 14a and (possibly 14b) have two questions in each line which makes the number of occurrences high for non-peak lines. Other non-peak occurrences are 10:3b, 9b; 11:8a, 8b; 14:8[9]a, 9[10]a. Nine of the non-peak occurrences come at the beginning of poems, suggesting another function, that of introduction. Deleting these gives the highest ratio to peaks. However, the difference is not sufficient to be statistically probable.

	Occurrences	Lines	Percent
Peak	2	60	3.3
Secondary	14	64	5.0
Non-peak	14–9=5	278	1.8

(Twenty-six Letters in a Line as a Feature of Prominence)

There are 22 poetic lines in Hosea that have 26 letters in a line following the lineage in this analysis. One poem has three 26-letter lines (4:5a, 6b and 7), two poems have two (1:4b and 5b, and 10:9b and 15a), and fifteen poems have one 26-letter line (1:2c, 2:1[3], 2:10[12]a, 2:16[18]b, 2:19[21]a, 2:20[22], 2:23[25]b, 6:4a, 8:14a, 10:6a, 12:7[8], 13:3a, 13:7, 13:10b, 14:3[4]b. All the groups are basically equal, so there is no statistical preference for peak lines. Four non-peak lines begin poems, which may indicate a special function, especially the first message line of the book in 1:2c. The others are 6:4a, 8:14a, and 13:7.

	Occurrences	Lines	Percent
Peak	3	60	5.0
Secondary	3	64	4.7
Non-peak	16	278	5.8

(Twenty-two Letters in a Line as a Feature of Prominence)

The following occurrences of MT lines with 22 letters was observed. The 8.3% for both peak and non-peak excludes statistical probability. However, it should be noted that the first peak line in 1:2, which is the second line of the first divine message, and the central peak line of the book in 8:2 both have 22 letters. This suggests a conscious counting of letters in these lines to tie the beginning of the book together with the center using the alphabetical symbolic number 22 that is basic in the structure of the book.

	Occurrences	Lines	Percent
Peak	5	60	8.3
Secondary	2	64	3.1
Non-peak	23	278	8.3

The peak and (secondary peak) occurrences are 1:2 (first episode); 5:(8a), 8b; 8:2 (central line of central poem); 10:5 (first of 7th block); and (12:12[13]b). Non-peak references are 2:2[4], 3, 8, 17a; 3:4a; 6:8, 9; 7:6, 12, 16b; 8:6, 13b; 10:8a, 12a; 11:8, 10b, 11b; 12:4[5b], 9[10]b; 13:11, 12, 14b; 14:2[3]c.

Summary of Features of Prominence

The difference between non-peak lines and both peaks likely and secondary peaks in many of the above examples is significant enough to claim that the structural analysis in this paper based on whether the poem is chiastic or homogeneous does identify peak lines. Secondary peak ratios come between peak and non-peak lines in thirteen of the above features (divine names, regular bicola, line length, single line strophes, switch to second person, imperatives, lists, anacrusis, syntactic complexity, dropping parallelism, and the related group of avoiding syntactic similarity, word pairs, and metaphor). Three features (avoiding rhyme, number switch and positive-negative contrast) show even greater differences between secondary peaks and non-peaks. For these sixteen features, Hosea's poetry consistently shows a relationship between structure and emphasis. A summary of the data percentages of those with statistical probability from the above features follows. Parentheses indicate where secondary peak figures were zero or one, and were therefore not included in the calculations.

Chart of Distribution of Features of Prominence

Features in Peak **Percent of Occurrences**

	Peak	Secondary	Non-Peak	Probability
Divine Names (LORD or God)	46.6	17.2	11.9	99%
Dropping Semantic Parallelism	20.0	12.5	4.7	99%
Unique Line Length in Poem	18.3	10.9	.7	99%
Single Line Strophe	13.3	9.4	3.2	99%
Switches of Number in a Line	11.7	(0.0)	1.8	99%
Imperatives (less poem openers)	15.0	4.7	5.4	97%
Lists of Three or More	11.7	9.1	5.4	99%
Enjambment	7.5	(0.0)	2.3	91%
Switches to 2nd Person	10.0	9.4	3.6	90%
Syntactic Chiasmus in Lines	15.0	6.1	6.8	99%
Repetition within Lines	11.7	(1.6)	5.0	99%

Features Where Peak has Low Counts **Percent of Occurrences**

	Peak	Secondary	Non-Peak	Probability
Irregular Bicola Not a Peak Norm	4.2	6.1	13.8	98%
Avoiding Parallelism of Syntax	5.0	6.1	14.4	88.7%
Avoiding Word-Pair Parallelism	20.0	27.3	37.4	93%
Avoiding Number-Switch Parallel.	5.0	3.0	11.2	90%
Avoiding Parallelism of Rhyme	15.0	9.1	21.6	*93%
(93% combines peak & secondary)				

Studies in Hebrew discourse analysis have identified turbulence or breaking of the norm as one feature of peak.[6] With the well-documented analyses of parallelism as the basis of Hebrew poetry, it is then to be expected that "dropping parallelism" and the related features of avoiding parallelism of syntactic similarity, word pairs, rhyme, number switch and gender switch are more typical of peak. On the other hand there are structural features more specifically used for giving prominence at peak than for being a general feature of Hebrew poetry, and are therefore countable positively. These might be described as an enhancement in peaks of a general poetic feature. "Repetition," "chiasmus," "regular bicola," "unique line length," and "lists" fit this expectation.

6. See especially Longacre, Discourse, 25–38.

Shoshany ("Prosodic," 171ff.) lists repetition as a feature of "weak" lines. However, it seems that repetition should be put together with word play as a strong feature rather than with parallelism as a "weak" line feature (201). Longacre (*Discourse*, 26) notes that "rhetorical underlining" with "extra words" is a feature of peak. This fits with including repetition as a feature of peak. In regard to narrative he describes Biblical Hebrew as typically restricting "explicit back reference to very rare and pivotal storyline marking functions" (443), and gives an illustration of Gen 39:5 as being "climactic as seen by its elaborate back-reference and verbal-nominal paraphrase" (456). Increased use of repetition at peak is also what comes out of this study of Hebrew poetry. As evidence of this feature note the following list of peak and secondary peak lines with repetition of their peak words within their respective poems: 1:2, (4b, 5, 6a,) 6b-7a, (7b), (10a), 10d-11a; 2:(1[3], 3[5]b,) 5[7], (7[9]b), 17[19], (20[22], 21[23]a,) 22–23[24–25](inclusio); 3:1, 5(inclusio); 4:(4b), 6, (9a, 11b, 14c); 5:4, (5a); 6:4–6; 7:5–6, (10), 12; 8:6, (9a), 11(with five of its seven words repeated), (13c,) 14; (ix 3, 7c, 10d, 11–12, 16a, 16b-17a, 17c; 10:14b); 12:(2a), 9, (12b); (13:15a); 14:1–2[2–3]a, (2[3]b, 5[6], 6[7]).

B. Overall Structure of Hosea

There is no scholarly consensus on an overall structure for Hosea besides the division between chapters 1–3 and 4–14.[7] The various proposals are normally based on thematic and discourse features. I am here proposing to add *numerical counts* to these basic criteria. I found that the book of Hosea can be divided into sections based on *the number of poetic lines* grouped in various multiples of 22, the number of letters in the Hebrew alphabet.[8] These blocks have been defined after having observed that breaks between

7. Garrett (*Hosea*,24–25) states what I have also found: "the Book of Hosea, albeit a text that is notoriously difficult to analyze and seemingly a series of fragments, is best understood when treated as a literary work, a complex whole, and not as an anthology of many separate parts." On p. 30 Garrett adds as an introduction to his critique of several scholars' analyses of the structure: "the various proposals have little in common besides noting that there is an apparent break between 3:5 and 4:1." And on p. 34 Garrett rejects the possibility of Hosea having no meaningful structure saying, "there are too many indications of care, precision, and artistry in this book for me to find this solution satisfactory." The question of whether any proposed overall structure came from Hosea, his collector, or a later redactor is debated (see Yee, Hosea, 42–43, 309–13 who proposes the final redactor, and discusses the history of similar proposals of K. Budde (p. 5), H. Frey (p. 13), and Willi-Plein (p. 20)).

8. Watson, (*Poetry*, 199) gives examples of "11-line and 22-line poems." Freedman ("Acrostic," 415) notes the significance of 22-line poems which are "nonalphabetic" as well as the acrostics.

poems are found every 44th poetic line, with a 50-line block in the center. The common literary division of Biblical material into five parts (note the Pentateuch and Five Books of Psalms, and see Bliese, "Joel," 73–76, and Christensen, "Jonah," 33–45) is realized when each successive block of 44 is combined with its partner to make four parts of 88 lines plus the center of 50 lines. That this is basic to the structure is indicated by the unique character of the first 88 poetic (excluding non-poetic) lines with the story of Hosea's life in chapters 1–3.[9] Strong support for recognizing these first units comes in the convergence of MT counts noted above especially in the first block of 44 poetic lines with 286 words equaling 22x13 and 11x26 in 1:1—2:8[10], and the second block of 44 lines with 390 lemmas equaling 13x30, 26x15, 10x39, 6x65 and 5x78 lemmas in 2:9[11]—3:5. The first and last parts of 88 lines are also the only structural parts with salvation as well as judgment poems. Note that the four occurrences of the lemma *yš*ʿ 'save' are patterned with two in each of these parts 1 and 5.

These combinations of blocks into parts are further supported by unique word patterns at junctures. Blocks one and two are tied together by anadiplosis (tail-head repetition) of "grain and wine" in 2:8[10] and 2:9[11]. The third and fourth blocks are tied by epiphora (tail-tail repetition) of "their deeds" in 5:4 and 7:2. The sixth and seventh blocks are tied by anadiplosis of "altar . . . pillars" in 10:1 and 10:2. The eighth and ninth blocks are tied together by the central peak of 12:9[10] in block eight being the same as the first line of block nine, "I am the LORD your God, from the land of Egypt." These connective devises are more obvious than the cohesion between other poems, and suggest an intentional effort to relate the blocks. The divisions can be charted as follows (the *non-poetic* lines of chapters 1–4 are not included in these counts):

9. Garrett (*Hosea*, 34) writes, "Hosea's rhetorical strategy may be derived from chaps. 1–3. The observation that Hosea 1–3 is programmatic for the whole book should startle no none. But in what sense is it programmatic?" Garrett then develops a parallel thematic structure between 1–3 and 4–14.

Structural Chart of Poetic Lines in Parts and Blocks in Hosea

A Part 1, 88 poetic lines of Judgment and Salvation

Block 1, 1:1—2:8[10]	44 poetic lines	7 poems
Block 2, 2:9[11]—3:5	44 poetic lines (22+22)	6 poems

B Part 2, 88 poetic lines of Judgment

Block 3, 4:1—5:4	44 poetic lines	6 poems
Block 4, 5:5—7:2	44 lines	6 poems

C Central Part 3, 50 lines of Judgment

Block 5, 7:3—8:13	50 lines	5 poems

B' Part 4, 88 lines of Judgment

Block 6, 8:14—10:1	44 lines (22+22)	3 poems
Block 7, 10:2—11:7	44 lines	4 poems

A' Part 5, 88 lines of Judgment and Salvation

Block 8, 11:8—13:3	44 lines	4 poems
Block 9, 13:4—14:9[10]	44 lines	4 poems
	Total 402 lines	Total 45

(The Total of 45 is made up of 44 messages and one introductory poem.)

This chart shows a symmetrical structure of five parts for the book. The central part 3 has 50 lines, representing the multiplication of *Y* 'ten' times *H* 'five.' Significantly there are also *five* poems in the central fifth block; the *central poem* has five lines; and the central line 8:2 has five words: "To-me they-cry MY-GOD we-know-you Israel," of which the central word is "God." The lemma "Elohim" for "God" comes **26** times in Hosea. The line has **22** letters, five of which are *y*, which is the first letter with the value of 10 in the name YHWH. Two of these are the eleventh letter from each end, thereby coming right in the middle of the line, and the five are distributed so that each of the five words has one *y*. Note that 10 and 5 are the values of the first two consonants in YHWH, corresponding to its shorter form YH. It may also be significant that this line is the thirtieth line in the block, with 30 having the factors 10 (x3), and 5x6 representing all the three letters of

YHWH. (See the discussion of the central poem 8:1–4a in chapter 4 below.) The total number of poems is 45, with 25 in the first two parts, and 15 in the last two parts, all with a factor of 5 numerically adding to the significance of the theological 5 (equivalent to the divine letter *H*) tying to those fives just noted that are found with the number of poems in the central part, the lines in the central poem, and the words in the central line.

Besides its central occurrence in 8:2, the surface form *ʾlhy* 'my-God' is found in 2:23[25] in the first confession "You are my God." It also comes in 9:8 (the thirteenth from the end of the **26** occurrences of "God"), and in 9:17. The key word in the central 8:2 *ydʿ* 'know' God (or its opposite "not knowing," or "forgetting") is repeated in many strategic peak lines and junctures throughout Hosea (see 2:20[22], 5:4, 6:3, 13:4). "Know" comes fifteen times in Hosea, which is another tie to the name *YH*=15. The central peak of 8:2 gets prominence by having the key personae of the book "My-God" and "Israel" together. *Yśr ʾl* 'Israel' comes 44 or **22**x2 times and has the value of 64 or **32**x2, giving it both alphabetical and theological marking. The key message of the major peak in 14:1[2] "Return Israel to God" is emphasized with these two main personae coming together with the key word *šb* 'return' which occurs **23** times. Both 32 and 23 are divine-name numbers based on *kbwd* 'glory,' as detailed in chapter 1 above.

The second block 2:9(11)—3:5 revolves around 22 with the first and second poems together having 22 lines, the second, third and fourth poems together having 22 lines, and the third through sixth poems together having 22 lines. This numerical device is also tied to the key word "Israel" occurring 44 times. The number 22 also comes in block 6 with the three-line 8:14 and the following nineteen-line 9:1–9 adding up to 22 lines, and the next or 33rd poem 9:10—10:1 being a **22**-line poem.

Part 1 has 13 poems, making a tie to the theological number set. These initial 88 poetic lines are parallel to part 5 (11:8 to the end of the book) with a return to the theme of God's mercy and promise of restoration. This is especially evident in the positioning of the positive *salvation poems* as the first and last major poems in the final part of 88 lines. The salvation poems in the first 88 lines are also interestingly placed—one after the introductory biographical section and five at the end. In contrast, the middle five blocks are mainly accusation and punishment.[10]

A symmetrically balanced arrangement such as this with 88s and 44s may seem unlikely. However, line counts in other minor prophets suggest

10. The juncture at 11:8 varies from that of Wolff (*Hosea*, 1965) and many followers (see Yee, *Hosea*, 142, 347) who put the major final break at chapter 12. Yee (*Hosea*, 246) makes the significant observation that chapters 1–2 and 12–14 also deal with the "marriage motif" while 4–11 have the "youth motif."

similar patterns. For example, I have analyzed Joel with five blocks of poems totaling respectively 44 lines (chapter 1), 22 lines (2:1–9), 33 lines (central 2:10–22), 44 lines (2:23—4:11) and 22 lines (4:12–21) (Bliese, "Joel," 73–76). Nahum has 34 lines (17x2 and 33+1) from 1:1—2:2[3], a central poem of 23 lines (22+1) from 2:2[3]–13[14], and 45 lines (44+1) in 3:1–9 (Bliese, "Nahum," 49). Obadiah divides at verse 11 with two sets of 22 lines plus a monocolon or 23 lines in each (Bliese, "Obadiah," 211). Habakkuk has a pattern of 30 (6x5), 33 (11x3), and 34 (17x2 and 33+1) lines in its three parts (Bliese, "Habakkuk," 47). The number of poems in Hosea also seems to be significant with 45 (44 prophecies and one introductory poem), when compared to Joel with 23 (22+1) (Bliese "Joel," 73) and Nahum with 11 poems and an introductory line (Bliese, "Nahum," 49).

In my studies I have also noted *key words* that occur in each part of various books. In Joel the key words "day of the LORD" occur once and only once in each of the five parts (Bliese, "Joel," 73). "Nineveh" and "against" occur once in each of the three parts of Nahum, (Bliese, "Nahum," 49–50); "Jerusalem" once each in the two parts of Obadiah, (Bliese, "Obadiah," 211); "holy" once in each of the three parts of Habakkuk, (Bliese, "Habakkuk," 48–49); and the noun "love" patterned with three in the first and last parts and once in each of the middle five parts in the seven parts of Song of Songs, (Bliese, *Count*, 57). Song of Songs follows the pattern of Psalms with *brwk YHWH* 'blessed be the LORD' three times in the first and last books and once each in the middle three books. Similarly, in Hosea the key words *bryt* 'COVENANT' and *ṭwb* 'GOOD' (with the vowel ô)[11] occur once and only once in each of the five parts. The central occurrence of each of them significantly occurs in the central poem of Hosea, with "COVENANT" the central word in 8:1, the line before the peak, and "GOOD" the central word in 8:3, the line after the peak. Note that "my-God" is the central word of the peak line. These three central key words if read vertically by lines in the original pre-Masoretic consonantal form would mean "the covenant of my God is good." It has prompted the main title of this book, *God's Good Covenant*. The vertical reading can be diagrammed as,

8:1 the-covenant-of

8:2 my-God

8:3 is-good.

11. There are also two occurrences of a related lemma, the noun *ṭwb* 'good/goodness' with the vowel û instead of ô in 3:5 and 10:11. These are not the same lemma and are not part of the five in the key-word pattern.

Besides this occurrence in the central part 3 at 8:1 "*covenant*" is also in the first lines of poems in part 1 at 2:18[20] "I will make for you a covenant" (of safety from animals and war), and part 2 at 6:7 "they transgressed the covenant." In part 4 it comes at 10:4 "with empty oaths they make covenants," and in part 5 in the last line of the poem at 12:1[2] making a covenant with Assyria while dealing with Egypt.[12] "*Good*" comes in part 1 at 2:7[9], in part 2 in 4:13 in a peak line, in the central part 3 at 8:3, in the last line of part 4 at 10:1, and in part 5 at 14:2[3] coming right after the central peak lines of that longest penultimate poem. The first occurrence in 2:7[9] is at the end of a stanza predicting the return to what is truly "good." The pattern has a message, *God's covenant is good, so return to God.*

The above patterns as I see it are more than chance arrangements, and likely are intentional efforts to put the poems into structured blocks with thematic components. With this in mind, blocks in Hosea have been compared, and tentative thematic words or ideas have been noted at the beginning of each block in the textual display.[13] The following notes on lexical patterns within the five parts of Hosea can give support to other evidence that the final document was put together with a chiastic plan, and is not a random collection of prophecies.

Words that Occur Chiastically Balanced Between Parts in Hosea

The following words occur *only* in the chiastically matched *parts* listed below.

Parts 1 & 5: the phrase *n 'm YHWH* 'says the LORD' (x4, three in part 1 at 2:15, 18, 23, one in part 5 at 11:11), *'šh* 'wife' (x5, 3 in part 1, two in part five), *'ḥ* 'brother' (x3, one in part 1, two in part 5), *yš'* 'save' (x4, two in part 1, two in part 5), *sws* 'horse' (x2, one each part 1 and 5), *'yn* 'eye' (x2, one each part 1 and 5), *'wd* 'yet' (x10 six in part 1, four in part 5), *rḥm* 'mercy' (x7, six in part 1, one in part 5), *śym* 'set/make' (x4, three in part 1, one in part 5), *šmn* 'oil' (x2, one in each part 1 and 5).

Parts 2 & 4: *'bl* 'mourn' (x2 one each in parts 2 and 4 at 4:3 & 10:5), *'lh* 'swear' (x2, one in each part 4:2 & 10:4 before 'mourn'), *'sp* 'gather' (x2 one in each part 4:3 & 10:10), *'l* 'not' x7 (six in part 2, 1 in part 4), *gb'h* 'hill/

12. Dearman (*Hosea*, 52) notes that in the five occurrences of covenant "Hosea employs the term *bĕrît* in two senses: one relates to political agreements between peoples, and the other represents YHWH's initiation of a relationship with Israel or another aspect of creation."

13. Eidevall (*Grapes*, 10) sees the book of Hosea as "a single, coherent and sophisticated, work of art. The various parts are connected and interwoven by means of lexical, thematic, and metaphorical links."

Gibeah' (x6, one "hill" and two "Gibeah" in each of parts 2 and 4), *hrg* 'kill' (one in each), *hr* 'mountain' (one in each, parallel to hill), *ṭm* ʾ 'unclean' (x3, two in part 2, one in part 4), *yṣ* ʾ 'go out' (one in each), *yrh* 'rains/waters' (one in each), *yrb* 'Jareb/great' (one in each), *kḥš* 'deceive/fail' (one in each), *m ʾs* 'reject' (x3, two in part 2 and one in 4), *m ʿllym* 'deeds' (x3, two in part 2, one in 4), *npš* 'greed/hunger' (one in each), *srr* 'stubborn/rebellious' (x3, two in part 2, one in 4), *ʿmq* 'made deep' (one in each), *pḥ* 'trap' (one in each), *qwm* 'rise' (one in each), *r ʾh* 'see' (x4, two in each), *r ʿh* 'evil' (three in each), *šm* ʿ 'hear' (x3, two in 2 and one in 4), *šḥr* 'dawn' (one in each).

Parts 1, 3 & 5 (none). (Also note there are 70 singletons in Part 3.)

Parts 1 & 3: *zhb* 'gold' (two in each of parts 1 and the central part 3), *m ʿṭ* 'little' (two in each), *pth* 'allure' (two in each), *qšt* 'bow' (x4, three in part 1, one in 3), *šbt* 'cease' (x3, two in part 1, one in 3).

Parts 3 & 5: *ʾp* 'anger' (x4, one in the central part 3, three in the final part 5 where the 1st and last are withholding anger), *ps* ʿ 'rebell' (x3, two in part 3, one in 5), *ʿgl* 'calf' x3, two in part 3, one in 5). The rest come once each in parts 3 and 5: *hpk* 'turn over/recoil,' *ḥrš* 'artisan,' *ywnh* 'dove,' *kly* 'vessel/article,' *kzb* 'lie/falsehood,' *pdh* 'redeem,' špṭ 'judge.'

Parts 1, 2, 4 & 5: (at least once in each of these parts) *bn* 'son/child/people,' *mṣ* ʾ 'find,' *škḥ* 'forget,' *ntn* 'give,' *yhwdh* 'Judah,' *ʾmr* 'say,' *lqḥ* 'take,' *drk* 'way,' *dbr* 'word,' and *yšb* 'inhabit, dwell.'

Words which occur at least once *in each of the five parts* are also worth noting: *kl* 'all,' *bryt* 'covenant,' *ywm* 'day,' *hlk* 'go, *ʾlhym* 'God,' *ṭwb* 'good,' *lb* 'heart,' *byt* 'house,' *yśr ʾl* 'Israel,' *mlk* 'king,' *yd* ʾ 'know,' *ʾrṣ* 'land,' *yhwh* 'LORD,' *ʿśh* 'make,' *śr* 'prince,' *pqd* 'punish,' and *šwb* 'return.'

"YHWH," and "return" also come in all nine *blocks*, "God" in all but block 7, "go" in all but 3, "land" in all but 4, "day" in all but 9, "Israel" in all but 4 and 6, which blocks correspond chiastically, "Ephraim" in all but 1 and 2, "know" in all but 3 and 11, "Judah" in all but 2, 5 and 9, *ʿm* 'people' in all but 8 and 9 (none in part 5). There is also consecutive cohesion in that "harlot/harlotry" occurs only in 1 to 4 and 6, "Assyria" only in 4 to 9, and "Egypt" only in 2, and 5 to 9.

Words that Occur Chiastically Balanced Between Blocks in Hosea

Along with the above lists of chiastic parts, other words relating chiastically between *blocks,* but that are not limited to these blocks, also show some interesting chiastic parallels for the book, as follows:

BLOCK 1 (1:1—2:8[10])	BLOCK 9 (13:4—14:9[10])
1:1 word	14:2[3] words (and Blocks 3 & 7)
1:1, 1 king(s)	13:10, 10, 11 king
1:2 take (Imperative Singular)	14:2[3] take (Imperative plural)
1:2, 3, 6, 8; 2:3[5] offspring, bear	10:1 birth (same root yld)
1:7 save	13:4 savior, 13:10 saves; 14:3[4] save
1:7 sword	13:16[14:1] sword
1:7 horses	14:3[4] horses (only these 2)
1:7 LORD their God, and	13:4 I am the LORD your God
1:10–11[2:1–2] children x3, & 2:4	13:13 son . . . children, and 13:15
2:1[3] brothers	13:15 brothers (only these and one "brother" in 12:3[4])
2:1[3] mercy & 1:6–7	14:3[4] (orphan finds) mercy
2:3[5] make her as a desert, and set her like a dry land	13:15 The wind of the LORD will arise from the desert, and his fountain will dry up, and his spring will go dry; and 13:5 land of drought
2:5[7], 7[9] lovers	14:4[5] love
2:6[8] way	13:7 way, and 14:9[10] ways
2:7[9] not find . . . return	14:1[2] return(twice) and 7, 8[8, 9] found, and 3[4] finds
2:8[10] But she didn't know that I gave her the grain, wine and oil	14: 4[5] not know any god, 6–8[7–9] olive, grain, wine . . . It is from me that your fruit is found
2:8[10] But gold they used for Baal (climax)	14:8[9] idols (end of next to last poem)
BLOCK 2 (2:9[11]—3:5)	**BLOCK 8 (9:8—13:3)**
2:10[12] hand	12:7[8] hand
2:12[14], 18[20] field	12:11[12], 12[13] field(s)
2:13[15] Baals . . . rings . . . jewelry Baal(s) 16[18], 17[19]	13:1–2 Baal . . . molten images, from their silver skillfully made idols
2:13[15], 16[18] & 21[23] says the LORD	11:11 says the LORD (only these four)
2:14[16] lead her to the desert, 15 and she will answer there as in the days of her youth, and as the day I brought her up from the land of Egypt	12:9[10] I am the LORD from the land of Egypt; again I will make you dwell in tents; 13[14] brought up from Egypt; land of Egypt also in 11:5, 11; and Egypt in 12:1[2], 13[14]
2:14[16] heart	11:8 heart

2:16[18] speak	12:4[5], 10[11]; 13:1 speaks
2:17[19] name(s) (Baal)	12:5[6] name (LORD)
2:18[20] covenant	12:1[2] covenant
2:18[20] birds	11:11 birds
2:19[21] justice	12:6[7] justice
2:19[21] loyalty	12:6[7] loyalty
2:23[25] "You are my people;" and he will say, "My God"	12:9[10] I am the LORD
3:1 love(s) (3 times)	12:7[8] loves
3:1 woman	12:12[13] wife/woman
3:3, 4 dwell	12:9[10] dwell
3:3 not be for a man	11:9 God not man
3:4 sacrifice	12:11[12] sacrifice
3:5 The children of Israel will return	11:11 And I will return them to their homes
3:5 goodness	10:1 goodness (the only two as nouns)
BLOCK 3 (4:1—5:4)	**BLOCK** 7 (10:2—11:7)
4:1 word	10:4 words (& above Blocks 1 & 9)
4:3 field	10:4 fields
4:4, 6, 9; 5:4 priests (only these and 6:9)	10:5 idolatrous priests
4:4, 6, 8, 9, 12, 14 people (*ʿam*)	10:5, 10, 14; 11:7 people
4:6 sons, 13–14 daughter	10:14 children; 11:1 son
4:6 destroy, destroyed	10:15 destroying destroy
4:7 sinned, 8 sins	10:8 sinned
4:7 glory	10:5 glory (and once in 9:11)
4:9 ways	10:13 way
4:11 takes	11:3 taking
4:13 good	8:3 good (adjective)
4:13 mountains	10:8 mountains (only these)
4:13, 14, 19 sacrifice	11:2 sacrificed
4:13 they burned incense	11:2 they burned incense (once more 2:13)
4:15 Bethaven	10:5 Bethaven
4:18 love	10:11; 11:1, 4 love
4:16 stubborn heifer	10:11 docile calf
4:19 shamed	10:6 shame . . . ashamed

5:1 king	10:3, 6, 7, 15; 11:5 king
5:1 judgment	10:4 judgment (justice root)
5:2 chastise	10:10 chastise (only elsewhere in 7:12, 15)
5:3, 4 know	11:3 know
5:4 they don't know	11:3 they didn't know
BLOCK 4 (5:5—7:2)	**BLOCK 6 (8:14—10:1)**
5:5; 7:1 iniquity	9:7, 9 iniquity
5:6 find	9:10 found
5:7 offspring (*bnym*)	9:13 sons (*bnym*)
5:7 devour (*ʾkl* 'eat')	8:14 consume (*ʾkl* 'eat')
5:8 Gibeah	9:9 Gibeah
5:9 day of chastisement (*twkḥh*)	9:7 days of punishment (*pqd*)
5:10 princes	9:15 princes
5:12 I am like a moth to Ephraim, rot to Judah	9:16 Ephraim is blighted their root is dried up
5:12, 14; 6:10 house	9:4, 8, 15 house
5:13 saw; 6:10 seen	9:10, 13 saw (only these)
5:13 Assyria	8:3 Assyria
5:13 great	9:7, 7 great
5:15; 6:1 return	9:3, 5, 5 return
6:3, 3 know	9:7 know
6:3 comes; 7:1 enter	9:7, 7, 10 come, came, 9:4 enter
6:4 do, 9 commit	8:14 Maker; 9:5 do, 16 yield
6:5 I killed them	9:16 I will kill their precious offspring
6:6 I desire loyalty and not sacrifices	9:4 nor please him with sacrifices
6:7 covenant	10:4 covenant (central of five is at 8:1)
6:9 man	9:7 man
6:10 harlotry	9:1 harlot
6:10 defiled (unclean)	9:3, 4 unclean, polluted
7:1, 2 evil	9:15 wickedness

These chiastically parallel words and themes show that it is important in the analysis to see that they can be meaningfully related to a *metrical structure of blocks* for the book as illustrated above.

C. Chiastic Symmetry Helps to Interpret Problematic Texts

Chiastic symmetry can help by giving guidelines in exegetical questions as illustrated by the following examples.

4:4b-9a is analyzed below as a chiasm with an inclusio of trimeters, following Lundbom ("Contentious," 52–70) who proposes that the two short lines at the ends are a "discontinuous bicolon." The final line is 9a "And it shall be like people, like priest." Its counterpart at the beginning 4b is therefore read, "your people are like contentious priests," instead of, "for with you is my contention, O priest" (NRSV, REB, NJPS, and GNT).

In 7:6 "their baker" (see *HOTTP*, 241; NJPS; and Andersen and Freedman, *Hosea*, 14) has been revised with the vowels changed to read "anger" (RSV, NRSV, GNT) or "passion"(NEB, REB, NIV). However, the beautiful chiastic structure clearly supports "baker." This also means that the "baker" (not "anger") is the one who metaphorically "burns like a flaming fire," showing a contrast to his "ceasing from stirring it up" in the parallel strophe in 4b.

7:12b is the center of the chiasm 7:8–16. The last two words of 12 read "according to the report to their assembly" (see NRSV). NIV has "When I hear them flocking together," and GNT in a revision of the MT has "the evil they have done." However, the last line of the chiasm speaks of "derision" as the result of their speech (their report), their "lies"(v. 13) and "insolence"(v. 16) against God. These references at the end of the poem support the meaning of "report" or "their bargaining" (NJPS) in the chiastic center. Centers and ends are often parallel.

The word "his counsel" (REB, see GNT) in 10:6b has been amended to "his idol" by NRSV and NIV. NJPS has "his plans." The parallel line in this chiasm is the derogatory 10:4a "they speak words, swear oaths, make covenants." This lends support to keeping "his counsel."

In 11:4 the MT has "yoke" (NJPS, NIV) while several translations (GNT, REB, NRSV) emend this to "baby" or "infant." Although the theme of "baby" is prominent in the first, middle and last lines of the chiasm, the first line also has a reference to "Egypt" which gives support to the reading of "yoke" in the last line.

A similar textual problem comes in 11:7 where the word "on high" (NJPS "upward," NRSV "Most High," NIV "God Most High") has the same consonants as "yoke" (see RSV, GNT). This word comes in the last line of the chiasm which begins with a reference to "Egypt" in the first line as in the previous poem. The following poem 11:8–11, the first in part 5 after the purely judgmental parts 2–4, also begins with a rhetorical question and ends with the answer of the assurance of the return from the exile referred to in 11:4–7. The emendation to "yoke" is therefore supported by the similar structure of inclusio in these three adjacent poems.

The first word "not" of the chiasm (11:5–7) is also controversial. RSV, NRSV, NEB emend *l'* 'not' to *lw* 'to him' as the object of the previous 'feed.' NIV has a rhetorical question keeping the negative, "Will they not return . . .?" NJPS translates with "No! They return . . . ." The following poem (11:8–11) has a parallel structure. It begins with a rhetorical question, "How can I give up Ephraim and hand over Israel?" (11:8). This is answered in the last line, "I will return them to their homes, says the Lord." The negative "not" fits well in 11:5–7 as part of another introductory rhetorical question, "Shall he not return to the land of Egypt?" which is answered by the last line, "So they are appointed to the yoke, and no one shall lift it." The first poem uses an introductory rhetorical question and final answer to emphasize the sureness of exile, and the second poem uses an introductory rhetorical question and final answer to emphasize the sureness of God bringing them back home. The change from judgment to salvation is marked by these two rhetorical questions of the poems on each side of the boundary of the last 88 lines. This is significantly the boundary where salvation oracles begin again, balancing the first 88 lines.

In 11:6 the MT "advice" is emended in the RSV to "fortresses." Support for keeping "advice" (NRSV "schemes," NJPS "designs," NIV "plans," GNT "what they themselves think best") is found in the speech act in the line which parallels this line in the chiasm, "Because they *refused* (*m'n*) to return" in 11:5b. (See Gen 37:35 "he refused to be comforted".)

D. Line Divisions that Show Sentence Boundaries

Several disputed sentence boundaries can get added support when defined by the metrical symmetry of their poem.

a. 4:2 "They break all bounds" distorts the balance with the hexameter in 4:3a if connected to the last clause of 4:2 as in RSV, NIV, and GNT. Chiastic metrical symmetry balances if it is the final verb filling the hexameter of the preceding list, "swearing . . . adultery break all bounds" (see Wolff, *Hosea*, 1965:65, NJPS "are rife," and NRSV "break out").

b. 4:10–11 In order to add to the short line, "wine" is better at the end of 4:10 as in BHS, not at the beginning of 4:11 as in the NJPS, NRSV, NIV, and GNT.

c. 4:11–12 "My people" fills the expected hexameter at the end of 4:11 (as in the BHS line, NJPS, and GNT). Putting it at the beginning of

4:12 as in RSV, NIV and NRSV distorts an otherwise perfect metrical chiasmus.

d. 14:6[7] "As Lebanon" (RSV "as the poplar") fits the rhythm better if moved from the end of 14:5[6] to read, "As Lebanon, his shoots will sprout" rather than "He will strike roots as Lebanon." (See NJPS, NRSV and NIV, who add tree(s) to clarify "Lebanon.") This change will make a three-foot line parallel to that at the end of 13:14.

Chapter 4

Structural Display and Analysis of Hosea 4–14

(Including symbolic numbers and patterns pointing to peaks)

Part Two 4:1—7:2

(88 Poetic Lines; Words: MT 533=13x41; Possible revision 534=6x89; Lemmas: MT 697=17x41, Possible revision 702=26x27, 13x54, 6x117)

Third Block 4:1—5:4, Key words: "Know the LORD" or "Spirit of Harlotry"

(44 Poetic Lines; Words: MT 276=23x12, 6x46; Lemmas MT 361, Possible revision 364 adding three lemmas, *w* in 4:10, and *m* in 4:18 and 4:19 for comparison of lemma counts in tables 4–7)

4:1a Introduction to the Following Poems

Hear the-word-of=the-LORD, children-of Israel. (4)

"The word of the LORD" repeats the words found twice in the opening of the book, now applying them to this new section, which is probably the rest of the book. The sentence does not fit into the following poem and is not counted as poetry. Both lemmas *dbr* 'word,' and *YHWH* have the highest theological value of **26**, and also occur together twice at the beginning of the book in 1:1–2. The initial *šmʿ* 'hear' has the value of 50, which may relate to YH by the multiples 10x5. The final *yśrʾl* 'Israel" has the value of

64 or 32x2. Note that the plural "words" occurs in blocks seven (10:4), and nine (14:2[3]), chiastically corresponding to the singulars in blocks one and three. These are significantly the only occurrences in singular or plural.

4:1b-4a Chiasm 576 3 675

(MT 38 word-stress units, or 39 for the following chiasmus; 68 lemmas, of which 19 or 27.98% have values that are multiples of 13, 17, 23, or 32 relating to God's name YHWH)

Indeed the-LORD has-an-*accusation*
  with=the-*inhabitants*-of the-*land*; (5)
For(+)there-is-no(=)faithfulness and-no(=)loyalty
  and-no(=)*knowledge-of(+)God* in-the-*land*; (6/7)

*

2 Cursing and-lying and-murder
  and-thievery and-adultery abound; (6)
And-<u>bloodshed</u> follows <u>bloodshed</u>. (3)

*

3 There=fore the-*land* withers,
  and-all=the-*inhabitants* in-it waste-away; (6)
The-beasts-of the-field and-the-birds-of the-sky
  and-also=the-fish-of the-sea are-dying. (7)

*

4 Only let-no=man *accuse*,
  and-let-no=man bring-charges. (5)

The repetition of "bloodshed" in the central peak is especially strong making up two of the three words in the line. Its lemma *dm* has the value of 17. Repetition is a common feature of prominence found in peaks in Hosea. "Bloodshed" also gets prominence as an expansion of the prominent central "murder" in the list of five sins in the previous line based on the ten commandments. Garrett (*Hosea*, 112) notes, "The emphasis on "bloodshed," however, has caught scholars' attention primarily because it seems unnecessary; the verse has already condemned murder." He then points out that *dm* 'bloodshed' also comes in 1:4 in the Jezreel oracle, and treats 4:1–4 as a recurrence that "looks back to the Jezreel oracle, just as the next two sections (4:4–14 and 4:15–5:15) look back respectively to Lo-Ammi and Lo-Ruhamah."

The peak line is also marked by its shortness of only three words. The third word is *ngʿ* 'touch, follow' which has the value of **33**. Both lines in the central strophe are tied together by the final plural û rhyme of "abound" and "follow." A metrical chiasm goes in tandem with semantic chiasmus, relating words symmetrically in the poem. "Accusation" in "YHWH has an accusation" in the first line has the same root as "accuse" in the final line making an inclusio, and emphasizing that only YHWH, not "man," has the right to accuse. "Land" and "inhabitants" come between them chiastically in both halves. Both have symbolic values with *ʾrṣ* 'land'=39, and *yšb* 'inhabitant'=33. The value of *ryb*, which is the same for both the noun "accusation" and the verb "accuse," is **32**, which is one of the four divine-name numbers. The pattern of 32s here helps to confirm that mathematical counts were in use with the final edition of Hosea. This is supported by the inclusio of *ryb* supplemented by a double occurrence of *ʾyš* 'man'=**32** in each colon of the final line before and after "accuse." The climax of the list in 4:2 *nʾp* 'adultery' also has the value of **32**. The chiasm can be displayed with the symbolic values of the lemmas as follows:

A accusation =32

B inhabitants, *yšb* 'inhabit'=33

C land, *ʾrṣ*=39 (4:1b)

D bloodshed=**17**

D' bloodshed=**17**

C' land=39 (in 4:3 and 4:1c)

B' inhabitants=33

A' accuse =32[1]

The semantic break after the peak is marked by the transitional word "therefore," shifting from accusation to punishment. Structurally the first half has only couplet parallelism, while the second half has internal parallelism in the first line of 3 and the final line. The second line of 4:4b fits better in the following poem following Lundbom ("Contentious," 52–70), resulting in a good metrical and semantic chiasm with 4:1b–4a as the boundaries of this poem. Both halves end with a shortened form: the monocolon in verse 2, and verse 4 without a second line for a couplet. The strophic structure is

1. Lemmas with symbolic values that are not cited in the discussion are *rṣḥ* 'killing'=46, prṣ 'abound, break out,'=55, *ʾml* 'waste away'=26, *kl* 'all'=23, *ḥyh* 'beasts'=23, *ʿwp* 'bird'=39, *ym* 'sea'=23, *ʾsp* 'die, gather'=33, and *ʾl* 'not'=13 x2. Those with multiples of 5 and 6 are *l* 'with/to'=12, *h* 'the'=5 x5, *ʾyn* 'not'=25 x3, *ʾmt* 'faithfulness'=36, *w* 'and'=6 x11, *dʿt* 'knowledge'=42, *ʾlh* 'cursing'=18, *kḥš* 'lying'=40, *kn* 'thus'=25 (with *ʿl* "therefore"), *ʾbl* 'wither'=15, *śdh* 'field'=30, and *ʾk* 'only'=12.

three regular couplets followed by a final single line strophe. The 39 revised word-stress units in the above display may also reflect a literary interest in symbolic numbers.

I see the phrase "knowledge of God" in the accusation in 1b as thematic for the block and for the whole book. It also connects this block to the previous one where the words *d ʿt ʾlhym* 'know God,' and *ḥsd* 'loyalty' are also together in 2:19–20, along with a cognate of *ʾmt* 'faithfulness.' Instead of knowing YHWH, Israel is under the control of a "spirit of harlotry." Block 3 ends at 5:4 with "Their deeds do not permit them to return to their God. For the spirit of harlotry is within them, and they do not know the Lord." 4:12 is similar, "Yes, a spirit of harlotry led them astray, and they harloted away from under God." This block 3 (4:1—5:4) has eight of the thirteen occurrences of *znh* 'commit harlotry,' and the only two *znwnym* 'harlotry' in the book after the four in block 1.[2]

4:4b-9a Chiasm 366 66 663

(47 words; 42 or 6x7 word-stress units as MT; 65 lemmas of which 7 or only 10.77% have multiples of divine-name values, but 8 of the 65 have multiples of 11, giving 12.31%, the 4th highest of the 45 poems for the alphabetic set, three 26-letter lines)

4b *And-your-people-are like-those-accusing a-priest.* (3)

* {13-letter line}

5 You-stumble by-day,

and-also=the-prophet stumbles

with-you by-night, {26-letter line}[2+2+2] (6)

And-I-will-destroy your-mother;

6 *my*-people are-destroyed

from-lack-of knowledge. [2+2+2] (6)

*

Because=you rejected knowledge, {13+13, 26-letter line}

then-I-reject-you from-being-a-priest for-me. (6)

And-you-forgot the-law-of your-God,

I=also will-forget your-sons. (6)

|#

2. Eidevall (*Grapes*, 236) gives as an example that "Some themes have a relatively restricted extension . . . Notice that whereas the theme of "whoring" (*znh*) is prominent in 4:1—5:7, it plays a marginal role in the following discourse."

7 The-more(*k*)-they-increased thus they-sinned=against-me;
they-exchanged their-glory for-disgrace. {26 letters} (6)
8 They-feed-on the-sins-of *my*-people,
and-to=their-iniquity they-lift-up his-greed. (6)

*

9 . . . *And-it-will-be as-the-people, so-the-priest.* (3)

This poem has an inclusio with the repetition and comparison of *ʿam* 'people' and *kohēn* 'priest,' following Lundbom ("Contentious," 52–70), who analyzes the two short lines at the ends as a "discontinuous bicolon." However, Lundbom's "contentious" has been disputed (see Garrett, *Hosea*, 116). "Contentious priest" can be read naturally in Hebrew as "those accusing a priest" as above, or "who bring charges against a priest" as in NIV, with "priest" as the object of the participle, rather than the subject as in Lundbom.[3] The lemma *ryb* 'accuse/contend' comes also in the line before this poem connecting the two poems by anadiplosis. There it is in a general admonition against accusing, which is now made specific regarding accusing priests. The whole poem switches focus repeatedly from accusations against both people and a priest or priests. It seems best to interpret the singular "priest" as collective for "priests."

The first line 4:6b of the central peak has 26 letters. This happens because there is an extra *alep* in *w ʾm ʾsk* 'and I reject,' making it *w ʾm ʾs ʾk*, which is not a normal spelling. This is the only poem by my analysis with *three* 26-letter lines, and it therefore has special prominence related to this primary theological number. Besides the one in the peak, 26-letter lines come in the first half in regard to the accusation of "stumbling," and in the second half in regard to "sinning." The first peak line repeats the thematic root word *khn* 'priest' from the first line with the verb *khn* 'be a priest.' The value of both the noun and verb *khn* is 30 or 10x3 and 6x5, factors that are numerically significant with reference to the three different consonants of YHWH. The peak also has the only divine name in the poem, "God." The word *d ʿt* 'knowledge'=42 or 6x7, comes in the peak and in the previous line and is thematic for this block. Eidevall (*Grapes*, 57) notes that "knowledge is [a]n important theme in the discourse."

The center begins with an emphatic "you," and ends with an emphatic *ʾny* 'I'=25 (see Kidner, *Hosea* 49–50.). The direct speech of the first stanza of the poem, which continues through the peak, shifts to indirect third person

3. A reconstruction of the MT changing "your people" to "with you," and making "priest" a vocative subject as in NRSV "with you is my contention, O priest" is followed by many.

plural "they" in 7–9. The peak also has parallel repetition in each line with "you rejected—I reject," and "you forgot—I will forget." The value of *škḥ* 'forget' is 40 with factors of Y=10 and H=5, the letters of YH. Willis ("Parallelism," 62) notes that the alternating parallelism in this "correspondence of the verbs . . . brings out sharply the direct connection between one's activities and the consequences which result from them." The first series in 6b has inverted parallelism in Hebrew with object-verb; verb-object in "knowledge-reject; reject-you." The verse ends with "from being a priest *for* me" with *l* 'for'=12. "Also" and "from" in the peak are repeated in 5A and 6A. The word "sons" (*bn*) in the central peak relates to the four repetitions of *'m* 'people,' two on each side. Garrett (*Hosea*, 1977:118) interprets "the threat against 'your children' in this verse as having dual significance" referring to both the priests and to the people, making a "link" between "*your* sons/children" in 6 and "*your* people" in 4. There is also rhyme in the peak with the first colon of each line ending in *-a*, and the end of each line *-î*.

The first word of this poem is "your people" and the next to the last word is "the people" in short secondary peak lines. "My-people" comes between them on each side of the central peak. Garett (*Hosea*, 114) notes that the repetitions of "my people" (*'ammî*) "look back to the Lo-Ammi oracle" in 1:9, marking a new section of accusations.

With the inclusio of trimeter lines, the poem may be considered chiastic in spite of the rest of the lines being hexameters. The total of word-stress units is 42 or 6x7 with no change from MT. The structure of two lines in the central peak also suggests secondary peaks in the first and last line. This applies nicely with the inclusio emphasizing the comparison of "people" and "priests." "As the people so the priest" in the last line is quoted in Isa 24:2 indicating its prominence. The first lemma of the poem is *w* 'and'=6, also occurring as an inclusio at the beginning of the last line. It also comes six other times. The preposition *k* 'like, as, so'=11 is part of the inclusio, coming once in the first line and twice in the last line, as well as the first lemma after the peak. The second word of the poem, "accuse" has the same lemma *ryb*=32 as the inclusio "accuse" in the previous poem. The last line also has the verb *hyh* 'be' with the value of 20 with factors of 10 and 5 as in *YH*.

Parallelism is developed both at the couplet and line levels, with the discontinuous bicolon having its own parallelism. This also gives a chiastic arrangement of strophes as follows:[4]

A Half Line

B Two Lines

4. See Renkema, "Lamentations," especially 344–45 for examples of concentric structural patterns.

C **Central Two Lines**

B' Two Lines

A' Half Line.

The lemmas for *kšl* 'stumble'=44 and *dmh* 'destroy'=22, which come twice each in 4:5, look like a play on key numbers in the alphabetical set, which are used in the structure of Hosea. The *w* preceding the perfect aspect *kšl* can be future tense both times as in NJPS and NRSV. However, the non-future interpretation of "stumble" fits the context better, since the second "destroy" and "reject" in the next line 4:6 have perfect aspect without *w*. See NIV "You stumble day and night, and the prophets stumble with you." This also applies to the first "forget" in 4:6 "you have forgotten" (NRSV), "have spurned" (NJPS), and "have ignored" (NIV). Also see 5:5 for the same non-future interpretation of "stumble" as an accusation with an imperfect verb followed by a perfect. "Destroy your mother" is best taken to refer to the "institutional" "hierarchy" of Israel as its mother rather than to a specific priest or some other person (see Garrett, *Hosea*, 117).[5]

In 7 "they exchanged their glory for disgrace" the value of *kbwd* 'glory' is **23**, which is one of the four divine-name numbers. This supports a divine interpretation for "glory" referring to YHWH here (see NRSV "glory of God," NIV "their glorious God," and Ps 106:20).[6] If *kbwd* is calculated by the mathematical value of 20 for *k* instead of the alphabetical 11, the value is **32** giving *kbwd* a double divine number reference along with 23. The line 4:7 with *kbwd* has **26** letters, which also adds weight to the divine interpretation of "glory" here. The lemma of the key word *ryb* 'accuse' in the first line with the alphabetical value of **32** adds a significant occurrence of this divine name number in the same poem (see the discussion on 9:11 below for a more concentrated grouping of these two numbers around *kbwd*). These are the only lemma values that have multiples of 23 and 32 in the poem. There is also only one multiple each of 17 and 26, which are the alphabetical and numerical values of *kbd*, the construct form that gave "glory" its numerical significance for divine-name numbers. The first is *qlwn* 'disgrace' with the value of 51, or **17**x3. It is the antithesis of *kbwd*, and follows *kbwd* in 4:7, and comes only once more in 4:13. In the last line *npš* 'greed/breath/spirit' has the value of 52, or **26**x2. It occurs only here in 4:8 and in 9:4. It seems

5. Dearman (*Hosea*, 158) notes, "Reference to the priest's *mother*, who will be destroyed, is likely metaphorical and not biological." He proposes either the "land" or "Samaria" for the meaning of "mother."

6. MT has "I will change" instead of "they changed" (see NJPS, RSV, and GNT). Dearman (*Hosea*, 160) notes that a medieval scribal tradition describes the change and gives the reason as to protect God's glory.

possible that these words were chosen for their numerical connection to *kbd/kbwd*. Other lemmas with theological numbers are *lylh* 'night'=39, *mwr* 'feed on'=39, and *ʾl* 'to'=13.[7]

There is a play on words with *ḥṭʾt* 'sin' also having the meaning of "sin offering," especially here in the context of "feeding on the sins/sin offerings of my people." The priests are presented as becoming "greedy for more iniquities" (Eidevall, *Grapes*, 58). The line also has prominence with number switches with the priests plural in "they feed" and "my people' singular, but in the second colon the people are plural in "their iniquity" and the priests are singular in "his greed."

Besides the metrical chiasmus, which has no changes from MT hyphenation, the poem has a chiastic pattern with a chaining development of repeated words in pairs. The pattern of repetition by doublets is more typical of homogeneous poems, and therefore in this case directs added attention to the final secondary peak. The fact that all normal lines are hexameters also gives a buildup to the final mutual judgment on people and priests. (Note that if the NRSV reconstruction of "people" to "with" in 4:4 is accepted, this word chiasm would be marred.)

A 4:4 <u>people</u>—<u>priest</u>=30

B 5–6 destroy=22 (your mother)—destroy=22 <u>my-people</u>

C 6 <u>knowledge</u>—<u>KNOWLEDGE</u>, <u>REJECT</u>—<u>REJECT</u> (<u>PRIEST</u>=30)

[capital letters show the central peak]

C' 6 <u>FORGOT</u>=40 (LAW OF GOD)—<u>FORGET</u>=40 (YOUR SONS)

B' 7–8 *ḥṭʾ* sinned—*ḥṭʾt* 'sin'=40 of <u>my-people</u>

A' 4:9 <u>people</u>—<u>priest</u>=30

4:9b-11a Three Hexameters

(19 words; MT 17 word-stress units; MT **26** lemmas, or revised 27 lemmas, adding *w* in 4:10 to "commit-harlotry;" of the 26 MT lemmas 7 or 26.92% have divine-name values)

9b And-I-will-punish him for-his-ways;

and-his-works I-will-turn <u>to</u>-him; (6)

10 And-they-will-eat and-*not* be-satisfied;

<u>commit-harlotry</u> and-*not* increase; (6)

7. Lemmas with symbolic factors of 6 or 5 are *h* 'the'=5 x3, *bly* 'lack'=24, *rbb* 'increase'=24, *kn* 'thus'=25, *ḥṭʾ* 'sinned'=18, *ʾkl* 'eat'=24, *ʿwn* 'iniquity'=36, and *nśʾ* 'lift up.'

For=they-forsook the=LORD

11 <u>to</u>-keep <u>harlotry</u> and-wine. [2+3] (5)

These three lines form a closely related unit of (1) announcement of punishment, (2) description of the punishment, and (3) reason for the punishment. There are **26** lemmas and **17** word-stress units in MT, giving strong theological symbolism. The first colon has two symbolic lemmas, *pqd* 'punish'=40 with theological factors of **10** and **5**, and *drk* 'way'=35 or 5x7. The final peak has the only reference to *YHWH* 'LORD' with its value of **26**. It also has prominence by being shorter than the other hexameters. Wolff (*Hosea*, 1965:82) notes "the express mention of 'Yahweh' emphasizes the abrupt antithesis." It is preceded in the peak with the object marker *ʾt* with the value of **23**. "Forsook the LORD" is noted by Wolff and Mays as climactic to the previous sections. Mays (*Hosea*, 71) comments, "The final sentence of the oracle gathers up all the charges against the priests in one final summary of the complaint: they have forsaken Yahweh to practice harlotry!" The last line as analyzed above has inverted parallelism in Hebrew with object–verb // verb–objects: "YHWH–forsook // keep–harlotry and wine."[8] The lemma *znwt* 'harlotry'=49 or 7x7 is strikingly juxtaposed in the same peak line with YHWH=**26**. "Harlotry" is repeated from the line before the peak where *znh* 'commit harlotry' has the value of **26** as does YHWH. The value of *yyn* 'wine' is 34 or **17**x2, and of *ʿzb* 'forsake' is 25 or **5**x**5**, giving further prominence in the peak. Repetitions of *lʾ* 'not'=**13** in 10a serve as a buildup leading to the final peak. Another repetition enhancing the peak is the preposition *l* 'to'=**12** making an inclusio with the final peak and the first line of the poem.

Another buildup comes with the first line 9b having four pronominal suffixes with final *waw*, and the second line 10a having four third-plural verbs with *waw*. The first of the latter is on the lemma *ʾkl* 'eat'=24 or **6**x4, the second is on *śbʿ* 'be satisfied' with the value of 39 or **13**x3, and the last is on *prṣ* 'increase' with the value of 55 or **11**x5 or 23+32. The first colon of the peak ends after this build-up to the peak with a plural verb with a final *waw*. The build-up of a repeated grammatical form ending on the final peak is typical of homogeneous poems (see 2:9–13 and Obad 19–21 in Bliese, "Obadiah," 224). The dropping of the *waw* alliteration in the last colon, which instead of *waw* ends with the *-n* of "wine," may also be seen as a means to give emphasis by breaking expectations after the buildup of

8. MT ends 4:10 with the verb *šmr* 'to keep' without an object. NRSV and NIV add the first word "harlotry" from 4:11 to fill the semantic gap. I have added both the first and second words "harlotry and wine" to give balance to the trimeter inclusio in the next poem.

waw. The lemma *w* 'and'=6 also makes a buildup with the final sixth *w* on "wine," the last word of the final peak. Syntactic complexity as a feature of prominence at peak is found with the initial *ky* 'for.' All lines have internal parallelism. Besides the peak line, the first line 9b also has inverted parallelism with the verbs "punish" and "turn" enclosing the nouns "ways" and "works." This gives prominence at the beginning of the poem.

4:11b-14 Chiasm 3575 7 5753
(58 words; 47 word-stress units as MT; 74 lemmas of which 22 or 29.73% have divine-name values, the 6th highest)

11b *And-new-wine takes=the-heart-of* (12)*my-people*. AB (3)

* . . .

12 He-inquires at-his-wood,
and-his-staff reports to-him. [2+3](5)
Yes, a-spirit-of *harlotry* led-them-astray,
and-they-*harloted* away from-under-God. (7)
13 *On*=the-tops-of the-mountains they-*sacrificed*,
and-on=the-hills they-burned-incense, (5)

*

Under oak, and-poplar, and-terebinth,
because its-shade is-GOOD. (7)

*

There=fore your-daughters become-*harlots*,
and-your-daughters-in-law commit-*adultery*; (5)
14 I-will-not=bring-punishment on-your=daughters
because they-become-*harlots*,
nor-on-your=daughters-in-law because
they-commit-*adultery*, (7)
Because=these-men-themselves go-aside with=*harlots*,
and-they-*sacrifice* with=*cult-prostitutes*. (5)

* . . .

And-a-people without=understanding will-be-ruined. BA (3)

Lundbom ("Rhetoric," 305–306) shows the relationship of the first and last line forming a "broken bicolon." This is the same structure he noted in

4b–9a above, and 8:9–13 below. All of these poems also have initial *waw* 'and'=**6** beginning both discontinuous cola. The first line has "takes the heart of my people," and the last, "a people without understanding," tying to the central sarcasm about a senseless choice.[9] *Lqḥ* 'take' in the first line adds prominence with the symbolic value of 39 or **13**x3, and three lemmas in the last line have symbolic numbers, *l'* 'not'=**13** (also in 14a), *byn* 'understanding'=**26**, and *lbṭ* 'be ruined'=**23**. *Lbṭ* occurs only here and in Pro 10:8, and 10. Its uniqueness suggests it was chosen because of its value of 23 as the emphatic last word of the poem following the **26**-value *byn*. Garrett (*Hosea*, 133) proposes "the probability that this is a proverb fragment that Hosea has used for concluding this section." Garrett supports this by noting that *lbṭ* comes otherwise only in Proverbs, that the line has "terse style" similar to a proverb, and includes the "wisdom" use of *byn* 'understanding.' *Byn* comes in Hosea again only in the wisdom closure twice in 14:9[10].

"Because its shade is good," in the central peak implies lack of sense in rejecting God's shade and thinking that of trees is "good" (Mays, *Hosea*, 74). The contrast is seen in that "shade" is used for God's protection in 14:7[8], and God is likened to a "green cypress" in 14:8[9]. Furthermore, the key word "GOOD" in this peak also comes in the same climactic poem at 14:2[3], and in the central poem of the book at 8:3 "Israel has spurned the GOOD." The lemma *ṭwb* 'good' has the value of **17**, which is a divine-name number, and *ṣl* 'shade' equals 30 with factors of Y=**10**, H=**5**, and W=**6**. The first word of the peak "*under* oak" repeats in a sarcastic way the first word of "from *under* God" in 12. *Tḥt* 'under' has the strong theological value of 52 or **26**x2. "Under every green tree" is found in the context of idolatrous sex under trees in 1–2 Kings, 2 Chronicles, Isaiah, and Jeremiah. The first two tree names in the peak also have identical symbolic values in the alphabetical set with *'lwn* 'oak'=33 or **11**x3, and *lbnh* 'poplar'=33. The third tree is *'lh* 'terebinth'=18 or **6**x3. All three trees have an *l*, giving alliteration.[10] The surface form of the final word of the peak line *ṣēllâ* has a geminated *l*, which enhances the alliteration. The two cola of the peak end in *la* and *lâ* giving rhyme. The lemma *ṣl* 'shade' has the value of 30, which has factors of **10**, **6**,

9. Garrett (*Hosea*, 133) writes about 4:14c, "The line has no logical connection to the poem that precedes it," but he continues on p. 134 by accepting the connection Lundbom makes with the boundaries of the first and last lines of 11b–14. I personally thank Lundbom for revealing these boundaries that fit my analysis as a metrical chiasm, and for making the logical connection in this discontinuous bicolon. Kinder (*Hosea*, 54) also notes that 14c "could well be coupled with the verse that introduced the paragraph," (p. 11).

10. Garrett (*Hosea*, 35) states with many examples: "The most noteworthy feature of chaps. 4–7 is the astonishing frequency of the number three." On p. 123 he adds concerning the three tree names "that the number three is significant again in Hosea."

and 5, as YHW of YHWH. The *list* of three trees also helps to give prominence to the central peak (note the agricultural list in 2:5[7]).

Lundbom ("Rhetoric" 305–306) also notes that the *centers* are special, and that 13b "is the only bicolon in the poem to lack parallelism." The central peak of 4:13b has two other features of prominence by *syntactic complexity*. The first colon is a prepositional phrase connected to the previous line, and the second colon is a subordinate *ky* 'because' clause. The sarcasm in both the list of trees in the peak and the idolatrous *ʿṣ* 'wood/tree'=34 or 17x2 and *mql* 'staff'=44 or 22x2 of verse 12 serves to emphasize the difference between true religion and the useless association with wood and trees. "Wood' in 12a and the trees in 13b also show the chiastic pattern of tying the beginning to the center of poems. Both lines of 12 have internal parallelism with the more specific information in the second cola, where "wood/tree" becomes "staff," and "astray" becomes "away from under God."

The center line is enclosed by the same root beginning the lines adjacent to it, *ʿal-* 'on'=28 or 6x7, and *ʿal=ken* 'therefore' with *ken*=25 or 5x5. These two lines both have word pairs, "mountains and hills" before, and "daughters and daughters-in-law" after the peak. *Gbʿh* 'hill' has the value of 26, *bt* 'daughters'=24 or 6x4, and *klh* 'daughters-in-law'=28 or 6x7. "Daughters" and "daughters-in-law" are repeated in 14a. There is also balance on each side of the peak with *zbḥ* 'sacrifice'=17 coming in both halves in 13A and 14C, and with the semantic similarity of "led astray" in 12 and "go aside" in 14. *Ky* 'because' in the peak comes three times in 14 and once as "Yes" in 12, tying the peak to the rest of the poem.

"People" *ʿam* forms an inclusio, being the last word of the first line and the first of the last line. "Heart" and "understanding" enclose them chiastically, indicated by ABBA above). "People" is also in the inclusio of the discontinuous bicolon in 4:4b–9a. *Znh* 'be a harlot'=26 comes four times. The third line 12b has *znwnym* 'harlotry'=64 or 32x2 followed by "*become harlots*," and the third and fourth from the end 14a–b have "*become harlots*" followed by "adultery" (*nʾp*=32). Two symbolic lemmas in verse 12 relate to 17, *šʾl* 'inquire'=34, and *rwḥ* 'spirit'=34.[11] Although these repetitions balance chiastically in this poem with a chiastic structure, the repetitions also serve as a terrace pattern in 12–14 with "harlotry-harlots, harlots-adultery; harlots-adultery, harlots-*cult prostitutes*." The first lemma *znwnym* 'harlotry' comes from the same root as the four *znh*, but the change to *qdš* 'cult

11. Other symbolic numbers with the factors of 6 and 5 are, *l* 'to'=12, *rʾš* 'top/head'=42, *h* 'the'=5 x4, *hr* 'mountain'=25, *pqd* 'punish'=40, and *hm* 'they'=18.

prostitutes'=49 or 7x7 at the end of the two series of four I see as emphasizing that the main accusation is the fertility cult.[12]

No changes in MT hyphens are necessary for this metrically chiastic poem 11b–14. Instead of the usual couplet parallelism, the strophic structure of this poem includes triplets, with two interrelated sets of three bicola on each side of the peak. The triplet after the peak has especially strong cohesion because of the above list of sexual sins. The triplet before the peak develops three themes of idolatry: inquiring of wood, harlotry, and sacrifice. This arrangement of strophes gives a chiastic pattern to the poem similar to 4:4b–9a above:

A monocolon

B three bicola

C central bicolon

B' three bicola

A' monocolon.

4:15–19 Chiasm 6445 5 5446

(47 words; MT 40 or 10x4 or 5x8 word-stress units, revision 43; 56 lemmas of which 18 or 32.14% have multiples with divine-name values, the 5th highest)

15 Though-you(=)play-the-*harlot*, you Israel,

don't=let-Judah become-guilty; [4+2](5/6)

And-don't=enter Gilgal;

and-don't=go-up to-Beth(+)aven; (5/4)

And-don't(=)swear

"As-YHWH(=)lives." (2/4)

*

16 Truly like-a-*stubborn* heifer

Israel is-*stubborn*; (5)

Will-YHWH now feed-them

like-lambs in-a-meadow? (5)

*

12. Eidevall (*Grapes*, 58) notes the various forms of the root *znh* that Hosea uses, and on page 59 describes "'going aside' with prostitutes, and sacrificing together with hierodules. These utterances can be read as literal descriptions of promiscuous behavior, apparently with some kind of cultic connection. Though the exact nature of these practices has been much debated, very little can be said with any certainty." On page 60 he lists the references in 4:10a, 13b, and 14 as "non-metaphorical" in contrast to 12b "metaphorical": "A spirit of harlotry has led them astray and they harloted away from under God."

17 Ephraim is-joined to-idols,
leave(=)him. (4/5)
18 Ending-their drunkenness
they-*indulged* in-*harlotry*. (4)
*
They-really love
the-dishonor-of her-shield [NIV "their rulers"]; (4)
19 A-wind(spirit) wrapped her <u>in</u>-its-wings;
and-they-are-shamed because-of-their-sacrifices. [4+2](6)

The center of 4:15–19 is highlighted by a rhetorical question, by the divine name *YHWH*=**26** directly in the center as the third of the five words, and by the simile "like lambs" with *k* 'like'=**11**, and *kbṣ* 'lamb'=34 or **17**x2. This is preceded in 4:16 by the opposite simile "Israel is stubborn like a stubborn heifer" with another *k* 'like' in the line before the peak. The word order puts the two "stubborn" adjacent making them prominent. The lemma *prh* 'heifer'=42 has a factor of **6**, and *srr* 'stubborn'=55 has **5**x**11** or **23**+**32**. The derogatory name "Bethaven" "house of evil" also has the value of 55. These are the two lemmas with the value of 55 that come most frequently at three times each among the seventeen 55s in Hosea. YHWH=**26** also comes in 15C. The preposition *b* 'in' comes in the peak and in the last line, a favorite pattern in chiasmus. *Yśr 'l* 'Israel'=64 or **32**x2 comes at the end of the first colon and at the end of the colon before the central peak. This is balanced by "Ephraim" at the end of the colon next after the peak. The reference to "Judah" in the second colon of the poem is looked upon as a possible later addition after the fall of the northern kingdom. Garrett (*Hosea*, 135) sees this poem as an expansion of the Lo-Ruhamah oracle with "I will have mercy on the house of Judah" in 1:7. Both poems are favorable to Judah in contrast to Israel. Semantically *'šm* 'guilt'=35 or **5**x7 in the first line is paired with *qlwn* 'dishonor'=51 or **17**x3 and *bwš* 'be ashamed' in the last two lines. "Play harlot" in the first line is matched by "indulged in harlotry" with *znh* twice as an infinitive absolute in 18 (see the same in 1:2c-d beginning the messages). The lemma *znh* has the value of **26**. The first and last lines have the same irregular 4+2 cola structure, forming a metrical inclusio. The chiastic balance can be illustrated as follows:

A be a harlot=26 . . . guilty 15 (4+2 cola 1st line)
B LORD=**26** 16b central peak
A' be a harlot=26 x2 . . . ashamed 18–19 (4+2 cola last line).

The first three lines are tied together by four negative commands with *ʾl* 'don't'=13 (two in the second line) suggesting a three-line strophe. The rest of the poem follows Hosea's normal groupings by couplets. Line-internal parallelism comes with "don't-don't" in 15b, and "stubborn-stubborn" in 16a. Other symbolic lemmas including four with 30 with factors of 10, 6 and 5 of YWH, are *yhwdh* 'Judah'=30, *glgl* 'Gilgal'=30, *ʿlh* 'go up'=33, *šbʿ* 'swear'=39, *ḥy* 'live'=18, *ḥbr* 'join'=30, *ʿṣb* 'idol'=36, *sbʾ* 'drink'=18, *mgn* 'shield'=30,[13] *rwḥ* 'wind/spirit'=34, *knp* 'wing'=42, *zbḥ* 'sacrifice'=17, *w* 'and'=6 x4, *h* 'the'=5, *l* 'to'=12, and *ʾt* object=23. WHM has *yhb* 'give'=17 as the lemma for *hb*, but Paratext has it as *ʾhb* 'love'=8, which emphasizes the preceding *ʾhb* as in the above translation "really love." The divine-name numbers are strong with the 5th highest percentage of 32.14%, reinforcing the central peak's focus on YHWH.

5:1–4 Eight Hexameters

(53 words; 49 MT word-stress units or 48=6x8 revised; 67 lemmas of which 17 or 25.37% have divine-name values)

1 Hear(=)this, O-priests,
    and-give-your-attention, O-*house-of Israel*; (5/6)
And-O-*house-of* the-king, listen,
    <u>for</u> the-judgment is-against-you. (6)

*

<u>For</u>=you-have-been a-snare to-Mizpah,
    and-a-net spread on=Tabor. (6)
2 And-a-slaughter[pit]=of rebels[Shittim] dug-deep;
    but-*I* will-chastise all-of-them. (6)

*

3 *I* <u>know</u> *Ephraim*,
    and-*Israel* is-<u>not</u>=hid from-me. (6)
<u>Yes</u>, now, *Ephraim*, you-have-<u>committed-harlotry</u>,
    Israel is-defiled. [4+2](6)

*

4 **<u>Their-deeds do-not</u> allow-them**

13. "Shield" is a metaphor for "ruler" (Ps 47:9) or God (Gen 15:1). It is also used for decorations (1Kgs 10:16–17). It is not clear what is meant here. NIV translates "their rulers dearly love shameful ways."

to-return to(=)their-God. (5/6)

<u>For</u>(+)a-spirit-of <u>harlotry</u> is-among-them,

and-they-<u>do-not</u> <u>know</u> the=LORD. (7/6)

The final peak line is enhanced by the only occurrence of YHWH, and is preceded by the similarly thematic colon with a divine name, "return to their God." "For/yes" comes four times, the last in the final peak line. "I know Ephraim" in v. 3 is emphatically reversed in the final peak line, "they don't know the LORD." Andersen and Freedman (*Hosea*, 391) note the "immense weight of the final statement of v. 4." The unity of all of v. 4 and its position as the final strophe of block three suggest counting both lines as the peak (note the extra lines in the final peaks in 3:5 at the end of block two, and in 11:7 at the end of block seven). The negative particle *l'* 'not' forms an inclusio for v. 4, being the first word and next to the last word of this expanded peak. Other features which highlight the first line of 4 are syntactic complexity with the infinitive of the key word *šwb* 'return,' which comes **23** times in the book, and rhyme with *-êhem* ending both cola. 5:1–4 has a terrace pattern pointing to the final peak as follows (verse numbers are in parentheses, the peak in caps, and words repeated in the peak underlined):

house-house (1) *byt*=34

<u>for–for</u> (1) *ky*

I (2) *'ny*–I *'ny* =25 (3) . . . <u>know</u> *yd'*=30 . . . <u>not</u> *l'* (3) . . . commit <u>harlotry</u> *znh*=**26** (3)

Ephraim, Israel (3a)–<u>Yes/for</u> *ky* Ephraim, Israel *yśr 'l*=64 (3b)

NOT (GOD) (4a) FOR HARLOTRY *znwnym*=64 . . . (YHWH) NOT KNOW (4b)

This peak has prominence by being tied to the central peak of the book in 8:2 "O God of Israel, we know you" where the people make a superficial claim to know God. Other repetition in 5:1–4 is "Israel" in 5:1, and *l'* 'not'=13 in 5:3. The lemma *l* 'to/for'=12 comes four times ending on the final peak and adding to the buildup. The number of symbolic lemmas in 4a-b also supports the whole verse to be called the peak. They are *ntn* 'allow/give'=50, *'l* 'to'=13, *rwḥ* 'spirit'=34, *'t* object=**23**, *YHWH*=**26**, *yd'* 'know'=30, *l* 'to/for'=12 and *'l* 'not'=13.[14]

14. Other symbolic lemmas in the poem are *šm'* 'hear'=50, *z't* 'this'=30, *h* 'the'=5, *khn* 'priest'=30, *w* 'and'=6 x7, *qšb* 'give attention'=42, *'zn* 'give ear'=22, *mlk* 'king'=36, *l* 'to'=12 x4, *mšpṭ* 'judgment'=60, *pḥ* 'snare'=25, *hyh* 'be'=20, *tbwr* 'Tabor'=50, *'mq* 'dig deep'=48, *mwsr* 'chastise'=54, *kl* 'all'=23, *kḥd* 'hide'=23, and *ṭm'* 'defile'=23.

The strophic pattern follows Hosea's normal couplets. Semantic parallelism is found in most couplets and in most lines internally. An important exception is in the first line of the peak where "Their deeds don't allow them to return to their God" drops the line-internal parallelism found in 5:3 "Ephraim you have committed harlotry//Israel is defiled." This sets off the peak line, and is typical of other peaks. However, *strophic* parallelism comes in the peak with an inclusio of *l'* 'not' plus verbs "don't allow//don't know" connecting both lines, and with "God" in the first line parallel to YHWH in the last line. The *-m* 'them' suffix also comes in both lines at the end of the first three cola.

There is a play on two words in 5:2 that occur only here in the Hebrew Bible: *šḥṭh* 'slaughter,' and *śṭ* 'rebel'=30. Puns with similar sounding words "pit" and "Shittim" are likely intended, following the pattern in 5:1 with "snare" followed by "Mizpah" and "net" followed by "Tabor." This produces a pattern of three traps and three places, along with identifying them as "rebels" who "slaughter." Garrett (*Hosea*, 142) points out that this "could be taken to refer to Mizpah, Tabor, and Shittim together" as places intended with "I will chastise all of them."

The first word *šm'* 'hear'=50 (or 10x5 equivalent to YH) of this last poem of block 3 is also the first word of the introduction to this block in 4:1, giving cohesion to the block with an anaphoric inclusio. "Spirit of harlotry" also occurs in this block at 4:12 as well as in this final peak, the only two places in the book, and "wind" or "spirit" (*rwḥ*=34) is also in the last line of the previous poem with possibly the same meaning, forming epiphora. The thematic word *yd'* 'know' in the final colon is also found at the beginning of this block in 4:1, making an inclusio for block 3. The thematic word "harlotry" ties this poem to the previous three poems in block 3 and to part 1. The juxtaposition of "harlotry" and YHWH in the final line of 4:10–11 is now repeated here, giving strong emphasis at the end of this block.

Fourth Block 5:5—7:2, 44 Lines, "Israel, Ephraim and Judah"

(Words: MT 257, Possible revision 258=6x43 by adding "begin" in 6:11; Lemmas MT 336=6x56, Possible revision 338 adding *k* in 6:5 and "begin" in 6:11, see table 4)

5:5–7 **Chiasm** 36 44 63

(33 words, or 30 if 5c is deleted; MT 28 word-stress units, revision **26**; 44 lemmas of which 10 or 22.72% have divine-name values)

5 *And-the-pride-of=Israel testifies against-him.* (3)

Both-*Israel*(+)and-Ephraim stumble in-their-guilt;

Judah=also stumbled with-them. (7/6)

*

6 **With-their-sheep and-with-their-cattle** {N

they-go(+)to-seek the=LORD. V:V'N'} (5/4)

But-they-will-not find-him;

he-has-withdrawn from-them. (4)

*

7 They-betrayed the-LORD,

for(=)they-bore alien children. [2+4] (5/6)

Now the-new-moon(+)will-devour-them with=their-fields. (4/3)

This new fourth block shifts from poems of condemnation of idolatry and fertility prostitution to the *politics* of Israel and Judah. The accusation is now that Israel "betrayed" or "dealt treacherously" with God. The word *bagad* significantly comes only in 5:7 and 6:7, both in this block. This first poem describes the futility of their turning to sacrifice to get God's help, when they had alienated him by their sins.

The first line of the central peak has a grammatical inversion with the verbs in the center and the nouns on the sides: "with sheep & cattle go–seek YHWH." The sequence "they-go(+)to-seek" is long for normally hyphenated sequences, although within parameters noted by others.[15] All the overloaded syllable counts in this first line of the peak serve as a poetic device emphasizing the greatness of their useless sacrificial ritual—a common theme in Hosea, see 6:6 and 8:11. Even the use of the optional object marker *ʾet*=23 before "YHWH" adds a syllable to the line. "And" also comes in the last line connecting the peak and end chiastically. (See Bliese, "Psalms 1–24," 269, 281, 298 on Pss 1:2; 8:3, and 17:14b for a similar overloading of syllables to show greatness.) In contrast, the second line of the peak emphasizes the "withdrawal" and "not finding" of the LORD by having no hyphenated words, all of which are short. Even *lōʾ* 'not'=13 is

15. Korpel and de Moor ("Fundamentals," 174) describe the metrical system as "free rhythm" where "stressed syllables could be combined with a considerable number of unstressed syllables or could be drawn out at will to make one word sound as long as a whole phrase." They also (p. 3) see eight syllables as the "largest foot." Van Grol ("Zephaniah," 191) proposes that "a metrical unit consists of one strongly stressed syllable (sometimes followed by a slightly stressed ultima) preceded by zero, one, two, three or four slightly stressed syllables."

read as a separate word, in spite of usually being hyphenated before a verb. The *b* 'with' prepositional phrases are emphasized by fronting them before the verbs. The word pairs "sheep-cattle" and "seek-find" are also significant in the central peak. The lemma *ṣʾn* 'sheep' has the value of 33. The peak also has prominence with the divine name, "YHWH"=**26**. "YHWH" is also repeated in the line after the peak. Other lemmas with symbolic values in the central peak are *l* 'to'=12, *bqš* 'seek'=42, and *mṣʾ* 'find'=**32**. The actions with movement "go, seek, not find" in the peak connect semantically with the double occurrence of the action *kšl* 'stumble'=44 in the first strophe. The reference "Judah also stumbled with them" is among those seen by some scholars as additions to the original text after the fall of Samaria when the book was used in Judah.[16]

The double center suggests secondary peaks in the peripheral lines. The first line has prominence by being repeated in 7:10 also as a secondary peak. The first four lemmas all have symbolic values: *w* 'and'=6 which also comes four more times, *ʿnh* 'testify/answer'=35, *gʾwn* 'pride'=24, and *yśrʾl* 'Israel'=64. In the last line the figurative language of the new moon "devouring them with their fields" gives prominence, and plays on the central theme of sacrificing (and devouring) "sheep and cattle." It may predict the imminent invasion described in the next poems. Eidevall, (*Grapes*, 73–74) proposes that "it is likely that the new moon festival is metaphorically portrayed as a personified agent in v. 7b, possibly as a predatory animal of some kind. The idea would be that the coming religious festival will bring destruction of the fields, instead of blessing on the crops." The last four lemmas all have symbolic values, *ʾkl* 'eat/devour'=24, *ḥdš* 'new moon'=33, *ʾt* 'with'=**23**, and *ḥlq* 'portion, field'=39, matching the first four of the poem, which also are all symbolic, thereby giving prominence to both lines.[17] The 39-valued *ḥlq* is also a singleton for Hosea, suggesting a conscious choice.

Internal parallelism with rhyme comes in the repetition of "stumble" and end rhyme with *-am* in both cola of the second line (5:5), and the *-dû* end rhyme of both cola of the second line from the end (5:7).[18]

16. Garrett (*Hosea*, 146) notes that the "triplet" structure of 5:5 indicates that the third line is "artificially added on," but sees Hosea himself as a likely source. In my above chiastic analysis the unusual "triplet" becomes a regular initial trimeter line balanced by a trimeter at the end and followed by a normal couplet with parallelism of "stumble." Dearman (*Hosea*, 175) states that the clause "may well be an editorial update," but "Whether it goes back to the prophet's own updating of his work or to one of his disciples at a later time cannot be determined."

17. Other symbolic lemmas in the poem are *pnh* 'against/face'=36, *ʿwn* 'guilt'=36, *yhwdh* 'Judah'=30, *zwr* 'alien'=33 (or *zr* =27), and *yld* 'bear'=26.

18. The BHS apparatus suggests deleting "both Israel" in 5 as a variant reading. See Mays, *Hosea*, 82. The deletion would make the line a regular hexameter, as does the

The six lines of the poem may be paired into couplet strophes. The central peak couplet has the strongest cohesion with the parallelism of "seek // not find." The first and last trimeter lines possibly fit together as a discontinuous unit as in 4:4b-9a and 4:11b-14 above. The lines relate as cause and effect, "And the pride of Israel testifies against him . . . Now the new moon will devour them with their fields."

5:8–9 Chiasm 4 55 4

(19 words; MT 19 word-stress units, revision 18 or 6x3; 23 lemmas of which 8 or 34.78% have divine-name values making it the third highest in the book)

8 *Blow(+)a-trumpet in-Gibeah,*
a-horn in-Ramah! (5/4)
Sound-the-alarm in-Beth aven;
behind-you, Benjamin! (5)
*
9 **Ephraim will-become a-desolation**
in-the-day-of chastisement. (5)
In-the-tribes-of Israel
I-proclaim what-is-sure. (4)

The two poems 5:8–9 and 5:10–11 possibly describe events from the Syro-Ephraimite war.[19] The poem divides in the center, with the first half the alarm, and the second half the pronouncement of judgment. "Behind you, Benjamin" is probably interpreted best as a warning cry identifying the attackers, parallel with "sound the alarm" in the first colon of the line. The two center lines are the high point for these two themes. "Desolation" (*šmh*) is a very strong word also translated "horror" in Deut 28:37 with its similar prediction of punishment.

added hyphen above. Keeping "Israel" gives further emphasis to the first line by the repetition. Gelston (2010:59*) in BHQ notes, "There is no evidence for the omission of this word in text or v[e]rs[ion]s."

19. See Mays (Hosea, 86–87), and Eidevall (*Grapes*, 79), who gives possible reasons on pages 80–81 that "these references to military conflict and devastation are parts of a drama dealing with the relationship between YHWH and the people." Similarly, Dearman (Hosea, 180) reviews some of the arguments for and against, and concludes "Perhaps it is best to see this subsection as concentrating on the people's encounter with YHWH against the backdrop of the Syro-Ephraimite war and its immediate aftermath."

The unity of 5:8–9 is supported by alliteration and rhyme. Word final -â is repeated at the end of the first two cola, and the end of the last two lines, plus once each within the first and third lines. The two cola of the central second line end with -n, and the two place names in this line begin with b. Since the central peak is a couplet, emphasis is also likely in the first and last lines. The initial imperative and final affirmation "sure" meet this expectation. The first three lines each have 22 letters. Garrett (*Hosea* 36) notes the list of Gibeah, Ramah, and Beth Aven typical of Hosea's groups of three. Note that the first two historical examples are in the initial secondary peak, and Beth Aven, the contemporary target, is in the central peak.

Lemmas with symbolic values occur in all lines. 5:8–9 has the third highest percentage 34.78% of divine-name lemma values among the 45 poems. The first line has *šwpr* 'horn'=64, *gbʻh* "Gibeah"=26, and *rwʻ* 'sound the alarm'=42. The central peak has *byt ʼwn* 'Bethaven'=55 which comes x3 in Hosea, *ʼḥry* 'behind'=39, *l* 'for'=12, *šmh* 'desolation'=39, *hyh* 'be'=20, and *twkḥh* 'chastisement'=52. The last line has *šbṭ* 'tribe'=32, *yśrʼl* 'Israel'=64, and *ydʻ* 'know, proclaim'=30. (Note that Bethaven is written three times as two words in MT as above, but for lemma counts WHM and Paratext who both count it as a single lemma name are followed.)

5:10–11 Chiasm 5 44 5
(18 words; MT 17 word-stress units, revision 18; 21 lemmas of which only 3 or 14.29% have divine-name values, the 8th lowest percentage of the 45 poems)

> 10 The-princes-of Judah are
>> <u>like</u>-removers of-boundaries; (5)
>
> **I-will-pour on-them**
>> **my-wrath <u>like</u>-waters.** (4)
>
> *
>
> 11 **Ephraim is-oppressed,**
>> **crushed (in)-judgment;** (4)
>
> Because he-was-determined to-go
>> after(=)a-command. (4/5)

As in the previous poem, 5:10–11 is made of two strophes, with the peak of each half in the center. The center has prominence with the key word *mšpṭ* 'judgment/justice'=60 or 10x6 or 5x12, by the simile "like waters" (*k* 'like'=11, *mym* 'water'=36 or 6x6), and by the word pair "oppressed" and "crushed." The same words come in the covenant curse of Deut 28:33, "you shall be oppressed and crushed." Wolff (*Hosea*, 114) notes about them, "The assonance of the passive participles gives a stirring quality to the lament over the already-present distress." Here the theme is punishment. The cause-effect development is chiastic by lines:

A because of the offense of Judah

B wrath poured like waters;

B' Ephraim oppressed and crushed in judgment

A' because of going after a command.

The chiasmus in the strophes helps define the passives "Ephraim is oppressed; crushed (in) judgment" as divine passives referring to God's punishment. Note that the previous line likely refers to God's wrath. The instrument God used for oppressing and crushing Ephraim would be Assyria. Garrett (*Hosea*, 153) proposes that the "command" refers to Menahem agreeing to pay tribute to Tiglath-pileser III, and "exacting the money from Israel" to get him to withdraw (see 2 Kgs 15:19–20).

The double lines in the center give expectation of emphasis on the ends as secondary peaks. The first and last lines of this poem have a striking pattern of Hosean singletons that match numerically. The first line has *swg* 'remove'=24 and *gbwl* 'boundary'=23, and the last line has *y ʾl* 'determine'=23 and *ṣw* 'command'=24. The fact that these four numerically paired singleton lemmas occur only in these structurally matching peripheral lines looks like an intentional plan.

The first line also has prominence in a *k* 'like' simile with these same words "like removers of boundaries." The preposition *k* 'like'=11 ties chiastically to the simile "wrath like water" in the central peak. The first line has two other lemmas with symbolic values, *hyh* 'be'=20, and *yhwdh* 'Judah'=30.

In the last line the numerically significant *ṣw* 'command'=24 has further prominence by being enigmatic in this context. The difficulty has prompted other translations such as "vanity"(LXX), "idols"(NIV), "dung"(*HOTTP*), and "nothingness" (Eidevall, *Grapes*, 83). It is in obvious contrast to "sure" at the end of the previous poem, giving literary epiphora. The lemma *ʾḥry* 'after/behind'=39 also comes in both poems at 5:8 and 5:11, tying them together.

MT has the divine-name number 17 for word-stress units, and a possible revision has 18 or 6x3.

5:12—6:3 Twelve Hexameters (with anacrusis before the last strophe)
(87 words; 123 lemmas of which 24 or 19.51% have divine-name values)

12 And-*I*-am like-a-moth to-*Ephraim*,
and-like-rot *to-the-house-of Judah*; (6)

*

13 And-*Ephraim* saw his=sickness,
and-*Judah* his(=)*wound*; (5/6)
Then-*Ephraim went to*=Assyria,
and-he-sent *to*=the-great king; (6)
But-he was-*not*(+)able to-*heal*(+)you;
and-he-did-*not*=cure your *wound*; (8/6)

*

14 For(+)I-am like-a-lion to-*Ephraim*,
and-*like*-a-young-lion *to-the-house-of Judah*; (7/6)
I, I will-*tear and-will-go*;
I-will-carry-away, and-no-one(+)will-rescue. [4+2] (7/6)

|#

5:15 I-*will-go*, I-will-*return* to=my-place,
until they=admit-their-guilt, and-seek(+)my-face; (7/6)

*

In-their troubles they-will-seek-me:
6:1 "*Come*, and-let's-*return* to=the-LORD, (6)
For he has-*torn*, but-he-will-*heal*-us;
he-has-hit, but-he-will-bandage-us. [4+2] (6)
2 He-will-*revive*-us after-two-days, AB
on-the-third(+)day he-will-raise-us-up; B'A'
that-we-may-*live* before-him. [2+2+2] (7/6)

*

3 **So-let-us-know,** (anacrusis) (1)
Let-us-press-on to-know the=LORD, VVN
like-the-dawn his-going-forth is-sure; N'V'V' (6)
And-he-comes to-us like-showers, AB
like-spring-rains that-water the-earth." B'A' (6)

The structure of these two stanzas in 5:12—6:3 is a work of art. This poem has overall unity in seven similes with the preposition *k* 'like'=11 about God: "moth" and "rot" in the first line, "lion" and "young lion" in the middle, and "dawn," "showers" and "spring rains" at the end. The last peak line has an ABB'A' inverted parallelism with the similes in the center and the verbs "comes" and "water" outside. The blessings of "showers" and "spring rains" is a reversal of 5:10 in the previous poem, "I will pour on them my wrath like water." The penultimate line, which here is counted as part of the peak, also has inverted parallelism shown above as VVNN'V'V' with two verbs "press on to know" followed by the noun "LORD," and the noun "dawn" followed by two verbs "going forth is sure." Anacrusis, "So let's know," sets off the final two lines as the peak, with the thematic lemma *yd*ʿ 'know'=30 with factors of Y=10, W=6, and H=5. It is repeated in "know the LORD." All of 6:3 is analyzed as the final peak. (See 3:5 and 5:4 above for similar long final peaks.) The third line from the end also has inverted parallelism with "revive" and "raise up" enclosing "after two days" and "on the third day," adding to the buildup to the end. The lemma *ḥyh*=23 is repeated, first as "revive," and then as "live." Eidevall (*Grapes*, 95) notes that the "emphasis lies on the healing activity" in relation to the previous "Ephraim saw his sickness, and Judah his wound" in 5:13 and God as a lion who tears in 5:14.

A terrace pattern in 5:12—6:3 helps to point to the final peak, with God's expressed desire that through punishment his people will "seek" him, resulting in their return where they really turn to know him so that his judgment can turn to blessing:

like (moth), like (rot) (verse 12)

Ephraim, to the *byt* 'house'=34 of Judah=30 (12)-Ephraim *ʾt*=23, Judah (13A)-Ephraim (13B)

ʾt mzwr 'wound'=46, *ʾl* 'to'=13, to, heal, wound (13)

went/go *l*ʾ 'not'=13, you-not, you (13c)

like(lion) to Ephraim, like (a young lion), to the house of Judah (14)

I-I (14B) (also 12 and variant in 14), tear (see "torn" in 6:1)

go (14B)-go (15A)

seek 15A (same letters *šḥr* as "dawn" in peak)

return, to (5:15a)-come/go, return, to YHWH=26 (6:1A)

torn, heal, -us—us (6:1B) (see "heal" in 13)

revive us-live (2B) (same root *ḥyh* for both)

day-day (2A)

KNOW-KNOW *ʾt* YHWH (3A)

LIKE-DAWN (3A) LIKE- LIKE (3C)

The final peak also has emphasis by synonyms, with the last two phrases "like showers" and "like spring rains that water the earth," and with the phrase "like dawn" in the first line of the peak referring back to "day" in 3. The last two words *yrh* 'water'=35 and *ʾrṣ* 'earth'=39 have symbolic values. The agricultural simile for God also relates to the climax of the final major poem in 14:5–8[6–9], "I will be as dew to Israel . . . I am like a green cypress; it is from me that your fruit is found."

Semantic balance between the proposed stanzas gives cohesion to the whole poem and may give emphasis to God's action in judgment in the center (the climax of the first stanza and beginning of the second). This can be seen in that the two stanzas are tied together by anadiplosis, "I will go," in the middle lines of the poem on each side of the juncture, and by the word *ṭrp* 'tear'=46 in the end of the first stanza and the middle of the second. There is interdependence with the metaphor of God as a wild animal who tears (*ṭrp*) and from whom no one will rescue/deliver (*nṣl*) in both 14b and in Ps 50.22 "Mark this, then, you who forget God, or I will tear you apart, and there will be no one to deliver." The warning has a reversal in the people's response in 6:1, "For he has torn, but he will heal us." The word "heal" is in the fourth line from each end, first negatively of Assyria, then positively in the peoples' expectation of God.

The proposed two halves of the poem are also structurally similar. Both have inclusions emphasizing their final lines. The first stanza (12–14) has the pronoun *ʾny* 'I'=25 (5x5) as the first word, and the last line (14b) has it repeated twice. (Note that the full form *ʾnky*=36 comes between them in 14a.) In the second stanza *hlk* comes with the first word translated "Go" in 5:15 speaking of God's departure. This is reversed with the first word of the last line the synonym *bwʾ* 'come' in "he comes to us" in 6:3, giving an emphatic antithetical inclusio.

The first six word-roots of the last line of the first stanza 14b all begin with *ʾalep*—the alliteration giving it prominence as the climax of the stanza. (Two of these words begin with the conjunction *w* 'and'=6 which comes a total of 18 times in the poem.) The last lemma of the first stanza is *nṣl* 'rescue' with the value of 44 giving prominence to the final "I will carry away, and no one will rescue." *Nśʾ* 'carry away' has the value of 36. Other lemmas with symbolic values in the first stanza are *l* 'to'=12 (x11 in the poem), *rʾh* 'see'=**26**, *ʾt*=23 object marker x2, *ḥly* 'sickness'=30, *ʾšwr* 'Assyria'=48, *ykl* 'able'=33, *ghh* 'cure'=13, and *ʾyn* 'no one'=25. The preposition *ʾl* 'to'=13 also has a buildup to YHWH coming twice in 5:13, once in 5:15 and finally before YHWH in 6:1.

The second stanza is the same length with six hexameters. The name *YWWH*=**26** comes in the second line from each end of this stanza, the only occurrences in the poem, with the latter in the peak. Two other key lemmas are repeated from 5:15 where God is the subject, but in 6:1 with Israel as subject (see Eidevall, *Grapes*, 93). They are *šwb* 'return' of God's departure in 5:15 and of Israel's return in 6:1, and the previously noted *hlk* 'go' of God in 5:15 with the opposite 'come' of Israel in 6:1. This stanza also has the same strophic structure as the first one, with a single bicolon where God describes his activities, followed by a three-line strophe on wounds not healed by Assyria, but healed by God in the reversal, and a final two-line strophe first with God the "lion" who "tears," and "goes," and then becomes the "rains" which "come" and "water the earth." This structure suggests the words of Israel in 6:1–3 are what God expects them to say when they are punished (see "saying" at the end of 15 in LXX), and should not be taken as true repentance at this stage in the book. It may be seen as a liturgical example of "shallow" repentance (Mays, *Hosea*, 94–95; *NIV Study Bible*, 1328), or as an "exhortation to repentance" which went "unheeded" as seen in 6:4–6 (Eidevall, *Grapes*, 93). (Also see chapter 3 B "Overall Structure" noting that salvation poems only come in parts 1 and 5, the first and last parts.) Other lemmas with symbolic values in the second stanza are *mqwm* 'place'=51, *ʿd* 'until'=20, *ʾšr* 'which'=42, *ʾšm* 'guilt'=35, *bqš* 'seek'=42, *pnym* 'face'=54, *hwʾ* 'he'=12, *nkh* 'hit'=30, *h* 'the'= 5, and *pnh* 'before'=36.

6:4–6 Four Hexameters and a Trimeter before the last line

(32 words; MT **26** word-stress units, possible revision 27; 42 lemmas of which 3 or only 7.14% have divine-name values, and 5 or 11.9% have values as multiples of 11)

4 *What shall-I-do=with-you,* Ephraim?
What shall-I-do=with-you, Judah? (26 letters) (6)
Your-<u>loyalty</u> is-like-a-morning(=)cloud,
and-like-dew that-goes-away early. (5/6)

*

5 There=fore I-cut-them-in-pieces by-the-prophets;
I-killed-them by-the-words-of(=)my-mouth; (5/6)
And-your[LXX my]-judgment goes-forth like-light. (3)

*

6 **For(+)I-desire loyalty, and-not=sacrifice;**

And-knowledge of-God more-than-burnt-offerings. (7/6)

The final line has prominence with the only divine reference, a repetition of *ḥsd* 'loyalty' from 4, and the thematic words "knowledge of God" as found in other strategic lines. Garrett (*Hosea*, 161) writes, "This is one of the great texts of the prophets." Kidner (*Hosea*, 66) calls it "the great verse 6" and the "climax" of the poem. The line also has prominence by being a well-known quotation from the "prophet" (v. 5) Samuel. (See 1 Sam 15:22, and 15:33 which has the prophet "hewing to pieces" King Agag.) Although parallelism is more predictable in non-peak lines, it should be noted that this peak is exceptionally well-formed. In this case the good parallelism of the first lines is broken by the trimeter short line before the peak, and then resumed in a strong parallelism in the last line. It also has gender switch, with "loyalty" and "sacrifice" masculine in the first colon of 4b, and "knowledge" and "burnt offerings" feminine in the second colon. The final word *ʿlh* 'burnt offerings' has the value of 33 and is a singleton, and the last word of the penultimate colon *zbḥ* 'sacrifice' has the value of 17, adding prominence to the peak. The conjunction *w* 'and'=6 has its last two of five occurrences in the peak line. Andersen and Freedman and Wolff also note the climactic position of the last line.[20]

The exceptionally short line before 6 also sets off this peak, similar to the anacrusis of the previous poem. Besides both poems being hexameters, they are tied to each other by chiasmus. The hope of "dawn" in 6:3a in the previous poem is turned to the "light" of "judgment" here in 6:5, and the hope of God as faithful "rain" in 6:3b is compared to Israel as unreliable *ʿnn* 'clouds'=44 and "dew" here in 6:4 (similes repeated in 13:3). The references to "morning" (*bqr* 6:4), "early" (*škm* 6:4), and "dawn" (*šḥr* 6:3) in these two poems helps to explain the ambiguous "light." (Also note the same consonants *šḥr* in 5:15 for "seek.") The prayer in 6:3 was that God's blessings would be as "sure" as the "dawn," but instead because of their unfaithfulness God's "judgment" will go forth on them as surely as the morning "light." Dearman (Hosea, 196) writes, "Just as light pierces the darkness, so divine judgment has come forth in Israel's history." Eidevall (*Grapes*, 98) notes that both metaphors of "dawn" and "light" as the "sun" have the same verb *yṣʾ* 'go forth.' Also note Andersen and Freedman (*Hosea*, 13, 429), "My judgment goes forth like the sun." A positive reading of "My *justice* goes forth like light" is linguistically possible. However, because of the context of judgment, most translations use the LXX "my *judgment*" in translating the Hebrew

20. Wolff (*Hosea*, 1965:120) states, "The saying reaches a climax in 6:6." Andersen and Freedman (*Hosea*, 430) call this verse, "the rhetorical climax of the entire section."

"your justice/judgments." The terse short line, the metaphor "light," and the ambiguous word *mšpṭ* 'judgment/justice'=60 all give prominence to this line as a secondary peak. The conjunction *w*=**6** begins this secondary peak line. The first four lines pair as two strophes, and the last peak line stands alone as a strophe. Also note the same structure in 11:12—12:1 [12:1–2].

MT has **32** words and **26** word-stress units, giving the poem numerical theological prominence. The first line has **26** letters, and two initial questions giving it prominence. The questions begin a terrace pattern leading to the final peak as follows:

> What shall I do with you? *mh* 'what'=18, *ʿśh* 'do'=42, *l* 'with/to'=12 (4a)
>
> What shall I do with you? *mh* 'what'=18, *ʿśh* 'do'=42, *l* 'with/to'=12 (4a)
>
> as—as *k*=11 (4b)
>
> (-I verb suffix), by—(-I), by (5)
>
> loyalty (4b)—LOYALTY *ḥsd* (6)[21]

6:7—7:2 Chiasm 65554 55 45(3)556
(The extra trimeter begins a final build-up; 68 words; MT word-stress units 64 or 32x2, revision 63; 83 lemmas of which **17** or 20.48% have divine-name values)

7 *But-they as[at]-Adam*
transgressed the-COVENANT;
<u>*there*</u> *they-betrayed(+)-me.* [2+2+2] (7/6)
8 Gilead is-a-city-of *doers*-of(+)evil,
tracked with-blood. (6/5)

*

9 And-as-those-who-wait for-a-man in-*bands*
are-the-company-of priests; (5)
They-murder on-the-road=to-*Shechem*;
yes, they-commit villainy. [2+3] (5)

*

10 In-the-house-of *Israel*
I-have-seen a-horrible-thing. (4)
<u>There</u> <u>Ephraim</u> has-harlotry;

21. Other symbolic lemmas are *yhwdh* 'Judah'=30, *škm* 'early'=45, *kn* 'them'=25, *ʾmr* 'word'=34, *ph* 'mouth'=22, and *lʾ* 'not'=13.

Israel is-defiled. (5)

*

11 **Also(=)Judah,**

he-has-set a-harvest for-you. [2+3] (4/5)

*

Whenever-I-would-restore the-fortune-of(+)my-people,

7:1 as-when-I-would-have-healing for-Israel, (5/4)

The-iniquity-of Ephraim is-revealed,

and-the-*evils*-of *Samaria.* (5)

*

Yes, they-deal falsely! (3)

And-thieves enter;

bandits raid in-the-streets/outside. [2+3] (5)

*

7:2 But-they-don't(=)say in-their-hearts

that-I-remember all=their-*evil*; (4/5)

Now their-works surround-them;

they-are before my-face. (6)

The metrical chiasm of 6:7—7:2 is supported by an overall semantic chiastic structure, mostly of names, which gives cohesion to the whole poem, and in the center emphasizes the key three words of the block, "Ephraim, Israel, Judah."

A They *hm*=18 . . . me -*y* suffix (of God) (first line)

B bands *gdwd*=17 (9) (third line)

C Shechem *škm*=45 (9) (fourth line)

D Israel yśr ʾl=64 (10a) (fifth line)

E EPHRAIM, ISRAEL=64 (10b) JUDAH =30 (11a) (6–7th lines)

D' Israel (11b) (fifth full line from end)

C' Samaria (1a) (fourth full line from end)

B' bandits *gdwd* (1c) (third line from end)

A' –their -*hm* suffix, -them . . . my -*y* suffix (of God) (last line)

The first cola of the first and last secondary peak lines have the third person plural "they/them/their," and the final cola of these lines have the divine first person "me/my" with the suffix *-y*, making a double inclusio of the major characters. The poem begins with the conjunction *w*=**6** connected to the emphatic full pronoun *hm* 'they,' which has the lemma value of 18 or 6x3 as well as **23** in its surface form *hmh*. The final line has the object suffix *-m* 'them,' and *-hm* 'their.' The grammatical switch from being the *subject* of transgressions in the first line to the *object* of being surrounded by "their deeds" at the end shows thematic development toward their accountability before God.

The initial word *šm* 'there'=34 of the peak is also in the first line of the poem, giving chiastic beginning-to-center cohesion. The peak has the only reference to *znwt* 'harlotry'=49 in this fourth block, tying this block to the theme of parts 1–2. The peak line words in "Ephraim has harlotry, Israel is defiled" are also in 5:3b, giving them significance by repetition. The lemmas *ṭm ʾ* 'defiled'=**23**, *Yśr ʾl* 'Israel'=64, and *Yhwdh* 'Judah'=30 give numerical prominence to the peak. The preposition *l* 'for'=12 comes three more times in the second half. The metaphor "harvest" (*qṣyr*) in v. 11 is ambiguous in Hosea, for blessing or judgment (Andersen and Freedman, *Hosea*, 443–44), and may have an intentional double meaning here in the peak. The meaning of blessing would understand the following line of the "restoration" as prophecy rather than unfulfilled hope (see Stuart, *Hosea*, 6:11–7:1a). Eidevall (*Grapes*, 107) argues for a "future retribution, possibly in the form of divine judgment." The lack of other salvation prophecies in the central blocks of Hosea supports the judgment interpretation as the main meaning. See GNT "I have set a time to punish you also for what you are doing."

There is a series of eight lemmas all with symbolic values in v. 9: *ḥkh* 'wait'=24, *ʾyš* 'man'=**32**, *gdwd* 'band'=**17**, *ḥbr* 'company'=30, *khn* 'priest'=30, *drk* 'road'=35, *rṣḥ* 'murder'=46, and *škm* 'Shechem'=45. "Priests," "murder, "Shechem," and "villainy" in v. 9 recall the Gen 34 deceitful murder of the men of Shechem by Simeon and Levi, the ancestor of the priests.

The strophic structure has typical couplets throughout the poem, except that the line with "Judah" in 6:11 stands alone, perhaps supporting that it is a later addition, similar to the list of kings of Judah in 1:1, and to the extra words in 1:7, which are also in a central peak with a double line in its present form.[22]

22. Dearman (*Hosea*, 199) writes: "The short sentence in v. 11a seems to stand alone, almost as an ejaculatory cry: 'You too, Judah!' As such it may be an editorial update, added later by Hosea or an editor. Surprisingly, the LXX does not preserve the name Judah in this verse."

Since the text has a double line in the center, the first and last lines are counted as secondary peaks. The ambiguous *ʾdm* 'Adam'=18 draws attention to the first line, with its possibilities of meaning (1) the first Adam, (2) humanity, or (3) the place where the Jordan River dried up at the beginning of the entry into Canaan with possible associations of transgressions such as at nearby Achor or Baal Peor.[23] The preposition *k* 'as'= also comes in verses 9 and 11. The key words "transgress the COVENANT" and "betray" also add prominence in the first line, as does "there" by being repeated in the central peak. Each colon of the first line has a *-w* 'they' subject suffix followed by *b* and *î*, giving rhyme.

The end of the poem is also emphatic. (The analysis here follows BHS, NRSV, and NIV in adding the first two words of 7:1a as the second colon of 6:11b. For the poem break after 7:2 note GNT, CEV, and NIV.) In support of the unity of the poem ending at 7:2, Eidevall (*Grapes*, 104) lists correspondences between 5:1–7 and 6:7—7:2, and refers to Andersen and Freedman's (*Hosea*, 433) statement that the two "need to be examined together." The fourth line from the end in 7:1c is only three words, beginning with the deictic *kî* 'Yes,' which is also in 6:9B. The line qualifies as a secondary peak because of its shortness, and by breaking the regularity of the metrical chiasm. It serves here as an introduction to the climactic end lines of this poem and block. (Note the similarity to the extended climax at the end of block 2 in 3:5, and in this block at 6:3.) The lemma *šqr* 'false'=60 comes in the short line along with the verb *pʿl* 'deal/do'=45, which also comes in the second line 6:8 as the participle "doers." Semantically the short line "Yes, they deal falsely" parallels "yes, they commit villainy" at the end of 6:9 in the first half of the poem. The value of *zmh* 'villainy' is 25, and of ʿśh 'commit/do' is 42.

Another significant marker pointing to the final climax of this poem is a series of inverted parallelisms in the last three lines. 1c has the verbs in the center, "thieves-*enter*; *raid*-bandits;" and the last two have verbs on the ends: 2a has "*say*-in hearts; evil-*remember*," and 2b has "*surround*-works; before my face-*they are*." The two poem-final lemmas have symbolic values, *pnym* 'face'=54, and *hyh* 'are'=20.[24] "Works/deeds" (*mʿll*) in the last line

23. Garrett (*Hosea*, 163) connects (1) and (3): "The prophet has made a pun on the name of the town and the name of the original transgressor. His meaning is, "Like Adam (the man) they break covenants, they are faithless to me there (in the town of Adam)." The pun obviously adds prominence to this initial secondary peak. Garrett also points out another pun in the second line of 6:8 where *ʿqb* 'tracked,' which only comes here in the Hebrew Bible, has the same root as "Jacob," a cognate of "heel."

24. Other lemmas with symbolic values are *w* 'and'=6 x6, *k* 'as'=11 x3, *ḥbr* 'company'=30, *glʿd* 'Gilead'=35, *dm* 'blood'=17, *byt* 'house'=34, *rʾh* 'see'=26, *šbwt* 'fortune/captivity'=51, *ʿwn* 'iniquity'=36, *glh* 'reveal'=20, *ḥwṣ* 'outside'=32, *ʾmr* 'say'=34, and *kl* 'all'=23.

summarizes all the transgressions, villainy, harlotry, iniquity and evils of the poem. Mays (*Hosea*, 103) says of 7:2, "What one line could better sum up the theological failure of Israel."

A terrace pattern also points to the climactic secondary peak at the end:

Israel-Ephraim-Israel (6:10)

restore-restoration (11)

Israel (11)-Ephraim, evils of Samaria (7:1)

-their—evil -their (2a)

-THEIR—THEM (same final -*m*) (2b).

Note that these four are the only occurrences of the "-them/their" suffix in the poem.

This fourth block begins in 5:5 with a cluster of "Israel-Israel-Ephraim-Judah," similar to the list here at the end, and these names are particularly prolific in this block. There is epiphora with "their deeds" at the end of both the third and fourth blocks in 5:4 and 7:2, tying these two blocks together as part two. "Their/his deeds" (*m ʿll*) is a key word coming also in 4:9; 9:15, and 12:3[4], or five times in Hosea, all in passages accusing Israel of evil deeds.

Central Part Three 7:3—8:13, Fifth Block, 50 Lines, "Kings and Princes"

(50 lines with factors of Y 10, and H 5; and Words MT 301, Possible revision 300=Y 10x30, H 5x60, W 6x50 by deleting "trained" in 7:15; Lemmas MT 357=17x21, possible revision for structural comparison has the same 357 by adding *h* in 7:16 covering the deleted "trained," see table 4)

7:3–7 Chiasm 557 66 755
(54 or 6x9 words; MT and revision 46 or 23x2 word-stress units; 66 lemmas of which 18 or 27.27% have divine-name values)

3 *By-their-evil they-delight(=)the-king,*

and-by-their-lies princes. (4/5)

4 *All-of-them* are-adulterers,

as a-burning oven. [2+3](5)

*

The-*baker* ceases stirring-it-up,

from-kneading the-dough until(=)it-is-leavened.

* [3+4](6/7)

5 **On-the-day-of our-king**

they-made the-princes-sick

from-the-heat(poison)-of the-wine. [2+2+2](6)

He-lifted(+)his-hand with=the-mockers,

6 **while=they-came-near as-an-oven,**

their-heart on-their-plots. [2+2+2](7/6)

*

All=night their-*baker* sleeps;

in-the-morning he burns like-a-flaming(+)fire. [3+4](8/7)

7 *All-of-them* are-hot as-an-oven;

and-they-devour their=rulers. (5)

All=their-kings have-fallen;

none=of-them calls to-me. {2+3](5)

The chiastic structure of this poem is one of the most artistically done in Hosea. Semantic chiasmus clearly supports the metrical chiasm of this poem. The participants of king, princes, baker, and mockers/assassins are arranged so that they come in not only lines, but also strophes which are chiastically arranged. "Our king" comes in the center of the chiasm in the first line of the central peak. There is also an inclusio with *mlk* 'king'=36 in the beginning, and "kings" in the final line. It is structurally significant that the important character, the king, is in both ends as well as the center since both peripheral lines are secondary peaks on the basis of the double line in the chiastic center. The central peak is the high point of the action, with the confrontation of the mockers and king. "Princes" in 3b also comes in the central peak, and is matched by "rulers" in 7b. "All of them" (*kullām*) begins the second line from each end, and *kl* 'all'=23 also comes without a suffix in the final line and the line after the peak. The "baker" *ʾph*=23 comes on each side in the line after and the second line before the center. In the central peak the rebels are identified as the 'mockers' (*lyṣ* =40). The preposition *ʾt* 'with' that is attached to *lyṣ* also has the value of 23. These three 23s connected to the baker and his cohorts look like a play on numbers, and may be related to the 46 or 23x2 word-stress units in the poem. "All of them," comes chiastically between the baker and the groups on the two ends of "kings/princes // rulers/kings" (see 13:10 for a similar combination of officials). "As an oven" also comes with "all of them" in 4a and 7a as well as in the central peak.[25] The preposition *k* 'as, like' has the value of 11, and besides being chiastically in the peak and second line from each end, it comes in the third line from the end. Besides these four lemmas of "king," "mockers," *ʾt*, and *k*, five other lemmas with symbolic values in the peak are *ḥlh* 'sick'=25, *ḥmh* 'heat'=**26**, *yyn* 'wine'=34, *mšk* 'lift'=45, and *ʾrb* 'plot'=**23**. The change from bicola with parallelism to tricola without parallelism marks the two peak lines.

The consistent structure recommends identifying all of the "them/their" suffixes in the poem with the assassins or "mockers" rather than with the immediate antecedents such as "princes" in 3 and "kings" in 7. *Lyṣ* 'mockers' in the central peak is the only nominal referent for all the "them/their" suffixes on both sides of the chiasm. It also seems likely that the ambiguous, "He lifted his hand," refers to the baker's complicity (see Andersen and Freedman, *Hosea*, 451–454), rather than to the king's naiveté. All third person singular verbs in the poem would then consistently refer to the baker. This would also mean that all four groups of the participants in the chiastic structure are gathered in the peak at 7:5 (see the "crowded stage" feature for peak described by Longacre, *Discourse*, 27). The arrangement of words referring to the "baker" is thereby chiastic with the nouns on the sides and the pronoun in the central peak. The referent for "our king" is not clear since he could be the deceived incumbent king (v. 3) celebrating some special "day" along with his princes who are lied to and made drunk by the rebels, or he could be the usurper (Pekah son of Remaliah as in 2 Kgs 15:25 or Hoshea son of Elah as in 2 Kgs 15:30), who after the assassination will celebrate his coronation later on this "day."[26] The beautiful word chiasm can be diagrammed as follows:

king (1st line)

princes

all of them as an oven (2nd line)

baker (3rd line)

KING, PRINCES, HIS HAND, MOCKERS AS AN OVEN

baker (3rd from end)

25. Dearman (*Hosea*, 205) writes concerning v. 6, "The term *like an oven* sits awkwardly in the first clause and could be deleted without detracting from either parallelism or basic meaning." This unexpected repetition adds prominence in this peak line. It also makes possible the above analysis of 2+2+2 tricola for both lines of the peak.

26. Dearman (*Hosea*, 205) writes, "perhaps the best is the assassination of Pekah and the resulting appointment of Hoshea as ruler by the Assyrians." Eidevall (*Grapes*, 110) sees the poem as a general condemnation of "moral decadence at the court" rather than a description of a specific assassination.

all of them as an oven (2nd from end)

rulers

kings (last line).[27]

The third lines from each end which have "baker" also have alliteration of *ʿr* in *mēʿîr* "stir-up" and *boʿēr* "burns" at the end of their first cola as the baker's *activity*, and of *yš* with *yšbt* 'cease' and *yšn* 'sleep' just after and before "baker," showing his *inactivity*. The numerical value of the latter two lemmas is the same, *šbt* 'cease'=45 and *yšn* 'sleep'=45. *Boʿērâ* 'burn' also comes in the second line, referring to the oven, balancing its occurrence at the end. Whoever the baker is, he apparently is involved with stirring up the plot, then "ceasing the stirring," or "sleeping" while it "ferments," and joining in the assassination with the "mockers," "burning" as they do in "hot" (*ḥmm*=34) rebellion.[28] Eidevall (*Grapes*, 114) identifies the topic of the metaphors of "fire," "hot," and "burning" in the poem as "hatred, which finds its outlet in acts of violence."

The double lines in the center point to emphasis in the peripheral lines. The first line, which is counted as a secondary peak, has three lemmas with symbolic values, *śmḥ* 'delight'=42, *mlk* 'king'=36, and *w* 'and'=6, which also comes once in the penultimate line. The final line is a didactic secondary peak climax with the lament of God, "None of them calls to me." The 2+3 exceptional cola structure gives it prominence, especially with the final emphatic "to me" of God's lament. Verse 7 has four pronominal suffixes "them/their" which have the referent of the assassins, the "mockers." The assassins are on the ends and the victims in the center. The last two make a concluding emphatic chiasmus in the secondary peak in 7b:

"A them, B their rulers; 7b B' their kings, A' them."

The final line has four lemmas with symbolic values, *kl* 'all'=23, *ʾyn* 'no'=25 (together they mean "none"), *qrʾ* 'call'=40, and *ʾl* 'to'=13.

Strophic structure is beautifully chiastic, with the opening and closing bicola couplets describing the interaction of the heated opponents hot as an oven with the king and princes. These are followed by single 3+4 heptameter bicola strophes about the baker in the middle of each side, and then a central strophe of two 2+2+2 tricola hexameters with the peak action involving

27. Garrett (*Hosea*, 1997, 168) lists "kings" and "all of them" in a similar chiasmus. He also has "day" and "night," but these do not fit in my above lineation. He assigns different roles to the participants in the assassination.

28. Other lemmas with symbolic values are *kḥš* 'lies'=40, *nʾp* 'commit adultery'=32, *ʿwr* 'stir up'=42, *lwš* 'kneading'=39, *bṣq* 'dough'=39, *ʿd* 'until'=20, *ḥmṣ* 'leaven'=39, *h* 'the'=5, *lylh* 'night'=39, *hwʾ* 'he'=12, *ʾš* 'fire'=22, *lhbh* 'flame'=24, and *ʾkl* 'devour'=24.

all the participants including the oven and the baker with "his hand." The large number of irregular cola seems intentional with two 3+4, two 2+2+2 and one 2+3 cola. The scene of disruption is conveyed by the irregular cola patterns within a carefully constructed strophic symmetry.

The first word *r ʿh* 'evil' repeats the same in 7:2 in the penultimate line near the end of the previous poem (anadiplosis), linking parts two and three. Kidner (*Hosea*, 69 and 139) also places a major juncture after 7:2.

7:8–16 Chiasm 456646645 6 546646654
(108 words, or 107 if "trained" is deleted in 15 to get 300 words in the central part, giving the factors Y 10x30, H 5x60, and W 6x50. "Trained" is not in LXX, see BHS; MT 97 word-stress units, revision 98 the sum of 17, 23, 26 and 32; 134 lemmas of which 23 or 17.16% have divine-name values)

8 Ephraim among-the-peoples
mixes himself. (4)
Ephraim is a-cake
not turned. (5)
*

9 Aliens devour his-strength,
and-he does-<u>not</u> know-it. (6)
Also=grey-hair[mold] is-sprinkled on-him;
and-he does-<u>not</u> know-it. (6)
*

10 *The-pride-of(=)Israel*
testifies against-him. (3/4)
But-they-do-<u>not</u>=return to=the-LORD their-God,
<u>nor</u>-do-they seek-him in-all-of=this. (6)
*

11 And-Ephraim is like-a-dove,
silly, without any-sense. (6)
They-call Egypt,
they-go to-Assyria. (4)
*

12 <u>As</u> they-go

I-will-spread my-net over-them; [2+3](5)

As-birds-of the-sky I-will-bring-them-down;

I-will-chastise-them as-the-report to-their-assembly. (6)

*

13 Woe to-them,

for(=)they-strayed from-me; [2+3](4/5)

Destruction to-them,

for=they-rebelled *against-me.* (4)

*

I would-redeem-them,

but-they speak lies *against-me.* [2+4](6)

14 And-they-do-not=cry to-me with-their-hearts,

while they-wail upon=their-beds. (6)

Over=grain(+)and-new-wine they-gash-themselves;

they-turn-away from-me. (5/4)

*

15 I trained(chastised),

I-strengthened their-arms;

yet-for-me they-plan=evil. [2+2+2](6)

16 Where-they-turn is-not upwards;

they-are like-a-treacherous bow. (6)

*

Their-princes fall by-the-sword

because-of-the-insolence-of their-tongues. (5)

This-is their-derision

in-the-land-of Egypt. (4)

This 19-line poem resembles the 19-line poem of 2:2–8[4–10] with a central peak, and secondary peaks in the center of each half. The central peak 12b has two similes, "as birds," and "as the report," which are arranged chiastically (Andersen & Freedman, *Hosea*, 464) with the verbs, "I'll bring them down" and "I'll chastise them," rhyming in the middle making an ABBA inverted parallelism. The lemmas of the peak-initial *k ʿwp* 'as birds' have the value of 11 and 39, and the penultimate *k šm ʿ* 'as report' has 11 and

50. *K* 'as' also comes in 7:11 with "*as* a *pth* 'silly'=44 dove," then in 12a with "*as* they go I'll spread my net over them," and in 7:16 "*as* a defective bow." *Yrd* 'bring-down' has the value of 34. The central words in each colon of the peak, "sky" and "hear/report," have alliteration by both beginning with *šm*. The article *h* 'the' on "sky" has the value of 5, and is the only *h* in the poem. "I'll chastise them as the *report*" in the peak connects with "insolence of their tongues" at the end, "Their princes fall by the sword because of the insolence of their tongues." Besides in the peak at 7:12b, *ysr* 'chastise'=45 is also found in 7:15 "train." Dearman (*Hosea*, 2010:211) points out that for God to "discipline" or "chastise" is part of the "covenant" common to Hosea and Deuteronomy. Having "chastise" in this peak in 7:12 adds prominence because of its connection with the key word "covenant" for the book. The lemma *ʿdh* 'assembly/congregation' has the value of 25. The preposition *l* 'to'=12 comes on "assembly" in the peak, and twice after the peak. The 2+3 irregular cola of the lines on each side of the peak also set it off. While the peak has inverted ABBA line parallelism, the line after it, v. 13, has strophic parallelism. More specific seconding typical of parallelism comes in 13 with "woe" becoming 'destruction'=25, and "strayed" becoming *pšʿ* 'rebelled'=54.

The mid-half strophe of 10 is counted as a secondary peak as in other long poems. The first line is the central line of the first half, and is a short tetrameter. It also gains prominence by having the same words as the secondary peak of 5:5, "And the pride of Israel testifies against him/in his face." All lemmas in 10a except *b* 'against/in' have symbolic values, *w* 'and'=6, *ʿnh* 'answer'=35, *gʾwn* 'pride'=24, *yśrʾl* 'Israel'=64, and *pnh* 'face'=36. The next line, although central to the first half only by strophe and not by line, can also be counted as a secondary peak since it has the only divine names in the poem, "LORD their God," and has the important thematic words "not return" and "not seek." These verbs are parallel and rhyme with both ending with *û*. *Bqš* 'seek' has the value of 42 or 6x7. The lemma *lʾ* 'not'=13 comes twice in the secondary peak in verse 10b, and four more times in the poem. It is also marked by coming 65 or 13x5 times in the book. The lemmas *ʾl* 'to' and *YHWH* have the values of 13 and 26. "To" also comes in 14 and 15 with "to me" referring to YHWH. The last two words in 10 are *kl* 'all'=23 and *zʾt* 'this"=30. Since "God" comes x26, and "return" comes x23, all lemmas in 7:10b except *b* 'in' have either symbolic values or total symbolic counts for the book. Through the first secondary peak (10) God is referred to in the third person; but from 12 to the end God is in the more personal first person.

Since a second line 10b is being counted as secondary peak after the central short line 10a in the first half, it is possible to consider adding 14a to the short 14b as a secondary peak in the second half. The whole verse 14 has ABBA chiasmus with A "they do not cry to me" and A' "they rebel against me" with "me" referring to God, enclosing B "wail on their beds" and B' "gash themselves" (as HOTTP, NRSV, GNT) referring to the idolatrous cult. "Not cry" has symbolic values of *l'*=13 and *z'q*=42, and *yll* 'wail=34. However, for closer consistency with other long poems I have chosen to keep the secondary peak in the second half limited to 14b, the short quarter line, rather than the whole strophe of 14. 14b repeats "grain and new wine," which was thematic in part 1, in an extreme form of worship, "gashing themselves." The long combination "over=grain(+)and-new-wine" proposed in 14b resembles the peak emphasis given by overloading syllables in the similar criticism of ritual worship in 5:6. The second colon, "They turn away from me," emphasizes the reason for their punishment. The final key word "against-me" with the preposition *b* in this secondary peak is repeated at the end of 13b, and three other prepositions with "me" describing offenses against God are concentrated in this half, totaling six references. "To me" (14a) and "for me"(15) are the same word with the lemma *'l=13*, coming on both sides of this secondary peak. The strophic structure falls into couplets except the secondary peak at 14b which is the last line of a triplet. These features all help to emphasize the secondary peak in 14b.

Overall unity besides the metrical chiasm is supported by the following correspondences of mainly synonyms rather than repeated words:

A peoples (1st line, second word) (8a)

B cake (*'ugâ*) not turned (2nd line) (8b)

C not (3rd line) (9a)

D they <u>don't</u> return . . . they <u>don't</u> seek (6th line) (10b)

E they go (line before peak) (12a)

F <u>AS</u> BIRDS . . . I'LL BRING THEM DOWN (12b)

F' I'LL CHASTISE THEM <u>AS</u> THE REPORT . . . (12c)

E' they strayed (line after peak) (13a)

D' they <u>don't</u> cry to me (6th line) (14a)

C' not (3rd line) (16a)

B' derision (<u>la 'gam</u> last line 1st colon) (16c)

A' Egypt (last line, last word). (16c)

"Egypt" in 11 and 16, *lb* 'sense/heart' in 11 and 14, and *šwb* 'return/turn' in 10 and 16 give further balance by having the same Hebrew words in each half.

The repetition of *whw' l' yd'* 'and-he does-not know' gives emphasis to 7:9. The lemmas all have symbolic values in the theological set, *w*=6, *hw'*=12, *l'*=13, and *yd'*= 30. The word *śybh* 'grey hair' may also be translated on the basis of an Akkadian cognate as "mold," which would continue the metaphor of the "cake" (see Andersen and Freedman, *Hosea*, 467 and Eidevall, *Grapes*, 117).

The reference to "their princes fall" in 7:16 ties this poem to the previous poem ("princes" in 7:3 and in the peak at 5, and "their rulers fall" in 7:7 as epiphora with 7:16). The "cake not turned" in 7:8 also ties this poem to the "baker" and his activities in 7:4–6 in the previous poem.

In the first line the lemma *bll* 'mix' has the value of **26**, and comes only this time in Hosea, suggesting authorial intent. Verse 13 has two lemmas with the value of **26** giving it prominence. The first is *pdh* 'redeem' in "I would redeem them," and the second is *dbr* 'speak' in "but they speak lies against me." *Kzb* 'lies' has the value of 20. Instead of just verbal suffixes, 13c also has emphatic full pronouns *'nky* 'I'=36, and *hm* 'they'=18 emphasizing the contrast between the two participants, God and Ephraim/Israel. The shorter full pronoun *'ny* 'I'=25 begins verse 15, again emphasizing the contrast. Other lemmas with symbolic values are *hpk* 'turn'=33, *zrq* 'sprinkle=46 or 23x2 (only here in Hosea), *qr'* 'call'=40, *'wy* 'woe'=17, *ndd* 'stray'=22, *yll* 'wail'=34 or 17x2 (only here in Hosea), *ḥzq* 'strengthen'=34 or 17x2 (only here in Hosea) (*zrw'* 'arms'=49), *ḥrb* 'sword'=30, *zw* 'this'=13, and *'rṣ* 'land=39.[29] Note the above "only here in Hosea" for the first 26 value, and for 46 (23x2) and two 34s (17x2), which may indicate choosing lemmas with divine-name factors. Also note that the revised count of 98 word-stress units is the sum of the four divine-name numbers 17, 23, 26, 32. The number 98 is also important in Song of Songs as a theological marker (see Bliese, *Count*, 63). The MT 97 word-stress is not symbolic. The two places where hyphens were found to be easily deleted (7:10a and 13a), and the added hyphen in 14b were done for chiastic balance without reference to a symbolic total.

8:1–4a Four Pentameters and a Final Hexameter, Central Poem of Book (But Chiastic Central Emphasis; 30 words; 115 letters; MT 27 word-stress units, revision **26**; 34 lemmas of which 10 or 29.41% have divine-name values, the 7th highest of the 45 poems)

1 To=your-mouth, the-trumpet;
as-an-eagle over=the-house-of the-LORD; [2+3](5)

29. Other lemmas with factors of 5 and 6 are *hyh* 'is' x2, *'gh* 'cake'=24, *bly* 'not'=24, *'kl* 'devour'=24, *w* 'and'=6 x12, *ywnh* 'dove'=35, *'yn* 'not'=25, *'šwr* 'Assyria'=48, *'šr* 'when/that'=42, *r'* 'evil'=36, *rmyh* 'treacherous'=48, and *z'm* 'derision'=36.

Because they-broke my-COVENANT,
and-against=my-law they-rebelled. (5)

*

2 **To-me they-cry, "My-God,**
we-Israel know-you!"
[or "**O-God-of Israel, we-know-you!**"] (22 letters) (5)

*

3 Israel spurned the-GOOD;
an-enemy will-pursue-him. (5)
4a They made-kings, but-not by-me;
they-made-princes, but-I-didn't(+)know. [4+2](7/6)

This poem is structurally central to the whole book, and although a homogeneous line analysis seems best metrically, the center line has more features of prominence than the expected final line. This reversal of expectations follows literary tendencies for exceptional features at the peak, in this case the central peak of the book. The central peak line is especially marked by syntactic complexity, with a singular "my" and plural "we" in the same sentence. This anomaly has prompted the alternative translation "God of Israel." If this reading is chosen, the poet's placing "God" in the center of the line may account for the "discontinuous construct phrase" (Andersen & Freedman, *Hosea*, 490). In support of the reading "my God," note the use of the phrase also in 2:23[25] (final peak); 9:8 and 9:17. The first word of the central line is *lî* 'to me' referring to God, and the last word ends in -*ēl* meaning 'God,' which gives a chiastic arrangement of divine references in three of the five words in the peak, with the main word "God" in the center. There are 22 letters in this line with *l*'s on the ends, and one *y* in each word. *Y* begins the second word from each end, the final word, and also comes in the middle being the eleventh letter from each end. This may be a cryptic reference to YHWH with its initial *Y*.[30] With the above hyphenation the total number of **26** word-stress units could also be a reference to the numerical value of YHWH. (Also see 1:6b–7a and 11:5–7.) As noted in the discussion on "Overall Structure in Hosea" in chapter 3, the central words "God," "Israel" and "know" are all thematically important in the book as a whole. "God" significantly occurs **26** times in Hosea, and this is the 11th,

30. The middle word *ʾlhy* 'God' has one of its middle letters *l*, which has been noted as the central line of some acrostics such as Pss 25 and 34 (Freedman, "Acrostic," 416).

which is the base of the 22 set.[31] *Yśr ʾl* 'Israel'=64 or 32x2 occurs 44 times, and this is significantly the 23rd, which along with 32 is one of the four numbers used to represent YHWH. It also occurs in the next line after the peak. "Know" comes 15 times, which numerically suggests the value of *YH*, 10+5. "Know" is also strategically placed chiastically as the last word of the poem where God says "I didn't know" as the tenth occurrence.[32] The lemma *yd ʿ* 'know' has the value of 30, which has factors of all three of the letters of YHWH, **10x3** for *Y*, and **6x5** for *W* and *H*. The claim in the peak to "know God" is best taken as superficial (see 5:4 "they don't know YHWH," and Garrett, *Hosea*, 181, "the texts that follow . . . will demonstrate that the people did not know Yahweh or have him as their God"). The preposition *l* 'to,' which occurs 143=11x13, comes in the MT here in 8:2 the 70th time or 10x7. Seventy combines the factor ten, which numerically represents the *Y* of *YHWH*, together with the well-known seven of fullness. The value of *l* as a lemma is 12, with a factor of *W*=6. The strong word "cry" only occurs elsewhere at 7:14 in the previous poem, which is also in this central block. There the same two lemmas "cry" and "to-me" come with a negative, "They do *not* cry to me" (from the heart, but they wail upon their beds). It has the same accusatory context in both references. The lemma *z ʿq* 'cry' has the value of 42 or 6x7, which combines the six of *W* with the seven of the fullness set.

The first and last lines are balanced by both having irregular colometry. The first two lines and last two lines each form a normal couplet strophe, leaving the central line alone, and making a chiastic arrangement of strophes. The second and last lines also have internal parallelism semantically, but the central peak third line significantly does not. The parallelism of the last line has each colon having a third plural verb with the suffix û followed by the conjunction *w* 'but'=**6**, and by *l ʾ* 'not'=**13** in "they made kings but not" // "they made princes but not." Either the MT line length of seven word-stress units or the proposed six set off the last line from the others, which are pentameters. "But-I-didn't(+)know" is more natural combining the negative and verb with a hyphen. In the above analysis the line is analyzed in this way, reducing MT 27 word-stress units to the theological

31. The short form אלה comes twenty times, and the full form "Elohim" comes six times.

32. Eidevall (*Grapes*, 129) states well the relationship of these two occurrences of "know" in commenting on the final one. "This is probably a way of saying that the deity had not been consulted, and that the kings and princes of Samaria therefore lacked divine legitimization. However, the formulation points to v. 2. While the people claim (erroneously, it appears) that they know their god, the deity is said to know nothing about their doings."

26. A possible terrace pattern may also give emphasis to the final line, even if it is not analyzed as the peak:

over (1a)-against (1b)(same in Hebrew)

Israel (2)-Israel (3)

not-not (4)

The first and last lines are chiastically tied to the center. The last word of the poem repeats "know" in the peak, and YHWH the last word of the first line connects to "God" in the peak. "To me" in the peak ties to "by me" in the last line. The words "kings" and "princes" in the last line tie to these key words in the first poem of this part 3, (note "princes" in the first central peak at 7:5). Especially the similarity of this last line (8:4a) with the last line 7:7, by epiphora of "kings," "me," and "them," lends support for the juncture after 4a. It also shows beginning-to-center chiastic repetition in the poems in part 3.

Inverted parallelism with verbs enclosing nouns is found in, "They broke my covenant and against my law they rebelled" in the second line. This relates thematically to "Israel spurned the good" in the second line from the end (see Mays, *Hosea*, 116), giving thematic chiastic balance by lines. "COVENANT" (*bryt*=54 or **6**x9) and "GOOD" (*ṭwb*=17) are the *two unique words occurring only once in each of the five parts of Hosea*, so the fact that in this central block they are arranged in the *center* of the two lines adjacent to the central line of this central poem is another example of Hosea's artistry. As noted in the discussion on overall structure, since the central word of the line between them is "my-God," it may be intended as a supplementary message reading vertically, "the COVENANT of MY GOD is GOOD." The horizontal reading as a discontinuous construct "God-of Israel" allows for a play on words on "God" as the central word of the book, either as "God-of" or "my-God." This vertical positive reading is supported by the very positive poem 2:18–20[20–22], in which the word COVENANT occurs for the first time. It also ties part 1 to the central part as is typical in chiasmus. Eidevall (*Grapes*, 144) states that in the discourse unit 8:1—9:9 "the *covenantal* model plays the most prominent role . . . In 8:1 the nation's apostasy is spoken of in terms of covenant breach." Dearman (*Hosea*, 38) writes concerning 8:1, "Covenant and instruction, what we might call in summary fashion the "covenantal ethos," is another of the linguistic and thematic connections between Deuteronomy and Hosea. They both use the term *bĕrît* ('covenant') to describe YHWH's acquisition of Israel and his binding of himself to them."

Other lemmas with symbolic values are *ʾl* 'to'=13, *šwpr* 'trumpet'=64, *k* 'as'=11, *nšr* 'eagle/vulture'=55 (only here in Hosea, note that besides the factors 5x11, 55 is the sum of the two divine name numbers 23 and 32 based on *kbwd*), *byt* 'house'=34, *YHWH*=**26**, *y ʿn* 'because'=40, *w* 'and'=6 x3, *pš ʿ* 'rebel'=54, *ʾyb* 'enemy'=13, *hm* 'they'=18, and *mlk* 'made king'=36. "House of YHWH" comes once more in 9:4, which is often interpreted as the temple. Many see it here in 8:1 also as the temple rather than the "land." Note Wolff (*Hosea*, 137), Mays (*Hosea*, 115), Andersen and Freedman (*Hosea*, 406, and Garrett *Hosea* 181). It is also pointed out that the term "land of YHWH" comes unambiguously in 9:3. Eidevall (*Grapes*, 127) finds "it unlikely" that "house of YHWH" "refers to the land," and prefers "temple" for 8:1. However, Dearman (*Hosea*, 217) notes the relationship to Deut 28:49, "The Lord will bring a nation from far away, from the end of the earth, to swoop down on you like an eagle, a nation whose language you do not understand," and states, "the 'house' in Hos. 8:1 is probably a reference to Israel (land and people) as YHWH's household." Dearman gives an analysis of the Hebrew *bayit* 'house' as also having the meaning "household" on p. 44 supporting this interpretation, and also applies this interpretation to 9:4 on pp. 46 and 240. I agree that the context supports Dearman's "land and people" here, but am less convinced about 9:4 where the immediate context is "sacrifices" and "the feast of the Lord."

The various ideas of this poem are repeated in many places throughout the book, showing the central importance of the poem. The implied imperative in the first line "To your mouth the trumpet" applies well to God's command to Hosea as "watchman" (see 9:9). The following lines are then the main themes of his warnings. This ties this central poem to part 1 with God's imperative commands to Hosea in the action prophecies (four in chapter one and one in chapter three in regard to his wife and children). "To your mouth the trumpet" beginning this central poem is the only other candidate for a direct speech command to Hosea in the book. The repetition of the direct commands and watchman role for Hosea in the *beginning and center* of the book are typical for chiastic structures.

8:4b–8 Chiasm 7655 4 5567

(56 words; MT and revision 50 or 10x5 word-stress units; 63 lemmas of which 6 or 9.52% have divine-name values, the second lowest of the 45 poems)

4b They-*made* their-silver and-their-gold

into-idols for-themselves,

so-that it-be-destroyed. [3+2+2](7)

5 Spurn your-calf, Samaria,
    my-anger burns on-them. (6)

*

Until=when will-they-not(+)be-able to-be-pure;
    6 for-they-are from-*Israel*? (6/5)
And-an-artisan *made* it;
    it is-not(+)God. (6/5)

*

Truly,=broken-to-pieces is
    the-calf-of Samaria. (4)

#

7 Truly, they-sow the-wind;
    and-they-reap the-whirlwind. (5)
The-standing-grain has=no head,
    it-*yields* no=meal. (5)

*

If it-would *yield*,
    aliens would-swallow-it;
8 *Israel* is-swallowed-up! [2+2+2](6)
Now they-are among-the-nations
    as-a-pot that(=)no-one wants. [3+4](6/7)

This poem shifts to the theme of idolatry. Placing the juncture before 8:4b as above, ties "idols" in 8:4b to the "calf of Samaria" theme of 8:5–6.[33] This juncture is also supported by the MT niphal (passive) masculine singular *yikkārēt* 'it will be cut off' agreeing with the thematic *ʿēgel* 'calf' in the next line and the peak.[34] There is anadiplosis at the juncture of the poems

33. Dearman (*Hosea*, 221) writes, "It is not clear whether the charge of idolatry in 8:4b–7 continues and elaborates upon the critique of the house of YHWH in 8:1–4a, or whether it is another passage now incorporated in a secondary collection of prophecies against Israel in ch. 8."

34. Although the verb is singular, which fits "calf," it is translated plural "to destroy themselves" in the LXX and Vulgate, and "to/for their own destruction" in NRSV, NIV, and GNT, and "To their own undoing" in NJPS. This presumably was done because of the plural references in 4a, which are carried over into 4b. The change of theme from making kings without God to idolatry for 8:4b–8 is minimized when 8:4a is taken as the conclusion to the previous poem rather than the opening line here.

with *hm* 'they' the first word in the last line of the previous poem, translated "themselves" in the first line of this poem. The word "he-spurned" in 8:5 has the same MT form (*zānaḥ*) as in 8:3, tying these poems together. The vocative context doesn't make sense with "he" so the imperative having the same consonants is proposed above as in NIV "throw out your calf-idol!" These are the only two occurrences of *znḥ* in Hosea.

The center is the shortest line, giving it emphasis, "Truly, broken to pieces is the calf of Samaria." The deictic "Truly" also sets it off. "Truly" also begins the following strophe at 7, and the same Hebrew word *kî* "for" begins 6 before the peak. This puts the chiastic peak occurrence in the center of the three. The reference to "calf" recalls animal references in other peaks (4:16; 5:6; 6:12). "Calf" and "Samaria" in the peak are repeated in the second line and they tie to "idols" in the first line. *Hyh* 'is' has the value of 20 in the peak. "Broken to pieces" (*šbbym*=48 or 6x8) is a singleton for Hosea giving it prominence in the peak. It ties chiastically to the graphic imagery of the "pot that no one wants" of the last line, and with "idols" "to be destroyed" in the first line.

Metrically the first and last lines have near balance with irregular cola structure of 3+2+2 and 3+4. The last colon in each is climactic. In 8:4b "That it be destroyed" is given as the *reason* for idolatry with the surprise *lm ʿn* 'so that.' *Lm ʿn* is a singleton with the value of 55 or 11x5 or 23+32, which suggests an intentional choice for metrical prominence. 8:4b also has a change from plural "idols" to singular "it," which gives prominence by the lack of agreement, and connects it with the "calf" in the next line and in the central peak.[35] *Yśr ʾl* 'Israel'=64 or 32x2 comes once in each half at 6a and 8a. "Made" (*ʿśh*=42) comes twice on each side of the central peak: in the first colon 4b, in 6b, and as "yield" in 7b and 7c.

A thematic change from condemnation of idolatry to agricultural and culinary imagery comes after the peak. There is a play on words with *ṣmḥ* 'standing grain'=39, and *qmḥ* 'meal'=40 in 7b. Dearman (*Hosea*, 227) notes the "alliteration" and "proverbial form." The consecutive values of 39 and 40 add a possible play on numbers for these words. "Whirlwind" following "wind" in 7a illustrates the more specific seconding of parallelism. The strophic pattern is regular couplets with the peak set off as a single line. MT and revised counts for word-stress units are 50 or 10x5 related to YH.

Other lemmas with symbolic values are *w* 'and'=6 x4, *l* 'to'=12 x2, *ʿṣb* 'idol'=36, *ḥrh* 'burn'=33, *ʿd* 'until'=20, *lʾ* 'not'=13, *ʾp* 'anger'=18, *mty*

35. See Andersen and Freedman (*Hosea*, 493), and Dearman (*Hosea*, 222) who discusses options including "a proleptic reference to the idolatrous calf explicitly mentioned in the next verse."

'when'=45, *ykl* 'be able'=33, *hw*ʾ 'it'=12 x2, *ḥrš* 'artisan'=49, *rwḥ* 'spirit'=34, *ʾyn* 'not'=25 x2, *bly* 'no'=24, *bl*ʿ 'swallow'=30, *k* 'as'=11, *kly* 'pot'=33.

8:9–13 Chiasm 3565 7 5653
(53 words; MT and revision 45 or 5x9 word-stress units; 60 lemmas of which 6 or 10% have divine-name values, the 3rd lowest of the 45 poems)

9 *Indeed,=they went-up to-Assyria . . .* (3)
Ephraim-is a-wild-donkey isolated(+)to-himself.
* [enjambment]
They-hired lovers. (6/5)
10 Even though(=)they-hire among-the-nations,
now I-will-gather-*them*. [4+2] (5/6)
And-they-will-begin to-diminish under-the-weight-of
the-king-of princes. (5)
#
11 **Indeed,=Ephraim multiplied altars for-sin,**
they-became=for-him altars for-sin. (7)
12 I-was-writing=for-him multitudes-of my-laws;
they-were-regarded as-something=alien. (5)
*
13 They-sacrificed the-sacrifices-of(+)my-loved-ones
and-ate flesh;
the-LORD is-not(+)pleased-with-*them*. [4+2] (6)
Now he-remembers their-iniquity,
and-punishes their-sin. (5)
. . . *They to-Egypt will-return.* (3)

The peak in 8:11 begins a thematic switch to sinful sacrifice. The play on the paradoxical meaning of the infinitive "altars to sin" rather than the expected "altars for sin" as a noun gives strong prominence.[36] Besides the repetition of the verb "sin/sinning" (*ḥṭ*ʾ=18 or 6x3) in the peak, the noun

36. Wolff (*Hosea*, 144) writes, "The statement is so astonishing and filled with excitement that its main catchwords are repeated: 'Altars for sinning!'" Lundbom ("Rhetoric," 306) also notes this repetition as an "embellishment" in the center of the poem.

comes in the next to the last line (*ḥṭ ʾt* =40 or 10x4 and 5x8). The repeated peak lemma *mzbḥ* ʻaltars'=30 (with factors of 10, 6 and 5) has the same root *zabāḥ* as "sacrifice," which comes twice in 13a, and has the value of 17. The preposition *l* ʻfor'=12 comes three times in the peak, twice with "for sin" and once between them with "for-him." "For-him" *lw* translated "to-himself" also comes in the first full line chiastically tying the beginning with the central peak. "For-him" is also in the next line making an ABABA pattern with "for-him, *for-sin, for-him, for-sin,* for-him" with the three central words in the peak. The central peak has further emphasis because of the deictic *kî* ʻIndeed,' which is also in the first line, in the third line as "though," and in the previous peak. "Ephraim" also comes in the second line as well as in the central peak. "Multiplied" in the peak has the same *rb* root as "multitudes" in the next line. The lemma *hyh* ʻbe' in the peak has the value of 20.

The characterization of Ephraim as a "wild donkey" gives a striking beginning to the poem. Eidevall (*Grapes*, 134–35) proposes applying the metaphor of Ephraim as a wild donkey who was isolated to himself "to the relation between people and God," where "independence can be seen as something negative." The wild donkey here "pictures the nation's arrogance in its attitude towards YHWH."

The first and last trimeter lines are counted as secondary peaks because of their shortness. The "discontinuous bicolon" of these first and last lines has been described by Lundbom ("Rhetoric," 300–308) and noted by Andersen and Freedman (*Hosea*, 502). They also note the inclusio "they," and the identical length (seven syllables) and chiastic structure of these two cola: "went up-to Assyria . . . to Egypt-return." The lemma *hm* ʻthey' has the value of 18, *ʿlh* ʻwent up' has the value of 33, and *ʾšwr* ʻAssyria' has the value of 48, giving prominence to the first line. Kidner (*Hosea*, 82) writes concerning the prominence of "return" in the last line, "perhaps the deepest thrust lies in the word ʻreturn.'"

Besides the inclusio "they," further chiastic patterns are seen in that the third line from each end has a final suffix "them," and an irregular cola [4+2] structure, giving symmetrical balance. The first "them" comes on *qbṣ* ʻgather,' which has the value of 39, and refers to God's judgment on *them*. This is balanced with the third line from the end "YHWH is not pleased with *them*." "Now" comes in the third line and the second line from the end. "Lovers" (*ʾhbym*) in the second line may relate to "my loved ones" (*hbhby*) in the third line from the end. The singleton root of *hbhby* is debated whether it is "give" (NIV) or "love" (RSV). "They" (*hm*) in the first and last lines of this 8:9–13 repeats 8:4a, the last line of the central poem of the book, and is anaphoric to "themselves" in the first line of 8:4b–8. Strophic divisions may be divided into 9a-b, 9c–10, 11–12 and 13, which with the enjambment are basically a couplet, a triplet, a couplet and a triplet. Note a similar pattern in 9:10—10:1 with two couplets followed by a triplet.

Other lemmas with symbolic values are *bdd* 'be isolated'=**10**, *w* 'and'=**6** x3, *ḥll* 'begin'=**32**, *mśʾ* 'weight'=36, *mlk* 'king'=36, *ktb* 'write'=35, *k* 'as'=**11**, *zwr* 'alien'=33, *YHWH*=**26**, *ʾkl* 'devour'=24, *lʾ* 'not'=**13**, *ʿwn* 'iniquity'=36, and *pqd* 'punish'=40. The revised word-stress counts for all five poems in this central part 3 are related to theologically symbolic numbers with (1) 46 or 23x2, (2) 98 as the sum of the four divine-name numbers 17+23+26+32, (3) the central poem with the most potent 26, (4) 50, with factors of 10 and 5, and (5) 45, with 5x9. MT differs in (2) with 97, and in (3) with 27.

This central block 7:3—8:13 has frequent references to "king(s)" and "princes," beginning with both in the first line 7:3, and coming again toward the end with "king of princes" in 8:10. The two terms come doubly also in 7:5 and as verbs in 8:4. In the center between the above doublets, "kings" in 7:7 and "princes" in 7:16 come individually. The *verbal* references of making kings and princes in 8:4 are thematically significant because of being the last line of the central poem condemning making rulers without God. All references refer to Israelite rulers, except the final reference in 8:10 which probably refers to the Assyrian "king of princes" in a final judgment in the series.

Part Four 8:14—10:1, 88 Lines

(Words: MT 496, Possible revision 495=11x41, 5x99; Lemmas: MT 626, Possible revision 625=5x125, see 9:6)

Sixth Block 8:14—10:1, 44 Lines, Key word "Multiply" for evil

(Words: MT 242=**22x11**, the alphabetical base; Lemmas MT 307, Possible revision 306=**17**x18, 6x51 deleting *l* at 9:6)

8:14 Three Tetrameters
(70 letters; 15 words; MT 13 word-stress units, revision 12; 21 lemmas of which 5 or 23.81% have divine-name values)

14 Israel(+)forgot his=Maker,
  and-built *palaces*. (26 letters) (5/4)
And-Judah multiplied
  fortified <u>cities</u>. (4)

But-I-will-send=fire on-his-cities,

and-it-will-consume her-*strongholds*. (4)

The setting of this block returns to times of prosperity before the Assyrian invasion portrayed in the previous two poems. The first colon of this new block, "Israel forgot his Maker," is thematic for the whole book in repetitions with "forget" or its parallel "not know." The final line of judgment is the peak of this homogeneous poem. The line comes from the repeated peaks at the beginning of Amos (1:4, 7, 10, 12, 14; 2:2, 5). Amos applies this punishment to seven nations around Israel, but continues with a different judgment prophecy for Israel; now Hosea adds these words to Israel a half century later. The prior knowledge of this line as an introduction to judgment prophecies was probably assumed by Hosea. The final shift to God as subject is significant, as well as the imagery of his "sending fire to consume."

Key words in the peak line with symbolic values are *ʾš* 'fire'=**22**, *ʾkl* 'consume'=24 or **6**x4, *ʿyr* 'city'=46 or **23**x2, and *ʾrmwn* 'stronghold'=54 or **6**x9. "City" is also in the previous line along with *bṣwr* 'fortified' with the same value of 46. The line has 25 letters, which may relate to the total of 70 in the poem and the 15 words, all with factors of 5. The peak is set off by a chiastic sequence *beginning in the first two lines* with synonyms and culminating in the two cola of the peak with "cities"; "palaces-cities; CITIES-STRONGHOLDS." (See Bliese, "Psalms 1–24," 268 and 291 on Pss 1 and 11 for other examples of this pattern.) The pronominal suffixes at the end of each colon in the final line have gender switch, with "his" in the first colon changing to "her" in the second, with apparently the same referents of Israel and Judah. Judah although masculine, resembles feminine nouns in -â. Such grammatical anomalies set off peak lines in Hosea (note 8:2 the central line of the book). "Judah" is considered by many as having replaced "Ephraim" after the book was brought south following the fall of Samaria.

The first line has **26** letters, which may be designed to emphasize the relationship of *ʿśh* 'Maker' to YHWH. "Maker" has the value of 42 or **6**x7. Eidevall (*Grapes*, 145) points to the "theme" of "making" for this section with references in 8:6–7 including "a workman *made* it; it is not God" in 8:6, and "the standing grain yields/*makes* no meal; if it would yield/*make*, aliens would swallow it" in 8:7, and "their Maker" here in 8:14. This divine name with a personal pronoun suffix is unique here in Hosea although it comes five times each in Job and Isaiah and twice in Psalms. In the central line the word "multiply" ties to the center of the previous poem, and its *rb* root is repeated twice in each of the following poems as another key word in the block.

Other lemmas with symbolic values in the poem are *w* 'and'=6 x5, *yśr 'l* 'Israel'=64, *škḥ* 'forget'=40, *'t* 'object marker'=23, and *yhwdh* 'Judah'=30.

9:1–9 Chiasm 445545666 5 (1)666545544
(114 words 6x19; MT 100=10x10 or 5x20 word-stress units, revision 96 or 6x16, deleting *l* at 9:6; 140 lemmas of which 34 or 24.29% have divine-name values)

1 Don't=rejoice, *Israel*,
unto=exalting like-the-nations; (4)
For you-have-played-the-harlot,
leaving your-*God*. (4)

*

You-have-loved harlot's-wages
on *all*=threshing-floors-of *grain*. [2+3](5)
2 Threshing-floor and-winepress will-not(+)feed-them,
and-*new-wine* will-fail(+)in-her. (7/5)

*

3 *They-will-not live*
in-the-land-of the-LORD; (4)
But-*Ephraim* will-return to-*Egypt*,
and-in-Assyria they-will-eat(+)unclean-food. (6/5)

*

4 They-will-not=pour-out *wine* to-the-LORD,
nor please=him with-their-sacrifices; (6)
It-will-be-for-them as-*bread*-of mourning;
all(=)who-eat-it will-be-polluted. (5/6)
For=their-*bread* is-for-their-throat;
it-will-not enter the-*house-of* the-LORD. [2+4](6)

*

5 What=will-you-do for-the-day-of the-festival,
and-for-the-day-of the-feast-of=the-LORD? (5)

#

6 Yes,=behold, (anacrusis) (1)

They-went-away from-destruction;
Egypt will-gather-them;
Memphis will-bury-them. [2+2+2](6)
Their-precious-things of-silver,
nettles will-possess,
thorns-will-be in-their-tents. [2+2+2](6)
7 The-days-of(+)punishment have-come;
the-days-of(+)paying-up have-come;
let-*Israel* know! [2+2+2](8/6)

*

"The-*prophet* is-a-fool,
the-man-of the-spirit is-mad," [2+3](5)
Because-of(+)your-great iniquity,
and-great hostility. (5/4)

*

8 He-is-the-watchman-of *Ephraim*,
the-*prophet* with(=)my-*God*. [2+3](4/5)
There-is-a-fowler's snare on=*all*=his-ways;
hostility in-the-*house-of*(+)his-*God*. (6/5)

*

9 They-became-deeply(=)corrupted
as-in-the-days-of Gibeah; (3/4)
He-will-remember their-iniquity;
he-will-punish their-sins. (4)

This 19-line chiasm resembles 2:2–8[4–10] and 7:8–16 in having a central peak, and secondary peaks in the middle of each half. The theme of agricultural produce is also common to all three poems. Dearman (*Hosea*, 236) notes that the theme of the "harlotry" of the "wayward wife" is also repeated from the poems in chapter 2. The central peak of 9:5 applies the end of agricultural produce in their land to their not having anything to offer on feast days, repeating the threat of 2:11[13]. As the climax of its previous stanza, the peak (9:5) is marked by the "abrupt change to second-person plural in this verse, the only occurrence of that person and number" (Andersen & Freedman, *Hosea*, 529). YHWH=**26** comes three times earlier, building up to the fourth YHWH in the peak. Four lemmas also have symbolic values: *mh* 'what'=18 or **6**x3, *'śh* 'do'=42 or **6**x7, *mw'd* 'festival'=39 or 13x3, and *ḥg* 'feast'=**11**. "Day" comes twice in the peak, twice in 7, and near the end in 9. The preposition *l* 'for'=12 or **6**x2 comes twice in the peak and seven times total concentrated in 4–6. The peak also has rhetorical questions beginning with, "What will you do?" with the expected answer that they will not be able to do the normal feasting.

Kl 'all'=**23** comes in the third line from each end as well as in 4B. There is also balance with "God" (1B), "LORD" (3A, 4A), and "house of the LORD" (4C) in the first half, and "God" (8A) and "house of his God" (8B) in the second half. *Byt* 'house' x2 has the value of 34. "Ephraim" also comes in both halves in 3B and 8A, "Israel" comes in 1A and 7A, and "Egypt" in 3B and 6A. The lines on each side of the center both have irregular cola structure with 2+4 and 2+2+2 instead of normal 3+3 hexameters, adding to the balance.

The secondary peak in the center (3a) of the first stanza is the strong condemnation "not live in the land of the LORD." The lemma of every word has symbolic value, *l'* 'not'=**13**, *yšb* 'live'=33, *'rṣ* 'land'=39, *YHWH*=**26**. This is the first of four YHWH, and it gives emphasis to this middle line of the first half. "Not" (*l'*) comes five times in the poem. This first stanza has a semantic pattern of chiasmus of words in the same semantic frame with this condemnatory secondary peak 3a in the center as follows:

A rejoice . . . exalt 1a — A' festival . . . feast 5
B God 1b — B' LORD 4c
C grain 1c — C' bread 4b,c
D new wine 2 — D' wine 4c
E LAND OF LORD 3a — E' Egypt . . . Assyria 3b

The second stanza, which begins in 9:6 after the peak, is set off by an initial two-word anacrusis hyphenated in MT, "Yes,=behold," (*ky* '*yes*,' *hnh* 'behold.' "Behold" has the value of 24 or **6**x4). There is a play on words in 9:6 with *tqbbṣm* 'she will gather them' and *tqbbrm* 'she will bury them,' which are identical except for one letter. The first strophe in this stanza is unique with all three lines tricola [2+2+2].[37] The warning "Let Israel know" is thematic for the book. Eidevall (*Grapes*, 142) notes that "'knowing' at the end of 7a provides a link back to the utterance in 8:2." As noted earlier, 8:2 is the peak of the central poem in Hosea. The secondary peak 7c in

37. Dearman (*Hosea*, 15) notes the first two of these three tricola, "An uncommon form is a verse with two tricola, as in 9:6."

the middle line of the second stanza is set off by being the only *second person singular* reference in the stanza, "Because of *your* great iniquity and great hostility." It relates to the first three lines of the poem with condemnations in the same second person singular. This secondary peak line has repetition of *rb* 'great/multitude'=22, the key word of the block, and of *'wn* 'iniquity'=36 in the last line, and of "hostility" in 8. The whole line also has syntactic complexity by being a prepositional phrase *'l* 'because of.' The lines on each side of the stanza center 7c have the exceptional cola pattern of 2+3 and the word "prophet" in common, setting off the secondary peak between them. A nice chiastic sequence with a word in each colon of this line and its two adjacent lines highlights this secondary peak as diagrammed below. The structure emphasizes the great offense of the people who have turned against the "prophet" and "man of the spirit," calling him "a fool" and "mad" in 7B. In the central line of the chiasmus, which is a secondary peak by being central to the second half of the poem, the people are accused of having "great iniquity" and "great hostility" in 7C. Then in 8A the "prophet" is identified positively as "the watchman" whom God has placed to guard them.[38]

A prophet 7Ba — A' prophet with my God 8Ab

B man of the spirit 7Bb — B' watchman 8Aa

C *great iniquity* 7Ca — C' *great hostility* 7Cb

The last line 9b with God as the subject who *remembers their iniquity* and *punishes their sins* is also climactic. The last two lemmas *pqd* 'punish' and *ḥṭ'ṭ* 'sin' both have the value of 40, which is used in the Bible as a general number for large quantities. This looks like a play on numbers showing the *greatness* of sin resulting in punishment. The end has the same theme as 9:7a with "punishment" and "days" twice including "days of paying up" coming in the climax of that strophe. "Punishment" *pqwdh*=45 (5x9), and *šlwm* 'paying-up'=52 (26x2), both occur only here in Hosea, suggesting a numerical choice to emphasize the concept. The final line in 9:9 has special prominence since the same Hebrew words come near the end of the previous block in 8:13, "He remembers their iniquity, and punishes their sin." Eidevall (*Grapes*, 125) lists nine various lexical correspondences between 8:1–13 and 9:1–9, which I see as a buildup by repetition ending with this repeated clause in both 8:13 and 9:9. The reference to "the days of Gibeah" in both 9:9 and 10:9 recalls the terrible account of

38. Dearman (*Hosea*, 246) observes, "Hosea's prophecies take on the role of a verbal shofar," relating the "watchman" with the *shofar* 'trumpet' in 8:1, which begins the central poem of the book by my analysis.

the rape of a concubine in Jdg 19–20, and also can refer to the historical origin of the first King Saul of Israel as the beginning of political evils (see Mays, *Hosea*, 131, 143). Support for this political application comes in 9:15 which begins with "Every evil of theirs began at Gilgal" and ends with "all their officials are rebels."

This poem including the peak line has strong internal parallelism as found in chapter 2. Strophic structure is chiastic with a triplet on each side of the peak, setting off the single peak line which stands in a strophe of its own. The beginning and end of the poem each have three couplets. Since couplets are the most common cola structure in Hosea the series of three [2+2+2] hexameters in the strophe after the peak gives an emphatic staccato affect to the description of the punishment.

Other lemmas with symbolic value are the first six lemmas *ʾāl* 'don't'=13, *śmḥ* 'rejoice'=42, *yśr ʾl* 'Israel'=64, *ʾel* 'to'=13, *gyl* 'exalt'=25, *k* 'as'=11 x3, *znh* 'played the harlot'=26, *ʾtnn* 'harlot's wages'=51, *w* 'and'=6 x7, *kḥš* 'fail'=40, *ʾšwr* 'Assyria'=48, *ṭm ʾ* 'unclean'=**23**, *ʾkl* 'devour'=24 x2, *nsk* 'pour'=40, *yyn* 'wine'=34, *zbḥ* 'sacrifice'=**17**, *lḥm* 'bread'=33, *ṭm ʾ* 'make unclean'=**23**, *npš* 'throat'=52, *šd* 'destruction'=25, *qbṣ* 'gather'=39, *mp* 'Memphis'=30, *yrš* 'possess'=51, *ḥwḥ* 'thorns'=22, *ʾhl* 'tent'=18, *h* 'the'=5 x6, *yśr ʾl* 'Israel'=64, *yd ʿ* 'know'=30, *šg ʿ* 'mad'=40, *ʾyš* 'man'=**32**, *rwḥ* 'spirit'=34, *ṣph* 'watchman'=40, *pḥ* 'trap'=25, *drk* 'road'=35, *ʿmq* 'make deep'=48, *šḥt* 'corrupted'=51, *gb ʿh* 'Gibeah'=**26**. MT word-stress units of 100 or 10x10 or 5x20 are notable. The revised count of 96 or 6x16 is less symbolic, but is the same as the revised count in the next poem.

The boundaries of 9:1–9 follow MT. My boundary at 8:14 is supported by a paragraph in GNT and CEV. It should be noted that 9:1–9 and the previous poem 8:14 together (the first two in block six) make 22 lines. This resembles block two 2:9[11]—3:5 in which its 6 poems fit together in two groups of 22 lines.

9:10—10:1 Chiasm 4453(1)654544 5 445(2)4563544
(**22** lines, the extra 1-foot and 2-feet introduce stanzas; 113 words; MT 98 or 17+23+26+32 word-stress units, revision 96 or 6x16; 146 lemmas of which 27 or 18.49% have divine-name values)

10 As-grapes in-the-desert
  I-found *Israel*. (4)
As-first-fruit on-a-fig-tree [in-its-first-season]
  I-saw your-fathers. ([5]/4)

*

They came to-Baal=peor,

and-consecrated-themselves to-shame; (5)

And-became as-disgusting as-the-thing-they-loved. (3)

#

11 *As-for-Ephraim,* (extra, anacrusis) (1)

Their-glory will-fly-away like-a-bird;

no-birth, no-pregnancy, no-conception. (6)

12 *Even if=they-raise their=children,*

I-will-bereave-them of-everyone. (5)

Yes,=also=woe to-them

when-I-turn from-them. (4)

|#

13 Ephraim when=I-saw-it,

was-Tyre[palm-trees] planted in-a-pasture. [2+3](5)

But-Ephraim will-bring-out

his-children to=the-slaughter. (4)

*

14 Give=them, O-LORD,

what(=)will-you-give? (3/4)

Give=them a-womb that-miscarries,

and-breasts that-are-dry. (5)

*

15 *All*=their-iniquity is-in-Gilgal;

yes,=there I-hated-them. (4)

Because-of(+)the-wickedness of-their-deeds,

I-will-drive-them out-of-my-house. (5/4)

I-will-not love-them again;

all=their-princes are-rebels. (5)

#

16 *Ephraim is-blighted*; (extra, as anacrusis) (2)

Their-root is-dried-up;

they-don't=yield fruit. (4)

Even if they-bear-children,
I-will-kill their-precious(+)offspring. (6/5)

*

17 *My-God will-reject-them,*
because they-didn't obey him. [2+4](6)
And-they-will-be wanderers among-the-nations. (3)

#

10:1 A-luxuriant vine is-*Israel,*
yielding fruit=for-himself. (5)
As-his-fruit *multiplied,*
he-*multiplied altars.* (4)
As-his-land prospered (became GOOD),
he-improved *pillars.* (4)

The total MT words of Block 6 (8:14—10:1) is a significant 242, or **11x22**, which are the first two numbers of the alphabetical set of symbolic numbers. This last poem of the block is the **33**rd poem in Hosea and significantly has **22** lines. It has a chiastic structure of five stanzas. The outer two stanzas (9:10 and 10:1) have "Israel" in their first lines, the second stanzas from each end have "Ephraim" in the first line (11 and 16), and the center has "Ephraim" beginning its first two lines (13). The first and last stanzas have the themes of fruitfulness turning to apostasy. For example, "first-fruit" comes in the second line, and "fruit" in the second from the end. "Vine" and "fruit" are also in the third line from the end, and "grapes" in the first line. Similarly, apostasy is described by "consecrated themselves to shame" and "Baal-peor" in the beginning, and the criticism "he multiplied altars" and "improved pillars" at the end.

There is a possible play on numbers in the first stanza 9:10, with *yśr ʾl* 'Israel'=64 in "As grapes in the desert I found *Israel*," and *šqwṣ* 'disgusting'=64 (**32**x2) in "they became as *disgusting* as the thing they loved." "Disgusting" is a singleton coming only in this short secondary peak in Hosea. Although the symbolic use of 32 and its double 64 has been considered a later development in biblical numerology, this poem gives evidence of its use in the existing text of Hosea. Note two 32-value lemmas before "Israel" in 9:10, *ʿnb* 'grapes'=**32**, and *mṣ ʾ* 'found'=**32**, and another after the second "Israel" in 10:1, *šwh* 'yield'=**32**, which is another singleton in Hosea. "Disgusting"=64 also comes in 9:10 giving it two 64s and two 32s. *Kbwd* 'glory' with its values of 23 and 32 comes in v. 11 between this chiastic inclusio in both peripheral lines. These are the only 64s and 32s in this poem, and the fact that two of them are singletons suggests that they were intentionally chosen for their numerical values. Furthermore, "grapes" comes only once more, in 3:1 in a similar context of "the LORD loves the people of Israel, though they turn to other gods and love *raisin* cakes." Eidevall (*Grapes*, 149–50) notes that "grapes in the desert" is an oxymoron since grapes do not grow in a desert. He adds that the "main function is to express divine joy." This is clarified by the accompanying figure of the *first-fruit* on a fig tree, which gives special joy. Dearman (*Hosea*, 251) notes that *bikkûrâ* 'first ripe fig' is a "delicacy," and is related to the root *bkr* 'firstborn child,' playing "on the privilege of Israel's adoption as firstborn" in the wilderness.

The second stanzas from each end (9:11–12 and 16–17) continue the chiastic parallelism with the themes of sterility and death of offspring. *Ldh* 'pregnancy' in 11 and *yld* 'bear'=**26** in 16 come from the same root in Hebrew. Note that the sixth lines from each end of the poem are 12a, "Even if they raise their children, I will bereave them of everyone," and 16c "Even if they have children, I will kill their precious offspring." These lines together with the hexameters beyond them (11–12A and 16B–17A) are counted as secondary peaks since they are the quarter lines in a long poem. The first lines of these mid-half stanzas both begin with a kind of anacrusis, having the word "Ephraim" followed with "their glory will fly away" in the secondary peak 11, and "Ephraim is blighted" in 16. This continues with "no birth, no pregnancy, no conception" in 11, and the word pair "their *root* is dried up; they yield no *fruit*" applied to "children" in 16 (see Eidevall, *Grapes*, 154–55). "Glory will *fly away*" in 11 is matched as an inclusio in the stanza 9:11–12 by "when I turned from them," supporting "glory" also referring to God (see Andersen and Freedman, *Hosea*, 542, and Garrett, *Hosea*, 200).[39] Note that *kbwd* 'glory' has both the theological value of **23** by the alphabetical sequence, and **32** by the mathematical count. It is also the 22nd word in the poem. "Glory" in the fifth line 9:11 is balanced in the fifth line from the end 9:17 with the only occurrence of "God," coming in the matching quarter secondary peak of 16b–17a. The referent for "glory" is thereby signaled chiastically to be God. This also adds support to an intentional use in Hosea of the two calculations of kbwd, 23 and 32, as divine-name numbers. Lemmas with **23** come four times, and those with **32** and 64 come three times each in this poem (counting both occurrences of "Israel"=64). The large total of ten forms relating numerically to *kbwd* suggest intentional choosing to use

39. For example, "their glory" is used as a divine circumlocution in Ps 106:20, "They exchanged their glory for the image of an ox that eats grass." Although I interpret "glory" as a reference to God, it could possibly also refer sarcastically to fertility cult idolatry or *fruitfulness* in regard to the name "Ephraim."

lemmas with the same values as *kbwd*. Besides those with the value of 32 and 64 listed above, those with **23** are *kbwd*, *ʾt* object marker, and *kl* 'all' x2. The construct *kbd* without *w* has the value of **17** for the alphabetical count, and **26** for the mathematical count. These are the basic theological numbers for YHWH, and they are also represented in this poem. **26** comes four times (*rʾh* 'see' x2, *YHWH*, and *yld* 'bear'), and **17** once *ʾwy* 'woe.' In verse 11 "bird" and "fly" both have the lemma *ʿwp* with the value of 39, and are preceded by *k* 'as' with the value of **11**. Also in 11 of this secondary peak the contiguous words *bṭn* 'womb'=25 (**5x5**), and the singleton *hrywn* 'conception'=55 (**5x11** or **23+32**) suggest a stylistic attention to symbolic numbers.

In the corresponding secondary peak of 16b–17a the symbolic lemmas *yld* 'bear'=**26**, and *šmʿ* 'hear/obey'=50 give prominence. These are followed in the short secondary peak 17b with *ndd* 'wanderer'=22, and *hyh* 'be'=20, which also comes in the corresponding short secondary peak in 10D "*became* as disgusting" matching "they *will be* wanderers" in 17b. Garrett (*Hosea*, 198) in a chiastic analysis with many of the same parallels noted above also notes that the reference to Tyre in 13 is parallel to Gilgal in 15. The lemma *ṣr* means Tyre (NIV), or as *HOTTP* recommends "a grove of palm trees" or as in NRSV "a young palm" based on an Arabic cognate. This fits the context of "planted in a pasture." MT spells it with a *waw* as *ṣwr*, which has the surface value of 44. This looks like another pun of a name with a related meaning as in 5:2 with Shittim and "rebels." The function here adds the place name Tyre in the second stanza to chiastically fit Gilgal in stanza four on the other side of the peak.

The bimeter extra line 16a "Ephraim is blighted" stands outside the metrical chiasm as an exception. The anacrusis serves to introduce its stanza. It is the fifteenth line of the poem, and perhaps significantly begins with *h*, the numerical equivalent of five, and has a *y* the equivalent of ten. (See 7:1b and 14:3[4]c for similar extra lines with possible cryptic numerical markings.)

The central peak of the poem is 14B, "Give them a womb that miscarries, and breasts that are dry." Garrett (*Hosea*, 198) writes, "the prophet's prayer is the pivotal point of the chiasmus." This prayer is especially prominent by referring to the descendants of Joseph in a reversal of the blessing Jacob gave to Joseph in Gen 49:25 "blessing of the breasts and of the womb" (see Garrett, *Hosea*, 202). Symbolic lemmas are *ntn* 'give'=50, *škl* 'miscarry'=44 (also as "bereave" in 12A), *šd* 'breasts'=25, and *ṣmq* 'dry'=50. This emphasizes the theme of sterility as God's punishment for their apostasy and their idolatry with fertility religion as noted in the end stanzas. The contiguous 25 and 50 suggest another play on the number *H*=5 as noted in 11. (Also note the singletons in the continuous words *štl* 'planted'=55 and *nwh* 'pasture'=25 in 13. There is also a contiguous *srr* 'rebellious'=55 and *nkh* 'blighted/stricken'=30 or 5x6 in 15–16. All three lemmas with the value of 55 including *hrywn* 'conception' are singletons, which gives support for seeing an intentional design to include lemmas linked to 55 as the sum of the two divine numbers 23 and 32 based on *kbwd*.) Andersen and Freedman (*Hosea*, 539) note the "climactic" centrality of this "prophet's prayer" in 14 in an overall chiastic structure that has different borders from that presented here. Concerning this peak they say, "The use of imperative verbs to issue peremptory commands to the deity is startling" (544). The repetition in 14 of "give-them" and "give" in the question in its previous line builds up to the same word in the peak. The break in thought with the question addressed to YHWH=26 "What will you give?" further sets off the peak line. The peak has well-formed semantic parallelism with "a womb that miscarries//and breasts that are dry." This is a reversal of normal patterns of dropping parallelism at peak. This parallelism ties the central peak to the final couplet where besides semantic parallelism every word matches its counterpart with alliteration and or rhyme in a beautiful structure:

כְּרֹב לְפִרְיוֹ הִרְבָּה לַמִּזְבְּחוֹת kĕrōb lĕpiryô hirbâ lammizbĕḥôt
As-his-fruit multiplied, he-multiplied altars.
כְּטוֹב לְאַרְצוֹ הֵיטִיבוּ מַצֵּבוֹת: kĕṭôb l᾿arṣô hêṭîbû maṣṣēbôt
As-his-land prospered, he-improved pillars.

The final two lines total 39 letters, and have four symbolic lemmas: *rb* 'multiplied'=22, *mzbḥ* 'altars'=30, *ṭwb* 'GOOD/prospered'=17, *ʾrṣ* 'land'=39.

The central stanza has a kind of inclusio with the first and last lines with nostalgia, "Ephraim when I saw it was to be palm trees planted in a pasture" (13) (translation following *HOTTP*, 250), and "I will not love them again" (15c). The second lines from the ends of this stanza also correspond, with "bring out" (13b) and "drive out" (15b). Besides the secondary peaks in the similar 5th and 6th lines from each end noted above, the overall poem is also tied together chiastically by the similarity of the short trimeter secondary peaks the fourth lines from each end, which both begin with the same Hebrew word *hyh=20* (in spite of the difference in translation): "And became as disgusting as the thing they loved" (10d), and "And they will be wanderers among the nations" (17b).

Other symbolic lemmas are the six more *k* 'as'=11 totaling seven, *mdbr* 'desert'=39, *bkwrh* 'first-fruit'=44, *tʾnh* 'fig-tree'=42, *hm* 'them'=18, *w* 'and'=6 x9, *l* 'to'=12 x10, *bšt* 'shame'=45, *ʾdm* 'man'=18, *ʾšr* 'that'=42, *ʾl* 'to'=13, *mh* 'what'=18, *glgl* 'Gilgal'=30, *šm* 'there'=34, *śnʾ* 'hate'=36, *rʿ* 'wickedness'=36, *byt* 'house'=34, *grš* 'drive out'=44, *lʾ* 'not'=13 x2, *ysp* 'again/add'=42, *ybš* 'dry up'=33, *bly* 'not'=24, *ʿśh* 'do'=42, *gpn* 'vine'=34, and the singleton *bqq* 'luxuriant'=40. The 98 MT word-stress units have the sum of the four divine name numbers, 17, 23, 26, 32. The revised 96 or 6x16 is the same as the previous poem.

The strophic structure is patterned with a stanza of two couplet strophes followed by a triplet stanza, on each end. The central stanza significantly has two couplet strophes and a triplet all in one stanza. The strophe of 15 has an inclusio of "all" beginning the first and last cola.

Beginning this poem at 9:10 follows MT and most translations. Ending it after 10:1 rather than as MT at 9:17 was chosen since it gives 44 lines and the key word GOOD for the block. It also fills the chiasmus of 9:10—10:1 better with an inclusio of "grapes" and "first-fruit on a fig tree" in 9:10, and "luxuriant vine" and "fruit" x2 in 10:1.[40] I also found that the metrical and thematic chiastic balance of the resulting poems gives support for the change.[41] The resulting symmetrical use of the root *rb* 'multiply' in the second line from each end of this block of 44 lines (5:14 and 10:1 x2) is noteworthy. It also comes twice as "great" in the secondary peak of 9:7, giving cohesion with references in all three poems of the block. We will see that the following poem 10:2–8 also has similar chiastic correspondences of words by using this juncture.

Seventh Block 10:2—11:7, 44 Lines, 254 words, "Be destroyed or Lifted up"

(Words: MT 254; Possible revision 253=23x11 deleting *'l* in 10:5 as LXX; Lemmas MT 319=11x29, Possible revision the same 319 by replacing the lemma by dividing "idolatrous priests" into *k* 'as' and "rebel," see table 4)

40. Garrett (*Hosea*, 198) by ending the poem at 9:17 lists an inclusio of only "A Israel found in the desert (v. 10a)" and "A' Israel a wanderer among the nations (v. 17b)" in his chiastic display, missing the repetition of fruitfulness. On 207 he notes the lack of connection to 10:2 (which is a new poem in my analysis) unless his interpretation of "Israel as a false vine that deceives its owner by yielding false fruit" is read in 10.1. Garrett writes, "Verse 2, which has as its premise that the heart of the people is deceitful, is a non sequitur unless one reads v. 1 as described above. That is, it is difficult to see any connection between an "abundant harvest" (implied in the traditional interpretation) and false hearts." By starting a new poem and block at 10:2 the traditional interpretation is fine, and fits the chiasmus of 9:17—10:1 well.

41. The first poem of block six has twelve word-stress units and the other two poems in this block have 96 units each (6x16). The fact that all three poems can be analyzed with word-stress units totaling multiples of six here in block six is interesting. The total for the block is 204, 6x34 or 12x17, with 17 being the short count for YHWH.

10:2–8 Chiasm 4556666 5 6666556 (long emphatic end)

(Words 90 or 10x9 and 5x6x3; word-stress units MT 80 or 10x8 and 5x16, revision 83, or 84 or 7x12 or 6x14 as the next poem if the central peak here is made a hexameter; 106 lemmas of which 16 or 15.09% have divine-name values)

2 Their-heart is-deceitful;

now they-will-bear-their-guilt. (4)

He will-break-down their-*altars*;

he-will-*destroy* their-*pillars*. (5)

*

3 Indeed, now they-say,

"We-have no(+)*king*. (6/5)

Indeed,[or 'For'] we-don't fear the=LORD,

and-as-for-a-*king* what=will-he-do=for-us?" [4+2] (6)

*

4 They-speak words

making COVENANTs with-empty oaths; [2+4] (6)

So-judgment sprouts like-poison

on the-furrows-of the-fields. (6)

*

5 Over-the-calves-of Beth Aven

the-inhabitants-of Samaria tremble. (6)

Indeed,=over-it mourn his-people,

and-his-idolatrous-priests over-it. (5)

* {note that indeed has no hyphen twice in 3}

They-wail over(=)its-glory,

because(=)it-departed from-it. (4/6)

6 Also=it will-be-carried to-Assyria,

a-tribute to-the-great *king*. (26 letters) (6)

*

Shame will-overtake Ephraim,

and-Israel will-be-ashamed of-its-counsel. (6)

7 The-*king*-of Samaria will-perish

as-a-chip on=the-face-of(=)the-water. (5/6)

*

8 And-the-high-places-of Aven will-be-*destroyed*,

the-sin-of Israel. (5)

Thorn and-thistle will-grow-up

on(=)their-*altars*. (4/5)

*

And-they-will-say to-the-mountains, "Cover-us;"

and-to-the-hills, "Fall on-us." (long end) (6)

This poem 10:2–8 has chiastic correspondences in *mzbḥ* 'altars'=30 in the second line from each end, and *mlk* 'king'=36 in the fourth line from each end. "King" comes again on each side in 3a and 6a. The center of this chiasm is the mourning over the idolatrous calf in 10:5–6. The line 6a second after the peak has **26** letters adding prominence along with the "great king," who will carry away the calf. The third masculine singular object *ʾwtw* 'him' referring to the calf has plene spelling rather than *ʾtw* (see Gen 39:12 and 2 Kgs 9:27). This gives emphasis to the calf relation to the peak, and makes the line have 26 letters. Besides "great" as in NRSV, RSV, NIV, GNT and CEV, *yrb* has also been translated as a name Ιαριμ LXX, or Jareb KJV and ASV, or as "patron" (king) in NJPS, or with a footnote "who will contend" in RSV and NRSV. The people's anarchy and irreligious attitude, or insincere words of repentance, in 3, is the basis of the punishment in 7. "No king" in 3 relates to "the king of Samaria will perish" in 7, and "what will he do for us" in 3b relates to a worthless "chip" in 7b, so it is not recommended to take "king of Samaria" in 7 as the calf as Mays suggests (*Hosea*, 142). Also see 10:15 "he will be completely destroyed, the king of Israel." Garrett (*Hosea*, 208) recommends that "We have no king" includes YHWH in a general rejection of "all royal rule." The fifth lines from each end correspond with useless speech, "speak words making covenants with empty oaths" in 4, relating to "ashamed of its counsel" in 6. "Counsel" (*ʿṣh*) is often used for political advice, good and bad (see 2 Sam 15:31; 16:20; 1 Kgs 12:8–14).

The *central peak* begins with the deictic "yes" (which is also in 3 twice as "Indeed" and once in 5b as "because"). Sarcasm gives it prominence with people mourning (*ʾbl*=15) over the idolatrous calves (*ʿgl*=36) of the previous line. The peak line is also chiastic with "over" enclosing "people" and "priests": "over it-his people; his idolatrous priests-over it." The four words all end in *–w*. The center line has further prominence with 22 letters. The term *kmr* 'idolatrous priests'=44 is also a very strong accusation, coming only here in Hosea. (Note that LXX reads it as a verb 'rebel.') "Aven," "Samaria" and *'mr* 'say'=34 have one occurrence in each half of the poem, giving balance. The first "Aven" comes in the derogatory name for Bethel, "Bet-aven," which has the total value of 55. The description of "the high places of Aven" as "the sin of Israel" is reminiscent of 1 Kgs 12:28–30 where Jeroboam's placing golden calves in Bethel and Dan "became a sin."

The final line 10:8c is long, and with its imperative direct quotations "Cover us" and "Fall on us" is also climactic. It also has assonance with four words ending in *û*, including the rhyming of both cola with -*nû*. The last word of the first colon has two *û* with kass*û*n*û* 'cover us.' There is also the word pair *hr* 'mountains'=25 and *gb 'h* 'hills'=**26**. The last root lemma is the preposition *'l* "on," which is also the last lemma in the central peak 5b "over" as well as coming once earlier in the peak. It significantly comes seven times in this poem making a build-up to the final climax. (Note that the LXX omits the second one in 10:5.) The dominance of hexameters throughout the poem may also indicate a buildup to this final hexameter climax. The lines group as strophic couplets except for the last long line, which although metrically one strophe, also has four syntactic units as the previous couplets. The single line strophe also gives prominence to the final line.

The connection with the previous poem should be noted. The second line repeats the sequence of "altars . . . pillars" found in the last two lines of the previous poem (anadiplosis). This serves to tie together the sixth and seventh blocks in part four of the book.[42] Cohesion in the other direction is also significant. The root *šdd* 'destruction' is in the beginning of this poem in 10:2, and twice at the end of the next one (10:14) giving thematic emphasis to this block. Synonyms *šmd* 'destroyed' in 8, and *dmh* 'perish'=22 in 7 and 'destroyed' in 10:15 in the next poem add to this theme.

Other lemmas with symbolic values are the first word *ḥlq* 'deceitful/slippery'=39, *'šm* 'guilt'=35, *hw'* 'he'=12, *mzbḥ* 'altar'=30 (which is in an ABBA near inclusio with *'mr* 'say'=34), *'yn* 'not'=25, *l* 'to'=12 x7, *l'* 'not'=13, *'t* object marker=**23** x2, *YHWH*=**26**, *w* 'and'=6 x8, *h* 'the'=5, *mh* 'what'=18, *'śh* 'do'=42, *dbr* 'speak'=**26**, *dbr* 'word'=**26**, *'lh* 'make an oath'=18, *bryt* 'covenant'=54, *prḥ* 'sprout'=45, *k* 'as'=11, *r'š* 'poison'=42, *mšpt* 'judgment'=60, *śdh* 'field'=30, *škn* 'inhabitants'=46, *gyl* 'tremble/exalt'=25, *kbwd* 'glory'=**23**, *glh* 'departed'=20, *'šwr* 'Assyria'=48, *ybl* 'carry'=24, *mnḥh* 'tribute'=40, *rb* 'great'=22 [or *yrb* 'Jareb'=**32**], *bšnh* 'shame'=42, *lqḥ* 'overtake'=39,

42. If the hyphen from *kî* 'indeed' in 5B is deleted as twice in 3, both this and the next poem can be analyzed with 84 word-stress units. This may be significant since they come in the *seventh* block and might refer to the multiplication of 7x12 equals 84. These follow two proposed 96-unit (or 6x16) poems in the previous *sixth* block, and might also relate to the 50-unit (5x10) poem in the *fifth* block.

yśr ʾl ʻIsrael'=64 x2, *ʿṣh* ʻcounsel'=39, *qṣp* ʻchip'=54, *pnym* ʻface'=54, *mym* ʻwater'=36, *bmh* ʻhigh place'=20, *ḥṭʾt* ʻsin'=40, *drdr* ʻthistle'=48, *ʿlh* ʻgrow up'=33. The total of 90 words with factors of 10 and 5, and of 80 MT word-stress units with factors of 10, 6, and 5 give theological prominence by the values of *Y*, *H*, and *W*.

10:9–15 Chiasm 57535464 6 46453575
(17 lines; 7 strophes; 97 words, or 96 if "Judah" is deleted in 10:11, see BHS 13; both MT & revision have 84=7x12 or 6x14 word-stress units; 119 lemmas of which only 15 or 12.61% have divine-name values)

9 From-the-days(+)of-Gibeah you-sinned, *Israel*;
there they-stood. (6/5)
Will-not(=)war overtake-them in-Gibeah
on(=)the-sons-of injustice? (26 letters) (5/7)

*

10 When-I-please I-will-<u>chastise</u>-them,
and-the-nations will-be-gathered *against*-them, [2+3] (5)
In-binding[<u>chastising</u>]-them <u>for</u>-their-double iniquity. (3)

#

11 But-Ephraim is-a-docile calf
loving <u>to</u>-thresh, (5)
And-I passed-by [or ʻput a yoke on' LUT, NIV, GNT, NEB]
her=fair neck. (4)
I-will-yoke Ephraim;
Judah will-pull-a-*plow*;
Jacob will-harrow=<u>for</u>-himself. [2+2+2] (6)
[or if Judah is deleted it becomes a 3+2 line:
I-will-yoke Ephraim, he-will-plow;][43]

*

12 Sow(+)<u>for</u>-yourselves <u>for</u>-*righteousness*;
reap <u>for</u>-the-mouth-of=loyal-love. (5/4)

43. Dearman (*Hosea*, 271) gives the reason of "the apparent intrusiveness of Judah in the context" for seeing it as "an editorial update," but also notes several other passages where Judah fits better, concluding that "a reference to Judah is thus plausible in Hosea's prophecies."

Till for-yourselves the-untilled-ground,

for-it-is-time to-seek the=LORD; (6)

Until=he-comes and-rains

righteousness for-you. (4)

#

13 You-*plowed*(=)wickedness;

you-*reaped* injustice;

you-ate the-fruit-of=lies. [2+2+2] (5/6)

Indeed=you-trusted in-your-way,

in-the-greatness of-your-strength. (4)

*

14 But-a-war-cry will-arise among-your-people,

and-all=your-fortresses will-be-destroyed, (5)

As-Shalman's destruction*-of Beth(+)Arbel* (4/3)

In-the-day-of battle

mothers dashed *against*=children. [2+3] (5)

*

15 Thus he-will-do to-you, Beth=el, (26 letter line)

because-of the-wickedness-of your-evil(*r ʿh* x2). (7)

When-dawn-comes he-will-be-completely destroyed(*dmh* x2),

the-king-of *Israel.* (5)

The seventeen lines of 10:9–15 point to a strong theological theme realized in the central peak with "it is time to seek YHWH."[44] This poem has beautiful chiasmus of metrics and words. Cola structure is chiastic with the third lines from each end having exceptional 2+3 units per cola, and the seventh lines both being tricola of 2+2+2. "Israel"=64 or 32x2 comes in the first line and is the last word of the poem, forming an inclusio. "Day" and "dawn" in these first and last border lines correspond as well. In the second lines from each end "Gibeah" corresponds to "Bethel," and synonyms of "evil" are found in both. The second lines also have **26** letters each, giving prominence to these lines and to the poem as a whole by having two 26-letter lines. The third lines both have *ʿl* 'against.' In the sixth lines "fair (*ṭwb*=17) neck" of the

44. Kidner (*Hosea* 91) writes, "The one gleam of light, the invitation of verse 12, is the *raison d'être* of the whole chapter." On p. 99 he notes that the phrase is taken up by a later prophet in Jer 4:3, "Break up your fallow ground."

calf corresponds to "greatness (*rb*=22) of your strength." The seventh lines both have "plow" (*ḥrš*), and the eighth lines have "righteousness" (*ṣdqh*=46 before the peak, and *ṣdq* after it making an inclusio for the strophe). "Reap" (*qṣr*) comes in the eighth line and the seventh from the end. This can be diagrammed as follows:

A "Israel" 9, lst line (Note also "day" and "Gibeah")

B "Gibeah" (*gb ʿh*=**26**) 9b, 2nd line (**26** letters)

C "against" 10, 3rd line

D "fair neck" of calf 11b, 6th line

E "plow" 11c, 7th line

F "righteousness" 12a, 9th line

G Center Peak 12b, 10th line:

"Till for yourselves the untilled ground;

for it is time to seek the LORD."

F' "righteousness" 12c, 9th line from end

E' "plow" 13a, 7th line from end

D' "greatness of strength" 13b, 6th line from end

C' "against" 14c, 3rd line from end

B' "Bethel" 15a, 2nd line from end (**26** letters)

A' "Israel" 15b, last word of poem (Also note "dawn" and "king.")

"Injustice" (*ʾlwh/ ʾwlh*=39), "war/battle" (*mlḥmh*=51), "children/sons," "day," "from" and "people" also come once in each half of the poem giving further balance.

The central peak has the only divine reference, YHWH=**26**. "YHWH" comes as a climax at its end, and is preceded by the symbolic lemmas, *drš* 'seek'=45 or 5x9, *l* 'to'=12 or **6**x2 twice, and the object marker *ʾt*=**23** in the phrase "seek the LORD." A synonymous phrase comes in 3:5 and 5:6 with *bqš* 'seek'=42. "Till the untilled ground" is a repetition with both the verb and noun lemmas of *nyr*=44. "Till" as a *metaphor* and as an *imperative* is prominent along with the preceding "sow" in 12a. Eidevall (*Grapes*, 161) proposes that "tilling uncultivated areas could be a rhetorical figure for making use of previously unexploited resources" and suggests "that this phrase alludes to the prospect of obtaining new blessings by obeying the divine will." The central strophe of 12 has the preposition *l* repeated six times of a total of ten in the whole poem. It comes 143 or **13**x**11** times in Hosea with the base numbers of the two major symbolic sets. Andersen and Freedman

(*Hosea*, 563) note the uniqueness of 12b, describing it as a "prose-like statement," which distinguishes it from the norm of parallelism as in 12a. All of these features are common ways used to give literary prominence.

The position of "righteousness" in the lines on both sides of the peak make this word prominent. The two are followed in 13 by three antonyms to "righteousness": "wickedness," "injustice," and "lies." The final strophe repeats a synonym of *rš*ʿ 'wickedness,' "Thus he will do to you, Bethel, because of the *wickedness* (*rʿh*) of your *evil* (*rʿh*)." Besides this doublet of *rʿh*, the following line has a doublet of *dmh* 'destroy'=22 in an infinitive absolute, giving prominence to the final line with this main alphabetical symbolic number 22. The contrast between Israel's ideal of *righteousness* and its actions of *wickedness* are the same as the two key root words (*ṣdq* and *rš*ʿ) in Ps 1. The lemma *ʿwlh* 'injustice'=39 comes only here in Hosea but 34 times in the Hebrew Bible.[45] The value of 39 for this singleton suggests that it was chosen to add numerical emphasis here with its sum of 13 and 26 and the third multiple in the 13, 26 theological set.

The three stanzas are also chiastic, with the first (which ends with the first short trimeter in 10) and the last (13–15) speaking of the punishment of war, and the center stanza (11–12) giving advice and hope. Since the positive stanza is the peak of a chiastic structure it has greater prominence than the negative stanzas, and shows the aim to "chastise" Israel in order that they turn from evil to good. The metaphor "Ephraim is a *docile calf* loving to thresh" that God as a farmer will "yoke" in order to "plough" in 10:11, is a reversal of 4:16 where Israel is likened to a "stubborn heifer" that God as a "shepherd" will not "feed in a broad pasture." The verb *ʿbr* 'pass by' in 10:11b can mean 'spare,' but the context with the following "yoke" in 11c supports "put on a yoke." Eidevall (*Grapes*, 160) gives the various proposals, but supports keeping the MT applying this to "the deity's 'discovery' of something valuable . . . Having spotted the animal's neck and observed the animal's working capacity, the divine farmer resolves to yoke it."

Secondary peaks come at the quarter points with the short trimeter lines in 10b and 14b. The two trimeter lines connect syntactically to their preceding lines, and except for their total length of eight units, which is not found elsewhere in Hosea, could be considered tricola. The first in 10c has a play on words with the surface *ʾsrm* 'tying them' of *ʾsr* 'bind'=36 having the

45. Eidevall (*Grapes*, 235) points out a contrast between Hosea and other prophetic texts such as Amos in that "it is striking that not a single formulation in this text mentions the poor groups within society. Neither solidarity with the oppressed nor sympathy with the victims of injustice is explicitly expressed."

same consonants as *ʾsrm* ‘I will chastise them’ of *ysr* ‘chastise’=45 in the previous line 10a. The LXX and many other translations (see RSV, NRSV, GNT) interpret both the same as “chastise” or “punish.” The lemmas after it have *l* ‘for’=12, *štym* ‘two’=66, and *ʿyn* ‘eye’=40. The qire reading of the last lemma is *ʿwn* ‘iniquity’=36, which is generally read instead of “eye.” The trimeter in 14b has four consecutive symbolic lemmas: *k* ‘as’=11, *šd* ‘devastation’=25, *šlmn* ‘Shalman’=60, and *byt- ʾrb ʾl* ‘Beth-arbel’=70. Since the last two come only here in the Hebrew Bible, and the event is not otherwise documented, they might be candidates for having been chosen as symbolic lemmas with 60 and 70 adding prominence. The strophic pattern follows the verse numbers, with couplets except in 11, 12 and 14, which are triplets. This sets off the triplet in 12 with the peak line in its center, and with two couplets and a triplet on each side of the central strophe.

Other symbolic lemmas are *h* ‘the’=5, *ḥṭʾ* ‘sinned’=18, *šm* ‘there’=34, *ʿmd* ‘stand’=33, *lʾ* ‘not’=13, *ʾwh* ‘please’=12, *w* ‘and’=6 x8, *ʾsp* ‘gather’=33, *l* ‘to/for’=12 x10, *ʿglh* ‘calf’=36, *ʾny* ‘I’=25, *ṣwʾr* ‘neck’=45, *rkb* ‘pull yoke’=33, *yhwdh* ‘Judah’=30, *ph* ‘mouth’=22, *ʿd* ‘until’=20, *yrh* ‘rain’=35, *ʾkl* ‘eat’=24, *kḥš* ‘lie’=40, *drk* ‘way’=35, *šʾwn* ‘war cry’=42, *kl* ‘all’=23, *rṭš* ‘dash’=50, *ʿśh* ‘do’=42, *pnh* ‘because/face’=36, *mlk* ‘king’=36.

11:1–4 Chiasm 754 5 457
(7 lines; 40 words; MT 39=13x3 word-stress units & revision 37; 56 lemmas of which 8 or 14.29% have divine-name values)

1 When Israel was-a-child I-*loved*-him,
  and-from-*Egypt* I-called my-son. (7)

*

2 They[LXX ‘I’]-called to-them;
  thus they-went from-before-them[LXX ‘me’]. [2+3](5)
They-sacrificed to-Baals,
  and-they-burned-incense to-idols. (4)

*

3 **But-I made-Ephraim walk;**
  he-took-them <u>on</u>=his-arms. (5)

*

But-they-didn’t know
  that I-healed-them; (4)

4 With-cords-of man I-led-them,

with-ties-of *love*. (5)

*

And-I-was to-them as-those-who-*lift*(+)the-*yoke*

on(+)their-jaws,

and-bent to-him feeding. (9/7)

There are many chiastic relationships in this poem. "Loved a child" with the verb *ʾhb* in the first line corresponds to "ties of love" with the noun *ʾhbh*=13 and "bent to him feeding" as to a child at the end, forming a semantic inclusio. The lemma *nʿr* 'child'=50 is theologically important with factors of 10x5 equivalent with *YH*. The central peak 11:3a also has the parent-child imagery of teaching to walk (*rgl*=35) and taking (*lqḥ*=39) in arms, fitting into the center of this chiastic structure. "Israel"=64 in the first line also is matched by the related "Ephraim" in the central peak. The central peak begins with *w* 'but'=6 connected to the emphatic full pronoun *ʾnky* 'I'=36. The switch of person in "*I* made-*Ephraim* walk; *he* took *them* on *his* arms," with "I" switching to "he," and the switch of number with "them" referring to "Ephraim," sets off the peak. Dearman (*Hosea*, 2010:282) writes, "Reference to YHWH's parental *arms* (*zĕrôa ʿōt*) evokes a rich assembly of images regarding YHWH's strong or outstretched arm." "On" (*ʿl*) comes chiastically in the peak and the last line. "Egypt" in the first line also corresponds to "yoke" in the last.[46] The lines on each side of the center are accusation: "sacrificed to Baals and burned incense to idols," (with *zbḥ* 'sacrifice'=17, *qṭr* 'burn incense'=48, and *psyl* 'idol'=54) in 2b, and "they didn't know" (with *ydʿ* 'know'=30) in 3b. The second lines each speak of movement, "went" (*hlk*) in 2a, and "led" (*mšk*=45) in 4a. According to the Hebrew the second lines also contrast the "call" (*qrʾ*=40) of idolatry to which they responded, with the "cords (*ḥbl*=22) and ties (*ʿbwt* 'ties'=46)" of God's love (*ʾhbh*=13). LXX switches the pronouns making it God's call in 11:2 as with *qrʾ* in the first line, with Israel going away from God (me). This is followed by many translations, especially "they went from before *me*."[47] Luther introduced a new subject for "they/them" of "someone" who calls, but from whom Israel

46. "Yoke" follows the MT *ʿūl* as in RSV, but NRSV has "infants" and NIV has "a little child" by changing the vowel to *ʿōl*. Dearman (*Hosea*, 283) gives many reasons for keeping the MT "yoke."

47. Eidevall (*Grapes*, 169) notes that *qrʾ* call' and *hlk* 'go' are word pairs in Hebrew. Eidevall (170–74) also analyses the metaphors that come after the initial parental verse 1 with "child," and "son," as agricultural "shepherd" in v. 3 and "farmer" in v. 4. However, I see the above semantic chiasm as good support for the traditional parental metaphor for the whole poem.

turns away. *HOTTP* recommends keeping "they/them," and suggests it may be a popular saying. This may account for the LXX translation using "I/me," thereby applying the saying contextually. The full suffix *-hem* 'them/their' comes at the end of each colon in this second line (2a), and twice in the first colon of the last line (4b) in a near double inclusio.

The strophic pattern is also chiastic with single line strophes on each end and in the central peak. These are separated by couplet strophes. The five parts have chiastic balance both with theme and with the single line strophes A, C, and A' having *singular* references to Ephraim, and B, C, B' and A' having *plural*. The singular is especially noteworthy in the chiastic beginning, center, and end, since singular is linguistically recognized as the more personal number, and thereby adds prominence. The two lines with both singular and plural are the center and end chiastically as follows with third person singulars underlined and plurals in italics:

A I called my son from Egypt

B *They* went to idols

C I made Ephraim walk, taking *them* on his arms

B' *They* didn't know that I healed *them*

A' I was as one who lifts *their* yoke, bending to him.

"I was" is the same form *ʾhyh* 'I am" as the divine name God gave to Moses in Exod 3:14, giving prominence to the final line.

The junctures forming this poem as 11:1–4 are generally found in the translations (see the headings before it and the blank lines after it in NRSV, NIV, and GNT). "Lift" (*rwm*=39) comes at the end of this and the next poem giving cohesion by epiphora. Other symbolic lemmas are *w* 'and'=6 x6, *l* 'to'=12 x7, *kn* 'thus'=25, *pnym* 'before'=54, *l ʾ* 'not'=13, *hyh* 'be'=20, *k* 'as'=11, *lḥy* 'jaw'=30, *ʾl* 'to'=13, *ʾkl* 'feed'=24.

11:5–7 Five Pentameters

(27 words; MT & revision 25 or 5x5 word-stress units; 37 lemmas of which 8 or 21.62% have divine-name values)

5 Shall-he-not return

to(=)the-land-of *Egypt*? [2+3] (4/5)

And-shall-not-Assyria be his-king,

because(+)they-refused to-return? (6/5)

*

6 So-the-sword will-whirl-through his-cities,

and-put-and-end to-its bars[his plans], (5)

And-eat their-advice.

* (enjambment)

7 But-my-people are-bent on-<u>turning</u>-from-me; [2+3](5)

So-<u>to</u>=the-*yoke*[or MT **"height"] they-called-him;**

<u>no</u> one will-*lift*-them-up. (5)

This poem has its first three words repeated in the final peak, "not" (*l'*=13), "return" (*šwb*), and "to" (*'l*=13). The end of the inclusio has each word separately in one of the three cola of the peak in the order "turning, to, no." "Return/turn" (*šwb*) is repeated three times in the poem, each with a different meaning, namely (1) "go back" in v. 5a, (2) "repent" in v. 5b, and (3) "go away from" in the peak v. 7a. The repetition suggests a terrace pattern pointing to a final climax. The climax then begins with the half line after the enjambment, "But my people are bent (*tl'*=35) on *turning* from me." Four more symbolic lemmas come in the final peak, *w* 'so/and'=6 x6 in the poem, *qr'* 'call'=40, *yḥd* 'one'=22, and *rwm* 'lift'=39.

The MT *'al* 'height' in 11:7 is translated as "upward" by NJPS, "Most High" by NRSV, and "God Most High" by NIV. However, RSV and GNT conjecture the vowel should be *'ol* 'yoke' keeping the consonantal letters. If this is followed as suggested in the above display, this poem has the same inclusio as the previous one in that the first line has "Egypt" and the last "yoke," both of which are metaphors for the coming exile. The final word "lift" comes in the last lines of these two poems as epiphora, along with the proposed "yoke." Another structure making an inclusio is the rhetorical question in the first lines "Shall he not return to the land of Egypt?" which is then answered in the last line "To the yoke they called him," verifying the exile. The next poem has the same feature addressing the return from exile with a rhetorical question in 11:8, "How can I give you up, Ephraim, and hand you over, Israel?" answered in the last line 11.11b, "And I will *return* them to their homes, says the LORD." The repetition of the key word "return" (epiphora) with a fourth meaning "bring back," is significant, as is the reversal from the surety of exile in 11:5–7 in contrast to the surety of "return" from exile in 11:8–11. These two poems are on each side of the boundary of the final part five in Hosea, and mark the thematic change from pure judgment poems to a return to some salvation poems as in part 1. The close relationship of these three poems with such semantic inclusions gives support to the conjecture "yoke" in 11:7.

Besides the terrace pattern and inclusio, the final peak is marked by a grammatical inversion, plural-singular; singular-plural of subjects and objects: "they called-*him*; no one will lift-*them*." This is particularly interesting since the pronouns thereby reverse number in each colon. This also resembles the previous peak in 11:3, "But I made *Ephraim* walk, taking *them* on his arms." The final emphasis fits the above metrical analysis as a pentameter homogeneous poem.[48] The third line has *ḥwl* 'whirl'=26, which occurs only here in Hosea and may have been chosen because of its numerical value. It also has a play on words in Janus parallelism with *bd*=6 having two meanings, "bars" relating to the previous "cities" (*ʿyr*=46), and "plans" relating to the following "advice." The fourth line has enjambment recalling many of the earlier poems in Hosea. The strophic pattern is basically couplets, although the line with enjambment serves as the other half of the couplet for each of its adjacent lines. This results in three repetitions of number switches for "people" with a singular-singular-plural pattern coming once in each strophe as diagrammed below. This grammatical terrace pattern therefore parallels the terrace of "return," and supports including the whole last strophe (all of 7) as the peak with the final occurrence of "turn" and the key word "my people" (*ʿmy*) in 7a.

Strophe 1 not he-return to his they return (5)

Strophe 2 his his their (6) (all 3 strophes with sing. sing. plural)

Strophe 3 MY PEOPLE TURN TO HIM LIFT THEM (7)

Other lemmas with symbolic numbers are *ʾrṣ* 'land'=39, *ʾšwr* 'Assyria'=48, *hwʾ* 'he'=12, *mlk* 'king'=36, *l* 'to'=12 x2, *ḥrb* 'sword'=30, and *ʾkl* 'eat'=24.

Part Five 11:8—14:9[10], 88 Lines

(Words MT 495=11x45, 5x99; Lemmas MT 646=17x38, Possible revised 644=23x28)

Eighth Block 11:8—13:3, 44 Lines, "I am the LORD your God"

(Words: MT 256, Possible revised 255=17x15, 5x51 by combining "roams with" to become "knows" in 11:12[12:1]; Lemmas MT 347, Possible revised 345=5x69 by deleting *w* in 12:2[3] besides the deletion in 11:12[12:1]; revisions increase symbolic numbers in structural counts, see tables 4–7)

48. Deleting the MT hyphen with *ʾl* 'to' in the first line is a suggestion how the pentameter rhythm could have been done in performance although MT is consistent with hyphens after *ʾl* in Hosea.

11:8–11 Chiasm 55644 4 44655
(11 lines; 56 words; MT & revision 52=26x2 word-stress units; 72=6x12 lemmas of which 19 or 26.39% have divine-name values)

8 How can-I-give-you-up, Ephraim,
and-hand-you-over, Israel? (5)
How can-I-give-you-up as-Admah,
and-treat-you as-Zeboiim? (5)
*
My-heart recoils in-me;
my-remorse is-completely aroused. (6)
9 I-will-<u>not</u> express
my-fierce anger; (4)
I-will-<u>not</u> *return*
to-destroy Ephraim; (4)
*
Because(+)I(-am) God
and-<u>not</u>(=)man; [hyphen moved to 1st colon] (4)
Holy in-your-midst;
and-I-will-<u>not</u>(+)enter the-city[in wrath]. (5/4)
*
10 They-will-go after(+)the-LORD;
he-will-roar like-a-lion. (5/4)
Yes,(=)he will-roar;
and-the-sons will-tremble from-the-west. (5/6)
11 They-will-tremble as-birds from-Egypt,
and-as-a-dove from-the-land-of(+)Assyria. (6/5)
*
And-I-will-*cause*-them-to-dwell in(=)their-homes,
says(=)the-LORD. (3/5)

As in the previous poem this one begins with a rhetorical question which is answered in the last line. Here "How can I give you up?" which is repeated twice in 11:8, is answered in 11:11 with "I will cause them to dwell in their homes, says the LORD." In 11:9 God also says he will "not *return* to destroy the city" using the same key word *šwb* as in 11:5–7 where it is said his people will not "return" because they "refused to return." A play on *šwb* comes in the last line 11:11 with the hiphil (causative) of *yšb* 'dwell.' The surface form *hôšabtîm* 'I will make them dwell' has the same consonants as *hăšêbôtîm* 'I will return them.' The consonantal identity in the original non-vocalic text would bring to mind the previous use of *šwb* in 11:9. RSV and NRSV achieve a translation of this play on words with "I will *return* them to their homes." Deut 29:23[22] with "the destruction of Sodom and Gomorrah, Admah and Zeboiim, which the Lord destroyed in his fierce anger" gives the background of Admah and Zeboiim in v. 8 and of "fierce anger," which is not carried out in v. 9. In v. 8 *hāpak* 'overthrow/recoil/change,' which is a technical word for the overthrow of the cities, is now applied to God's change of heart. The change from the purely judgment prophecies of the middle five blocks to the mixture of judgment and salvation in the two blocks at each end is significantly marked by these questions and answers. The reversal is also evident in the simile of "lion," which instead of destroying Israel as in 5:14 is now calling them back to their homeland by roaring.

Other chiastic correspondences are as follows:

A How can I hand you over? (question) (1st line)

B Admah . . . Zeboiim (2nd line)

C <u>Not</u> express fierce anger (4th line)

D <u>Not</u> return to destroy Ephraim (5th line)

E *ʾnky* 'I'=36 (AM) *ʾl* 'GOD'=13, *w* 'AND' *l ʾ* '<u>NOT</u>'=13 *ʾyš* 'MAN'=32

D' <u>Not</u> enter the city (5th line from end)

C' Roar like a lion (4th line from end)

B' Egypt . . . Assyria (2nd line from end)

A' I will return them to their homes (answer to question) (last line)

The center has the poem's only occurrence of "God," and comes in the striking positive-negative characterization, "I am God and not man." It emphasizes the "freedom of God" to not bring about a deserved punishment (see Dearman, *Hosea*, 291). God is *qdwš* 'holy,' meaning completely unique in God's divine nature. God is not bound by any human expectations of what God should do. Eidevall (*Grapes*, 177) notes that "several exegetes have unpacked their superlatives" to describe this "utterance in v. 9" as a high point in Hosea and even in the "whole of prophecy." Garrett (*Hosea*, 229) uses the term "remarkable" to describe this verse, and points out, "This refusal to enter the city is an act both of judgment and of mercy." Eidevall (*Grapes*, 80) also points out that the "utterance affirms the incomparability of YHWH" and implies "that all metaphors based on human analogies are, in the last resort, insufficient and inadequate as portrayals of the divine." *Every* lemma except the first *ky* 'because' have symbolic lemma values as diagrammed above. The subordinate "because" gives prominence to the peak line with its syntactic complexity. "Not" in the peak is repeated in the two lines before the peak and the line after the peak. YHWH=**26** comes in 10A and is also the last word of the poem in the concluding phrase "says the LORD," structurally balancing block two where the first poem has the same ending in 2:13[15]. YHWH at the end here relates chiastically to "God" in the center.

Thematic cohesion supports five strophes with a triplet on each side of the peak, and a single final line strophe that answers the initial question in the first couplet strophe. The MT juncture after the final "says the LORD" is generally followed in the versions.

The proposed theme of block eight "I am the LORD your God" is reinforced by the double "YHWH" and central "God" in this initial poem of the block. Both MT and the revision have 52 word-stress units, or double the 26 count for *YHWH*. The eleven lines as the base of the alphabetical set of 22 suggest special care in structuring this first poem of the final part five. The 72 or 6x12 lemmas add to the numerical beauty of the poem.

Other lemmas with symbolic values are *ʾyk* 'how'=22 x2, *ntn* 'give'=50 x2, *mgn* 'deliver up"=30, *yśr ʾl* 'Israel'=64, *k* 'as'=11 x5, *ʾdmh* 'Admah'=**23** a singleton, *śym* 'treat, set'=44, *hpk* 'recoil, change'=33, *yḥd* 'completely, together'=22, *kmr* 'arouse, grow warm'=44, *nḥwmym* 'compassion'=64 a singleton, *l ʾ* 'not'=13 x4, *ʿśh* 'express, do'=42, *ḥrwn* 'fierce'=48, *ʾp* 'anger'=18, *l* 'to'=12, *w* 'and'=6 x5, *šḥt* 'destroy'=51, *qdš* 'holy'=50, *ʿyr* 'city'=46, *ʾḥry* 'after'=39, *š ʾg* 'roar'=25 x2, *ʾryh* 'lion'=36, *hw ʾ* 'he'=12, *ḥrd* 'tremble'=**32** x2, *ym* 'west/sea'=**23**, *ywnh* 'dove'=35, *ʾrṣ* 'land'=39, *ʾšwr* 'Assyria'=48, *yšb* 'dwell'=33, and *byt* 'home, house'=34. The singletons "Admah"=**23** and "compassion"=64 or 32x2 are noteworthy since they are the numbers used to represent God that are based on the two calculations, alphabetical and mathematical, of *kbwd*.

11:12—12:1 [12:1–2] Four Hexameters with a Trimeter before the last one (31 words; 27 word-stress units; 41 lemmas of which 8 or 19.51% have divine-name values)

11:12[12:1] Ephraim surrounded-me *with*-lies,
  and-the-house-of Israel *with*-deceit; (6)
But-Judah still goes <u>with</u>=God

and-<u>with</u>=the-holy-ones is-faithful. [4+2] (6)

*

12:1[2] Ephraim herds the-wind,

and-pursues the-east-wind all=the-day; (6)

He-increases falsehood and-violence. (3)

*

And-they-make a-COVENANT <u>with</u>=Assyria,

and-oil is-carried to-Egypt. (6)

The structure of this poem is four well-formed hexameter bicola with parallelism, and one trimeter. The five lines divide into two strophes with couplets, leaving a final peak line as a strophe by itself. The trimeter line creates a break in the pattern, which serves to set off the final peak line with its specific offense of making and breaking covenants with foreigners. Four lemmas in the final peak have symbolic values, all with the factor of 6, *bryt* 'covenant'=54 or 6x9, *ʾšwr* 'Assyria'=48 or 6x8, *šmn* 'oil'=48, and *l* 'to'=12 or 6x2. The key word "covenant" comes its final fifth time in this peak. Instead of keeping their covenant with God, Ephraim has gone after useless and violent alliances with Assyria and Egypt. Dearman (*Hosea*, 274) notes that the contents of the English 11:12, which is 12:1 in Hebrew, "clearly go with the material that follows" as above. The boundaries above follow the Hebrew verse numbers. The switch from singular references "he" in the first part of the poem to the plural "they" in the last line resembles the similar pattern repeated three times in 11:5–7. The poem has the same structure as 6:4–6 above.

There is close parallelism in all four bicola. The final peak even has three elements in a repeated parallel structure of (a) noun (b) prepositional phrase (c) verb in each colon, which is especially marked by having final verbs. It also has grammatical switches with "covenant" feminine and "oil" masculine, and "they make" plural and "is carried" singular. The Hebrew forms of Assyria (*ʾšwr*) and Egypt (*mṣrym* ending with *-ym*, which is a plural suffix elsewhere) also suggest a number switch, and are a common word pair in Hosea. They are also in 11:11, the last verse of the previous poem, forming epiphora. Although parallelism is a *general* feature of Hebrew poetry rather than an *exceptional* feature emphasizing peak, the number of parallel features in this peak line suggests special care in its formation. The resumption of the pattern of parallelism from the first lines, after the break at the trimeter 1b, seems to be a device setting off the final peak as in 6:6.

Repeated prepositions and synonyms suggest a terrace pattern pointing to the final peak as follows:

with-with (12a) (Hebrew *b*)

with-with (12b) (*ʿim*)

COVENANT WITH=ASSYRIA-EGYPT (1c) (*ʿim*).

The line 11:12b[12:1b] "But Judah still goes with God and with the holy ones is faithful" is translated negatively in NIV: "And Judah is unruly against God, even against the faithful Holy One." Garrett (*Hosea*, 230–31) defends the NIV, although Dearman (*Hosea*, 297) considers the NRSV positive reading as above "the more natural sense of the Hebrew text" and agrees with those who see it as "an example of Judean editing."

Lemmas with symbolic values are *kḥš* 'lie'=40, *mrmh* 'deceit'=51, *byt* 'house'=34, *w* 'and'=6 x7, *yśr ʾl* 'Israel'=64, *yhwdh* 'Judah'=30, *ʿwd* 'still'=**26** x2, *rwd* 'roam, go'=30, *ʾl* 'God'=13, *qdwš* 'holy,=50, *rwḥ* 'wind'=34, *qdym* 'east wind'=46, *kl* 'all'=**23**, *h* 'the'=5, *kzb* 'falsehood'=20, and *šd* 'violence'=25.

12:2[3]—13:1 Chiasm 36655536675 5 57663555663

(5 stanzas, 11 strophes, 23 lines [11 + 1 in peak + 11]) (138 or **23**x6 words; 123 MT word-stress units, revision 119 or 17x7; 188 lemmas of which 36 or 19.15% have divine-name values)

2 *And-the-LORD-has an-indictment with=Judah . . .* (3)

And-to-punish Jacob according-to-his-ways,

according-to-his-deeds *he-will-repay him.* (6)

*

3 In-the-womb he-took-his=brother by-the-heel,

and-in-his-manhood he-wrestled with=God; (6)

4 And-he-wrestled with=an-angel and-prevailed;

he-wept and-asked-for-favor=from-him. (5)

|#

He-finds-him at-Beth=el,

and-there he-speaks with-us[him]. [2+3] (5)

5 *And-the-LORD, the-God of-hosts,*

the-LORD is-his-name[zkr 'remembrance']. (5)

*

6 *And-you by-your-God return*; (3)

Keep(guard) loyalty and-justice,

and-hope on=your-God continually. (6)

|#

7 A-trader with-false scales in-his-*hand*,

he-loves to-oppress; (26 letters) [4+2] (6)

8 And-*Ephraim* said,

"*Ah*, I'm-rich;

I've-found wealth for-myself; [2+2+3] (7)

All=my-gains won't incur=to-me

guilt which-would-be=sin." (5)

*

9 **But-I-am the-LORD your-God**

from-the-land-of Egypt. (5)

Again I-will-make-you-dwell in-tents

as-in-the-days-of the-festival(meeting). (5)

10 And-I-spoke to=the-*prophets*,

and-I multiplied visions,

and-by-the-*hand*-of(+)the-*prophets* I-give-parables.

|# [2+3+2] (8/7)

11 If=Gilead is-evil they-are *surely*=worthless,

in-Gilgal they-sacrifice(+)bulls; [4+2] (7/6)

Also their-altars are-as-heaps

on the-furrows of-the-field. (6)

*

12 *And-Jacob fled to-the-fields-of(+)Aram,* (4/3)

And-Israel served for-a-wife,

and-for-a-wife he-guarded; (5)

*

13 And-by-a-*prophet* the-LORD brought-up

Israel from-Egypt, (5)

And-by-a-*prophet* he-was-guarded.

|# (enjambment)

14 *Ephraim* provokes bitterly, [2+3] (5)

So-he(LORD)-will-leave his-bloodguilt on-him,

and-his-*Lord will-return(+)to-him* his-contempt. (7/6)

*

13:1 When-*Ephraim* spoke there-was-trembling,

he was-exalted in-Israel; (6)

. . . *And(But)-he-became-guilty by-Baal, and-died.* (3)

This poem 2:2[3]—13:1 looks like those above which Lundbom ("Contentious") described as having a discontinuous bicolon as an inclusio (4:4b–9a, 11b–14 and 8:9–13). All of them have trimeter initial and final cola which begin with *waw* 'and.' In this case the semantic connection is with the correlates "indictment" and "guilty" in the inclusio: "The LORD has an indictment with Judah" (12:2[3]a) . . . "and he became guilty by Baal, and died." (13:1b)[49] The special guilt of idolatry "by Baal" (*b ʿl*=30) in the final secondary peak relates the end to the covenantal statement in the central peak, "I am the LORD your God." There is also a play on words with a synonym for ba ʿal 'master' coming as *ʾdwn* 'lord'=25 in 14[15]b. The last line is also climactic with the final "and died" following "guilty by Baal."

The central peak 9[10]a is a thematic ritual formula with both divine names, "I (am) YHWH, your God." It is also found at the beginning of the last block in 13:4. Andersen and Freedman (*Hosea*, 597) note that this verse is "more prose-like than the rest of the chapter." This change in style has the function of setting it off as the peak. "YHWH" in the first short secondary peak line ties to "YHWH" in the peak. "YHWH" and "from Egypt" are repeated in 12:13[14] as well as in the peak, and the emphatic full pronoun *ʾnky* 'I'=36 is in 10[11] as well as the peak. "YHWH" and "God" are also found two and three times respectively in 5[6]–6[7]. The peak has *ʾrṣ* 'land'=39 connected to "Egypt." Dearman (*Hosea*, 310) points out that this "self-presentation of YHWH . . . is like the prologue to the Decalogue" in

49. If "Judah" in 12:2[3] is considered having been introduced by a Judean redaction, an original text with "Israel" instead of "Judah" in the first line would balance "Israel" at the end (13:1) and be symmetrical to the references to "Jacob" in 12:2[3] and 12:12[13]. This would add to seeing the first line completed by the last lines with "Israel" in each. As for symbolic numbers, the MT count of 44 for "Israel" and 15 for "Judah" is good, as would be 45 for "Israel" and 13 for "Judah" in a presumed text with deletion at 11:12b[12:1b] and substitution at 12:2[3] as proposed by BHS apparatus, and Dearman (*Hosea*, 299). If there is substitution in both places 46 or 23x2 for Israel would also be good. MT has the balanced count of three occurrences of both "Israel" and "Ephraim" in this poem.

Exod 20:2 and Deut 5:6, "I am the Lord your God, who brought you out of the land of Egypt." Dearman adds that it thereby relates to the establishment of the covenant—a basic theme in Hosea.

12:5[6] is the mid-point of the first half and thereby a secondary peak, as is 6[7]a because of its shortness. The reference to "YHWH God of hosts" plus the repetition here of both "YHWH" and "God" gives very strong prominence to the lines. "Hosts" (*ṣb ʾ*) is a singleton in Hosea. Besides the **26** of *YHWH*, the article *h* 'the'=**5** comes on "hosts." Garrett (*Hosea*, 241) notes that "YHWH God of hosts" is prominent in Amos who influenced Hosea, and writes, "It is a grand name that calls to mind all the majesty and power of God." "YHWH" significantly comes 5 times in the poem. Dearman (*Hosea*, 308) points to Hosea's knowledge of the YHWH divine-name tradition in Exod 3:14–15 with the use of *zkr* 'remembrance' there as here. Dearman (*Hosea*, 308–309) also notes that *šwb* 'return' in 6[7]a relates to the previous verse with Bethel, the place where God promised to *šmr* 'keep' Jacob and *šwb* 'bring him back,' and Jacob in turn made the vow that YHWH would be his God if God *šwb* 'brought him back' in peace (Gen 28:15–20). These intertextual references give added prominence to the short secondary peak line 6[7]a. In the context of this favorable encounter with God the good name Bethel "House of God" is used rather than the derogatory Beth-Aven "House of Evil" (See Kidner, *Hosea*, 109).

The corresponding midpoint of the second half is 12:12[13]. It gets emphasis by internal repetition of "wife" and external repetition of *śdh* 'field'=30, *yśr ʾl* 'Israel'=64, *šmr* 'guarded'=54, and "Jacob." All of the repeated pairs in stanza four suggest a buildup to the key message of the stanza in 12:13[14] "the-LORD brought-up Israel from-Egypt." This statement of salvation history is highlighted by being enclosed chiastically with "guard, prophet, prophet, guard." Kidner (*Hosea*, 113) notes the repetition of "guarded," which implies a contrast between Jacob's "limited" guarding and God's. The references to YHWH and "Egypt" are also in the peak at 9[10]. Other symbolic lemmas in the secondary peak 12:12[13] are *brḥ* 'flee'=30, *ʿbd* 'serve'=**22**, and *w* 'and/but'=**6** which comes three times in 12[13], plus at the beginning of the central peak and first secondary peak, and totals **25** in the poem.

"He will repay him" in the second line (12:2[3]), is the same Hebrew as "will return to him" in the third line from the end (12:14[15]). *ʾl* 'God'=**13** in the third line (3[4]) corresponds to *YHWH*=**26** in the third line from the end, and *YHWH* comes in the sixth line and the fifth line from the end. "Hand" comes in the ninth line and in the tenth line from the end. The ninth line 12:7[8] also has **26** letters, and a play on words with the double meaning of the singleton *kn ʿn*=55 for 'Canaan' and 'trader.' It also has *mrmh* 'false, deceitful'=51 or 17x3, which comes only here and in the previous poem in 12.1[2] in Hosea. "Return/repay" comes twice in each half in 12:2[3]b, 6[7]a, 9[10]b, and 14[15]b. "Ah/surely" (*ʾk*=12) comes on both sides in 12:8[9]a and 11[12]a, and *dbr* 'speak'=**26** comes once before and twice after the central peak. "Guard" (*šmr*) is in the eighth line and in the fourth and fifth lines from the end. Besides the metrical chiasm and semantic balance, there is also symmetry in cola structure. The ninth lines match being exceptional with 4+2, and the tenth lines are both tricola heptameter.

The poem has five stanzas. The first and last have legal terms—12:2[3] has *ryb* 'indictment'=**32**, *pqd* 'punish'=40, and the key word *šwb* 'repay,' which comes **23** times in Hosea; and the final two verses have *dm* 'blood-guilt'=**17**, *ḥrph* 'contempt'=50, and *ʾšm* 'guilty'=35. The second and fourth stanzas have historical references from Genesis about Jacob's trip via "Bethel" (4[5]) to "Aram"=34 (12:12[13]).[50] The central stanza is divided into two strophes. The first describes Israel's guilt, and the second with the peak line describes how the LORD God faithfully brought them from Egypt. It goes on stating how God continues to speak to them through the prophets, and assuring them of a future time with tents as in a festival.

In the second strophe of the first stanza Holladay ("Chiasmus," 53–64) notes a chiastic structure, A/ 12:3[4]a "brother," B/ 3[4]b "God;" // B'/ 4[5]a "angel" 4[5]b A'/ "him" (brother). The chiasmus supports identifying the antecedent to the ambiguous pronoun "him" at the end as "brother." Dearman (*Hosea*, 306) notes that the chiastic analysis "has the advantage of shared vocabulary" of "weep" and "seek mercy" "between Hosea and the Genesis material." The interruption of the antecedent is intelligible because chiasmus clarifies it for readers used to such inversions. Garrett (Hosea, 238) sees a double meaning, relating to Esau with the chiastic structure, but relating to God with the preceding and especially the following line "asked for favor from him." Similarly, all six verbs in 12:3[4]–4[5]a have Jacob as subject. Holladay ("Chiasmus," 58–61) also notes the change of focus between the first two stanzas with the boundary after 12:5[6]a, in that aspect or tense is changed from perfect to imperfect "finds" and "speaks," and the subject of the verbs is changed to "God." The second stanza begins with a reversal of the expected cola pattern having 2+3, and the third and fourth stanzas begin with exceptional 4+2 cola structures. The double reference of "prophets" in 12:10[11] and "prophet" in 13[14] both come at the end of stanzas as epiphora. The last stanza begins with enjambment between the

50. Garrett (*Hosea*, 28) gives a list of references showing eleven common historical events in Genesis and Hosea including the "story of Jacob" in Gen 25–35. He summarizes this, "In short, Hosea's critique of his generation is founded entirely upon the Pentateuch."

end of 13[14] and the beginning of 14[15]. The half lines of the enjambment each join with their adjacent line to make couplets. Enjambment is a feature noted in several early poems and at 11:6 as a possible trademark of Hosea.

Divine names significantly each occur five times coming at the centers of stanzas one, two, three, and five, and at the climactic end of stanza four. The poem also has theological prominence with three divine-name counts: **23** lines, 138 or **23x6** words, and 119 or **17x7** revised word-stress units. The **11** strophes relate to the alphabetical set.

WHM (1991) lists the plural *tmrwrym* 'bitterness' in 14[15]a as a lemma, making it the only lemma with a value of more than 100 in Hosea. Its value is highly symbolic with 104, or **26**x4 and 13x8. The surface word is the same as the lemma, highlighting the 104 value. Dictionaries list the lemma as the singular *tmrwr* with the non-symbolic value of 81. Besides its single occurrence in Hosea it occurs only three more times in the Hebrew Bible in Jeremiah. These three are also in the *plural* supporting the WHM (1991) analysis. Having this the highest valued lemma gives special emphasis to the word and to the seriousness of Ephraim's sin called *dm* 'blood-guilt'=**17** in the next line. Other lemmas with symbolic values are *l* 'to'=12 x8, "Judah"=30, *k* 'as'=11, *drk* 'way'=35, *bṭn* 'womb'=25, *ʾt* 'with/object'=**23** x3, *śrh* 'struggle'=46 x2, *ykl* 'prevail'=33, *bkh* 'weep'=18, *ḥnn* 'favor'=36, *mṣʾ* 'find'=**32** x2, *šm* 'there'=34, *h* 'the'=5 x7, *mšpṭ* 'justice'=60, *šmr* 'guard'=54, *qwh* 'hope'=30, *ʾl* 'to'=13, *ʾmr* 'say'=34, *ʾk* 'ah/surely'=12 x2, *kl* 'all'=**23**, *ʿwn* 'guilt'=36, *ʾšr* 'which'=42, *ḥṭʾ* 'sin'=18, *ygyʿ* 'gain'=39, *lʾ* 'not'=13, *ʿ*wd 'again, still'=**26**, *ʾhl* 'tent'=18, *mwʿd* 'festival'=39, *ḥzwn* 'vision'=35, *dmh* 'gave parables'=22, *glʿd* 'Gilead'=35, *hyh* 'be'=20, *glgl* 'Gilgal'=30, *zbḥ* 'sacrifice'=**17**, *mzbḥ* 'altar'=30, *gl* 'heap'=15,[51] *ʿlh* 'brought up'=33, *kʿs* 'provoke'=42, *nṭš* 'leave'=44, *rtt* 'trembling'=64 (only here), *nśʾ* 'exalt/lift'=36, and *hwʾ* 'he'=12.

13:2–3 Chiasm 56 7 65

(31 words; MT 30 or **10**x3 and **5x6** word-stress units, or revised 29; and 45 lemmas of which 5 or 11.11% have divine-name values, the 5th lowest of the 45 poems)

2 And-now they-continue to-sin,
    and-make(+)<u>for-them</u>selves molten-images, (6/5)
From-their-silver skillfully-made idols,
    all the-work-of artisans. (6)

51. Dearman (*Hosea*, 312) notes the play on words with *gl* 'pile' and the names *glgl* 'Gilgal' and *glʿd* 'Gilead' (witness pile) in the account of the covenant between Laban and Jacob in Gilead (Gen 32:23–54).

*

<u>To-them they</u> speak,

those-who-sacrifice men,

kiss calves. [3+2+2](7)

*

3 Therefore they-will-be as-a-morning=cloud,

and-as-dew-of the-morning which-goes, (**26** letters) (6)

As-chaff which-swirls *from*-a-threshing-floor,

and-as-smoke *from*-a-window. (5)

The central peak is the longest line of the poem, and may be analyzed as a tricolon with the abomination of human sacrifice in the center. It is also distinguished by the sarcasm of "sacrificing men and kissing calves," instead of the proper reverse. The Hebrew also adds prominence by inverted parallelism of verb-object // object-verb with "those-who-sacrifice men // calves kiss."[52] There are six symbolic lemmas in the peak, *l* 'to'=12, *hm* 'they'=18, *ʾmr* 'speak/say'=34, *zbḥ* 'sacrifice'=17, *ʾdm* 'man'=18, and *nšq* 'kiss'=54. The first two words in the central peak make a repetition of *hm* 'them/they,' first as a pronominal suffix, and then as the full pronoun "they," adding prominence by repetition. The peak line is also marked by five words ending in -*m*, and the previous line has four. The strophic structure of the poem sets off the central peak with a couplet on each side of the tricolon. These couplets are also unique in having only one long sentence each per couplet. "From" occurs once in the first strophe and twice in the last line making a near inclusio.

The penultimate line 13:3a has **26** letters and is repeated from 6:4b, giving it emphasis.[53] In 6:4b "morning cloud" and "dew" are a criticism of their lack of "faithfulness," while here it is a metaphor of being ephemeral and a prediction of their destruction and disappearance. 13:3a has the following

52. "Sacrifice men" follows MT as do NIV and NEB. Others see human sacrifice as unlikely since it doesn't come elsewhere in Hosea. One proposed change is to make the final *y* into a *w* to make an imperative "sacrifice" (NRSV). Another proposal is to have the verb modify "men" as "men who sacrifice." However, keeping the strong MT reading is supported by the above analysis which places "those who sacrifice men" in the prominent center of the peak of the poem.

53. The count of 26 letters here depends on the participle of *hlk* 'goes' being written without a *waw*. In the minor prophets *hlk* comes only in Zech 2:2[6] besides in Hos 6:4 and 13:3, but four times with the plene spelling *hwlk* in Jonah 1:11, 13; Mic 2:7; and Hab 1:6. Andersen ("D62," 288) notes that the manuscript D62 originally had the plene form, but was corrected to *hlk* in Hos 13:3.

lemmas with symbolic values: *kn* 'thus'=25 (together with *l* as *lkn* 'therefore'), *hyh* 'be'=20, *ʿnn* 'cloud'=44, *škm* 'morning'=45. Other lemmas in the poem with symbolic values are *w* 'and'=6 x4, *ysp* 'continue'=42, *l* 'to'=12 x4, *ḥṭʾ* 'sin'=18, *ʿśh* 'make'=42, *ʿṣb* 'idol'=36, *mʿśh* 'work'=55, *mskh* 'molten image'=44, *k* 'as'=11 x5, *kl* 'all'=23, *sʿr* 'swirl'=51, *ʿšn* 'smoke'=51. MT word-stress units are noteworthy as 30 with *YHWH* factors of 10, 6 and 5.

The first and third peaks of this eighth block speak of the uniqueness of the LORD God and his special relationship to his people. This theme is also repeated in the secondary peak in 12:5–6[6–7]. The peaks of the second and fourth poems are accusations for apostasy: "covenant with Assyria" (12:1[2]), and idolatrous "calves" (13:2).

Ninth Block 13:4—14:9[10], 44 Lines, "The LORD and Fruit"

(Words: MT 239, Possible revision 240=10x24, 6x40, 5x48 by dividing "droughts" into "no houses" in 13:5; Lemmas MT 299=13x23, possible revision keeping the same 299 by offsetting the change in 13:5 by deleting *k* in 13:8, see tables 4–7)

13:4–6 Four Pentameters and a final short emphatic line
(25 or 5x5 words; MT 24 or 6x4 word-stress units, revised 22; 34 or 17x2 lemmas of which 9 or 26.47% have divine-name values)

4 And-*I*-am the-LORD your-*God*
    from-the-*land*-of Egypt. (5)
You-will-not(+)*know* any-*god* except-me,
    and-no-savior besides(+)me. (7/5)

*

5 *I knew*-you *in*-the-desert
    in-the-*land*-of drought. (5)
6 In-the-way-I-pastured-them they-became-*full*;
    they-became-*full* and-their-heart was-lifted-up. [2+3](5)
There=fore they-forgot-me. (2)

The first line "And I am the LORD your God from the land of Egypt" is the same as the peak of 12:9[10] giving cohesion with both blocks of part five. There is a nice interlocking terrace pattern of words occurring twice in this poem and pointing to the final peak:

ʾnky 'I' (first word, verse 4)— *ʾny* 'I'=25 (v. 5)

ʾlhym 'God' (4a)—'god' (4b)

ʾrṣ 'land' (4)—'land'=39 (5)

ydʿ 'know' (4)—'know'=30 (5)

b 'in' (5)—'in' (5)

śbʿ 'full' (6a)—'full'=39 (6a)

There=fore (*kn*=25) they forgot (*škḥ*=40) me. (6b)

The thematic "forgot" is the climactic final word in the short last line. It is the antithesis of "know," which comes in 4 and 5.[54] Note that "forgot" is also the key word in the final peak in 2:13[15], the first poem of block two, and "know" comes its last two times here before the final *ydʿ* in the wisdom poem of 14:9[10]. The first of fifteen "know" is in 2:8[10], the last verse of block one. Other key words end in this poem. "Desert" (*mdbr*=39) comes here its last of five times with the first in 2:3[5], and "Egypt" its last here with the first of thirteen in 2:15[17]. The next to the last line has inverted parallelism "them-full // full-them," which also gives prominence to the end of the poem along with the 39 value of *śbʿ* 'full/satisfied.' The strophic juncture after v. 4 makes a balanced framework of each strophe beginning with the full pronoun "I" (first with *ʾnky* and then with *ʾny*), and each ending with the suffix "me" for God. The final peak is an exceptional triplet strophe.

Other lemmas with symbolic values are *w* 'and'=**6** x5, *ʾnky* 'I'=36, YHWH=**26**, *lʾ* 'not'=**13**, *ʾyn* 'not'=25, *blty* 'besides me'=46, *k* 'as'=**11**, *rwm* 'lift up'=39. The number of words is symbolic with 25=5x5, and of word-stress units with MT 24=6x4 or revised with 22.

13:7–11 Chiasm 666 4 666

(44 or 22x2 words, or 43 if *kî bî* 'that against-me' is changed to *mî* 'who?' in 9 as in LXX, NRSV, and GNT; MT 38 word-stress units, revised 40 as 10x4

54. Dearman (*Hosea*, 34) clarifies the Hebrew meaning of "know" in 13:4: "The 'knowing' that the prophet attributes to both YHWH and Israel is a relational term that excludes other intimates from the covenantal bond." Also see Dearman's discussion of "know" as "intimacy of the national covenant" on p. 321. On p. 322 Dearman quotes Deut 8:10–14 which has the same theme of forgetting God as in Hos 12:4–6, including the common vocabulary of "Lord your God," "became full," "heart lifted up," and "forget," which comes twice along with "became full." Garrett (*Hosea*, 257) notes the "significant change" from the "First Commandment" "'You shall *have* no other gods' (Exod 20:3) to "'you shall *know* no other gods.'" He calls this "a deliberate modification by Hosea meant to focus attention on the significance of the word 'know.'"

and 5x8; 59 lemmas of which 8 or 13.56% have divine-name values, the 7th lowest of the 45 poems)

7 And-I-will-be to-them as=a-lion,
    as-a-leopard I-will-watch on=the-way. {26 letters}(6)
8 I-will-attack-them as-a-bear robbed-of-her-cubs,
    and-I-will-tear open their-chest. (6)
And-I-will-devour-them there as-a-lion,
    as-a-beast of-the-field would-tear-them. (6)

*

9 **<u>Your</u>-destruction, Israel,**
    is-that=you-are-<u>against</u>-me, <u>against</u>-<u>your</u>-help. (4)
[or: I-will-destroy-you Israel;
        who will-be-your-helper? (see LXX) (4)]

*

10 Where now is-<u>your</u>-king?
    and-he-who-saves-<u>you</u> <u>in</u>-all(=)<u>your</u>-cities? (5/6)
And-<u>your</u>-rulers of-whom you-said,
    "Give=me a-king and-princes." {26 letters}(6)
11 I-gave(=)<u>you</u> a-king <u>in</u>-my-anger;
    and-I-took-away <u>in</u>-my-wrath. [4+2](5/6)

This is the strongest portrayal of God's punishment, and significantly comes last before the long summary poem of Hosea. "Destruction" (*šḥt*=51 or 17x3) in 9 (the central peak) is dramatized in 7–8 with four similes of ferocious "wild animals" (*ḥyh* 'beast'=23, *h* 'the'=5, *śdh* 'field'=30). All four have the preposition *k* 'as'=11. They begin and end with synonyms for "lion." The four are *šḥl* 'lion' (also in 5:14), and three others that include four singletons in Hosea: *nmr* 'leopard,' *db* 'bear' *škwl* 'robbed of her cubs'=50, and *lby*ʾ 'lion'=25. The verbs graphically describe God's wrath on Israel—"attack," "tear open the chest" (*qr*ʿ 'tear open'=55 is a singleton, *sgwr* 'chest'=44), and "devour" (ʾ*kl* =24) as a wild beast watching on the "way" (*drk*=35). The poem has two 26-letter lines 7 and 10b, which adds to its theological impact.

The first line 7 has a play on words with the surface ʾ*šwr* 'I will watch/lurk' only distinguished from ʾ*šwr* 'Assyria' by the doubling of the *š* in "Assyria." "On the way watching" thereby gives a clue to the location of the punishment by "Assyria." There is a reversal with the lemma *šwr* 'watch' at the end of the next poem at 14:8[9] where God "watches" positively by "looking after" (NRSV) Ephraim. These are the only two occurrences of *šwr* in Hosea. The word-play in this inclusio in the first line 13:7 of this poem and the next to the last line 14:8[9] of the next poem ties these two poems together.

The tetrameter central peak 13:9 is the shortest line of the poem, all the rest being pentameters or hexameters. The first colon has *yśr ʾl* 'Israel' with the value of 64 or **32x2**, and the second colon has their "help" (*ʿzr*) as God. Repetition is found in the double preposition "against," and in the pronominal suffix "your" on the first and last word of the peak. The prepositions translated "in" once in 10 and twice in the last line are the same as *b* 'against' in the peak. "Your/you" comes four times more in 10 and once in the final line adding emphasis. The peak line also has syntactic complexity being elliptical, by not specifying "is that you are" but only "against me." Dearman (*Hosea*, 324) describes 13:9 as "tersely formulated and difficult to render."

Strophic structure is symmetrical with a triplet on each side of the single line strophe of the central peak. Both triplet strophes begin with the ambiguous word *ʾhy*, which in the first line means "I will be" and in the line after the peak means "where," but also suggests the reading "I am your king" (see Eidevall, *Grapes*, 199). The first triplet has cohesion with "lion, leopard, bear, lion," and the final triplet has cohesion with the chiastic series "king, rulers, king, princes, king."[55] The value of *mlk* 'king' is 36 or **6x6**.

"Saves" (*yšʿ*) in 13:10 gives cohesion with 14:3[4] in the next poem (and with "savior" in 13:4 of the previous poem), and as an inclusio for the book with the double occurrence in block 1 at 1:7 since these are the only four occurrences of *yšʿ*. God the Savior as a shepherd feeding them in the previous poem at 13:6 in striking contrast to God as wild animals devouring them here in 13:7–8 also gives cohesion to the first two poems in block nine.

Other symbolic lemmas are *w* 'and'=6 x8, *hyh* 'be'=20, *l* 'to'=12 x3, *šm* 'there'=34, *ʾpwʾ* 'where'=25, *kl* 'all'=**23**, *ʿyr* 'city'=46, *ʾšr* 'which'=42, *ʾmr* 'say'=34, *ntn* 'give'=50 x2, *ʾp* 'anger'=18, and *lqḥ* 'take'=39. There are 44 or 22x2 MT words relating to the alphabet, and 40 revised word-stress units with factors of 10 and 5 possibly relating to *YH*.

13:12—14:8[9] Chiasm 5755637445542 77 2455(3)447365575

(29 lines; 154 or **22x7** or 11x14 words, of which 54 or **6x9** are in 13:12–15, and 100 or **10x10** and 5x5x4 in 14:1–8[2–9]; MT 143 or **13x11** word-stress

55. Dearman (*Hosea*, 325) notes that Israel's request for a king is in 1 Sam 8:4–20, and "Hoshea's subsequent capture by Shalmaneser III would qualify as YHWH's *taking away in wrath*."

units, revised 141 not symbolic; 186 lemmas of which 38 or 20.43% have divine-name multiples, 16 or 8.6% have multiples of 11.)

12 *Bound-up is-the-iniquity-of Ephraim;*
stored-up is-his-sin. (secondary peak) (5)

*

13 Pangs-of birth come to-him;
he-is=a-child without wisdom. (7)
For=at-the-time he-does-not(=)stand
at-the-breaking(forth) of-children. (4/5)

*

14 Shall-I-ransom-them from-the-hand-of Sheol? A
Shall-I-redeem-them from-death? B (5)
I-will-be[Where-are] your-plagues, Death! B'
I-will-be[Where-is] your-destruction, Sheol! A' (6)
Compassion is-hidden from-my-eyes. (secondary peak) (3)

|#

15 *Though he-be a-child-of his-brothers bearing-fruit,*
the-east-wind will-come; (secondary peak) [5+2] (7)
The-wind-of the-LORD
will-arise from-the-desert, (4)
And-his-fountain will-dry-up,
and-his-spring will-go-dry. (4)

*

He/it will-strip the-treasury
of-all=things precious. (5)
16[14:1] Samaria will-bear-her-guilt
for she-rebelled against-her-God. [2+3] (5)

*

They-will-fall by-the-sword;
their-babies will-be-dashed-to-pieces, (4)
And-his-pregnant-women will-be-split-open. (secondary pk) (2)

|#

14:1[2] **Return, Israel,**
to(+)the-LORD your-God, (central peak)
for you-have-stumbled in-your-iniquity; [2+2+3] (8/7)
2 **Take words with-you,**
and-return to=the-LORD; (central peak)
say to-him: [3+2+2] (7)
*

"Forgive all=iniquity. (secondary peak) (2)
Accept=GOOD, and-we-will-pay
(as-)bulls[LXX fruit of] our-lips. (4)
*

3 Assyria will-not save-us,
we(+)won't-ride on=horses; (6/5)
And-we-won't=say again, 'Our-God'
to-the-work-of our-hands; (26 letters) (5)
It-is=in-you that-the-orphan finds-mercy." (extra 3)
|# (secondary peak)
4 I-will-heal their-back-sliding(turning);
I-will-love-them freely, (4)
For my-anger
returned from-him. (4)
*

5 *I-will-be as-dew to-Israel;*
he-will-blossom as-a-lily,
and-strike his-roots. (secondary peak) [3+2+2] (7)
6 *As-Lebanon his-shoots will-sprout,* (secondary peak) (3)
And-his-beauty will-be as-the-olive,
and-he-will-have fragrance as-Lebanon. (6)
*

7 They-will-return dwelling in-his(my)-shadow;
they-will-grow grain; (5)
And-they-will-blossom as-a-vine;

his-remembrance-will-be as-wine-of Lebanon. [2+3] (5)

*

8 Ephraim, what still=do-I[he LXX]-have-to-do with-idols?

I answer and-watch/look-after-him. {2:21[23]; 13:7} (7)

I am-like-a-green cypress;

it-is-from-me that-your-fruit(+)is-found. (sec. peak) (6/5)

The application of symbolic numbers in 13:12—14:8[9] is wonderfully beautiful. There are 154 words, which has factors of **22x7** and **11x14**. These factors amazingly combine the alphabetical set of 11–22 with the 7–14 fullness set for this last poem before the wisdom closure. The 154 words divide at the chapter break with 54 or **6x9** in 13:12–15, and 100 or **10x10** and **5x5x4** in 14:1–8[2–9]. Note that these factors of 54 and 100 give a full representation of the 10, 5, 6, 5 values of YHWH. MT word-stress units are also highly symbolic with 143 or **13x11** units, combining the base 13 of the 26 theological set with the base 11 of the 22 alphabetical set. The number 143 is also the total of the letter *l* in Hosea.

The central peak of this longest 29-line poem in Hosea has prominence by being a heptameter tricola couplet with chiastically structured cola 2+2+3; 3+2+2. It is set off by two-foot lines on each side. This is significant since heptameters are the longest and bimeters the shortest lines in Hosea. The divine names "YHWH your-God" come in the exact center of the first line of the peak, and "YHWH" also comes in the central colon of the second line of the peak, and in 13:15 with "wind (*rwḥ*=34 or 17x2) of YHWH." *ʾlhym* 'God' comes significantly **26** times in Hosea, and YHWH with the value of **26** comes 44 times after the two occurrences in the introduction, or a total of 46 or **23x2** times (Andersen and Forbes, *Vocabulary*, 276, 330). *Šwb* 'return' occurs in each line of the central peak, with a total of five times (including one noun form) in 14:1–7[2–8] (see Yee, *Hosea*, 133). The focus here is on the "return" of Israel to God in repentance. This is emphasized by the two *šwb* in the peak.[56] The final **23**rd occurrence of *šwb* in 14:7[8] is

56. Eidevall (*Grapes*, 237) points out that significant "themes are characterized not only by their frequency, but by their variability as well. Moreover, they tend to appear in pivotal positions." On p. 210 he notes, "With regard to content and function, the passage 14:2–4 is strongly reminiscent of 5:15—6:3. In both cases, a proposed prayer is introduced by an exhortation, and in both contexts the verb *šûb* plays a prominent role." Eidevall on p. 237 notes that tracing a theme through the text can produce a "narrative" giving "continuity." On pp. 241–42 he shows how the various meanings of *šûb* are used to "express the idea of 'reversal.'" Although the effect of God's departure is disaster as in 9:11–12, on p. 250 Eidevall points out that "Through his withdrawal, YHWH hopes to bring about repentance," and on p. 252 he states that "the final hopeful vision . . . focuses

in a play on the consonantal similarity of *yšbw yšby* 'they-will-return the-dwellers' (in my shadow), recalling the play on the same two lemmas in 11:7. "Israel"=64 or **32x2**, the second word of this major peak, also comes in the secondary peak 14:5[6], and occurs 44 or **22x2** times in the book. There is a repeated parallel sequence in the two central peak lines and extending into the next short line: "return-to the LORD-iniquity; return-to the LORD-iniquity." The first "to" is *ʿd*=20 with factors of **10** and **5**, and the second is *ʾl*=**13**. "Iniquity" (*ʿwn*=36 or **6x6**) besides coming in the peak and the short line after it, is also in the first line of the poem as is common in chiastic structures. *Kšl* 'stumble'=44 or **22x2** in the peak comes again as the next to last word in the book. The first line of the peak has second person singular throughout: "*Return*, Israel, to YHWH *your* God, for *you* have stumbled in *your* sins." This is matched in the last colon of the poem "from me *your* fruit is found." This adds prominence to these lines since singular is more personal than plural. *W* 'and/but'=**6** (x12 in the poem) comes on "and return to YHWH" in the peak and also comes in the secondary peaks in 13:16[14:1] and 14:5[6]. The enigmatic *dbr* 'word'=**26** in the peak should be seen in line with the overall symmetry of the book, with "word" in the beginning of blocks one and three, bad "words" in block seven, and now good "words" in block nine. Its value of 26 matches that of YHWH in the next colon. This puts an occurrence of the noun *dbr* in each of the five parts except the central part 3. *Lqḥ* 'take=39 in the peak and "accept" with the same root in the second line after the peak, recall the second word of the first command of God to Hosea in 1:2 "take a wife," which is the second and shortest poem in Hosea, in contrast to this second from the end longest poem. The four *imperatives* "return, take, return, say" give syntactic emphasis in the peak. "Say" (*ʾmr*=34) comes again in 14:3[4] after the peak. "Take words" in the peak, and the next "we will pay as bulls *our lips*" indicate that the best offering to God is not the *bulls* of sacrifice but *words* from the *lips* of those faithful to the commitments of God's good covenant.[57] The *words* of this model prayer begin with confession "Forgive all iniquity." All three lemmas of this short secondary peak 14:2[3]b have symbolic values, *kl* 'all'=**23**, and *ʿwn* 'iniquity' and *nśʾ* 'forgive' both have the value of 36 or **6x6**.

"Ephraim" comes in the first line of the poem and again as a vocative climax in the second line from the end, the first line of the last strophe. (It comes 37 times in Hosea.) The vocative "Ephraim" makes this final plea of God very personal (see 6:4 "What shall I do with you, O Ephraim?").

on the return of the people" rather than on the return of a "disappearing deity."

57. To clarify the double objects of bulls and lips, *HOTTP* recommends adding 'as,' to "bulls." Prepositions are often omitted in Hebrew poetry. LXX has "we will pay the fruit of our lips" presumably based on *pry* 'fruit' instead of MT *prym* 'bulls.'

"Ephraim" in the first colon of the first line also has its root meaning "fruit" repeated in the last colon of the poem, where it is connected to the thematic concept of God as the source. Since the center has two lines, secondary peaks are to be expected at the ends, making the occurrence of the fruit theme in these lines more significant. The final line 14:8[9] also has prominence from the mixed metaphors of God as a "green cypress" targeting faithfulness, not fruit, but ending with "it is from me that your *fruit* is found" relating better to the "olive" in 14:6[7] or the "vine" in 14:7[8]. The first line is also set off as the only single line strophe in the poem. Also in the first line the words "bound-up" and "stored" are significant as an old Canaanite (Ugaritic) word pair.[58] Another word pair in this first line is "iniquity" (*ʿwn*=36) and "sin" (*ḥṭʾt*=40). The widely held meaning is that God preserved a record of Ephraim's sin (see Eidevall, *Grapes*, 200).

There is an ABBA sequence of "Sheol–death–death–Sheol" in 13:14 which emphasizes the theme of death culminating in the atrocities of an invasion in 13:16[14:1]. "Ransom from Sheol" (*šʾwl*=40 with factors **10** and **5**) and "redeem (*pdh*=**26**) from death" in the fourth line (13:14), correspond antithetically to "grow," literally *ḥyh* 'make live'=**23**, in the fourth from the end (14:7[8]). The fifth line has *ʾhy* 'I will be' translated twice as a question "Shall I be?" In contrast, the LXX has 'Where?' possibly based on a Hebrew *ʾyh*. This is the basis for 1 Cor 15:55 and NIV translating the whole verse 13:14 positively with the challenge "Where?" However, the context in Hosea is condemnation, supporting the Hebrew and NRSV "Shall I?"

"God" occurs in the eleventh lines (13:16 and 14:3[4]b). 14:3[4]b is a **26**-letter line, and besides "God" has the following symbolic lemmas: *w* 'and'=6, *lʾ* 'not'=13, *ʾmr* 'say'=34, *ʿwd* 'again'=**26**, and *mʿśh* 'work'=55. The repetition of "return" and the "LORD-God-LORD" sequence in the central peak was noted above, filling in the center of the semantic chiasmus formed by the above matching lines.

"Fruit" (*pry*) in the last line, besides forming an inclusio with "Ephraim," is also connected to the verb *prh* 'bear fruit'=42 or **6**x**7** in the seventh line (13:15), which is a secondary peak as the middle line of the first half of the poem. *Prh* is matched by the plant references in 14:5[6] in the middle of the second half, especially *prḥ* 'blossom'=45 or **5**x9, which has the same *pr* sequence as in "Ephraim," "bear fruit," and "fruit." ("Blossom" is also in 14:7[8].) *Nkh* 'strike'=30 with factors of **10**, **6**, and **5** also comes in 14:5[6]. Note that these secondary peak mid-lines are long, heptameters, like the central peak. The trimeter line which follows, continues the same plant-growth theme, and because of its shortness is also counted as

58. See Greenfield (551) and Korpel and de Moor ("Fundamentals," 174).

a secondary peak, as are the other trimeter and bimeter lines. The contrast between the dry "east wind" (*qdym*=46 or 23x2) of the midpoint (13:15) in the first half, and "dew" in the midpoint secondary peak (14:5[6]) in the second half, points out the basic shift from judgment to salvation.

The first word in 14:5[6] *ʾhyh* 'I will be' is the same as the name "I AM," which God gave to Moses at the burning bush in Exod 3:14. This gives strong prominence to this secondary peak, "*I will be* as dew to Israel; he will blossom as a lily, and-strike his roots." The lemma *hyh* has the value of 20 with factors of 10=Y and 5=H. The only other place *hyh* comes in the poem is in the next verse 14:6[7] where the result of God being as dew causes them to blossom and has the result that Israel's "beauty will *be* as the olive." In the book the divine-name word *ʾhyh* 'I am/I will be' comes two more times. The first is in the condemnation in 1:9 "*I will* not *be* for you," which is reversed in this final positive form as an inclusio for the book. The second is another positive "*I will be* as one who lifts up the yoke" in 11:4. The eight *k* 'as'=11 prepositions in the poem begin with "I will be *as* dew" in 14:5[6] and end with God saying "I (am) as a green cypress" in 14:8[9] with only the pronoun "I," while the verb "am" is understood. The six *k* between them are comparisons describing Israel with its resulting bounty and beauty. This includes the short secondary peak 14:6[7]a which begins with "*as* Lebanon" *lbnwn*=48 or 6x8, which comes twice more in this half including another "*as* Lebanon" in 14:6[7]b. Lebanon is a well-known symbol of beauty and plant growth. The last *k* preposition on "I (am) *as* a green cypress" is the final 78th *k* in the book. The number 78 is highly symbolic as the product of 26x3, 13x6, or 39x2 and the sum of 13+26+39 the first three numbers in the 26 theological set.

The synonyms in the trimeters ending the first and third stanzas, the biblical hapax *nḥm* 'compassion'=35 and *rḥm* 'mercy' x7 in Hosea, both have the same final two consonants, giving further cohesion between the halves. Besides "compassion" the trimeter secondary peak 13:14c has another symbolic lemma *ʿyn* 'eye'=40. Metrically the spacing of the six long heptameters is significantly between the shortest lines in the center, the next to the shortest at mid-half, and the third shortest at the ends. This helps to give prominence to the heptameters in the center and mid-halves.

The poem divides into two parts just before the center—chapter 13 deals with punishment, and chapter 14 with blessing. In the above analysis the first short two-foot line in 13:16[14:1] marks the end of the first half, and an extra three-foot line the end of the third stanza, "It is in you that the orphan finds mercy." The function of this extra line in 14:3[4] goes beyond closure of the stanza. It is also the closure of the model prayer of repentance given to Israel.[59] The word "mercy" relates back to the prophetic name "(No) Mercy" at the beginning of the book, and "orphan" relates to "(Not) My People." The only hope for orphaned Israel is in God who has "mercy." The extra line has special emphasis by coming outside the regular chiastic structure, and by its intertextual relation to Ps 10:14 "you have been the helper of the orphan."[60]

The four stanzas are distinguished by the pronouns for God in a concentric structure of "I–he–he–I." Thematically they can also be divided chiastically as follows:

Stanza Themes	**Divine Pronouns**
A The sin of Ephraim brings death	I
B Rebellion brings punishment	He
B' Repentance brings mercy	He
A' The love of God brings life	I

The proposed analysis of 13:12—14:8[9] as a single poem is supported by this thematic chiasmus as well as by the metrical chiasmus in the 29 lines. The balanced long and short lines in the two halves of the poem are especially impressive.[61] Dearman (*Hosea*, 2010:334) describes chapter 14 as "a reversal of Israel's eminent demise as depicted in ch. 13" noting the correspondences: "Israel's 'iniquity' (13:12) will be taken away (14:2); neither king (13:10) nor Assyria will 'save' Israel (14:3); Israel will not deify the

59. Garrett (*Hosea*, 272) describes this last line as "terse," which "because of its distinctive form and brevity, stands out from the rest of this strophe and should be regarded as the linchpin." Kidner (*Hosea*, 123) calls it a "trustful climax."

60. The last two words of 14:3 begin with *y*, which as the first letter of YHWH, may cryptically emphasize that the "you" is YHWH. This would be similar to the central peak of the book in 8:2 with three words beginning with *y*. The two *y*'s may also be a device related to the irregular placement of this line, since it is the twentieth line from the beginning of the poem. The numerical equivalent of *y* is ten, with the two tens suggesting a correspondence with the exceptional twentieth line. Note similar extra lines in Hosea's chiastic poems: the first in 7:1b, the tenth line of the poem with one *y* in the line near the end of block 4, and the second in 9:16a, the fifteenth line of the poem with one *y* and two *h*'s (*h* has the value of five) near the end of block six. The final extra line in 14:3[4]c is possibly the climax of a buildup (10–15-20) of these exceptionally placed lines.

61. Eidevall (*Grapes*, 210) notes, "Several observations reveal that the hopeful vision in 14:2–9 has been purposefully constructed as a reversal of the dark vision in 13:1—14:1. Lexemes, themes, and metaphorical expressions from 13:1—14:1 recur, but they are employed in order to convey an altogether different message." Eidevall details this further in footnote 14 referring to other related studies and listing nine "lexical reversals." Most begin earlier in chapter 13, but *ʿāwōn* 'iniquity' comes chiastically in the first line and central peak of this poem 13:12—14:8[9].

'work' of their hands (13:2; 14:3); YHWH's 'anger' (13:11) will be removed (14:4); YHWH will be the 'dew' (13:3; 14:5) to sustain Israel." Dearman continues: "These characteristics suggest that ch.14 is one of the latest compositions in the book" either by Hosea or "the book's editors." I propose that this longest 29-line metrical chiasmus in Hosea is likely the result of such a later addition. The added 100 words (note the number) in chapter 14 begin with a central peak with the plea to "return" that is followed by lines that were matched to have the same length as the earlier lines in chapter 13. The exceptionally short two-foot line after the peak lines served as a signal of the reversal by matching the two-foot end line of chapter 13, thereby creating the metrical chiasm 5755637445542 77 2455(3)447365575. Note that only four proposed changes to the MT hyphenation, as noted in the display above, are required to show this extraordinary chiasmus.

Six strophes may be defined on each side of the central peak strophe. The first line 13:12 is the first strophe. After it comes a couplet, two triplets and two couplets. After the couplet peak there are a couplet, a triplet, a couplet, a triplet, and two couplets. This gives balance with two triplets on each side, as part of the six strophes on each side.

The phrase "I will love them freely" (*ndbh*=25) in 14:4[5] emphasizes that the reestablishment of the God's good covenant is ultimately based on *ʾhb* 'love' without any other requirements. Israel's history of repeated backsliding and rebellion will not deter God's love. There is a play on the meanings of *šwb* in 14:4[5]: the '*backsliding*' of Israel is reversed by God's healing, and God '*turns back*' anger freely in love.

This last ninth block begins in 13:4 with what I propose as the theme of the eighth block, "I am the LORD your God" (11:9; 12:9[10]). There is a build-up to the climactic final plea in 14:1[2] "Return, Israel, to the LORD your God." The theme of "Ephraim" or "fruit" comes repeatedly in this longest poem. It is also related to the imagery of God turning desert (*mdbr*=39) to fullness in the poem 13:4–6, or fruit to desert here in 13:15. The last stanza 14:5–8[6–9]brings this theme of "fruit" to a climax with God described as "dew," the one who brings "shoots like Lebanon," makes them to "blossom (*prḥ*=45) as a vine" (*gpn*=34) with the fragrance of "wine" (*yyn*=34), to "grow (*ḥyh*=23) grain," and "gives them "beauty (*hwd*=15) as the olive (*zyt*=39)." "Dwell" (*yšb*=33) in his shadow (*ṣl*=30)" adds to the garden imagery with God as a tree giving shade as well as fruit.[62] This is brought to a climax in the final secondary peak line of the poem, "I am like a green (*rʿnn*=64) cypress (*brwš*=49 whose factors suggest a 7x7 fullness),

62. Dearman (*Hosea*, 342) notes that the reference to God in "his shadow" is a typical "switch" from "his" also referring to *Israel* before and after "his shadow." This is clarified in NRSV by "my shadow."

it is from me that your fruit is found (*mṣ* ʾ=32)." Eidevall (*Grapes*, 219) notes that the strange combination of "a coniferous tree with edible fruits" emphasizes "the permanent and protective character of divine providence," which is also "bountiful." Eidevall goes on to note that commentators see this as a reference to the Garden of Eden with YHWH as the tree of life. The lesson of the block is that it is YHWH alone who brings fruit. The final word of the poem "found" with Israel finding fruit from God gets emphasis by association with the earlier occurrence in 9:10 where God *found* Israel as special fruit in the desert. The word *ṭl* 'dew' in 14:5[6] is enhanced by the reversal from a symbol of unfaithfulness in 6:4 and of annihilation in 13:3, to a simile of God who is the source of moisture producing growth.

The cohesion between part 1 and this major poem in part 5 are also worth noting. As was already noted, the second poem of Hosea is the shortest with only two lines, and this second from the end is the longest with 29 lines. Word repetitions provide a summary, giving an inclusio effect for the book. The key word "return" comes in the peak of the last poem of part 1 at 3:5 and twice in the peak of 14:1–2[2–3]. "Have mercy" (*rḥm*) comes six times in part 1—twice in the peak of 1:6b–7, once in the secondary peak of 2:1[3], once in 2:4[6], and twice in 2:23[25]—and then the seventh time in the secondary peak of 14:3[4]. The six include the passive form that comes in the name of Hosea's daughter, Lo-Ruhamah "Not having mercy." "Forgive" comes twice in the peak of 1:6 and once in the secondary peak at 14:2[3]. These are the only three places where the six *nś* ʾ=36 (or 6x6) have the meaning of "forgive." "Love" comes nine times in part 1 (four times in 3:1, three times in 2:9–13[11–15], twice in 2:5–7[7–9]), and now in 14:4[5] as the 18th (or 6x3) final time. "Answer" (*ʿnh*=35) is the key word of 2:21–22[23–24] and comes six of its nine times in part 1. It comes now in the final 14:8[9]. "Desert" comes two of its five times in 2:3[5] and 2:14[16], and comes finally in 13:15. "Grain and wine" come twice in the anadiplosis 2:8–9[10–11] and in 14:7[8]. "Horses" (*sws*=36)comes in the secondary peak in 1:7 and 14:3[4], the only two in the book. "Remember" (*zkr*) is in the peak of 2:17[19] and the noun "remembrance" comes in 14:7[8]. God's taking away the agricultural produce in 2:8–9[10–11] because they attributed the source to Baal, is now reversed in 14:8[9] with God as the recognized giver, saying "what have I to do with idols." The double emphatic *ʾny* 'I'=25 in 14:8[9] where YHWH is described as the true God who "answers" and "watches/takes care of" them, and is the source of their "fruit" contrasts with their unfaithful trust in Baal. As noted in the previous poem the lemma *šwr* 'watch/takes care of' is a reversal and play on words with the meaning "watch/lurk" for God as a leopard to kill them in 13:7 (see Dearman *Hosea*, 343). "Good/

better" (*ṭwb*=17) in 2:7[9] "I will go and return to my first husband, for it was *better* with me than than now" is repeated finally in part 5 in a poem with a theme of returning. "Accept that which is *good*" in 14:2[3]c should also be seen in relation to its unique occurrence only once in each of the five parts of the book as with "covenant." The first occurrence of "covenant" in 2:16[18] is also in the poem with the first occurrence of five of its good qualities: righteousness, justice steadfast love, mercy, and faithfulness in 2:19–20[21–22]. God promised these in part 1, and now Israel is to respond asking God to accept that which is "good" on their part in part 5.

The references to "Assyria," and "horses" (implying Egypt) in 14:3[4] recall the condemnation in 12:1 "they make a covenant with Assyria, and oil is carried to Egypt." Similarly, no longer saying "our God" to "the work of our hands" is a denial of their idolatrous relationship to Baal. In contrast, the "covenant" between God and Israel is "good." A significant intertextual parallel comes with "cypress" in the last line of the last major poem and also in the last verse of Second Isaiah at 55:13. This possibly relates to the identical list of kings in Isa 1:1 and Hos 1:1. Dearman (*Hosea*, 2010:344) notes that this is the only time in the Hebrew Bible where YHWH "is compared to a tree." This unusual simile adds prominence to the final secondary peak.

Other symbolic lemmas are, *ḥbl* 'pangs'=22, *yld* 'give birth'=**26**, *l* 'to'=12 x6, *hwʾ* 'he'=12 x3, *lʾ* 'not'=13 x6, *ḥkm* 'wisdom'=**32**, *ʿmd* 'stand'=33, *šʾwl* 'Sheol'=40, *dbr* 'plague'=**26**, *qṭb* 'destruction'=30, *ʿlh* 'arise'=33, *ḥrb* 'dry up'=30, *ʾwṣr* 'treasury'=45, *kl* 'all'=**23** x2, *kly* 'thing'=33, *ḥmdh* 'precious'=30, *ʾšm* 'bear guilt'=35, *ḥrb* 'sword'=30, *ʿwll* 'baby'=46, *rṭš* 'dash'=50, *hryh* 'pregnant'=40, *šlm* 'pay'=46, *ʾšwr* 'Assyria'=48, *rkb* 'ride'=33, *ʾšr* 'that'=42, *ytwm* 'orphan'=51, *ʾp* 'anger'=18, *mh* 'what'=18, and *ʿṣb* 'idol'=36.

14:9[10] Chiasm 6 3 6

(16 words; 15 or 5x3 word-stress units as MT; 20 lemmas with 7 having divine-name values 23, 26, 32, 51, or 64, giving 35%, *the second highest in the book*)

9 Who-is wise?
  and-let-him-understand these-things,
    discerning, and-let-him-know-them. [2+2+2] (6)

*

Truly,=right are-the-ways-of the-LORD; (3)
And-the-righteous go in-them;
  but-transgressors stumble in-them. (6)

This final wisdom poem begins with the question "Who?" thereby applying this book to all readers by addressing not Israel or Judah but anyone. This first lemma *my* 'who?' has the divine-name value of **23**, and the second lemma *ḥkm* has the value of **32**, the two divine-name numbers based on *kbwd*. The next two cola each have the strongest theological number 26 in an unexpected repetition of *byn* 'understand/discern'=**26**, which looks intentional to make two 26s. These cola also have the theologically valued lemmas *ʾlh* 'these'=18 or **6**x3, and *ydʿ* 'know'=30 or **10**x3 or **5**x**6**, the factors equivalent to *Y*, *H*, and *W*.

Each of the three feet of the short *central peak* has lemmas with symbolic values. The first is a combination of the deictic *ky* 'truly' connected by a hyphen to *yšr* 'right'=51 or **17**x3 with the short 17 count for YHWH. It is followed by *drk* 'way'=35 or **5**x7. The peak line ends with the divine name which is the basis of all theological numbers, *YHWH*=**26**. This is the final 46th (or **23**x2) occurrence of YHWH in the book, thereby tying 26 to the divine-name number 23. Dearman (*Hosea*, 345) points to the thematic importance of the key words "right (*yāšār*) are the ways of the LORD," in the central line, stating: "the emphasis is not only to set forth the folly of Israel as a negative example from which to learn, but also to confess the integrity of YHWH in his ways of dealing with his world."

The lemma *ṣdyq* 'righteous' second after the peak has the value of 51 or **17**x3, the same as *yšr* 'right,' the second in the peak. The first and last lines both have two *w* 'and/but'=**6** conjunctions, and the first and last cola of these lines all end with *-m*, giving symmetry and cohesion to the poem. The last colon also has *pšʿ* 'transgress' with the value of 54 or **6**x9.

The next to last word of this final poem is *kšl* 'stumble'=44 or **22**x2. This is the only lemma with a multiple of 11 in the poem, making it significant as a metrical closure for the book since 44 is important in the structure of the book with eight blocks with 44 lines each. "Stumble" is also in the peak of the previous poem, tying the two poems together. Also *ḥkm* 'wise/wisdom' comes near the beginning of these last two poems, forming anaphora, and together giving a strong admonition to take action. The previous "wisdom" comes in 13:13, "Pangs of childbirth come to him; he is a child without wisdom. For at the time he does not stand at the breaking forth of children." Then 14:9[10] asks finally, "Who is *wise*? Let him understand these things." These are the only two occurrences of *ḥkm* in Hosea. The value of *ḥkm* is **32**, the largest of the four divine-name numbers 17, 23, 26, and 32. All four numbers come in this short final poem as multiples, as do the values of the individual letters of *YHWH* (*Y*=10, *W*=6 and *H*=5). Besides the YHWH in the peak, the repeated lemma *byn* 'understand' adds two more occurrences making *three* for the value of **26**. The poem has two lemmas, *ṣdyq* 'righteous' and *yšr* 'right,' with the value of 51 and a factor of **17**, and two references to **23** with the initial word *my* 'who' with the total occurrences of 46 or **23x2** for YHWH.

The same lemmas "Who," "wise," "these," and "understand/consider" end a long account of punishment and blessing of Israel at Ps 107:43, "Who is wise, let them give heed to these things, and consider the steadfast love of the Lord." The initial *my-ḥkm* 'Who-wise' comes only in these two places in the Hebrew Bible giving strong intertextual cohesion.[63]

The initial question "Who is wise?" begins a tricolon line forming the first strophe. This is followed by three cola in the second strophe with the peak a monocolon and the final line a bicolon. This gives balance with three cola in each of the two stanzas. Lineation is chiastic with hexameters enclosing a short three-foot central peak.

The percentage of lemmas with divine-name values is 35%, the *second highest* in the book. This forms a numeric inclusio with the first poem of Hosea's message in 1:2c-d, which has the *highest* percentage at 56.25%. Besides this, each poem has one YHWH=**26**, and the first has *znh* =**26** twice, and the last has *byn* 'understanding'=**26** twice. This conjunction of YHWH with the contrasting key word of each poem, all with the strongest theological value of 26, is a beautiful artistic device. The special attention to symbolic numbers significantly elevates the status of this last poem as a beautiful wisdom conclusion.

63. In addition, *yšr* 'right/upright/straight' comes twice in Ps 143, once in v. 7 referring to the way God leads, and in v. 42 referring to the "upright" who see God's blessings and rejoice. *Drk* 'way' comes 4 times in Ps 143 including "straight way" in v. 7 paralleling "straight ways" here. This is evidence that if Hos 14:9[10] is a later addition, the person who wrote the conclusion to Hosea was acquainted with Ps 143 and its similar message, and found its conclusion applicable to Hosea. Or otherwise, the author of Ps 143 was acquainted with Hos 14:9[10] and appropriated it there.

Chapter 5

Translating Peak and Chiasmus

RECOGNIZING AND APPLYING STRUCTURAL and grammatical features which give prominence to literary peaks in Hebrew can add to the effectiveness of a translation. Obviously the same features cannot be reproduced one for one in a different language. One important thing for a translator to realize is that Hebrew has many ways to point out what the author wanted to emphasize. Some of these, such as repetition of the same word or root in the same line work nicely in some languages, but in other languages such as English would be considered bad style rather than good.[1] The feature of "rhetorical underlining" or using "extra words" and "tautologies" at peak (Longacre, *Discourse*, 26) is probably a universal of the grammar of discourse, but the question of whether to repeat the same word as in Hebrew, or choose synonyms, is language specific.

Hebrew sound devices such as alliteration, either consonance where words in a sequence have the same consonant, or assonance where they have the same vowel, may be a recognized marker if the translation is done in poetry. But it may also seem like a tongue-twisting game rather than a way to mark something important. The principle, however, is relevant, that peak lines are likely to have more care in bringing out striking sound patterns. Rhyme, although not a required feature in Hebrew, may be one of the most widely used markers of elevated style.

Number and gender switches are likely to be confusing rather than pleasing since they sometimes give different grammatical markers for the same thing, as seen in ambiguous passages in Hebrew noted above. However, the principle of exceptional grammar and unusual features which call

1. I have analyzed features such as repetition in the Ethiopian language of Afar in "Afar Songs," and "Afar Drum Song" noted in References.

attention to the peak line is valid in any language. Change of pace is another feature likely to be a discourse universal giving prominence. It is shown in Hebrew by more or less syllables in the stress units, the exceptional length of peak lines, or departure from normal couplet strophes. Knowing the metrical system of a language including its poetry helps to determine what is normal and how pace is changed.

It has been shown above that parallelism is a regular feature of Hebrew poetry, and therefore decreases at peak in order to show exceptional style. However, parallel syntactic structures are common for marking high points in many languages, including Hebrew. The important thing for the translator, is to analyze his own language to find what the *general* features of the receptor language poetry are, and then to see whether they are decreased at peaks. This will help to identify what features of peak are used by good writers and speakers. The function of the Hebrew form may then be replaced by an entirely different form which does the same thing—give prominence to peak.

Chiasmus is obviously one of the most difficult things to deal with in translation. The simplest form is the arrangement of parts of speech in adjoining clauses so that they come in an ABB'A' or similar inversion. This is easy to do in some languages with free word order—but the question is, "Does it mark something important?" If the function is not recognized, there is no point in it, and another feature of prominence should be found. Another form of chiasmus is the listing of words or synonyms in mirror image usually meeting in the central peak. Since Bible translators generally try to stay close to the order of the original sequences, the result will often be similar. It is useful to have first recognized which key words are repeated in the original language, so that they may also be repeated in the translation. However, one should never sacrifice meaning or collocation in the translation in an effort to repeat key words. The point then is, "Will this chiastic inversion of a series of words be recognized as pointing to the peak, or not?" If not, it may be useful to use italics or bold print to mark them as I have done in these Hosea texts. The use of printing style to mark text is already done to some extent in choosing prose or poetry format. The use of bold print in section headings is also common, and could well be added to peak lines and emphatic words in the text. Another less effective help would be to add a note explaining the function of the repeated words. Chiastic relationships between stanzas in a poem can also be shown by well-worded section headings. Longer chiastic structures such as in a block, or even a book, should be noted in the introductions.

Metrical chiasmus is likely to be the most difficult to translate in its function of giving prominence at peak. No translation will show whether the original poem was chiastic or homogeneous, a feature which this study describes as essential to knowing whether to expect the central or the final line as the peak line in each poem. Language typology shows that verb final languages prefer to have a buildup to the main point at the final climax. This makes the translation of homogeneous poems with similar line length easier in these languages. The effective translation of chiastic poems, however, may require sequential restructuring in order to put the peak at the end. Especially if the translation is being done into poetry, such reordering of verses can be considered in languages where chiastic structures are not appreciated.

The Hebrew use of lemmas with symbolic numbers to enhance a text or a peak line is good to be aware of when translating. Although the Hebrew alphanumeric system cannot be transferred, the places to which it gives prominence can be seen as places to add special stylistic features of prominence in the receptor language. The placement of the full name "the LORD" in a high point rather than a pronoun, may be one feature that can be transferred.

I am convinced that *emphasizing peaks* in some equivalent receptor language form will be a major help for the reader to see the main intent of the original. The peak of the poem will become clear to the modern reader as it was to the Hebrew audience, who could hear in the recitation whether the poem was chiastic or homogeneous. Although a listening audience will not be helped by seeing printed format changes; an oral reader can immediately note which line is the peak and can add articulatory emphasis. This will bring the translation closer to a "functional equivalence" (de Waard and Nida, *Language*) for a very important stylistic feature.

Appendix

A Test of Textual Variants to See if they Produce More Symbolic Numbers

The textual variant suggestions in BHK, BHS, and BHQ were tested to see if any would improve the symbolic counts of words and lemmas within the structural parts and blocks of Hosea proposed in this study. These apparatuses are a collection of textual criticism from many scholars. My criterion for accepting a variant was not its level of validity as a likely earlier text, but only whether it improved the counts. Some of the chosen variants are supported by current scholarship, while others are not. Details of the textual support for each are listed after the next table.

In the following tables the *alphabetical* number factors **11** and **22** and the *theological YHWH* number factors **13**, **17**, **23**, **26**, **32**, and **10**, **6**, and **5** are in bold.[1] *MT numbers* that are maintained are also in bold along with their symbolic factors. In table 4 the textual location of the proposed revisions are listed at the end of the line of the block in which they occur.

Table 4: Revised Word and Lemma Counts in Blocks and Parts

Blocks	Revised Words	Revised Lemmas; & Location
1st, Title—2:8[10]	**286=22x13, 11x26**	377=**13**x29; at 2:1[3]
2nd, 2:9[11]—3:5	272=**17**x16	391=**17**x**23**; at 2:16[18]
Part 1 totals	558=**6**x93	768=**6**x128

1. There are no counts with 32 as a factor in table 4. This may reflect an earlier period when 32 as a "mathematical" count was not developed.

3rd, 4:1—5:4	**276=23x12, 6x46**	364=**26x14, 13x28**; at 4:10, 18, 19
4th, 5:5—7:2	258=**6x43**	338=**13x26**; at 6:5, 11
Part 2 totals	534=**6x89**	702=**26x27, 13x54, 6x117**
5th, 7:3–8:13 & Part 3	300=**10x30, 6x50, 5x60**	**357=17x21**; at 7:15, 16
6th, 8:14—10:1	**242=22x11**	306=**17x18, 6x51**; at 9:6
7th, 10:2—11:7	253=**23x11**	**319=11x29**; at 10:5
Part 4 totals	495=**11x45, 5x99**	625=**5x125**
8th, 11:8—13:3	255=**17x15, 5x51**	345=**5x69** at 11:12[12:1], 12:2[3]
9th, 13:4—14:9[10]	240=**10x24, 6x40, 5x48**	**299=13x23** at 13:5, 8
Part 5 totals	495=**11x45, 5x99**	644=**23x28**

Note that the *revised block 2* multiples 272 and 391 introduce the divine numbers **17** and **23**, following those in block 1 (286 and 377) that introduce the 22 (11 base) and 26 (13 base) symbolic sets. In the column with Revised Words the central block five has all three of the *Y*=10, *W*=6, and *H*=5 small numbers, and these factors are repeated chiastically by coming in both the 5th central block and in the final ninth block. Block nine has two lemma changes, but retains the MT **13x23** lemma count, relating chiastically back to the opening blocks with 13 and 23. Lemma counts in both blocks three and four and their sum in their part 2 all have factors of **26** and **13** setting off this highest theological number set in a special way.

The above fifteen proposed revisions to the MT show that it is possible to make all of the twenty-eight structural numbers in table 4 have a symbolic factor. I repeat that the aim of this exercise was not to choose the best text but simply to see if the various changes proposed by scholars can produce symbolic numbers where MT does not have them. However, an added result is that in many cases the proposals do support generally accepted changes. The sources for these possible revisions as well as some of those who propose or used them follow in the 15 numbers below. I have also added the NJPS data, which is usually consistent with MT.

1. In 2:1[3] to add one lemma by moving the final plural suffix *m* from "your brothers" making it "your brother" and adding it to "my people" as the preposition *m* 'from, of' (the second plural *m* on "your sisters" would also be moved making it "your sister," adding the *m* to the next word "mercy" making it a participle, which does not change lemma

counts), (see singular "brother" and "sister" in LXX, NRSV, BHK, and BHQ, where Gelston (2010:55*) presents both sides of the argument as follows, "The weight of the evidence favors reading both nouns in the pl., while it is easy to see why they should have been assimilated to the sg. of the proper names in 1:6, 8 and 9, which are repeated here without the negatives." NJPS has plural.)

2. In 2:16[18] to add *lî* 'to me' (lemma and word) before "my-husband" as in the following clause in 16[18]b (see NRSV, LXX, Syriac, Vulgate, BHK, BHS, and BHQ, 56*; NJPS has [Me] in brackets.)
3. In 4:10 to add *w* 'and' to *ḥznw* 'commit-harlotry' (see BHS "2 Mss," and BHQ noting the Targum, although preferring MT. NJPS has no "and.")
4. In 4:18 to add a lemma by reading the first letter of the last word not as part of "shield" but as the preposition *m* 'than' (as in LXX, see NRSV, BHK, BHS, and see BHQ, 58* with *mg'wnh* 'than her glory' for the basis of the LXX reading; NJPS translates the last word as "gift.")
5. In 4:19 to add another *m* to the preposition *m* 'from' (NRSV translates 'because of') to make *mzbḥwtm* 'their altars' (as in LXX, Syriac, and Targum, see BHK, BHS, and BHQ, 59* although BHQ also gives support for MT; NJPS has "from their sacrifices" without an extra *m*.)
6. In 6:5 to add the preposition *k* 'as' before "light" by moving the *k* 'your' suffix, which is not a lemma, off of "judgment" as in LXX, Syriac, and Targum, with Vulgate translating it in both, (see NRSV, BHK, BHS, and see BHQ, 60*, "This reading is also preferred because it is identical with the consonantal text of M, and avoids the awkward change of speaker implied in M's word division." NJPS keeps "your.")
7. In 6:11 to add "begin" (word and lemma) as in the Targum (LXX has "beginning of" instead of "set," see BHQ, 61*, "it is interesting that T's paraphrase includes the verb שריאו ('have begun')." NJPS does not have "begin.")
8. In 7:15 to delete the first verb "trained" (word and lemma) leaving only "strengthened" as in LXX (see BHK, BHS, and BHQ, 62*, suggesting it was possibly omitted "because it was either not understood in the context or thought to be synonymous with the second.") NJPS keeps two verbs.
9. In 7:16 to add an article lemma *h* on *rmyh* 'defective' (bow) as in Dead Sea Scroll (see BHQ, 62*, "The only textually significant variant is the addition of the art. in 4QXIIg.") NJPS does not have "the."

10. In 9:6 to delete the preposition *l* 'to, of' from "silver" as in LXX, (see BHK and BHS, which suggest replacing it with a genitive on "treasure," BHQ, 64* gives another explanation, the LXX "omits the preposition ל before the second noun because it construes it in the next clause." NJPS has "[with] the silver.")

11. In 10:5 to delete the word *ʿl* 'on' and divide the previous word "idolatrous priests" making its initial *k* into "as" and leaving the verb "they rebelled" (thereby keeping the same number of MT lemmas), following the LXX καθὼς παρεπίκραναν αὐτόν (see BHQ, 66*). NJPS has "priestlings . . . Mourn over it."

12. In 11:12[12:1] to delete a word (and lemma) by combining "roams with" to become "knows" (see LXX, RSV, BHQ, 69*, "G[reek] read the two words together and either read the first letter as י or deliberately interpreted it as though it were י.") NJPS keeps both words and has no "knows."

13. In 12:2[3] to delete the lemma conjunction *w* 'and' before *lpqd* 'punish' as in LXX (see BHK, BHS, and see BHQ 69* as follows, "G may presuppose a *Vorlage* without it, but may simply have avoided rendering it for translational reasons.") NJPS has "And punished."

14. In 13:5 to add a word (and lemma) by dividing "droughts" into "no houses" following LXX ἐν γῇ ἀοικήτῳ (see BHQ, 71*, "Tov (Text-Critical Use, 137–38) suggests that G might have thought of לא-בת, which is graphically similar to M. S[yriac]'s second rendering agrees with that of G and V[ulgate]." NJPS has "In a thirsty land."

15. In 13:8 to delete the lemma *k* 'as' from "lion," see BHQ, 71*, "The real significance of G's rendering is its omission of כ in common with S[yriac]. Both remove the simile and make the lion(s) the subj[ect]." NJPS keeps "as a lion."

Twelve of the fifteen suggested changes are based on the LXX, and one on a Dead Sea text. Although some of these suggested revisions are questioned, as noted with some of Gelston's BHQ quotes, they are what I propose as possibilities for illustrating the numerical value gained by such revisions. Other changes could presumably also get these or other symbolic counts. There are only *six* proposed word changes to the 2,382 total MT words, and *nine* lemma changes to the 3,092 total MT lemmas. In comparison to these totals, the small number of changes needed to make all structural units have numbers with symbolic factors gives credence to proposing that such patterns were integral to the structure.[2] It also affirms the high integrity of the MT.

2. Song of Songs has the advantage of needing only *one* well-attested textual variant

In the above table 4 the large number of twenty-eight revised large number (11, 13, 17, and 23) symbolic multiples compared to the small numbers (5, 6, 10) with eighteen symbolic multiples is statistically significant.[3] A matrix using the same categories as in tables 1 and 2 above with categories of **1028** (potential for 11, 13 and 26) and **2329** (potential for 5, 6 and 10), compared to groups of **16** (hits for multiples of 11, 13 and 26 in table 4) and **17** (hits for multiples of 5, 6, and 10 in table 4) produces Yate's chi-square of 20.44 with a p-value of 0.000006 or nearly 100% positive probability. This is slightly higher than the 99% of MT in table 1. The fact that this high percentage was maintained by adding numbers based on a set of variant readings proposed by textual scholars gives further support that the system of symbolic numbers focusing on the large symbolic numbers is integral to all the blocks and parts defined here in Hosea.

We now return to the question of whether the plan for symbolic numbers included *cumulative* numbers. Table 5 shows the cumulative totals for the *revised* words and lemmas for each block. Table 6 gives a summary of this data for cumulative *words*, and table 7 a summary for cumulative *lemmas*. Results will be discussed after table 7.

Table 5: Cumulative Revised Word and Lemma Sums by Blocks and Parts

Blocks/Parts	Cumulative Words	Cumulative Lemmas
(Block 1, Title—2:8[10]	286=**22x13, 11x26**	377=**13x29**)
Block 2, Part I, Title—3:5	558=**6x93**	768=**6x128, 32x24**
Block 3, 4:1—5:4	834=**6x139**	1132 not symbolic
Block 4, Part II 4:1—7:2	1092=**26x42, 13x84, 6x182**	1470=**10x147, 6x245, 5x294**
Block 5, Part III 7:3—8:13	1392=**6x132**	1827 not symbolic
Block 6, 8:14—10:1	1634 not symbolic	2133 not symbolic
Block 7, Part IV 8:14—11:7	1887=**17x111**	2452 not symbolic
Block 8, 11:8—13:3	2142=**17x126, 6x357**	2797 not symbolic
Block 9, Part V, 11:8–14:9[10]	2382=**6x397**	3096=**6x516**

in 2:13 adding a *qire* lemma *l* to make its word and lemma numbers come out in numerous meaningful theologically symbolic patterns (see Bliese, *Count*, 50).

3. The counts including more than one symbolic factor are 26x4, 23x5, 22x2, 17x5, 13x6, and 11x6 for large; and 10x2, 6x9, and 5x7 for small.

The following table 6 for words and table 7 for lemmas summarize symbolic numbers in the two groups tabulated above: (1) the MT data and (2) the proposed "Revised" text data. Each category is listed with two lines, "MT" followed by "*Revised*" indented and in italics. All the data comes in two columns, one for parts and the other for blocks. The first three categories are the totals in the literary units themselves and last three categories are the *cumulative* totals which progress from the beginning of the book to the end. Both of these sections have the same three groups: (1) the number of parts and blocks that have any symbolic number, large or small, (2) the number of parts and blocks with the large numbers 11, 13, 17, 22, 23, 26, or 32, and (3) the total of large symbolic factors with corollaries or multiple symbolic factors for one number. (Parts are the same as blocks in cumulative counts, so cumulative parts with corollaries are in parentheses and are not counted.)

Table 6: Summary of *Word* Counts in MT & Revised, Plus Cumulative

	Parts	Blocks
MT, all symbolic word counts	2 of 5	4 of 9
Revised, *all symbolic word counts*	*5 of 5*	*9 of 9*
MT with large 11, 13, 17, 22, 23, 26, 32	2 of 5	4 of 9
Revised with large 11, 13, 17, 22, 23. 26, 32	*2 of 5*	*6 of 9*
MT large number totals with corollaries (multiple factors)	2	+7=9
Revised, large number totals with corollaries	2	*+11=13*
MT cumulative, all symbolic word counts	4 of 5	7 of 9
Revised Cumulative *all symbolic word counts*	*5 of 5*	*8 of 9*
MT cumulative with large 11, 13, 17, 22, 23, 26, 32	2 of 5	5 of 9
Revised Cumulative, large 11, 13, 17, 22, 23. 26, 32	*2 of 5*	*4 of 9*
MT cumulative large number totals with corollaries	(2)	=8
Revised Cumulative, large numbers with corollaries	*(3)*	*=8*

Table 7 is a summary of MT and "Revised" *lemma* counts including cumulative counts for each as in table 6 for words.

Table 7: Summary of *Lemma* Counts in MT & Revised Plus Cumulative

	Parts	Blocks
MT, all symbolic lemma counts	3 of 5	5 of 9
Revised, *all symbolic lemma counts*	*5 of 5*	*9 of 9*
MT with large 11, 13, 17, 22, 23, 26, 32	3 of 5	4 of 9
Revised with large 11, 13, 17, 22, 23. 26, 32	*3 of 5*	*8 of 9*
MT large number totals with corollaries	3	+6=9
Revised, large number totals with corollaries	*4*	*+11=15*
MT cumulative, all symbolic lemma counts	2 of 5	3 of 9
Revised Cumulative *all symbolic lemma counts*	*3 of 5*	*4 of 9*
MT cumulative with large 11, 13, 17, 22, 23, 26, 32	2 of 5	3 of 9
Revised Cumulative, large 11, 13, 17, 22, 23. 26, 32	*1 of 5*	*2 of 9*
MT cumulative large number totals with corollaries	(3)	=4
Revised Cumulative, large numbers with corollaries	*(1)*	*=1*

First, the success of the revision to improve the counts is shown in that all five parts and all nine blocks for both words and lemmas have symbolic factors, as shown by 5 of 5 and 9 of 9 for the revised counts in the second lines in both summary tables 6 and 7. It was noted after table 2 that cumulative symbolic factors are significantly higher for MT *words than for lemmas.* In table 5 comparing the five "not symbolic" lines in the lemma column to only one in the word column shows that the difference is even greater than MT after the proposed revisions. This is also shown in table 6 (in the fourth pair from the top) in the summary for cumulative MT words with 4 of 5 parts symbolic and 7 of 9 blocks. In contrast cumulative MT *lemmas* in table 7 have only 2 of 5 parts and 3 of 9 blocks symbolic. The difference is also seen in tables 6 and 7 by comparing the line of revised cumulative large factors (second pair from the bottom) for words in table 5 which has 2 of 5 for parts and 4 of 9 for blocks, with table 7 where revised cumulative lemmas have 1 of 5 for parts and only 2 of 9 for blocks. This shows that the proposed text revisions, which make the individual parts and blocks more symbolic, did *not* also make better cumulative numbers for *lemmas.* The contrast is also seen in the third pair from the end of the table 6 summary for words, which shows a slight improvement over MT in that *word* revisions produced 5 of 5 symbolic numbers for parts, and 8 of 9 for blocks after MT's 4 of 5 part numbers and 7 of 9 block numbers.

However, in table 7 (third pair from the bottom) revised *lemmas* have only 3 of 5 for parts and 4 of 9 for blocks. Even more clearly, the revisions *add* to the number of *large number factors,* from MT 9 to revised 13 for words (table 6 third pair), and keep 8 for cumulative large number word totals as in MT (table 6 sixth pair). However, although revisions increase large factor *lemmas* from MT 9 to 15 (table 7 third pair) for *part and block* totals, *cumulative lemmas decrease* from MT 4 to revised having *only one* large number (table 7 last pair). Revisions improved *cumulative word* counts indicating they originally may have been coordinated with the block numbers, but lowered *lemma* counts indicating they were not coordinated. It is easier to count words, which are surface forms, than to count lemmas, which require an analysis before counting. This may account for the greater use of *words* in forming symbolic number patterns in Hosea.[4]

The improvement of cumulative counts for *words* after the proposed revisions gives support to the proposal that there is an underlying symbolic number pattern since the effect on cumulative counts was not involved in the decisions when the revisions were chosen. They were only chosen to improve the counts within each block and part. Therefore, any changes that were not in line with the underlying pattern would have produced random changes that would reduce the percentage of symbolic numbers. Instead the improvement in sectional totals brought an improvement in their cumulative counts, indicating that *words* were likely adjusted for both sectional totals and cumulative counts to fit an underlying pattern.

4. This also applies to Song of Songs, which has five of its seven parts with symbolic totals for words, but only three of seven for lemmas. Its *cumulative* book *totals* are symbolic for both words and lemmas, but *part* cumulative numbers are too low for probability with only three of seven for words and four of seven for lemmas (see Bliese *Count*, 59–61).

References

Alter, Robert. "Ancient Hebrew Poetry." *The Literary Guide to the Bible*, edited by R. Alter and F. Kermode. Cambridge: Belknap, 611–24, 1987.

———. *The Art of Biblical Poetry*. New York: Basic, 1985.

———. "Psalms." *The Literary Guide to the Bible*, edited by R. Alter and F. Kermode. Cambridge: Belknap, 255–58, 1987.

Andersen, Francis I. "The Orthography of D62." In David N. Freedman, A. Dean Forbes, Francis I. Andersen, *Studies in Hebrew and Aramaic Orthography*. Winona Lake, Eisenbrauns, 1992.

Andersen, Francis I, and A. Dean Forbes. *The Vocabulary of the Old Testament*. Rome: E.P.I.B., 1989.

Andersen, Francis I, and David N. Freedman. *The Anchor Bible: Hosea*. New York: Doubleday, 1980.

Andersen, Francis I, and David N. Freedman. "Another Look at 4QSamb." In David N. Freedman, A. Dean Forbes, Francis I. Andersen, *Studies in Hebrew and Aramaic Orthography*. Winona Lake, Eisenbrauns, 1992.

Andersen, Francis I, and David N. Freedman. "The Orthography of 4QTestimonia." In David N. Freedman, A. Dean Forbes, Francis I. Andersen, *Studies in Hebrew and Aramaic Orthography*. Winona Lake, Eisenbrauns, 1992.

Andersen, T. David. "Problems in Analyzing Hebrew Poetry." *East Asia Journal of Theology* 2, 68–87, 1986.

(BHK) *Biblia Hebraica*. Edited by Rudolf Kittel. *XII PROPHETARUM* edited by O. Procksch. Stuttgart: Deutsche Bibelgesellschaft, 1954.

(BHQ) *Biblia Hebraica Quinta: editione cum apparatu critico novis curis elaborato. Vol 13, The Twelve Minor Prophets: Introduction and Commentaries on the Twelve Minor Prophets*. Prepared by Anthony Gelston. Stuttgart: Deutsche Bibelgesellschaft, 2010.

(BHS) *Biblia Hebraica Stuttgartensia. Liber XII Prophetarum*. Vol. 10, edited by K. Elliger and W. Rudolph. Stuttgart: Wuerttembergische Bibelanstalt, 1970.

Bliese, Loren F. "The Afar Drum Song." *Proceedings of the Eleventh International Conference of Ethiopian Studies*. Vol 1, edited by Bahru Zewde, Richard Pankhurst, Taddese Beyene. Addis Ababa: Addis Ababa University, 1994, 583–94.

———. "Afar Songs." *Northeast African Studies* 4.3 (1982–83) 51–76.

———. "Chiastic and Homogeneous Metrical Structures Enhanced by Word Patterns in Obadiah." *Journal of Translation and Textlinguistics* 6.3 (1993) 210–27. http://www. sil.org (then do a search for Loren F Bliese and click on the Obadiah article, and then click on JOTT06(3).pdf).

———. "Chiastic Structures, Peaks and Cohesion in Nehemiah 9: 6–37." *The Bible Translator* 39.2 (1988) 208–15.

———. *Count God In: Theological Numbers in the Song of Songs*. Eugene: Wipf and Stock. 2018.

———. "A Cryptic Chiastic Acrostic: Finding Meaning from Structure in the Poetry of Nahum." *Journal of Translation and Textlinguistics* 7.3 (1995) 48–81. Paper first presented to the SIL Seminar on the Discourse Structure of Biblical Hebrew in Dallas, Texas, 1993. http://www. sil.org (then do a search for Loren F Bliese and click on the Nahum article, and then scroll down to "Is Part Of" and click on the Journal, and then on JOTT07(3).pdf).

———. "Metrical Sequences and Climax in the Poetry of Joel." *Occasional Papers in Translation and Textlinguistics* 2.4 (1988) 52–84. http://www. sil.org (then do a search for Loren F Bliese and click on the Joel article, and then click on OPTAT02(4).pdf).

———. "Metrical and Word Patterns in the Structure of Zephaniah." *Journal of Translation and Textlinguistics* 17 (2004) 36–68. Also presented to the 1998 United Bible Societies Afrescot workshop in Nairobi and the 1998 Society of Biblical Literature International Conference in Krakow. http://www. sil.org (then do a search for Loren F Bliese and click on the Zephaniah article, and then scroll down to "Is Part Of" and click on the Journal , and then on JOTT17.pdf).

———. "Numerical and Lexical Patterns in the Structure of Micah." *Journal of Translation and Textlinguistics* 16 (2003) 119–43. Also presented to the 1996 United Bible Societies Afrescot workshop in Mombasa and the 1997 Society of Biblical Literature International Conference in Lausanne. http://www.sil.org/resources/archives 7734, or sil.org (then do a search for Loren F Bliese and click on the Micah article, and then scroll down to "Is Part Of," and click on JOTT16.pdf).

———. Review of David E. Orton, *Poetry in the Hebrew Bible: Selected Studies from Vetus Testamentum*. (Boston: Brill, 2000). Available to Society of Biblical Literature members on www.sblcentral.org. Search for Loren Bliese, then click on *Poetry in the Hebrew Bible* by David Orton, then scroll down to Reviewers and click on Sign In to Read.

———. "The Poetics of Habakkuk." *Journal of Translation and Textlinguistics* 12 (1999) 47–75. https//www.sil.org/resources//archives/41131.

———. "Structural Prominence in Second Isaiah 40, 45 and Servant Poems." Unpublished paper presented at the UBS 1992 Afrescot workshop in Nairobi.

———. "Structurally Marked Peak in Psalms 1–24." *Occasional Papers in Translation and Textlinguistics* 4.4 (1990) 266–321, first presented at an SIL Old Testament Seminar in Nairobi, 1988. http//www.sil.org (then do a search for Loren F Bliese and click on the Psalms 1-24 article, and then click on OPTAT_04(4).pdf).

———. "Symmetry and Prominence in Hebrew Poetry: with Examples from Hosea." In *Discourse Perspectives on Hebrew Poetry in the Scriptures*, edited by Ernst R. Wendland. (New York: United Bible Societies) Monograph 7, 67–94, 1994. (Includes the structural analysis used in this current study.)

———. "Translating Psalm 23 in Traditional Afar Poetry." In Lynell Zogbo and Ernst R. Wendland, *Hebrew Poetry in the Bible: A Guide for Understanding and for Translation*, 185–94. New York: United Bible Societies, 2000. A Spanish translation is "La Traducción del Salmo 23 en la poesía Afar Tradicional." In *La poesía del Antiguo Testamento: pantas para su traducción*, translated and adapted by Alfredo Tepox Varela, 235–47. Miami: Sociedades Biblicas Unidas, 2003. A French translation is "Traduire le Ps 23 en afar." *Le Sycomore* 8.2 (2015) 25–34, www.ubs-translations.org/sycomore.

Boadt, Lawrence. "Reflections on the Study of Hebrew Poetry Today." *Concordia Journal* 24 (1998) 156–163.

Breck, J. "Biblical Chiasmus: Exploring Structure for Meaning." *BTB* 17 (1987) 70–74.

(BDB) Brown, Francis, S. R. Driver, and Charles A. Briggs. *Hebrew and English Lexicon of the Old Testament*. Oxford: Clarendon, 1907.

Buss, M. *The Prophetic Word of Hosea: A Morphological Study*. Berlin: Topelmann, 1969.

Christensen, Duane L. "Narrative Poetics and the Interpretation of the Book of Jonah." In *Directions in Biblical Hebrew Poetry*, edited by Elaine R. Follis, 29–48. Sheffield: *Journal for the Study of the Old Testament Supplement Series* 40, 1987.

Collins, T. *Line-forms in Hebrew Poetry: A Grammatical Approach to the Stylistic Study of the Hebrew Prophets. Studia Pohl*: Series Maior 7. Rome: Biblical Institute Press, 1978.

Dearman, J. Andrew. *The Book of Hosea*. New International Commentary on the Old Testament, Grand Rapids: Eerdmans, 2010.

Eidevall, Göran. *Grapes in the Desert: Metaphors, Models, and Themes in Hosea 4–14*. Coniectanea Biblica Old Testament Series 43. Stockholm: Almqvist & Wiksell, 1996.

Emmerson, Grace L. *Hosea: An Israelite Prophet in Judean Perspective*. Sheffield: *Journal for the Study of the Old Testament Supplement Series*, 28, 1984.

Forbes, A. Dean. "A Tutorial on Method: A Guide for the Statistically Perplexed." Chapter 2 in David N. Freedman, A. Dean Forbes, Francis I. Andersen, *Studies in Hebrew and Aramaic Orthography*. Winona Lake, Eisenbrauns, 1992.

Freedman, David N. "Acrostic Poems in the Hebrew Bible: Alphabetic and Otherwise." *Catholic Biblical Quarterly* 48 (1986) 408–31.

———. "Another Look at Biblical Hebrew Poetry." *Directions in Biblical Hebrew Poetry*, edited by Elaine R. Follis, 1–28. Sheffield: *Journal for the Study of the Old Testament Supplement Series* 40, 1987.

———. "The Evolution of Hebrew Orthography." Chapter 1 in In David N. Freedman, A. Dean Forbes, Francis I. Andersen, *Studies in Hebrew and Aramaic Orthography*. Winona Lake, Eisenbrauns, 1992.

———. "Prolegomenon." In George B. Gray, *The Forms of Hebrew Poetry*. New York: KTAV, i–lvi, 1972.

Freedman, David N., A. Dean Forbes, Francis I Andersen. *Studies in Hebrew and Aramaic Orthography*. Winona Lake, Eisenbrauns, 1992.

Garrett, Duane A. *Hosea, Joel: An Exegetical and Theological Exposition of Holy Scripture*. The New American Commentary, 1997.

Gelston, Anthony. *Biblia Hebraica Quinta, Fascicle 13: The Twelve Minor Prophets*. Stuttgart: Deutsche Bibelgesellschaft, 2010.

van Grol, Harm W. M. "Classical Hebrew Metrics and Zephaniah 2–3." *The Structural Analysis of Biblical and Canaanite Poetry*. Eds., Willem van der Meer and Johannis C. de Moor, 186–206. Sheffield: *Journal for the Study of the Old Testament Supplement Series* 74, 1988.

Halle, Morris and John McCarthy. "The Metrical Structure of Psalm 137." *Journal of Biblical Literature* 100.2 (1981) 161–67.

Harper, W. *The International Critical Commentary: Amos and Hosea*. Edinburgh: Clark, 1905.

Holladay, William L. "Chiasmus, the Key to Hosea XII 3–6." *Vetus Testamentum* 16 (1966) 53–64.

(*HOTTP*) *Preliminary and Interim Report on the Hebrew Old Testament Text Project: Prophetical Books II*, Vol. 5, edited by D. Barthelemy, A. Hulst, N. Lohfink, W. McHardy, H. Ruger and J. Sanders. New York: United Bible Societies, 1980.

Kidner, Derek. *The Message of Hosea*. Intervarsity: Downers Grove, 1981.

Korpel, Marjo and Johannis de Moor. "Fundamentals of Ugaritic and Hebrew Poetry." *Ugarit-Forschungen* 18 (1986) 173–212. (Also in van der Meer and de Moor, eds., *The Structural Analysis of Biblical and Canaanite Poetry*, 1–61. Sheffield: *Journal for the Study of the Old Testament Supplement Series* 74, 1988).

Kosmala, H. "Form and Structure in Ancient Hebrew Poetry." *Vetus Testamentum* 14 (1964) 423–45.

Kugel, James. *The Idea of Biblical Poetry: Parallelism and its History*. New York: Yale, 1981.

———, ed. *Poetry and Prophecy: the Beginnings of a Literary Tradition*. Ithaca: Cornell, 1990.

Labuschagne, Casper J. *Numerical Secrets of the Bible: Rediscovering the Bible Codes*. North Richland Hills: Bibal, 2000. Also available www.labuschagne.nl/z%26oz/Numerical_secrets_2008.pdf. Reprinted Eugene: Wipf and Stock as *Numerical Secrets of the Bible: Introduction to Biblical Arithmology*, 2016.

———. "On the Structural Use of Numbers as a Composition Technique." *Journal of Northwest Semitic Languages*, 12 (1984[1986]) 87–99.

———. "Significant Compositional Techniques in the Psalms: Evidence for the Use of Number as an Organizing Principle." *Vetus Testamentum*, 59.4 (2009) 583–605.

Longacre, Robert. *The Grammar of Discourse*. New York: Plenum, 1983.

———. "Two Hypotheses Regarding Text Generation and Analysis." *Discourse Processes* 12 (1989) 413–60.

Lundbom, J. "Poetic Structure and Prophetic Rhetoric in Hosea." *Vetus Testamentum* 29 (1979) 300–308.

———. "Contentious Priests and Contentious People in Hosea IV 1–10." *Vetus Testamentum* 36.1 (1986) 52–70.

Margalit, B. "Introduction to Ugaritic Prosody." *Ugarit-Forschungen* 7, edited by K. Bergerhof, M. Dietrich and O. Loretz, 287–313. Neukirchen: Butzon & Bercker, 1975.

Mays, James Luther. *Hosea: A Commentary*. Philadelphia: Westminster, 1969.

van der Meer, Willem and Johannis C. de Moor. *The Structural Analysis of Biblical and Canaanite Poetry*. Sheffield: *Journal for the Study of the Old Testament Supplement Series* 74, 1988.

de Moor, Johannis C. "The Art of Versification in Ugarit and Israel I: The Rhythmical Structure." *Studies in Bible and the Ancient Near East Presented to S. E. Loewenstamm*, edited by Y. Avishur and J. Blau, 119–39. Jerusalem, 1978.

The NIV Study Bible. Grand Rapids: Zondervan, 1985.

O'Connor, M. *Hebrew Verse Structure*. Winona Lake: Eisenbrauns, 1980.

Paratext: Scripture Translation Software. United Bible Societies and SIL International, updated 2021.

Renkema, Johan. "The Literary Structure of Lamentations (i)–(iv)." *The Structural Analysis of Biblical and Canaanite Poetry*, edited by Willem van der Meer and Johannis C. de Moor, 294–396). Sheffield: *Journal for the Study of the Old Testament Supplement Series* 74, 1988.

Sawyer, John F. A. "A Change of Emphasis in the Study of the Prophets." *Israel's Prophetic Tradition: Essays in Honour of Peter R. Ackroyd*. Eds. R. Coggins, M. Phillips, M. Knibb, 233–46. New York: Cambridge, 1982.

Schedl, Claus. *Baupläne des Wortes. Einführung in die biblische Logotechnik*. Wien, 1974.

Schoekel, L. Alonso. *A Manual of Hebrew Poetics. Subsidia Biblica* 11. Roma: Editrice Pontificio Istituto Biblico, 1988.

Shea, William. "Chiasmus and the Structure of David's Lament." *Journal of Biblical Literature* 105.1 (1986) 13–25.

Sherwood, Yvonne. *The Prostitute and the Prophet: Hosea's Marriage in Literary-Theoretical Perspective*. Sheffield: Sheffield Academic, 1996.

Shoshany, Ronit. "Prosodic Structures in Jeremiah's Poetry." *Folia Linguistica Historica* 7.1 (1986) 167–206.

Stuart, Douglas. *Studies in Early Hebrew Meter*. Harvard Semitic Monograph 13. Missoula: Scholars, 1976.

———. *Hosea-Jonah: Word Biblical Commentary* 31. Digital. Word: Waco, 1987.

Tängberg, K. A. "A Note on *pištî* in Hosea II, 7, 11." *Vetus Testamentum* 27 (1977) 222–24.

Watson, Wilfred G. E. *Classical Hebrew Poetry*. Sheffield: *Journal for the Study of the Old Testament Supplement Series* 26, 1984.

de Waard, Jan, and Eugene A. Nida. *From One Language to Another: Functional Equivalence in Bible Translating*. New York: Nelson, 1986.

Wendland, Ernst R,. ed. *Discourse Perspectives on Hebrew Poetry in the Scriptures*. UBS Monograph Series, No. 7. New York: United Bible Societies, 1994.

(WHM) Westminster Hebrew Morphology. Data disk, 1991. Abbreviated as WHM.

Willis, John T. "Alternating (ABA'B') Parallelism in the Old Testament Psalms and Prophetic Literature," edited by Elaine R. Follis, 49–76. Sheffield: *Journal for the Study of the Old Testament Supplement Series* 40, 1987.

Wolff, Hans W. *Hosea. Hermeneia*. Translated by G. Stansell. Philadelphia: Fortress, 1974.

Yee, Gale A. *Composition and Tradition in the Book of Hosea: A Redaction Critical Investigation*. Society of Biblical Literature Dissertation Series 102. Atlanta: Scholars, 1987.

Youngblood, Ronald. "Divine Names in the Book of Psalms: Literary Structures and Number Patterns." *Journal of the Ancient Near Eastern Society* 19 (1989) 171–81.

Zevit, Ziony. "Psalms at the Poetic Precipice." *Hebrew Annual Review* 10 (1986) 351–66.

Author Index

Alter, Robert, 3, 5, 225
Andersen, Francis I., 5, 23, 24, 36, 37, 39, 46, 48, 54, 62, 69, 110, 128, 139, 142, 143, 146, 149, 152, 153, 156, 158, 160, 164, 170, 172, 179, 192, 196, 203, 225, 227
Andersen, T. David, 3, 225

(BHK) *Biblia Hebraica* (Kittel), 16, 65, 217, 219, 220, 225
(BHQ) *Biblia Hebraica Quinta*, 16, 132, 217, 219, 220, 225
(BHS) *Biblia Hebraica Stuttgartensia*, 3, 4, 6, 16, 38, 40, 42, 48, 54, 62, 63, 65, 67, 111, 131, 143, 148, 177, 192, 217, 219, 220, 225
Bliese, Loren F., 1, 5, 7, 12, 13, 17, 18, 22, 32, 39, 49, 54, 68, 80, 96, 97, 101, 104, 121, 130, 152, 162, 221, 224, 225, 226
Boadt, Lawrence, 5, 227
Breck, J., 6, 227
Buss, M., 38, 53, 65, 227

Christensen, Duane L., 5, 101, 227
Collins, T., 48, 227

Eidevall, Göran, 106, 116, 117, 120, 125, 131, 132, 134, 136, 138, 139, 142, 143, 146, 147, 152, 154, 155, 156, 160, 162, 165, 166, 170, 179, 180, 182, 187, 188, 200, 203, 205, 207, 209, 227
Emmerson, Grace L., 37, 69, 227

Forbes, A. Dean, 23, 39, 62, 203, 225, 227
Freedman, David N., 3, 5, 23, 23, 36, 37, 46, 48, 54, 69, 70, 100, 110, 128, 139, 142, 146, 149, 152, 153, 156, 158, 160, 164, 170, 172, 179, 192, 225, 227

Gelston, Anthony, xi, 132, 219, 225, 227
Grol, Harm W. M. van, 3, 54, 130, 227

Halle, Morris, 5, 227
Harper, W., 48, 62, 228
Holladay, William L., 194, 228
(*HOTTP*) *Hebrew Old Testament Text Project*, xi, 110, 134, 151, 171, 172, 183, 204, 228

Korpel, Marjo, 4, 130, 205, 228
Kosmala, H., 6, 228
Kugel, James, 3, 228

Labuschagne, Casper J., 7–8,17, 21, 23, 228
Longacre, Robert, 80, 86, 87, 88, 92, 99, 100, 146, 213, 228
Lundbom, J., 5, 6, 53, 110, 115, 117, 122, 123, 124, 159, 160, 192, 228

Margalit, B., 3, 228

Mays, James Luther, 26, 37, 43, 46, 57, 63, 64, 69, 121, 123, 131, 132, 138, 144, 155, 156, 167, 175, 228
McCarthy, John, 5, 227
Meer, Willem van der, 5, 227, 228, 229
Moor, Johannis C. de, 4, 5, 130, 205, 227, 228, 229

Nida, Eugene, A., 215, 229
NIV Study Bible, 138, 228

O'Connor, M., 4, 5, 228
Orton, David E., 226

Paratext, 65, 127, 133, 228

Renkema, Johan, 118, 229

Sawyer, John F. A., 5, 229
Schedl, Claus, 8, 21, 229
Schoekel, L. Alonso, 80, 229
Shea, William, 6, 229
Sherwood, Yvonne, 32, 35, 36, 46, 57, 229
Shoshany, Ronit, 6, 80, 91, 92, 100, 229
Stuart, Douglas, 36, 57, 80, 142, 229
Watson, Wilfred G. E., 3, 29, 80, 100, 229
Waard, de, Jan, 215, 229

(WHM) Westminster Hebrew Morphology, xi, 41, 65, 127, 133, 195, 229
Willis, John T., 4, 118, 229
Wolff, Hans W., 37, 40, 43, 52, 57, 65, 103, 111, 121, 134, 139, 156, 159, 229

Yee, Gale A., 43, 100, 103, 203, 229
Youngblood, Ronald, 80, 229

Zevit, Ziony, 3, 229

Subject Index

11: 1, 2, **8**, 18, 169
13: 1, 2, **7**, 18, 21
17: 7, **8**, 10, 19, 22, 49, 65, 115, 155, 218
22: 2, **8**, 12, 13, 19, 21, 27, 28, 33, 50, 57–58, 98, 100, 102, 103, 133, 153, 167, 169, 217
22-letter lines, 28, 98, 102, 133, 153, 175
23: **8**, 10, 19, 21, 22, 23, 70, 119, 170, 188, 190, 195, 211, 218
26: xii, 1, 2, 3, 7, 9, 10, 11, 13, 14, 19, 21, 22, 26, 28, 29, 31–32, 35, 42, 58, 60, 63, 64, 75, 80, 97, 117, 119, 121, 126, 152, 204, 211, 212, 218
26-letter lines, 97
32: **8**, **9–10**, 19, 22, 44, 45, 50, 65, 79, 115, 119, 124, 140, 169, 170, 211
39: 20, 21, 60, 131, 158, 172, 180, 198, 204
52: 20, 39, 119, 123
55: 8, 20, 22, 79, 126, 133, 156, 158, 171, 172, 199
64: 9, 20, 29, 30, 33, 44, 60, 128, 169, 170, 188, 208
78: 2, 13, 20, 21, 45, 76, 206
104: 2, 20, 21, 31, 195
143: 14, 39, 60, 75, 154, 179, 203
286: 1–2, 13, 14, 25

accuse, 9, 115, 118
alphabetical counts, xii, 2, 8, 9, 12, 22, 27, 32, 33, 98, 119, 123, 170, 180, 203, 217–18
anacrusis, 4, 28, **90**, 136, 165, 170

"blessed be YHWH" in Psalms, 134
blocks, **13**, 105, 107–9, 116, 129, 130, 144, 155, 161, 162, 173, 176, 188, 197, 200, 204, 209, 217–18, 221

central peak, 6, 26, 32, 36, 41, 47, 54, 60, 71, 101, 103, 114, 117, 123, 124, 130, 145–146, 149, 153, 171, 179, 192, 196, 200, 203, 208, 212, 214
chiasm(us), (parts): 105–6, (blocks):106–9, (metrical): 26, 32, 35, 46, 50, 110–111, 144, 164, 177, 186, 190–91, 200–8, (word): 115, 120, 126, 134, 141, 146–47, 151, 165, 166, 170, 179, 183, 187, 207
chronology, 23
climax, 5, 6, 29, 52, 57, 61, 67, 139, 143, 184, 215
clitic, 21, 23
competence, 17
count, ix, x, **3**, 12, 13, 21–23, 39, 51, 63, 224
covenant, 9, 38, 49, 54, 58, 59–**60**, 63, 75, **104–5**, **155**, 189, 208, 210
cumulative, **15–17**, 221–24

desert, 9, 44–45, 55–57, 78, 93, 107, 167, 169–70, 172–73, 197–98, 201, 208–9, 227

divine name, 2, 8–10, 21, **22–23**, **80**, 229 (also see the discussion of the individual poems with divine names)

enallage, 88
enjambment, 34, 36, 40, 43, 49, 50, 53–54, 58, 68, **90**, 184, 185, 194–95
exile, 23–24, 69, 110–11, 184

faithfulness, 9, 59, 60, 70, 75, 114, 116, 205, 210

God, 3, 6, 8, 9, **10–11**, 23, 32, 35, 39, 41, 51, 59, 61–62, 74, 80, 99, 101, **102–104**, 106, 107, 116, 123, 128, 139, 150, 153, 155, 165, 170, 187–88, 190, 192–93, 194, 197, 203, 205, 207, 208, 210

hapax (also see singleton), 2, 9, 206
homogeneous, ix, **3–6**, **71–72**, 80, 120–21, 215, 225 (also note the discussion of the fifteen homogenous poems)

imperatives, **89**, 107, 133, 156, 158, 172, 176, 179
inspir(ation), 18
intent(ional), 9, 10, 11, 14, 15, 21, 22, 29, 40, 42, 50, 51, 101, 105, 134, 148, 152, 158, 170, 172, 211, 215
inverted parallelism (see under parallelism)
(ir)regular colometry, 4, 48, 50, **84–86**, 126, 148, 150, 158, 160, 165
Israel, 3, 9, **10**, 11, 26, 33, 41, 49, 60, 65, 68, 88, 103, 129–30, 141,44, 153, 162, 169, 178–80, 181, 186, 202, 210

Judah, 19, 26–27, 35–37, 40–41, 51, 74, 106, 125–26, 129, 130–31, 133–34, 135–36, 138, 141–42, 144, 161–62, 177, 188, 190, 192

judgment, 52, 56, **101–2**, 109, 111, 127, 132, 134, 139, 142, 162, 184, 187, 206

kbwd, **8–9**, 10, 19, 22, 24, 32, 79, 119, 169, 170–71
key to formatting, 25
key word, 2, 10–11, 25, 29, 32, 35, 36, 41, 48, 49, 50, 51, 53, 59, 60, 61, 65, 68, 70, 71, 73–79, 103, **104**, 113, 119, 123, 128, 133, 143, 144, 150, 155, 161, 162, 166, 173, 184, 185, 187, 189, 194, 198, 209, 211–12, 214

lemma, ix, x, 1, **2**, 3, 9, 10–12, **13**, 14, 15–16, **17–24**, **27**, 28–29, 81, 101, 212, 215, 217, 218–20, 223–24
line length, ix, **4**, 6, 26, 50, **72**, 76, 77, **86**, 110, 117, 130, 139, 140, 151, 158, 180, 196, 200, 203, 205–8
line(ation), **3–4**, 6–7, 26, 29, 33, 34, 38, 39, 50, 52, 63, 68, 118–19, 197, 212
lists, 9, 27, 36, 46, 50, 54, 60, 69, 74, 79, **89–90**, 99, 114, 121, 124–5, 133, 144, 210
love, **10**, 11, 54, 64–65, 70–71, 104, 108, 127, 160, 170, 172, 182, 207–8, 210
loyalty, 58, 60, 75, 108, 116, 139–40, 191

maqqep, 6
Masoretic/MT, 6–7, 9, 10, 12, **13**, 14, 15, 16, 17, 23–24, 25, 27, 28, 38, 39, 40, 43, 55, 57, 58, 65, 110, 111, 118, 121, 125, 133, 140, 154, 157, 158, 167, 169, 173, 184, 188, 200, 203, 208, 218–20, 222–24
mathematical counts, xii, 8–9, 22, 24, 32, 64, 79, 115, 119, 170–71, 188, 217
mercy, 9, 34–36, 37, 39, 40–41, 46, 58, 59–60, 61–63, 74–75, 103, 105, 107, 202, 206–7, 209, 219

metaphor, 29, 36, 44, 49, 56, 76, 77, **96**, 98, 105, 110, 119, 125, 127, 131, 137, 139, 140, 142, 147, 152, 160, 179–80, 182, 184, 188, 196, 205, 207, 227

metrical chiasm(us), 3, 4, 5, 7, 26, 32, 34, 35, 48, 65, 112, 115, 120, 123, 141, 143, 145, 151, 171, 194, 207–8, 214

overall structure, ix, 1, 28, 50, 63, **100–5**, 138, 153, 155

parallelism: 4, 5, 6, 41, 43, 45, 47, 54, 56, 63, 68, 115, 118, 125, 127, 129, 131–32, 139, 154, 167, 172, 189, 228, 229; avoiding/dropping, 29, 80, 81, **91–96**, **99**, 124, 146, 180, 214; inverted, 36, **82–84**, 118 121–22, **136**, **143**, 149, 155, 196, 198; Janus, 185; seconding/more specific second line, 45, 56, 65, 78, **92**, 124, 150, 158

parts, viii, 12, **13**, **15**, 17, 49, 101, **102**, 103, 104, 105–6, 110, 209–10, 217, 221–24

peak, **6–7**, 25, 71–100, 213–15, 226, (also see the discussion of each of the 45 poems)

peak: central of book, **102–4**, **152–6**

perform(ance), 6–7, 32

peripheral lines, 33, 72, 74, 77, 131, 134, 145, 147

plene, 175, 196

plethora, 9, 79

positive-negative (antithetical parallelism), 77, **96**, 187

prominent/prominence, ix, x, 5, 6, 72–73, **79–100**, (also see the discussion of each of the 45 poems)

quarter line peaks, **6**, 45, 48, 151, 170, 180

redact(or/ion), 10, 24, 27, 37, 100, 192, 229

repetition, 4, 9, 26, 29, 33, 36, 38, 41–42, 45–46, 48, 53–54, 57, 59–61, 65–67, 71, 74, 77, 79, **81**, 92, 99, **100**, 101, 114, 117–18, 120–21, 124, 128, 131–32, 139, 142, 146, 151, 155–56, 159, 162, 166, 172–73, 179, 184–85, 193, 196, 200, 205, 209, 211, 213

return, **10**, **11**, 48, **51**, 67, **70**, 103, 105–9, 111, 116, 128–29, 135–36, 138, 148, 150–51, 159–60, 163, 184–87, 191–94, 202–5, 208–9

rhetorical questions, **97**, 110–11, 126, 165, 184, 186

salvation, viii, 35, 56, 60, 101, **102**, **103**, **111**, 138, 142, 184, 187, 206

secondary peak, **6**, 25, 27, 33, 35, 48, 50, **72–79**, 79–98 (also see the discussion of many in other poems)

sequential (counts), 10–12

short lines, 4, 6, 27, 45, 48, 49, 50, 53, 72, 77–78, 82, **86**, 90, 93, 110, 115, 117–18, 139–40, 143, 150–51, 158, 160, 169, 171–72, 180, 192–93, 197–98, 200, 203–8, 211–12

single line strophe, 4, 76, **87**, 98–99, 116, 176, 183, 200, 205

singleton (hapax), 2, 9, 19, 20, 23, 33, 45, 50, 58–60, 76, 78–79, 106, 131, 134, 139, 158, 160, 169–73, 180, 188, 193, 199

Song of Songs, ix-x, 7, 9, 13, 17–18, 21, 24, 32, 39, 49, 104, 152, 220, 224, 226

structure/al, v, ix-x, 1, **3–8**, 10, 12, **13–15**, 17–18, 21, 23, 25, 26–28, 33–34, 36–39, 42, 43, 45–51, 54, 59–63, 65–67, 71–73, 79, 82, 84–86, 91–92, 98–99, **100–5**, 109–11, 113, 115, 118–19, 122, 124–26, 131, 133–34, 136–38, 140–42, 144–48, 151, 153, 155–56, 158, 160,

structure/al (continued) 165–67, 169, 172–73, 178, 180, 182, 184–85, 188–89, 194, 196, 200, 203–4, 207, 211, 213–15, 217–18, 220, 225–29
switches: person, 87, 98–99, 182; number, 57, 88, 94, 98–99, 120, 185, 189, 213; gender, 95, 139, 162, 189, 213
symbolic number, ix-x, 1, 2–3, **7–10**, 11–23 (also identified in the discussion in each poem)
symmetry, iv, ix, 1, 5, 50, 52, 84–85, 110–11, 148, 194, 211, 226
syntactic chiasmus or inverted parallelism (see under parallelism)
syntactic complexity, 65, 79, **91–92**, 98, 122, 124, 128, 153, 166, 188, 200

Table 1: MT Word and Lemma Counts in 9 Blocks and 5 Parts, 13
Table 2: Cumulative MT Word and Lemma Sums by Blocks and Parts, 15
Table 3: Total Counts of Lemmas Having the Same Value, 18
Table 4: Revised Word and Lemma Counts in Blocks and Parts, 217
Table 5: Cumulative Revised Word and Lemma Sums by Blocks and Parts, 221
Table 6: Summary of *Word* Counts in MT & Revised, Plus Cumulative, 222
Table 7: Summary of *Lemma* Counts in MT & Revised Plus Cumulative, 223
terrace, **4–5**, **29**, 53, 57, 61, 67, 69, 124, 128, 136, 140, 144, 155, 184–85, 190, 197
theme, **10–12**, 35, 47, **49**, 56, 59, 65, 70, 75, 103, 109, 110, 116–17, 125, 130–32, 134, 142, 156–57, 162, 164, 166, 169–71, 176, 178, 183, 188, 193, 197–98, 203, 205, 207–8, 210
title, 1, 13, 15, **26**, 27, **104**

value, ix-x, **xii**, 1, 2, 3, 7–10, **17–24**, (also see discussion in the 45 poems)

wisdom/wise, 9–10, 94, 123, 198, 201, 203, 210–12
word, ix, 1, 2, 3–4, 6, 9–12, 13, 15–17, 23, 25, 90, 104–11, 213–14, 217–24 (also see discussion in the 45 poems)
word-stress, x, 3–7, 9, 14, 71 (also see details in the 45 poems)

YH, 22, 47, 49–50, 57, 65, 102–3, 113, 118, 129, 154, 158, 182, 282
YHWH, xii, **1**, 2–3, **7–10**, 11, 21–22, 75, 102, 104, 106, 217 (also see discussion in the 45 poems)

Scripture Index

Abridged for Hosea

Genesis

15: 1, 4 26
37:35 111
39:5 100
39:12 175

Exodus

3:14–15 7, 38, 183, 193, 206
6:4–7 38, 60
20:2 193
20:3 198
29:43 8
33:18, 22 8

Numbers

14:22 8
23:18–24 80

Deuteronomy

3:1–10 21
5:6 193
5:24 8
6:4 21
8:10–14 198
28:33 134
28:37 132
28:49 156
29:12–13[11–12] 38
29:23[22] 187
30:2, 10 12

1 Samuel

8:4–20 200
15:22, 33 139

2 Kings

9:27 175
15:19–20 134
15:25, 30 146
19:15 22

Nehemiah

9 54

Psalms

Five Books 101, 104
1–24 7, 68, 80,130, 162, 226
1 162, 180
1:2 130
1:6 80
2:7 80
3:3[4] 8
3:7–8 68, 80
4:8 80
5:8 80

Psalms (continued)

8:3 130
9:16 80
10:14 78, 207
11 162
11:4 80
12:5 80
13:3 80
15:4 80
16:7 80
17:14b 130
23 7, 226–7
25 153
34 153
47:9 127
50:22 137
79 21
85 80
106:20 119
107:43 94, 212
119 8
137 5, 227
143 212

Song of Songs

6:12 39

Isaiah

1:1 210
11:12 43
24:2 118
37:20 22
40:13, 18 97
43:5 43
45:11 97
50:8 97
55:13 210

Jeremiah

4:3 178
11:2–4 38

Hosea (Abridged)

(Poems and Primary References in **Bold**)

1:1—3:5 (Part 1) **25**, 101, 142
1:1—2:8[10] (Block 1) **25**, 101, 107
1:1–2a Chiasm 25, **26–27**, 113
1:1 64, 86, 90, 107, 142
1:2c-d Homogeneous **2**, **28**–30, 32–34, 38–39
1:2 1, 9, 27, 36, 39, 46, 50–51, 64, 70, 97–98, 107, 126, 204, 212
1:3 **30**, 34, 50
1:4b–5 Chiasm **31–34**, 68, 73, 97
1:4 2, 35–36, 114
1:6a 30, **34**
1:6b–7 Chiasm **34**–37, 39, 41–42, 68, 74, 83, 153, 209
1:6 39, 41–42
1:7 39, 59, 107, 126,142, 200, 209
1:8–9a 20, **37**, 41
1:9b-d Homogeneous **38**–40, 39, 42, 72, 206
1:10—2:1[3] Chiasm **40**–43, 41, 51, 62–63,74, 102, 209
1:10–11 [2:1–2] 84, 107
2:1[3] 25, 42, 209, 217–18
2:2–8[4–10] Chiasm **43**–51, 73, 149, 164
2:2[4] 2, 21, 44–46, 50, 77, 88–89
2:5–7[7–9] 209
2:5[7] 124
2:7[9] 44, 105, 210
2:8–9[10–11] 209
2:8[10] 13, 44, 47–**49**, 59, 101, 107
2:9[11]—3:5 (Block 2) **51**, 102–3, 107, 167
2:9–13[11–15] Homogeneous **51**–54, 121, 209
2:9[11] 54, 57, 63, 70, 77, 101
2:10[12] 53, 97, 107
2:12[14] 54, 107
2:13[15] 52, 59, 198, 107, 188

2:14–23[16–25] Three Love Poems 54
2:14–17[16–19] Homogeneous 5, **54–58**
2:14[16] 56–57, 63, 107, 193, 209
2:15[17] 43, 56, 93, 198
2:16[18] **51**, 56, 97, 108, 210, **219**
2:17[19] 59, 108, 209
2:18–20[20–22] Chiasm **58–61**, 62, 155
2:18[20] 40, 59–60, 84, 91, 105, 108
2:19–20[21–22] 116
2:19[21] 57, 60, 88, 97, 108
2:20[22] 59, 97, 103
2:21–23[23–25] Homogeneous **61–63**
2:21–22[23–24] 209
2:22[24] 5, 62
2:23[25] 39, 43, 97, 103, 153, 209
3:1–5 63, 108
3:1b-d Chiasm 1, 9–11, **64–65**, 70
3:1 9–11, 70, 83, 108, 170, 209
3:3b–5 Homogeneous 62, **66–70**, 120
3:4 69–70, 103, 107–8
3:5 11–12, 63, 65, 70–71 100, 104, 136, 179, 209
4:1–2:8[10] (Part 2) 102, **113**
4:1–5:4 (Block 3) 102. 106–7, **113**
4:1–10 5
4:1 1, 100, 108 **113**, 129
4:1b-4a Chiasm 9 ,**114–16**
4:2 72, 82, 105, **111**, 115
4:4b-9a Chiasm **97**, 110, **116–20**, 124–25, 132, 192
4:5 119
4:6 82
4:9b-11a Homogeneous **120–22**
4:9 83, 108, 144
4:10–11 82, 111, 129
4:10 5, 120–21, 219
4:11b-14 Chiasm 5, **122–25**, 132, 192
4:11–12 111
4:12 112, 116, 129
4:13 49, 83, 94–95, 105, 108
4:15–19 Chiasm **125–27**
4:16 83, 97, 108, **126**, 158, 180
4:18 65, 108, 113, 219
4:19 108, 113, 219
5:1–4 Homogeneous **127–29**
5:1 109, 129
5:2 109, 172
5:3 83, 109, 128–29, 142
5:4 93, 103, 109, 116, 144
5:5 7:2 (Block 4) **129**
5:5–7 Chiasm **129–32**
5:5 109, 119, 131, 144, 150
5:6 82, 109, 151, 158, 179
5:7 109, 130–31
5:8–9 Chiasm **132–33**
5:8 76, 109, 134
5:10–11 Chiasm 132, **133–34**
5:10 76, 109, 136
5:12—6:3 Homogeneous **134–38**
5:13 109, 136
5:14 173, 187, 199
6:3 49, 139
6:1 109, **135–38**
6:2 83, 94
6:3 103, 109, 136–37, 139, 143
6:4–6 Homogeneous 10, **138–40**, 189
6:4 109, 139, 196, 204, 209
6:5 109, 129, 139, 219
6:6 93–94, 109, 130, 139, 189
6:7—7:2 Chiasm **140–44**

Hosea (continued)

6:7 76, 105, 109, 130, 140
6:9 109, 143
6:10 109, 144
6:11 96, 129, 142, 219
7:1 109, 144, 171
7:2 83, 101, 143–44, 148
7:3—8:13 (Part 3, Block 5) 102, **144**, 161
7:3–7 Chiasm 4, **144**–48
7:3 76, 94, 152, 161
7:5 84, **146**, 155, 161
7:6 110
7:7 152, 155, 161
7:8–16 Chiasm 73, 110, **148**–52, 164
7:10 76, 131
7:12 110, 150
7:14 5, 154
7:15 144, 150, 219
7:16 144, 152, 161, 219
8:1–4a Homogeneous Central 60, 103–4, 109, **152**–56
8:1 104–5, 109, 155–56, 166
8:2 Central 28, 49, 61, 80, 87–88, 91, 93, 98, 102–3, **153–55**, 162, 165
8:3 49, 88, 104–5, 108–9, 123, 158
8:4a 155, 157, 160–61
8:4b–8 Chiasm **156**–59
8:5 157–58
8:6–7 98, 162
8:9–13 Chiasm 5, **159**–61, 192
8:9 22, 161
8:10 94, 161
8:11 81, 88, 130, **159**
8:12 83, 93
8:13 81, 94, 166
8:14--11:7 Part 4) 102, 109, **161**
8:14—10:1 (Block 6) 102, 109, **161**, 169
8:14 Homogeneous 95, 103, 109, **161**–63, 167
9:1–9 Chiasm 72–73, 103, **163**–67
9:1 89, 109
9:3 109, 156
9:4 109, 119, 156
9:5 109, 164
9:6 94, 163, 165, 220
9:7 109, 173
9:8 103, 153
9:9 94, 109, 156, 166
9:10—10:1 Chiasm **167**–73, 103, 161
9:10 9, 56, 109, 169, 173, 209
9:11 8, 81, 119, 170
9:15 109, 144, 167
9:16 94, 109
9:17 103, 153, 170, 173
10:1 9, 49, 101, 105, 107–8, 169, 173
10:2—11:7 (Block 7) 102, 108, **173**
10:2–8 Chiasm **174**–77
10:3 109
10:4 105, 108–10, 114
10:5 8, 83, 88, 98, 105, 108, 173, 176, 220
10:6 82, 108, 110
10: 8 43, 89, 108
10:9–15 Chiasm 4, 73, **177**–81
10:9 166
10:10 105, 109
10:11 68, 104, 108, 177, 180
10:13 83, 108
10:14 83, 108, 176
10:15 108, 175–76
11:1–4 Chiasm **181**–83
11:1 11, 87, 96, 108
11:2 94, 108, 182
11:3 88, 108–9, 185
11:4 38, 110–11, 206
11:5–7 Homogeneous 111, 153, **183**–85, 187, 189
11:5 97, 107, 109

11:6 111, 195
11:7 108, 110, 128, 184, 204
11:8--14:9[10] (Part 5) 102, **185**
11:8—13:3 (Block 8) 10, 102–3, 107, **185**
11:8–11 Chiasm 110–11, **186**–88
11:8 98, 103, 107–8, 111, 184, 186
11:9 108, 186, 208
11:11 52, 105, 107, 186–87, 189
11:12—12:1 [12:1–2] Homogeneous 140, **188**–90
11:12[12:1] 185, 189, **220**
12:1[2] 78, 105, 197, 210
12:2[3]—13:1 Chiasm 73, **190**–95
12:2[3] 78, 83, 185, 192, **220**
12:3[4] 92, 107, 144, 194
12:5[6] 79, 91, 93, 108, 193, 197
12:6[7] 83, 89, 108
12:7[8] 97, 107–8, 193
12:9[10] 101, 107–8, 197, 208
12:10[11] 83, 194
12:11[12] 94, 108
12:12[13] 79, 83, 88, 98, 108, 193–94
12:13[14] 78, 193
12:14[15] 2, 21, 193
13:2–3 Chiasm **195**–97
13:2 82, 86, 197
13:3 83, 90, 196, 208
13:4—14:9[10] (Block 9) 102–3, 107, **197**
13:4–6 Homogeneous 5, **197**–98, 208
13:4 107, 192, 198, 208
13:5 56, 107, 197, **220**
13:6 72, 83, 200
13:7–11 Chiasm **198**–200
13:7 46, 83, 97, 107, 200, 209
13:8 197, **220**
13:9 52, 87–88, 200
13:10 35, 107, 145, 200
13:12—14:8[9] Chiasm 14, 73, **200–10, 207**
13:13 10, 211
13:14 94, 112, 205
13:15 107, 203, 206, 209
13:16[14:1] 107, 204–6
14:1–8[2–9] 203
14:1[2] 11, 80, 84–86, 103, 107, 201–2, 209–210
14:2[3] 11–12, 49, 78, 85, 89, 105, 107, 114, 123, 204, 207
14:3[4] 35, 78, 97, 107, 171, 200, 204–10
14:4[5] 11, 88, 107, 208–9
14:5[6] 38, 112, 204
14:6[7] 83, 112, 205–6
14:7[8] 11, 123, 203, 205, 209
14:8[9] 9, 14, 73, **76**, 97, 107, 123, 200, 205–6
14:9[10] Chiasm 2, 10–11, 28–29, 72, 87, 89, 92, 94, 107, 123, **210**–12

Joel

2:26C–27 68

Amos

1:4, 7, 10, 12, 14; 2:2, 5 162

Obadiah

11 104
19–21 121

Jonah

1:11, 13 196

Micah

2:7 196

Nahum

1:6; 3:19 97

www.ingramcontent.com/pod-product-compliance
Lightning Source LLC
Chambersburg PA
CBHW060559230426
43670CB00011B/1896